AF776621

The Power and Politics of Art in Postrevolutionary Mexico

The Power and Politics of Art in Postrevolutionary Mexico

Stephanie J. Smith

The University of North Carolina Press CHAPEL HILL

This book was published with the assistance of the Anniversary Fund of the University of North Carolina Press.

© 2017 The University of North Carolina Press
All rights reserved
Set in Espinosa Nova by Westchester Publishing Services
Manufactured in the United States of America

The University of North Carolina Press has been a member of the Green Press Initiative since 2003.

Library of Congress Cataloging-in-Publication Data
Names: Smith, Stephanie J., author.
Title: The power and politics of art in postrevolutionary Mexico / Stephanie J. Smith.
Description: Chapel Hill : University of North Carolina Press, [2017] | Includes bibliographical references and index.
Identifiers: LCCN 2017007227 | ISBN 9781469635675 (cloth : alk. paper) | ISBN 9781469635682 (pbk : alk. paper) | ISBN 9781469635699 (ebook)
Subjects: LCSH: Artists—Political activity—Mexico—History—20th century. | Women artists—Political activity—Mexico—History—20th century. | Partido Comunista Mexicano—History—20th century. | Art and state—Mexico—History—20th century. | Mexico—History—Revolution, 1910–1920—Influence.
Classification: LCC HX521 .S575 2017 | DDC 701/.03097209041—dc23
LC record available at https://lccn.loc.gov/2017007227

Cover illustration based on 1930 arrest photographs of Tina Modotti (courtesy of Archivo General de la Nación, Dirección General de Investigaciones Políticas y Sociales, Caja 259, Exp. 34).

For Eva and Jim, both accomplished scholars,
and both fiercely dedicated to the transformation
of wrongs into rights

Contents

Illustrations

Acknowledgments

This is the book I always wanted to write. The intriguing topic of Mexico's radical artists first grabbed my attention during my previous career as an artist, and the story of their complicated lives continued to inhabit my imagination throughout my current life as an historian of the Mexican Revolution. As I consider these acknowledgments, though, the future looks especially unclear. The 2016 presidential elections are not even two weeks in the past, and the larger-than-life leader of the Cuban Revolution, Fidel Castro, just lost his final battle on earth. The artists throughout this book also faced a murky path forward as they struggled to create a more equitable society through their striking political images. Even if their efforts resulted in fewer political changes than they expected, the art they produced still provides a legacy that confirms the power of culture in times of uncertainty.

Throughout this project, I have enjoyed the support of exceptionally skilled librarians and archivists. As the Associate Curator for Special Collections and the Latin American and Iberian Studies Librarian at The Ohio State University library, José Díaz carried out the impossible—not once but twice—by obtaining obscure but key materials, including the microfilm of the Taller de Gráfica Popular Records, Mexico City, 1937–1960. David Lincove, the History Librarian at Ohio State, also helped enormously by acquiring the Comintern Archives: Files of the Communist Party of Mexico, 1919–1940. I am grateful to work at a university with such talented colleagues and scholars in their own right. Additionally, I would like to express my gratitude to the various Mexico City archives and the knowledgeable staff who generously provided their support and access to documents. Of particular mention are the archivists at the Archivo General de la Nación who furnished much needed assistance; working at the old penitentiary, with its numerous cats that roamed the halls, was magical. I also would like to thank the Archivo Diego Rivera y Frida Kahlo, the Centro de Estudios del Movimiento Obrero y Socialista, and the other fine archives throughout Mexico's lovely capital. Certainly, this book benefited from the archivists at the beautiful Internationaal Instituut voor Sociale Geschiedenis in Amsterdam, and of course the Pompidou Center,

Bibliothèque Kandinsky. And without doubt, the remarkable people and resources found in various U.S. institutions, including the Hoover Institution Library and Archives, also significantly strengthened this work.

In Mexico City, those at the Red Tree House, including owners Craig Hudson and Jorge Silva, guaranteed that staying in Mexico's busy capital was both productive in terms of research, but also the best time ever. Craig and Jorge graciously opened their home for delicious dinners and the company of their friends. In 2011, I first began working with my research assistant, Lorena Marcela Botello Ibarra, and her work proved hugely helpful during the years that followed. As a scholar of art history and history, Lorena now curates art shows in Mexico City, and she also writes her own innovative work on Mexico's artists.

Throughout the writing of the book, I have benefited from the thoughtful insights of friends and colleagues. Susan Gauss has been a longtime friend and fellow scholar of Mexico since our days in graduate school. Our discussions on a number of academic issues and nonrelated topics generated exceptionally valuable feedback and fun. At Ohio State, my fellow historians have been a solid source of support. Jennifer Siegel, Margaret Newell, and I shared many meals together, and life in Columbus is so much better because of their friendship. I also would like to thank Lilia Fernández (now at Rutgers University), Robin Judd, Birgitte Søland, Nathan Rosenstein, Katherine Marino, David Brakke, Bert Harrill, Tina Sessa, Chris Otter, Theodora Dragostinova, Mytheli Sreenivas, Bruno Cabanes, Susan Lawrence, Daniel Rivers, and Ying Zhang. Our friends and neighbors, Keith Speers and Micheal Carroll, offered entertaining nights out in the neighborhood and hours of conversation that covered a wide variety of topics. And finally, thank you to Andrea Ottone for his help in securing the documents from Italy.

Various funding sources allowed me to complete the research and writing of this book. Ohio State's Mershon Center for International Security Studies twice awarded funding, once to visit the Hoover Institution Archives and then for travel to Mexico City. OSU's College of Arts and Humanities awarded the Grant for Research and Creative Activity in the Arts and Humanities to begin this project, and they also funded international travel for research. I especially would like to thank the Department of History for its generous support, including the Merton Dillon Fellowship for Research as well as the teaching releases that enabled me to write this book. Additionally, the Center for Latin American Studies at OSU provided a Faculty Travel Grant for Professional Development.

I owe a great debt to Elaine Maisner and the staff of the University of North Carolina Press. Elaine, a superb editor, also was the editor of my first book; working with her again was such a pleasure. Elaine not only offered her valuable advice, but also her wonderful friendship. The two manuscript readers gave insightful comments, and their suggestions made the book substantially stronger.

Since the publication of my first book, my daughter, Eva Smith Pietri, has grown into a scholar in her own right, and now produces promising research in Social Psychology that addresses gender, ethnicity, and diversity in the STEM fields. My husband, James Genova, a fellow historian, continues to offer the gift of friendship and scholarly support, and our respective research trips remain a source of exceptional enjoyment, even while we work. I look forward to seeing Jim's and Evie's forthcoming research, and certainly the future will be better for their studies. This book is dedicated to Jim and Eva.

The Power and Politics of Art in Postrevolutionary Mexico

Introduction

Imagining a Red Path Forward

In 1948, David Alfaro Siqueiros gave a talk titled "The Art of Mexico in the Ranks of the People: 37 Years of Struggle by the Mexican Painters" at a rally organized by the *Partido Comunista Mexicano*, or Mexico's Communist Party (PCM).[1] Diego Rivera, Siqueiros's "partner in art," joined him at the symposium, along with about three hundred other participants. Mexico's internal security inspectors No. 20 and 58 infiltrated the event to report on the "suspicious" activity, and according to the agents' accounts, twenty-five women, who were "more or less all decent looking" and dressed well, also attended the artist's presentation. In addition, quite a few foreigners and Spanish refugees circulated among the crowd, and many gathered to chat below the prominent Communist Party flag with the legendary hammer and sickle. Once the audience settled into their seats, and only after a robust cheer of "viva el Partido Comunista," Siqueiros began to speak. Throughout his address, Siqueiros focused on three main points, all of which stressed the links between culture, politics, and Mexico's contemporary art. First, Siqueiros argued that the country's artistic culture originated from the Mexican Revolution and then evolved under the direction, structure, and soul provided by the Mexican Communist Party. Second, Siqueiros stressed that the current development and life of Mexican art depended on the continued growth of the Communist Party, which reflected the genuine politics of the proletariat as a class. Third, the muralist claimed that the transformation of bourgeois democracy into popular democracy and, ultimately, socialism would result in culture's escape from the increasing decadence that plagued all parts of the world. Only a strong and vigorous Communist Party, grounded in the doctrines of Marx, Lenin, and Stalin, could lead this struggle.[2]

At the time of Siqueiros's lecture on art, Mexico's Communist Party had yet to readmit Rivera following his expulsion from the Party in 1929. Indeed, after several requests, the PCM only approved the muralist's return in 1954. Still, by 1948, Rivera often spoke at PCM meetings to profess his loyalty to the Party and admit his multitude of prior political errors. Just a few days following Siqueiros's talk, Rivera and his wife, Frida Kahlo, attended a local meeting of Mexico City's Communist Party to support both the PCM and Siqueiros in his capacity of first secretary. To publicize the occasion, *El Machete*, the PCM's newspaper, proudly displayed the bright red headline splashed across its front page: "June 6! The most significant day in the political moment for the Mexican proletariat and the immediate future of our country."[3] Once again, internal security representatives closely documented this event, and according to the agents, the audience roundly applauded Rivera's arrival at the assembly. Just moments before the muralist's boisterous entrance, Siqueiros stood at the podium to announce the Party's program. He barely uttered a sound, however, before Rivera joined him at the front of the crowd of eight hundred participants. Speaking with great flourish, Rivera proclaimed he was glad to be back among comrades at a time when Mexico needed a mass party capable of guiding the people in their struggle against reactionaries. Rivera continued that because the Mexican Revolution had evolved into a capitalist agrarian democracy, it was now time to advance to the next stage, which represented an authentic popular democracy. After Rivera continued his lengthy discourse without an apparent end in sight, Siqueiros finally passed him a note insisting that Rivera stop in order to return to his own presentation.[4]

Rivera's and Siqueiros's interactions at the two meetings illustrate the central role the PCM played in the artists' concepts of culture and politics. As addressed in his 1948 talk, "The Art of Mexico in the Ranks of the People," Siqueiros specifically employed the term "culture" when he argued that Mexico's contemporary "pictorial culture was the result of the Mexican Revolution and direct work of the Mexican Communist Party."[5] In this manner Siqueiros well understood that culture—or for Siqueiros the visual arts (the focus of this study)—moved beyond the material object and instead conveyed an intentional political program, in this case that of the PCM.[6] By referencing the Mexican Revolution in the abstract, Siqueiros suggested revolutionary ideology, but he also alluded to nascent governmental structures. In this manner, Siqueiros underscored culture as a processual relationship, in constant flux between "regimes of symbolic practice" and "regimes of power."[7] Immersed in the interaction of cultural production, leftist politics, and shifting state policies, Siqueiros and Rivera produced images meant to impart a revolutionary message to a receptive audience, but the ensuing "meaning" of the works shifted between interpretation and the artists' intent.[8]

Despite Siqueiros's and Rivera's historically rocky relationships with the Party and each other, the future seemed exceptionally bright during the early 1920s when the muralists first joined the PCM. Along with other painters, artists, and intellectuals, Siqueiros and Rivera recognized the potential of the Party to influence Mexico's political future, and they understood the value of culture within political movements. The PCM also acknowledged the artists' usefulness in disseminating revolutionary concepts through their art, and as early as 1922, Party members met with Rivera and others to discuss the possibilities of collaborative art shows and posters created specifically for the popular classes.[9] Vanguard artists, including Rivera, Xavier Guerrero, Siqueiros and his wife, the writer Graciela Amador, the Italian photographer Tina Modotti, and others played a central role in the PCM in the years following the Party's creation in 1919.[10] As an indication of their growing commitments to the PCM, Rivera joined the Party's Executive Committee during its Second Congress in April 1923, and soon afterward, Siqueiros assumed the position of secretary of trade unions on the National Committee.[11] Moreover, in 1924, Siqueiros, Rivera, Guerrero, and Amador established the publication, *El Machete*, which the PCM recognized as their official organ only a year later during the PCM's 1925 Third Congress.[12] The muralists, photographers, and printmakers dedicated their artistic skills to Party activities, but they also formed close friendships that would last a lifetime. Within the PCM meetings and informal gatherings alike, artists discussed the meaning of art and the appropriate images and style for the broad dissemination of political concepts. The dynamic interchange of dialogues reflected their determination to merge art, ideologies, and everyday life in a strikingly persuasive manner. Even today, the artistic and political implications of their art, with its revolutionary images, continue to impact significantly the global audiences that flock to view the Mexico City murals and paintings.

Given the historical importance of the artists' deeply rooted ideological positions, an understanding of the interactions between these creative intellectuals and the postrevolutionary Mexican state remains incomplete without a careful consideration of Mexico's Communist Party. Despite the deep ties of many of Mexico's most important innovative thinkers to the PCM, the historiography of this period largely ignores the centrality of the Party within their lives. This study rethinks previous works to highlight the complex relationship between the artists and the Party and trace their complicated collaborations throughout the first half of the twentieth century. In this respect this book builds upon Barry Carr's seminal research to argue that despite the PCM's marginal membership in terms of actual numbers, this relatively small group of revolutionary artists and intellectuals played an outsized role in the intellectual life of the country and significantly influenced Mexico's political culture and cultural production through art dedicated to the restructuring of Mexican society.[13] Indeed, the artists enjoyed a stunning level of popularity among the elites and everyday people, and overflowing crowds turned out for art openings and public debates. Members of Mexico's Communist Party—and at this early point, the Mexican state as well—recognized the wide appeal and propaganda value of Rivera's and Siqueiros's paintings, and the potential of the artists to expand the PCM's influence, especially in the urban areas.

In return, many of Mexico's historically and artistically significant artists also embraced Marxist ideology as official PCM members, and others participated as sympathizers. An analysis of the reasons as to why some artists remained on the sidelines while the others enthusiastically joined Mexico's Communist Party reveals a number of complicated concerns. For one, Rivera, Siqueiros, Kahlo, Modotti, and the painter Aurora Reyes, along with Amador and the singer Concha Michel, originally joined the PCM during the 1920s, at a time of tremendous excitement and potential following the Mexican and Russian revolutions.[14] For these artists, communism specifically represented the path of the future, at least during these exceptional years. Second, personal reasons led some to understand more fully the legacy of poverty. For example, Reyes's family experienced financial and political difficulties that forced them to live with few financial resources during her childhood in Mexico City. Reyes never forgot her past, and she worked to change society through her subsequent participation with the PCM, unions, and the *Liga de Escritores y Artistas Revolucionarios*, or the League of Revolutionary Writers and Artists (LEAR), established in 1934.[15] Third, many artists referenced the legacy of the Mexican Revolution and their desire to uphold the revolutionary principles as their impetus for joining the Party. For example, Kahlo claimed that at age thirteen she enrolled in the Young Communists based largely on her firsthand experiences as a child during the Mexican Revolution.[16] Siqueiros's involvement in the revolution also served as a foundational element that supported his desire to join the Party.[17] However, as Leonard Folgarait confirms with his analysis of the difficulties in locating the formation of Siqueiros's political nature, the ultimate reasons why people act at particular times often remain situational or obscure to history.[18]

Beginning with the founding of Mexico's Communist Party in 1919, this study analyzes the roles of the PCM to uncover the political contingencies that shaped the artistic community within the country during the

1920s, 1930s, and the 1940s. Indeed, as members of the PCM, the artists developed a sophisticated interpretation of Marxist ideology that not only contributed to their understandings of Mexico's national distinctiveness during the 1920s, but also alerted them to the growing dangers of fascism during the subsequent decades. Generally considered the "postrevolutionary" years, the era represented, as Rick López rightly argues, less an indication of the Mexican Revolution's conclusion, but rather "a historical moment when intellectuals, state officials, artists, reformers, and sectors of the popular classes seized on the recent popular upheaval as an opportunity to formulate new cultural ideas, as well as repackaging many Porfirian ideals and infusing them with new urgency."[19] In this respect the artists visualized an emerging world of opportunities, constructed on the rubble of a corrupt past and guided through the unknown future by the light of the PCM.

Mexican nationals and international artists maintained radical political connections, but a closer analysis of the artists, the PCM, and government officials reveals complex constellations of relations in flux. Although artists assumed high-level positions within the PCM leadership, not all remained Party members throughout their careers. State officials' attitudes toward the PCM also shifted over time as Mexican presidents and high-level administrators either worked with the artists associated with the PCM or fiercely defended more conservative strategies by imprisoning or deporting anyone suspected of maintaining connections with the Party, especially by the end of the 1920s. Artists also lacked a single consensus on the meaning or purpose of art as well as a definition of culture. What this meant was that even while the artists included in this study generally identified with the left, they still held contrasting political and artistic views, especially with regard to the Leon Trotsky affair. More importantly, not all artists were muralists, even though scholars and tourists alike have showered the greatest attention on those who practiced this form of expression. And not all Mexican citizens, especially ordinary people and residents living outside of the capital, viewed the murals located in government buildings or large museums. Still, everyday women and men often were aware of the newspapers' widely published accounts of the artists' escapades, or saw art and photographs depicted on posters and broadsheets plastered around cities in parks, universities, and other easily accessible locations. Art spilled out from official and state-sanctioned locations and into the streets, as did the artists' visibility as they led popular protests, organized exhibitions, or participated in contentious debates covered widely in the popular media. Reflecting a high level of recognition among a diverse group of Mexico's citizens, the artists disseminated culture and political content to the poor and rich, and to the workers and the popular classes alike.

Culture as a Revolutionary Weapon: Art and Mexico's Communist Party

The role of culture in revolution historically has played out in a number of theaters. Following V. I. Lenin's 1920 proclamation that public education and art should be "imbued with the spirit of the class struggle being waged by the proletariat," many of Mexico's artists put great faith in the centrality of culture within revolutionary struggles.[20] During the 1920s, a number of Mexico's artists thus found inspiration in the Soviet Union's campaign to create art that illustrated the fight against oppression, figuratively depicted by realistic images of heroic popular classes and workers. After all, both Mexico and the Soviet Union recently experienced grand revolutions and the two countries now were constructing exciting new futures. Moreover, Mexico and the USSR established diplomatic relations in 1924, and soon afterward, the Soviet Union opened an embassy in Mexico City.[21] Mexico's artists and PCM members expressed a desire to experience the land of the Russian Revolution firsthand, and the establishment of the embassy within the country facilitated the ease of traveling to the USSR.[22]

In some ways, the Russian cultural path provided a model for Mexican artists. To be effective, of course, the newly formed Soviet government needed to widely disseminate visionary and revolutionary concepts through easily comprehensible images. In order to move beyond a narrow bourgeois reception and instead reach a large number of people, 1920s Soviet artist organizations rejected easel painting in favor of public murals.[23] The October group (or Oktyabr), formed in 1928 in the Soviet Union, specifically promoted a mass-produced public people's art, or a proletarian art, that combined "highly qualified professional art" with workers' "amateur art."[24] Members of the October group included Diego Rivera, who lived in the Soviet Union from late 1927 to 1928; Rivera's contact with Oktyabr left a lasting impression on the painter and influenced his subsequent work.[25] The October group also counted as members various Soviet photographers, architects, designers, and filmmakers, including Sergei Eisenstein, who would move to Mexico in 1930 to film his iconic, but unfinished work, *Que viva*

México.[26] While the organization's members aligned to promote the spatial arts as a form of ideological propaganda to engage the proletariat, they still argued for the necessity of education to teach the masses the principles of art.[27]

In the early 1930s, the Soviet Union adopted socialist realism—"realism in form and realism in content"—as communism's official aesthetic.[28] Loosely defined, the term "socialist realism" thus combined class-based content and Party loyalty (socialist) with "truthfulness" (realism) to create an idealistic vision for the future.[29] After the 1932 creation of the Moscow section of the Union of Soviet Artists (or MOSSKh), socialist realism predominated as the approved artistic expression, and writers and intellectuals endorsed the program of socialist realism during the 1934 First All-Union Congress of Soviet Writers.[30] Although theories on socialist realism continued to evolve over time, the 1934 constitution of the Union of Writers stated that socialist realism should depict a "true and historically concrete" revolutionary reality "combined with the task of educating workers in the spirit of Communism."[31] Instead of abstract modernism, proponents of socialist realism favored art visually accessible to the masses, with images portraying historical themes easily readable by the popular classes.[32] Moreover, supporters of socialist realism promoted the concept of the collective over the individual, and some also argued for the importance of proletarian art, or paintings and drawings produced by amateur, untrained workers.[33] In this manner, the artist's revolutionary (or proletarian) qualifications and Party loyalty could weigh more heavily than the ultimate quality of the subsequent art produced, especially during the early years.[34] Soviet officials still understood the importance of accomplished painters, and in response, during the 1930s, they also established academies and exhibitions with the purpose of training artists in the fine arts and displaying their work.[35] By the 1940s, during the exigencies of war, the exhibitions of large paintings continued, but the artists also produced posters that contained images of combat for greater dissemination.[36]

In Mexico, elements of socialist realism, including the concept that art should teach the central messages of the Mexican Revolution to the masses, influenced creative thinkers of the postrevolutionary era. Most importantly, even though Mexico's radical artists disagreed on the exact nature of revolutionary art, they nonetheless shared a common belief in the potential of art to be revolutionary. Not only did their faith in the power of art influence their decisions to join the PCM but their dedication to Mexico's

Communist Party, at least during the Party's early years, also shaped their art. Here, much as in the Soviet Union, the artists argued for the importance of understandable art created for the benefit of the popular classes rather than traditional paintings owned solely by the bourgeois rich. In a similar vein, Mexico's artists, and most especially the printmakers of LEAR and the Taller de Gráfica Popular, or the Popular Graphic Art Workshop (TGP) established in 1937, argued for the notion of the collective, or realistic art produced within a shared workshop, and they also produced posters that revealed the horrors of fascism.[37] As inspiration, LEAR artists looked to the Soviet Union, which, according to LEAR's founding principles, was the only country "where culture . . . is the Torch that points the way forward for the proletariat of the other countries of the earth." LEAR hoped to recreate the same emphasis on culture in Mexico, and contribute their artistic skills toward the liberation of the proletariat as they broke the chains of oppression.[38] From 1934 until 1936, LEAR artists even planned exhibits that combined the work of professional artists with those with little training, including amateur art hung next to their own prints.[39] Overall, throughout these years, serious disagreements hampered the artists' relationships with the PCM, and certainly some took the commitment to the growth of international communism more seriously than others. But for the artists considered in this study, most remained convinced in the centrality of art's role in reaching the popular classes and communicating their notions of the Mexican Revolution.

Still, not all artists approved of socialist realism as the appropriate doctrine to embrace. For example, by the end of his visit to the Soviet Union, Diego Rivera reversed his earlier position and adamantly denounced socialist realism as "bad nineteenth-century academicism."[40] Moreover, significant differences also existed between political postrevolutionary art in Mexico and the Soviet Union. In Mexico, the artists associated with the PCM often portrayed the uprising of the oppressed, or the masses of the struggling popular classes, led by an organic intellectual. Most often devoid of the heroic images of state figureheads that were depicted in Soviet images, the art represented the people from below rather than an official vision from above.[41] As Deborah Caplow notes in her study of the printmaker Leopoldo Méndez, although Mexico's artists and intellectuals referenced images of revolutionary workers, at times they also criticized the failures of the Mexican Revolution to promote great change. Thus, Caplow argues that rather than socialist realism, with its close connections to the Soviet state, "social realism" better describes the work of Mexico's artists who at times fiercely attacked the policies of the Mexican government, but at other times also supported presidents, including, for example, Lázaro Cárdenas (1934–1940) and the Popular Front during the mid-1930s.[42]

Artists disagreed on the "true" meaning of art throughout the lively postrevolutionary years, and similar debates continue even today. My own interest in the subject of art within a historical context originated from my interdisciplinary training, first as a professional artist for twelve years in New York City and currently as a historian of Mexico and the Mexican Revolution. After earning my MFA in drawing, I promptly moved to New York City to become a working artist. During my subsequent time in New York, the art and poetry scene fascinated me with all its complexities of ideas and theories. Artists, poets, and intellectuals often met to discuss the significance of art in the modern era, and first and foremost they insisted upon the independent nature of art, or that artists should be free from influences that dictated the content of their images. Still, the 1980s and early 1990s also was the era of revolutionary possibilities, and artists from Nicaragua and other Latin American countries firmly insisted that art should exist for the service of the "revolution" or the popular classes. As one activist artist argued, paintings of colorful butterflies, or art for art's sake, ignored the exploitative nature of capitalism at a time when the United States sponsored the burning of Central America's communities and the killing of its peoples. Much as Siqueiros and Rivera had discussed before, contemporary artists now debated the age-old questions concerning the obligations of artists to the people and state, and they also considered the right of artists to decide, without state interference, what kind of art they produced. Despite the specificity of their situation, in many ways an analysis of the creative intellectuals who lived in Mexico during the postrevolutionary era reflects the complexities that even today continue to impact the relationship of artists with government policies and their societies, both on a national and international level.

This study combines my previous background in art with my current research as a historian to analyze the negotiations between the artists, the PCM, and the postrevolutionary state. To unpack the complex positions of Mexico's radical postrevolutionary artists, this work stresses a multidisciplinary approach in its dual consideration of Mexico's cultural developments and the historically relevant political environment in which the artists operated.[43] Through a close examination of archival documents and historical contingencies, combined with a consideration of the development of art

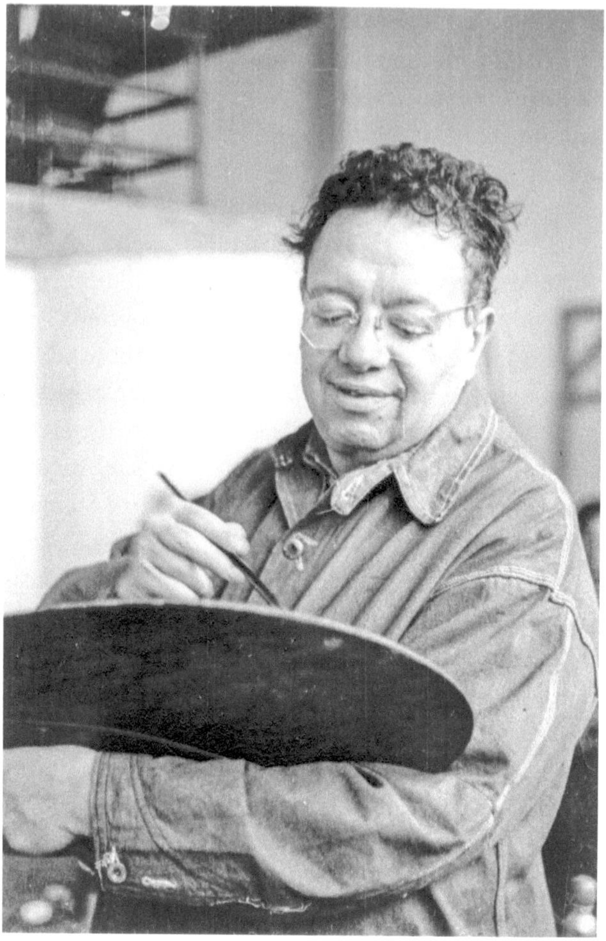

Diego Rivera with a paint palette. Alexander Buchman Papers, envelope G. Courtesy of the Hoover Institution Library & Archives, Stanford University.

forms, images, and techniques, this book constructs a bridge between academic disciplines and listens carefully to the dialogue generated as a result. By stressing the importance of situating culture within a historical context, as well as the ways in which history is shaped by culture, I build upon recent innovative studies that contextualize the production of art throughout the postrevolutionary era, highlight the role of art and artists in shaping Mexico's governmental policies, and explore the ways government officials and a shifting global political environment influenced the construction of art in return.[44] An approach that utilizes history, art, and art history allows the reader to "see" the lively postrevolutionary period in novel ways and situate the relationship between the artists and Mexico's Communist Party as a key element of this crucial era.

The Construction of Mexico's Postrevolutionary Identity

Following the bloody years of armed struggle during the Mexican Revolution, officials linked the reconstruction of the country, free from dependence on its imperialist neighbor to the north, to the creation of an "authentic" Mexican national identity incorporating both a present and a past.[45] After more than a decade of violent warfare, during the early 1920s, Mexico's political leaders looked to culture as a powerful educational and nation-building tool in the struggle to unite a country fractured by years of regional fighting.[46] The question remained, however, as to who would create the "official" representations of Mexico in the twentieth century and how the revolutionary history would be illustrated. As John Mraz argues, "History is a fundamental element of identity but, again, it is a question of *how* the past is represented."[47] Moreover, the process of identity formation remained in constant flux, or as Mraz again clarifies, "it is constructed, deconstructed, and reconstructed endlessly."[48] For Mexican officials, large-scale murals, posters placed strategically in public locations, and widely accessible public art exhibitions represented the appropriate path to assimilate national identity, especially in a country where many still could not read or write.[49] Besides its educational purposes, the postrevolutionary government also understood that nationalistic art and stirring images could mobilize loyalty—a love of nation—within the heart of the popular classes.[50]

As the first director of the *Secretaría de Educación Pública*, or the Ministry of Public Education (SEP) from 1921 to 1924, José Vasconcelos well understood the impact of culture on the politics of the day and the power of art to "uplift" the popular classes. As Rick López notes, Vasconcelos actively promoted government involvement in the production of art, while further endorsing the state's support for the arts and the government's superior capacity to "direct and systematize artistic production."[51] In his push to instigate a new nationalism through art, Vasconcelos first pressed Rivera to explore "Mexican" themes in his murals.[52] To carry out this objective, Rivera—as well as other artists—turned to a particular image of an "eternal Indian woman" with her hair styled in long braids and her arms hugging flowers or her child. Rivera, Fernando Leal, and Jean Charlot, as well as the photographers Modotti and Edward Weston, discovered the look they desired in the model Luz Jiménez and her baby Concha. In murals, paintings, and photographs, the artists portrayed Jiménez in a wide variety of poses, including that of a rural teacher, at a picnic with Zapatistas, nude, pregnant and grinding corn, as a mother, as a servant, at a market, or occupied with other "traditional" chores.[53]

Thus drawing upon his vision of an "authentic" Mexico, during the early 1920s, Vasconcelos commissioned Rivera and others to paint images inspired by Mexico's glorious indigenous past or the country's striking future possibilities.[54] Presented in a large mural format on the walls of public buildings, Rivera's art represented the importance of the Mexican Revolution and revolutionary ideals, theoretically educating ordinary people in the class struggles of the rich versus the poor and inspiring them to action in response. In the same manner that *indigenismo* both celebrated a glorious past but denigrated Mexico's living indigenous population as primitive, Vasconcelos later would reject traditional popular art forms in favor of a modernist perspective.[55] Debates surrounding the portrayal of indigenous women and men in art also divided the muralists in general, and arguments over the definitions of national art specifically exacerbated the simmering tensions between Rivera and Siqueiros. With his support of the Soviet Union and its focus on industry and the proletariat during the 1920s and the early 1930s, Siqueiros's work focused less on *indigenismo* ideology.[56] Instead, Siqueiros privileged the mestizo in art over the indigenous and criticized Rivera's early adoption of Vasconcelos's visual program as indicative of the painter's tendencies to acquiesce to government directives.[57]

Despite the conflicts between Rivera and Siqueiros, government officials and artists alike recognized the significance of culture as a propaganda tool, but so did members of Mexico's Communist Party. Following the PCM's active recruitment of artists during the early 1920s, and even after the PCM expelled Rivera in 1929 and Siqueiros in 1930, artists and intellectuals from Mexico and abroad continued to produce political art while enthusiastically participating in the PCM throughout the 1930s and 1940s. Marxist ideology informed their work, and their commitment to the Party structured much of their existence. Members socialized with other comrades or Party sympathizers, and their lives often revolved around meetings, PCM activities, and painting, photography, or printmaking. But even as their left-wing politics were at odds with the Mexican government's policies, many of the artists—although not all—continued to pursue the financial patronage that came from their cooperation with Mexican government officials. Thus, state recognition represented a double-edged sword for both artists and government officials. For the creative intellectuals, the financial rewards could be alluring, but they risked the appearance of co-optation by working with the government. And even as the Mexican state recognized the importance of revolutionary art as a propaganda tool, for the most part the artists maintained ties to the PCM as supporters if not actual members.

Within this contested environment, state officials appropriated the artists' images as a means to promote nationalist education, but also as a path to disseminate the glory of a Mexican postrevolutionary national identity to larger audiences at home and abroad. In return, artists constructed work predicated on the notion that "political" art still could have intrinsic artistic value, or even more, that genuine art must carry a social message. Despite seemingly disparate ideologies, PCM artists and state officials often held similar ideas of what represented appropriate images of Mexico. Indeed, following the tumultuous revolutionary years, artists' representations of an idealized Mexico, complete with tropical flowers, indigenous mothers dressed in colorful blouses, and heroic revolutionaries, provided a valuable state resource as Mexico's elites attempted to once again attract foreign investment. Aesthetics and the transformation of society thus marched hand in hand as artists and intellectuals produced images that imagined a glorious past or an even more exciting future. Looking backward with pride, murals illustrated Mexico's indigenous heritage as an awe-inspiring foundational inheritance. And gazing forward with optimism, the art and writing of the period foretold a modern future illuminated by the bright lights of prosperous industries supported by the labor of productive workers well satisfied as a result of Mexico's transformation. The on-again, off-again marriage of convenience between the state and artists continued throughout the first half of the twentieth century as both conservative bureaucrats and members of the political left continued to draw upon the resources of the other. Even as politicians increasingly implemented a series of assaults against the artists, by the late 1920s, in their attempt to suppress the Communist Party, this international group of intellectuals and artists continued to popularize revolutionary rhetoric through their artwork and writings.[58]

Still, as Barry Carr points out, the muralists who belonged to the Party both "challenged and confirmed . . . state goals."[59] In this manner, art and state policy overlapped or even merged in a complex pattern of mutual accommodation alternating with state repression and the artists' resistance. Much as popular knowledge and official discourse reinforced and reproduced the other through the process of negotiation, so did art and the sanctioned interpretation of Mexico's revolutionary past and future.[60] But as compromise is more difficult when staring down the barrel of a rifle, the painters, photographers, printmakers, and others could experience serious opposition as well. Many of the artists associated with Mexico's Communist Party sought to radically transform Mexico's existing economic and political structures, and in response, government officials punished their actions with harsh measures, including prison sentences and expulsion from the country. In other words, to speak of negotiation is not to negate the difficult conditions and sanctioned state violence that often plagued the artists, especially from 1929 until 1934. Thus, at times, the artists represented a serious threat to the official narrative through their radical images and involvement in politics, while at other points, they intentionally joined forces with the Mexican state, for example, to fight the growing threat of fascism as part of the Popular Front.

Ultimately, this book neither situates art as *only* part of a project to legitimize the state, nor as *only* a revolutionary social project.[61] Through a close reading of a wide variety of historical sources, in addition to an exploration of the multiple meanings involved in the production of art, this study complicates the connections between art and the postrevolutionary state and moves the analysis beyond traditional accounts that take substantially divergent but equally incomplete positions: (1) the state co-opted revolutionary art and artists in the creation of Mexican state hegemony, or (2) the radical nature of the artists resulted in an ideological gulf that essentially separated their art from the services of the government.[62] Instead, the complex negotiations between the leftist artists, the PCM, and the postrevolutionary state resulted in a hybrid, but generally accepted national identity reinforced by salient images representing well-crafted historical narratives.

Who Creates the Cultural Revolution?

As an exceptional time in Mexico's history, the postrevolutionary era opened spaces in both art and politics for increased women's participation. Women from Mexico and other countries seized upon the new opportunities to push artistic boundaries, and they also embraced involvement in radical activities with passion. Tina Modotti, the writer and art historian Anita Brenner, Frances (Paca) Toor, the Mexican painters Aurora Reyes and Frida Kahlo, and the photographer Lola Álvarez Bravo, all occupied central roles within the artistic movements that sought to reshape Mexico's politics and culture.[63] Lupe Marín, Rivera's former wife, certainly took center stage within Mexico City's artistic and literary scene. The U.S. muralists and LEAR members, Grace and Marion Greenwood, traveled to

Mexico in the early 1930s. While there, they painted murals in Taxco, Morelia, and most importantly, in the Mercado del Carmen (later named the Rodríquez Market) in Mexico City.[64] The singer "Conchita," or Concha Michel, and Graciela Amador originally joined the PCM during the early 1920s, and both contributed significantly to politics and culture. In Mexico, as female activists broke new ground with their revolutionary views on the restructuring of society, they also refused to abide by the traditional sexual and gender norms of the times. In many ways, their radical political and social viewpoints allowed them to utilize the unique intellectual and artistic opening created in the aftermath of the Mexican Revolution to produce powerful images that reflected both the political and the personal. This study highlights women's contributions throughout its pages, but it also devotes two chapters to focus on women artists and their often highly contested connections to Mexico's Communist Party.

As with women's involvement, the cultural environment in which Mexico's leftist artists operated blossomed significantly with the inclusion of painters, photographers, and printmakers from different parts of the world. Certainly the 1917 Russian Revolution, followed by the expansion of communism and the creation of Comintern in 1919, led to the emergence of political and ideological leftist movements throughout Mexico and Latin America as well as other regions around the world.[65] During the 1920s, 1930s, and 1940s, Mexico City radiated a creative exuberance that attracted women and men from many parts of the world. Besides the excitement of an international art scene within a postrevolutionary environment, Mexico also provided a safe haven for those escaping political oppression or the growing threats of fascism.[66] After arriving in the country, these artists quickly assumed roles within Mexico's artistic and political organizations, including the PCM, and they also solidified friendships among other internationals and with their Mexican counterparts. Throughout its pages, this work interweaves the input of these global intellectuals and artists; indeed, a study of Mexico's postrevolutionary nation-making mission would be incomplete without the inclusion of the many influences provided by those who originated from outside Mexico's national boundaries.[67]

Even as Mexico attracted the world's most notable artists, many of Mexico's radical artists and intellectuals also traveled *to* other countries, including the United States, the Soviet Union, and Spain, among others. The Soviet Union played a particularly important role as a revolutionary model during the 1920s, as artists such as Rivera, Siqueiros, Guerrero, the painter and printmaker Pablo O'Higgins, and others journeyed to the country for training, to participate in conferences, or be a part of the revolutionary excitement. With the advent of the Spanish Civil War in 1936, artists and intellectuals also traveled to Spain to participate in the battles against the fascist forces. Siqueiros, for example, left Mexico in late 1936 for Spain, where he remained for the most part until 1939.[68] Additionally, artist groups, including LEAR printmakers, sent expositions and delegations to Spain, where the artists and writers collaborated with those already working there.[69] After returning to Mexico, the artists' subsequent writings and creative productions reflected their exposure and reactions to "foreign" political and artistic discourses. Such circular interactions profoundly influenced Mexico's art and politics during the postrevolutionary era. Indeed, the merging of international ideologies with Mexican revolutionary thought ultimately produced a powerful artistic movement that sought to place art at the service of the fight against tyranny, teach the masses the principles of revolutionary reform, and challenge prevailing notions of traditional art.

In many ways, Mexico's capital during the 1920s served as the nexus of radical artists—from Mexico and abroad—who met, organized, and created their works in this lively city. Given the close proximity of the United States, as well as its historical trends in conservatism, many creative U.S. intellectuals flourished in Mexico City's artistic circles. For example, Paca Toor traveled to Mexico City in 1922 to attend university classes, but soon Mexico's vibrant art and culture fascinated her, and by 1925, she decided to remain to establish *Mexican Folkways*, a journal that highlighted Mexico's folk art and indigenous population. Toor's home provided a dynamic space for those wishing to partake in passionate political and artistic discussions, and throughout its existence, Mexican and transnational intellectuals and artists collaborated on the journal.[70] Joseph Freeman, a member of the U.S. Communist Party and cofounder of *The New Masses*, first arrived in Mexico City in 1929 as a correspondent for the Telegraph Agency of the Soviet Union, or TASS, and quickly sought out Toor. As Freeman explained, "she [knew] everybody worth knowing in Mexico. The contributors of her government subsidized publication [*Mexican Folkways*] were officials and scholars of some standing in the republic; her house was the mecca of all good Americans who wished to drink from the fountain of Mexican culture or to make profitable connections of various kinds."[71] Freeman even met his future wife, the painter Ione Robinson, when she lived in Modotti's apartment as her roommate.[72]

Artists also arrived from many other countries besides the United States. Among others, Carlos Mérida from Guatemala and Jean Charlot, originally from France, joined the *Sindicato de Obreros Técnicos, Pintores y Escultores* (Union of Technical Workers, Painters, and Sculptors, SOTPE), founded in the early 1920s. Originally from Italy, Modotti arrived in Mexico in 1922, joining the PCM in 1927 and becoming close friends with Guerrero, Rivera, Charlot, Siqueiros, and Vasconcelos.[73] Modotti and Toor rented apartments on the fifth floor of the same Mexico City building as the offices of *Mexican Folkways*, and Modotti's home functioned as a "salon" for both Mexican comrades and delegates of the Communist International from Cuba and other parts of the world.[74] After being exiled from Mexico in 1930, and following a brief stay in Germany, Modotti moved to Moscow where she remained until she traveled to Spain to participate in the Spanish Civil War during the mid-1930s. Not long after Modotti left the country, the Soviet filmmaker Sergei Eisenstein journeyed to Mexico during December 1930 to make *¡Que Viva México!*, funded by Upton Sinclair and his wife, Mary. As an inauspicious start to his trip, Mexican police briefly detained him in late 1930, just a few days after his arrival.[75] Once Sinclair withdrew his financial support of the film a year into the project, and after the Soviet government repeatedly sent orders that he apply his talents in his home country, Eisenstein returned to the Soviet Union in mid-1932—but not before U.S. officials stopped him at the U.S.-Mexico border on his way home via the United States.[76] Although Modotti and Eisenstein never met in Mexico City, they later would have the opportunity in Moscow.

By the 1930s the fascist terror added an additional dimension for the artists, writers, and the intellectuals who arrived in Mexico City from wide-ranging parts of the world. Not only did they travel to Mexico to join the country's burgeoning cultural movement, but they also sought safety from the horrors of fascism. The influx of refugees from the Spanish Civil War, along with artists and intellectuals from France, Germany, and other parts of Europe, transformed Mexico City into a vibrant center of antifascist resistance. While living and working in Mexico's capital, transplanted activists actively participated in debates on art, its place in revolution, and the appropriate style that would appeal to the greatest number of people. For these artists and intellectuals, Mexico not only represented their home of choice, at least temporarily, but a political refuge as well. Along with their families and belongings, the transnational population brought their revolutionary ideals and beliefs. Through their art and writings, they contributed significantly to the emergence of leftist movements, as well as to the creation of a postrevolutionary national identity during their years in Mexico.[77]

Two artists' organizations assumed particularly noteworthy roles in the fight against fascism: LEAR and the TGP. After their arrival in Mexico, transnational artists from a variety of countries joined LEAR and the TGP and united around the production of particularly powerful posters and prints with images that directly challenged and warned of the violence of fascism.[78] Ultimately, the artists' time in Mexico ranged from a couple of years to decades. Among others, O'Higgins participated in LEAR, as did the U.S. muralists Marion and Grace Greenwood, the Cuban artist Clara Porset, and the French artist Jean Charlot. O'Higgins also played a key role in the TGP, as did Mariana Yampolsky, originally from the United States, although she never joined Mexico's Communist Party. In 1939, Hannes Meyer, the former Bauhaus director, arrived in Mexico as well, and in 1942, he assumed the role of the Taller's business manager. Artist Elizabeth Catlett moved to Mexico City in 1946, and she soon became an integral member of the TGP. As a black woman, Catlett positioned her identity as a key element in her art, but she also transcended national borders, adopting Mexican culture as an integral element of her being.[79]

Not all political exiles were welcomed equally to Mexico. And without doubt, Leon Trotsky's early 1937 arrival in Mexico represented one of the country's most controversial refugees. As this study explores, Trotsky's short years in Mexico ripped apart the fragile political fabric that initially united those involved in Mexico's Communist Party. By the end of the 1920s and throughout the 1930s, Mexico's artists largely split between those who backed Stalin, most importantly Siqueiros, and the Trotsky supporters, including Rivera. Even before Trotsky landed on Mexico's shores, years of differences came to a head with the widely publicized and heated public debate in 1935 between Siqueiros and Rivera that took place in the *Palacio de Bellas Artes* (Palace of Fine Arts).[80] The following year Rivera successfully promoted Trotsky's asylum in the country, and the Russian moved into Kahlo's family home in Coyoacán. Despite Rivera's assistance in bringing Trotsky to Mexico City, within a few short months Rivera drifted away from the Fourth International, an act that distressed the older man. In early 1939, Trotsky even wrote an impassioned letter to Kahlo, begging her to intercede in his deteriorating relationship with her husband. Although Trotsky referred to Rivera as an "authentic revolutionary," he nonetheless deemed Rivera "absolutely unfit" to assume a bureaucratic position within the Fourth International. Rivera soon resigned from the organization in anger, an act that Trotsky categorized as a "heavy blow."[81] Still, upon Trotsky's assassination, Rivera sent a telegram from San Francisco to Trotsky's widow,

Natalia, stating, "I ask you in spite of our great differences in political opinions to permit me to express my deep condolences on the death of Liev Davidovitch."[82]

Sources and Overview

This work utilizes extensive historical research uncovered in archives, libraries, and museums located in five countries—Mexico, Holland, France, the United States, and Italy—to understand better Mexico's place as a center of art and politics. In Mexico City, I examined various document groups found in the *Archivo General de la Nación* (Mexico's National Archives); the *Centro de Estudios del Movimiento Obrero y Socialista, A. C.* (Center for Studies of the Labor and Socialist Movement); the *Centro Nacional de Investigación, Documentación e Información de Artes Plásticas* (National Center for Research, Documentation, and Information on Fine Arts); and the *Archivo Diego Rivera y Frida Kahlo*, among others. The *Archivo Diego Rivera y Frida Kahlo*, which only recently opened its doors to investigators, is home to letters, posters, drawings, and other valuable items relating to Rivera and Kahlo. In Amsterdam, I researched at the *Internationaal Instituut voor Sociale Geschiedenis* (International Institute of Social History), which holds a number of document groups relating to communism in Mexico. In the United States, I worked at the Hoover Institution Library and Archives at Stanford University to examine several significant collections, including the Leon Trotsky Collection; the Bertram David Wolfe Papers (1903–2000); the Joseph Freeman Papers; the Rodolfo Echeverría Martínez Collection, 1911–1986; the Alexander H. Buchman photos; and others. I also researched at New York University's Tamiment Library; at the Houghton Library at Harvard University to investigate the Leon Trotsky Exile Papers; and the Getty Research Institute to examine the Siqueiros Papers. From Italy, this work utilizes police files on Tina Modotti housed in Rome's *Archivio Centrale dello Stato*, or the Central Archive of the State, Italy's National Archives. And from France I uncovered documents on Frida Kahlo's time in Paris at the Bibliothèque Kandinsky in the Pompidou Center. Additionally, my work benefits from material found within the microfilm series of the Comintern Archives: Files of the Communist Party of Mexico, 1919–1940; and the Taller de Gráfica Popular Records, Mexico City, 1937–1960.

Mexico's intelligence service documents from the recently released internal memos on the artists' "seditious activities" provide exceptionally rich sources to examine the government's surveillance of the radical artists.

From 1918 forward, internal security agents monitored the movements of Mexican nationals and transnational artists and intellectuals with equal zeal, although at times, "foreign" influences and possible threats appeared especially ominous with respect to national security. To analyze the ways in which the Mexican officials viewed the artists as a serious concern, even while they simultaneously supported the arts, this study utilizes records from the *Dirección General de Investigaciones Políticas y Sociales*, 1920–1953 (DGIPS), and the *Dirección Federal de Seguridad* (DFS). Both contain security files detailing the movements and activities of the artists, but because the DFS covers more recent events, this study makes limited use of the latter group. As Aaron W. Navarro points out in his history of the Mexican intelligence services, Mexico employed several intelligence services at the same time; for example, the Secret Service of the Chief of Police for Mexico City and the DGIPS.[83] Even more complex, the DGIPS adopted different bureaucratic names over the years, making it difficult to state definitively the appropriate titles for a particular year.[84]

Scholars only recently have incorporated these spy reports, especially because the Mexican government first declassified the collection in 2002. With the exception of Navarro's study, there are few works that explore the inner workings of Mexico's political intelligence agencies. Sergio Aguayo Quezada, however, pioneered the study of Mexico's intelligence services, providing groundbreaking studies on the subject.[85] Tanalís Padilla and Louise E. Walker also edited an immensely useful collection on the topic in the *Journal of Iberian and Latin American Research*.[86] Given the exceptionally valuable material found in this document group, scholars increasingly will mine this rich source for information not available elsewhere. Not only do the files offer a record of the artists' participation in PCM meetings, protests, or other potentially "threatening" activity, but they also present colorful insights into the artists' everyday and seemingly mundane activities. This study utilizes the DGIPS documents throughout its pages; they enrich the overall narrative and also add significantly to our understanding of Mexico's postrevolutionary anxieties.[87]

CHAPTER 1 FOCUSES on the founding of Mexico's Communist Party in 1919, and the Party's links to the influential national and international artistic movement active in Mexico throughout the 1920s. Chapter 2 analyzes the complex and often contradictory gendered positions of women artists associated with Mexico's Communist Party during the first decades of the twentieth century. This chapter first examines the Party's official stance toward women from 1919 to the 1940s, and the changing global and national political framework in which the PCM operated. Chapter 2 also highlights the artistic and political contributions of Tina Modotti, while recognizing her ambivalent position within postrevolutionary society. Chapter 3 considers the Rivera-Siqueiros debate and the arrival of Leon Trotsky in Mexico in January 1937 to analyze the artists' major political and artistic differences.[88] This chapter also utilizes the Trotsky incident to highlight a crucial time in Mexico's history when the artists influenced Mexico's politics in profound and lasting ways. Chapter 4 explores the manners in which women artists and intellectuals, including Brenner, Kahlo, Reyes, Toor, and others moved beyond traditional gendered stereotypes to assume positions within the vanguard of radical politics and revolutionary change, especially throughout the 1930s and 1940s. The significance of chapter 5 is threefold: (1) to analyze the interactions of Mexico's printmakers, including those belonging to LEAR and the TGP, with state officials, (2) to situate Mexico as a vital space within the international struggle against the spread of fascism, and (3) to understand better the transnational influence on culture and politics during Mexico's postrevolutionary period. And finally, the conclusion comes full circle to consider the multiple meanings of Rivera's return to Mexico's Communist Party in 1954 as well as Siqueiros's conflicted relationship with the PCM during his final years.[89] In the end, both Rivera and Siqueiros completed their careers much as they started: with a passion for creating art and a fascination with revolutionary change.

CHAPTER ONE

Art and the Creation of Mexico's Communist Party, 1919–1930

In 1922, Diego Rivera joined the *Partido Comunista Mexicano*, or the Mexican Communist Party (PCM). Citing the inability to paint *and* work for the Party, he only would last three years before he resigned. Although Rivera returned the following year in 1926, he still faced expulsion from the Party in 1929, and this time it would be 1954 before the PCM agreed, after much discussion, to readmit Rivera.[1] As he grew older, Rivera readily acknowledged his past "political" mistakes, and he admitted that the Party's decision to expel him was fair and reasonable, especially given his "mental confusion and political blindness" at the time. Rivera's embrace of Leon Trotsky ranked high among his list of grave errors, and accordingly, he identified his 1934 *Palacio de Bellas Artes* mural, *Man, Controller of the Universe*, with its inclusion of Trotsky and workers holding the Fourth International flag, as the best example of the "degree of degeneration" to which a Marxist could fall. According to Rivera, because an artist could not separate content from form, the paintings completed during the time when he maintained connections to the Fourth International also corresponded to his weakest work.[2]

Rivera's fellow muralist, David Alfaro Siqueiros, also experienced a complicated relationship with the PCM. Although Siqueiros demonstrated greater loyalty to the Party's Marxist ideology throughout much of his career, his artistic nature, unwillingness to submit to the Party's directives, and years spent outside of the country as an exile created tensions between the painter and various PCM members. Siqueiros's refusal to follow the Party's mandate to terminate his relationship with Blanca Luz Brum, the Uruguayan poet, and his "undisciplined" behavior, ultimately resulted in his expulsion from the Party in March 1930.[3] Although Siqueiros maintained that the PCM's Central Committee quickly recognized the error of its ways, even reinstating him and placing him in charge of the International League Against War and Fascism, the Party only officially readmitted him in 1946.[4] Still, Siqueiros's unorthodox activities continued to color his interactions with the PCM throughout the rest of his life. To many communists, the artist often lacked self-control, especially after his 1940 attack on Trotsky, then living in Mexico City. Indeed, after Siqueiros's arrest for orchestrating the assault on the Trotsky compound, the PCM categorically denied any link between current Party members and the "uncontrollable elements and provocateurs" involved in the unsuccessful attempt on Trotsky's life.[5]

The groundbreaking historical events of the early twentieth century—both within Mexico and on a transnational level—influenced the revolutionary views of the artists in many ways. Indeed, the birth of Mexico's Communist Party in November 1919 marked the beginning of an era of transformation in Mexico's history. Although Mexico's own great revolution officially ended in 1917 after seven long years of struggle, the ensuing state government apparatus revealed cracks and weaknesses that allowed revolutionary change to continue. Outside of Mexico, the formation of the PCM reflected the role of powerful global movements that rocked many parts of Latin America during this era. Certainly the 1917 Russian Revolution and the spread of communist ideals radicalized workers and provided a blueprint for other countries to follow. Thus, an enervated central state, combined with workers and intellectuals who continued to demand radical change within Mexican society, resulted in a fertile ground for the growth of radical ideas and international revolutionary movements that circulated during the years following the Mexican Revolution. By 1920, Mexico's Communist Party began to take root within Mexico's postrevolutionary politics.

Focusing on Rivera and Siqueiros, this chapter analyzes the interactions of the artists, the PCM, and the Mexican state within the context of the vibrant postrevolutionary era. Although during these early years, the Party's official membership numbers remained relatively insignificant, this chapter argues that the extraordinary influence of these creative participants, both female and male, on the politics of the period was far from trivial.[6] As Barry Carr points out, during the 1920s, the PCM derived a great deal of prestige from its association with the muralists and the arts, and as a result, Mexico's lively political and artistic scene attracted the attention of writers, photographers, artists, and great thinkers from all over the world.[7] The relationship between Mexico's PCM and radical transnational and local artists only grew stronger during the initial years following the creation of the PCM. Art and politics intertwined as artists played major roles in political affairs, and politicians appropriated the arts to transmit the "official" national history.[8] Indeed, during the exhilarating years of postrevolutionary Mexico, the political and cultural capital of the artists associated with the Communist Party—either the PCM or those from other countries—clearly influenced Mexico's future for years to come. Despite the seemingly warm marriage between the artists and the PCM, however, not all comrades approved of the artists' involvement within Party politics. One disgruntled former PCM member complained that soon after its founding, the Party inappropriately aligned with a group of "publicity seeking painters," including Diego Rivera, who understood little of the communist doctrine.[9] Still, as this chapter discusses, the artists and the PCM built a powerful coalition, and one whose influence would endure long beyond the 1920s.

The shifting relationship between the radical artists, the PCM, and the postrevolutionary state proved to be tempestuous throughout the 1920s. As the artists associated with the Communist Party utilized resources at their disposal to disseminate antigovernment propaganda, state officials repressed members of those groups, including the PCM, who agitated against the growth of an increasingly capitalist postrevolutionary economy. Despite the conflicting objectives of the artists' radical rhetoric and the government's recurrent crackdowns on the PCM, this chapter nonetheless reveals the points of confluence between the various groups, and argues that, at times, both artists and representatives of the state operated with similar long-term objectives. For example, the politicians appropriated the artists' images in such a way as to appeal to the masses and create a shared vision of a nationalist future built on a revolutionary past. And in return, artists sought government funding and sponsorship, even while they contributed pieces to publications that criticized politicians and economic practices.

The Founding of Mexico's Communist Party

The relatively small Mexican Socialist Party initially laid the foundation for the creation of a communist party.[10] During its First National Congress, held from 25 August to 5 September 1919, some sixty delegates voted to affiliate with the Third International, adopt a program that called for the dictatorship of the proletariat, and further endorse the seizure of power by "revolutionary mass action."[11] Members also approved a "program of action" that specified particular objectives to be implemented in the near future. Not surprisingly, the general organization of the Party ranked high on the list of priorities, and affiliates soon formed a provisional Executive Committee, constituted with elected representatives, who were to return to their communities to establish local parties. To carry out their reforms, organizers considered the creation of schools, libraries, and newspapers that would communicate revolutionary socialist directives. Specifically addressing the issue of unions in the factories and of agricultural workers, representatives recommended the use of propaganda to unify the proletarian forces.[12]

In line with its program of action, members of the congress also nominated three delegates who would represent the new party at the next meeting of the Third International. According to the organizers, responsibility for the "complete emancipation" of the working class lay with the Third International; consequently, the National Committee declared its "total solidarity" from this point forward. Even as committee members praised the Comintern, they harshly criticized many of Europe's socialist parties for being no more revolutionary than liberal, bourgeois political groups. According to some Party members, in their worst moments the socialist parties assumed a decidedly hostile attitude toward social revolution during World War I, and even at their best, they remained inactive or irresolute. As a result of such grave failures to support the working class, the organization declared a break with the past, thus pronouncing "We have nothing in common with the Second International."[13] Despite the strong language put forward at the First National Congress, the group remained socialist. Still, various factions soon developed over the nature of the Party and its future direction.[14]

Responding to such growing concerns, and after considerable discussion, in November 1919, the Socialist Party officially changed its name to the *Partido Comunista Mexicano*. Not all members of the Socialist Party approved of the Party's new direction, although it would appear that they remained a minority.[15] After all, members of the Socialist National Congress already had aligned with the Comintern and had nominated delegates to attend its next meeting as well.[16] Nonetheless, the Party's transition signaled a meaningful move; from this point forward Mexico's young Communist Party clearly aligned with Moscow and endorsed the terms "communist and communism." Organizers made clear that the new turn—from socialism to communism—did not imply "a change in principle or politic"; it simply clarified their political position.[17] Soon afterward, the Party established the Latin American Bureau of the Third International to spread propaganda throughout Latin America, "to unify the proletarian movements in those countries and to pave the way for the Social Revolution in all of them."[18] By the end of November, José Allen, then secretary general of Mexico's Communist Party, wrote directly to the secretary general of the Third International in Moscow to rationalize the Party's revolutionary intentions and ask for the Comintern's official recognition, which they soon received.[19]

To secure ties with the international communist movement, the PCM promptly sent delegates, including Manabendra Rath Roy (who traveled under the assumed name of Roberto Allén), Roy's wife, Evelyn Trent (Helen Allén), and Charles Phillips (who went by the name of Frank Seaman) to Moscow, where they began the process of sending out statements announcing the PCM as Mexico's official communist party.[20]

In his bid to publicize the existence of Mexico's PCM, and to establish regular connections outside of Mexico, José Allen reached out to members of the United Communist Party of the United States. In his letter dated September 1920, and written in English, Allen wrote that it was "high time for us to be in touch." Still, he cautioned that Mexico's great distance from the United States resulted in a lack of understanding concerning the "psychology" of the Mexican people. In his attempt to rectify the situation and explain the PCM's position, Allen wrote that Mexico's young Communist Party hoped to send comrades to the United States, but only after they resolved their money matters. Meanwhile, he suggested that both parties communicate through a complicated system of smuggled letters and a third party named "Mr. Palacios." He also boasted that while their organization was not perfect, they had made headway throughout the country, especially with a number of disaffected army officers who had weapons.[21]

As the PCM communicated with communists in other countries, members of the Comintern, in return, also took an active interest in Mexico's fledging communist party. Given Mexico's strategic geographical location in relationship to the rest of Latin America, Comintern agents considered Mexico to be an especially important jumping-off point in the development of movements in Cuba, Central America, and South America.[22] Moreover, Mexico's shared border with the United States, as well as its recent revolutionary activity, made the country an attractive location to train the ideological soldiers in the battle against capitalism within the Western Hemisphere. Shortly after the establishment of the Third International, several representatives visited Mexico to help organize the party and train the leadership.[23] More agents followed in 1921, and soon Sen Katayama journeyed to the country.[24] Born in Japan and educated in the United States, Katayama's politics radicalized after 1917, and eventually he traveled the world "for the cause."[25] Despite his diverse life experiences, Katayama quickly discovered that building a communist party was no easy task. To cover his identity, he often operated under the assumed names, H. Kiyoda or "Yavki." Beginning in 1920, he also faced political persecution while in the United States, with questioning by government officials, threats of arrests, and detectives often stopping by his home.[26] Anxiously reporting from New Orleans on the eve of his trip to Mexico, Katayama expressed his hope for a better existence, writing that he soon would "be in a freer country."[27]

Katayama arrived safely in Mexico City from New York during late March 1921. Through his numerous letters to comrades around the world, Katayama reported on his situation in Mexico and expressed relief at being in the capital. Conveying a certain level of optimism with the PCM in Mexico, he still observed that there were few actual Party members in Mexico, and the newly established organization lacked sufficient funds to carry out "effective propaganda work."[28] Katayama further noted that various Party and labor union structures lacked the necessary organization and membership. Funding for publications and organizing also remained a problem, with few affiliated locals paying dues. On the local level, industrial or farm laborers rarely could read, and the skilled workers regularly aligned with the foreign capitalist companies where they often worked. Even worse, although Mexico had experienced its great revolution, the movement failed to produce leaders who could support the "Communist struggle." The task at hand thus remained the introduction of communism to a largely uninformed populace though the use of publications, pamphlets, and leaflets written in clear language.[29]

Although Katayama anticipated greater political freedom in Mexico, the situation soon changed in his adopted country. By mid-1921, suspected "foreign Red agitators" faced increased harassment by Mexican state officials. Pressure from the U.S. government as well as foreign businesses precipitated the shift in Mexico's policy, although internal national politics and Mexico's attempts to appear tough on radicals also played a role.[30] In May 1921, Katayama wrote about the arrest and probable deportation of twelve or fourteen of "those comrades we sent to the country as propagandist[s]," and he feared his own apprehension would follow. The deteriorating political climate forced Katayama into hiding, where he constantly moved from one house to another.[31] One letter to a fellow comrade began with the ominous account, "The forgoing report was made from a dark den in the Chinese quarter of this City where I was temporarily located. Naturally I was rather deppressed [*sic*] with vague fear [that] something may happen at any moment."[32] Katayama's situation was made worse by the fact that he was Japanese in a city with very few other citizens from Japan. As Katayama pointed out, his ethnicity and lack of Spanish language skills made him an easy target when he left his secluded location to wander into the streets.[33] Ultimately, he only remained in Mexico a few months longer before leaving for Moscow in October.

To address serious questions about its future direction, the PCM held its first congress at the end of December 1921. The Party's participation in elections and its role in the organization and leadership of labor unions ranked high among the key issues.[34] Although Katayama had left the country by the time of the congress, another Comintern agent, Louis Fraina, took an active role in the meetings. A founding member of the U.S. Communist Party of America, Fraina arrived in Mexico to offer guidance to the PCM in July 1921. Born in Italy but raised in the United States, Fraina maintained a rather contentious relationship with the U.S. communists. Indeed, by the time he arrived in Mexico, he faced a number of serious accusations, including charges of being a spy and abusing funds. Even though Fraina eventually abandoned communism altogether in 1922, during his short time in the country, he contributed his organizational skills to the strengthening of the PCM.[35] His records on the activities of the congress as well as on the interactions of Mexico's communists provide a compelling account of the issues facing the PCM as they struggled to build a communist foundation in a country with a largely agrarian population who often lacked education beyond the most rudimentary level.

According to Fraina's report on the 1921 congress, the twenty-one delegates who attended represented approximately seven hundred to one thousand members from all over the country. Moreover, members of various labor groups, including agrarian and industrial workers, participated in wide discussions on topics that covered many of Mexico's problems. First, and much to Fraina's dissatisfaction, representatives argued against the Comintern's position on parliamentary elections and voted instead to disregard the ballot box, as least for the time being, because of widespread corruption within the political system. Second, the PCM debated the possibility of a "new revolution," or one where the workers took up weapons for an armed struggle. Again, Fraina opposed this idea, arguing that even while the workers experienced deep discontentment, their lack of a united structure doomed any possible uprising to a "bloody disaster." Instead, Fraina pushed for "peaceful constructive labor organization activity and propaganda," and members eventually incorporated the later concept in their congressional resolutions. Third, Party members, as well as Fraina, emphasized the need to agitate for the unification of Mexico's labor unions in one national federation in order to strengthen the labor movement. Besides these more concrete suggestions, members of the congress also discussed the issue of "theoretical education," or possible ways to teach the theories and practice of communism to the PCM members, most of whom remained unfamiliar with the principles of Marx.[36]

Even with the tangible recommendations put forward by the PCM's first congress, Fraina expressed a pessimistic outlook for Mexico's potential for radical change, and the Party's ability to lead such a transformational movement. He stressed that social revolution occupied no place in Mexico's immediate future, and, in fact, the country was "far from it." Although he predicted that Mexico's oppressed workers would struggle aggressively for improved conditions, Mexico lacked leadership, even within the ranks of a communist party "weak in membership and leaders," who effectively could guide the "masses." To correct the deficiently in guidance, Fraina suggested that the Comintern send a Russian comrade who could provide direction to Mexico's inexperienced Communist Party. Besides Russia, Fraina recommended that comrades from the United States also reach out to the Mexican Party to offer "moral encouragement and a certain amount of direction." Fraina left Mexico soon after he wrote his report in January 1922.[37]

As a new organization, the PCM leadership grappled with innovative ways to attract additional members and spread propaganda. They also needed to present their ideas in a manner that would appeal broadly to the largely undereducated masses. Widely published propaganda pamphlets with revolutionary images provided at least part of the solution to broadening the appeal of the newly created Party. Moreover, the artists, and especially Diego Rivera, occupied a popular place within the public imagination, meaning they presented a possible solution to some Party members who desired to reach a larger audience. Although, at this early point, politics married culture in a union of convenience, the resulting radical artistic movement proved to be a powerful element in the postrevolutionary nation-building process.

Enter the Artists

During the early 1920s the art and writings of three of Mexico's finest artists, including Diego Rivera, David Alfaro Siqueiros, and Xavier Guerrero, increasingly revealed a shift toward radical, revolutionary politics. Certainly Rivera, Siqueiros, and Guerrero linked their notions of artistic value with the legacy of Mexico's revolution and the unique culture of their country of birth. For example, as early as 1921, Siqueiros published his manifesto, "Three Appeals for the Current Guidance to the New Generation of Painters and Sculptors of the Americas," in *Vida-Americana*, a journal he helped to produce while in Barcelona.[38] Although the publication only released one issue, Siqueiros's guidelines laid the ideological foundation for the Mexican muralists as well as the avant-garde in Mexico in the subsequent years.[39] In this work, Siqueiros argued for the retrieval of Mexico's indigenous cultural inheritance, but without resorting to an exotic "Indian" past. Addressing this point, and referencing early Maya and Aztec painters and sculptors, Siqueiros wrote: "Our proximity . . . with them will allow us to assimilate the constructive force of their works in which there is a clear understanding of the elements of nature, which can serve as a starting point for us. We adopt their synthetic energy, without reaching, naturally to the lamentable archeological reconstructions (Indianism, Primitivism, Americanism) so fashionable among us."[40]

Siqueiros, Rivera, and Guerrero grew increasingly close to the PCM, in terms of both ideology and politics, and toward the end of 1922 and early 1923, the artists joined the Communist Party.[41] But their attraction to the PCM was not a one-way street; early on, Party members expressed an enthusiastic interest in the artists as well. In fact, in November 1922, the PCM contacted Diego Rivera and other painters and sculptors to discuss the possibility of working together. First the communists proposed an exhibition of popular revolutionary art held in the Arteaga salon. Afterward, they anticipated the artists would design a series of "Russian style" propaganda posters to distribute throughout the countryside and in various city locations. According to the PCM, Rivera and many of these artists agreed, at least theoretically, with the work of the Communist Party, although a few comrades still questioned whether their ideas would be carried out in practice.[42] Despite such reservations, others welcomed the presence of the artists. For example, Party member María del Refugio García, or Cuca García, remarked that she met the painter Rivera in person. According to García, Rivera had the appropriate references, especially because he already was a personal friend of several comrades.[43]

The artists' presence within the Communist Party increased rapidly during the initial year of their membership. Reflecting their growing influence with the PCM, members even elected Rivera to the Party's Executive Committee during its Second Congress in April 1923. The PCM placed Rivera, along with two others, in charge of politics and agriculture, while Rivera also administered *Plebe,* an anarchist newspaper then utilized by the communists to publish their essays.[44] Not long after Rivera took his place, the committee lost several members and alternates as some left town and others failed to fulfill their positions. In view of the "complete ineptitude" of the comrades who were unable to carry out their duties, the PCM nominated two additional comrades to help with the work of the National Committee. At this point, Siqueiros occupied the position of secretary of trade unions, and Guerrero the secretary of agrarian issues.[45] Female artists also played a role at the Second Congress. For example, the singer and PCM member "Conchita," or Concha Michel, was named to the position of temporary treasurer, and the Party's *Sección Femenina* (Women's Section), which included a group of female intellectuals and workers, also constituted a lively program. Once again, Michel occupied a place on the organizing committee of the *Sección Femenina* along with three other women.[46]

Following their decision to dedicate their art and time to the transformation of society, artists associated with the PCM came together with other like-minded radical thinkers to launch the *Sindicato de Obreros Técnicos, Pintores y Escultores*, or the Union of Technical Workers, Painters, and Sculptors (SOTPE) in December 1922.[47] PCM representative Rosendo Gómez Lorenzo attended the SOTPE's early meetings to explain the "ABC's" of class struggle. According to Siqueiros, under Gómez Lorenzo's direction, the artists first discussed political issues for three days. Later they also examined the matter of aesthetics and their work.[48] The union's formation allowed Siqueiros, Rivera, Guerrero, José Clemente Orozco, Fernando Leal, and others to demand, as workers, better working conditions and increased wages.[49] Through the act of unionizing, the artists came together as a powerful working group to promote art and politics on a national level. Additionally, the union offered space for both women and artists from other countries. For example, two women, Nahui Olín and Carmen Foncerrada, joined the Union, as did Carlos Mérida from Guatemala and Jean Charlot, originally from France.[50] Although political differences led to the eventual breakup of the Union in December 1924, the legacy of the artists' group survived well beyond its short life.[51]

Siqueiros, the Union's intellectual spearhead, wrote the SOPTE's manifesto in 1922, which the artists later signed.[52] Reflecting the group's commitment to social justice and art, all members of the Union, including Rivera, Orozco, Guerrero, Jean Charlot, Ignacio Asúnsolo, Fermín Revueltas, Roberto Montenegro, Carlos Mérida, and others agreed with the declaration.[53] In their manifesto, the artists clearly elucidated their belief in the inseparability of art and politics as well as the beauty of Mexico's indigenous population. Siqueiros made this point clear when he wrote, "With their admirable and extraordinary *talent to create beauty, peculiar to themselves, the art of the Mexican people is the most wholesome spiritual expression in the world*."[54] Even more important was the declaration that artists should reject the "bourgeois individualism" of easel painting and instead produce "ideological" art that would educate people in revolutionary principles.[55] Of course, large-scale public murals provided a plausible strategy to present powerful political declarations and revolutionary concepts within easily accessible images.

Beginning in March 1924, the Union of Technical Workers, Painters, and Sculptors established, and then produced, their newspaper, *El Machete*, which they dedicated to the union's views on art and politics. Although the publication started as a bimonthly publication, by August Graciela Amador, Siqueiros's wife and the only woman working with the paper, proudly announced that given the "importance of the fight against the bourgeoisie," *El Machete* now would become a weekly with increased circulation.[56] Revealing the close ties between Guerrero, Siqueiros, Rivera, and the PCM, the newspaper also acted as the Communist Party's only propaganda organ, although an unofficial one, for its first year.[57] Siqueiros, Rivera, and Guerrero composed the executive committee, while Graciela Amador acted as the paper's administrator. Additional communists from Mexico and other countries advised the artists, and others wrote articles for the paper. Because the group followed a model based on the notion of a "socialist" or group production rather than the individualist work associated with a bourgeoisie press, the paper rarely identified their articles or art by author.[58] During the first few months, *El Machete* reached three thousand readers, and by December the number grew to an impressive six thousand.[59] Workers in a variety of fields made up the paper's intended target audience, including those involved in carpentry, metalworking, and the railroad.[60] Indeed, PCM members argued that *El Machete*, if circulated properly at the factory, was a crucial means to attract new members and supporters, and also a way to spread news of the workers' issues and achievements.[61]

The artists devoted the first issue of *El Machete* to a variety of current topics, and they also presented their political justifications for publishing their new newspaper. Guerrero, writing in the name of the executive committee, forcefully described the paper as a publication for the "People."

He further vowed that *El Machete* would fight for those who still lacked access to land or justice, who did not have enough to eat, and whose bodies were poisoned by their work in the factories. Once again linking art to revolutionary ideals, Guerrero declared that their art would have a social function, and in a similar vein, their newspaper would promote proletarian brotherhood by providing the people of Mexico with the pride of belonging to a great cause.[62] Diego Rivera's piece on the 1924 assassination of Felipe Carrillo Puerto, Yucatán's revolutionary governor, ran on page one of *El Machete*'s first edition. In addition to Guerrero's declarations and Rivera's article on Carrillo Puerto, the paper also dedicated much of page three to Siqueiros's manifesto for the Union of Technical Workers, Painters, and Sculptors. As artists, the layout directors artfully wrapped the copy around the newspaper's publishing information combined with a drawing of a powerful clenched fist, accompanied by the motto: "Director: La [drawing of a fist] del Pueblo," or the power of the people.[63]

In many ways, Siqueiros's manifesto read as a literary punch that left the reader reeling from the force of the artist's convictions. Certainly, Siqueiros refused to soften his statements or blunt his boldness as he described the Union of Technical Workers, Painters, and Sculptors as an organization of immense importance within Mexico's national life, most especially by performing the "miracle" of bringing together a group of Mexican intellectuals and artists dedicated to social action. In this regard, though, Siqueiros sharply delineated the boundaries between the artists associated with the *Sindicato* and other more "parasitic 'artists'" who, at the expense of others, adopted a rabidly individualistic existence no better than "social masturbation." All too aware that painters and sculptors must refuse a lifestyle that stressed the personal, Siqueiros instead emphasized the collective role of artists as their primary function. Accordingly, meeting common human needs and beauty assumed a greater role than personal work in a true artist's life. In highlighting joint action, Siqueiros underscored the union's connections to communism. Indeed, Siqueiros proudly proclaimed that SOPTE provided the artists with a means of participating in a "communist action of production."[64]

Throughout the next few years, the artists wrote a number of hard-hitting articles for publication in *El Machete*. Although many of the illustrations remained unsigned, the artists occasionally included their names with their editorials. Their subject matter covered a wide variety of topics, much of it critical of Mexico's bourgeoisie and the country's political leaders. For example, in May 1924 Siqueiros contributed a piece that questioned the frenzied commercialism and construction of public buildings with the "people's" money.[65] Just a month later, Siqueiros continued with the topic of fiscal concerns by providing a scathing assessment of politicians who wasted workers' scarce financial resources on cars, liquor, prostitutes, and all sorts of decadent activities.[66] Both articles represented the recurrent concerns of the newspaper, especially with the careless spending by government officials and "los ricos" on extravagant and personal items. Besides internal concerns, *El Machete* also critically examined transnational issues, including the growing threat of fascism in Europe, U.S. imperialism, and Mexico's dependent relationship with the United States. Stories on the success of the revolution in the Soviet Union, as well as its great achievements, also figured prominently within the paper's pages, and the editors roundly applauded the Soviet way of life.

In addition to their *El Machete* commentaries, the artists also provided illustrations to accompany various essays. Although significant because of their narrative images and broad appeal to workers, the art also represented the cultural contributions of some of Mexico's most preeminent and historically important artists. Indeed, the blending of radical politics and culture in *El Machete* provided a noteworthy opportunity for the readers of the paper to integrate radical communist ideology presented as appealing propaganda. With their stark black-and-white contrasts and bold lines, the woodcuts worked well to catch the viewer's eye. Additionally, the newspaper provided the artists with the opportunity to experiment with new techniques and artistic approaches. Drawing upon the previous style and content of one of Mexico's most influential printmakers, José Guadalupe Posada, while also utilizing a woodcut technique familiarized by Jean Charlot, artists including Rivera, Siqueiros, and Guerrero created a highly effective means of communicating ideology and culture to a growing audience.[67]

As a remarkable example of the blending of art with politics, starting with its third edition, *El Machete* included a play titled, *The Fall of the Rich and the Construction of the New Social Order*. Written by Siqueiros and Amador, the paper presented the work in a serial format over the next few months.[68] Dedicated to soldiers, workers, and peasants—as the three victims and brothers—each group represented an attribute of revolution. For example, a young soldier signified "energy," the old worker symbolized "experience," and peasants denoted "faith."[69] Throughout the various issues, the artists richly illustrated the theatre piece with striking black-and-white woodcuts. For the first act, Siqueiros presented the soldier, worker, and peasant, each in their appropriate uniform, marching hand-in-hand while singing the *International*. Backed by a large group of similarly dressed men, all represented classes wore similar determined expressions.[70] Utilizing the same woodcut process as Siqueiros, Guerrero provided the next arresting print for the second scene of the first act of the play. For this section the artist depicted a group of workers who gathered around a leader/teacher in overalls leaning on a table that held an open book, a hammer, a sickle, and a star. The men appeared to be listening intently, almost reverently, to the slightly larger and powerful worker who read to them. With the workers' bowed heads and clasped hands, in many ways Guerrero's scene reminded the viewer of a religious scenario, but with the communist symbols replacing traditional crosses and the Bible.[71] Ironically reflecting their position as artists, in July, the newspaper continued its serial production with the first scene of the second act titled "The mummies and bats give their opinion about the revolutionary paintings." Once again, *El Machete* illustrated the play with a woodcut, although this time the artist remained unnamed. Much like the whimsical title, the art depicted a muralist hard at work painting a hammer and sickle on a large star mural while two soldiers, portrayed as mummies, flank him with menacing looks, rifles, and bandoleers. Three huge bats flew near the top of the woodcut, with the center one holding a banner that read, "reactionary."[72]

While the artists provided art and articles for *El Machete*, they simultaneously worked on murals for the Mexican government. But as the politics of Siqueiros, Guerrero, and other PCM members grew more radical, their pointed critiques of Mexican officials led to conflicts not only between the artists and the authorities, but also among the artists themselves. Moreover, although the previous minister of public education, José Vasconcelos, supported the muralists during his time in office, his late 1924 replacement, Manuel Puig Casauranc, expressed little of Vasconcelos's tolerance of art that criticized government policies or politicians. After Casauranc issued his ultimatum to the artists to refrain from painting such negative representations, the muralists' responses divided between two groups that signified an essential ideological split. In this respect, Rivera represented those who cooperated with the government and continued to accept commissions, while Siqueiros and his group refused to compromise their politics.[73] Lacking the government contracts as a source of income, the latter alliance of artists found it increasingly difficult to support themselves.[74] As they faced financial hardships for their stance on artistic and political self-determination, many criticized Rivera for continuing to work with a government that increasingly opposed the communists. Ultimately, the conflict between Rivera and

Siqueiros foreshadowed the many years of disagreements over the meaning of politics and art that would continue for the next several decades.

Siqueiros and Guerrero expressed serious reservations with Rivera's individualism and lack of dedication to communist ideology, but members of PCM's Central Committee questioned the abilities of all three artists—Rivera, Siqueiros, and Guerrero—to carry out their duties as high-level Party members. Bertram Wolfe, the U.S. communist and early member of the PCM, described the election of the artists as a pivotal event in the early history of the Party that transformed the PCM from a "party of revolutionary politicians" to a "party of revolutionary painters."[75] As a member of the Party's Central Committee, Wolfe certainly meant for his remarks to criticize, even as they praised the muralists' involvement in the PCM. Wolfe, who later published a biography on Rivera, reserved his greatest concerns for Rivera and his unwillingness to devote his time to necessary Party business, especially because he preferred to paint. Wolfe even contended that Rivera "was a very poor Central Committee member . . . for he was constantly forgetting what day of the week it was and what hour of the day, so absorbed in his painting that he missed his committee meeting and even his speaking dates."[76] According to Wolfe, Rivera displayed a remarkable ability to influence other comrades, even when his ideas "were so far wrong that they might as well be laying plans for work in another country or on another planet."[77] Clearly Wolfe admired Rivera's formidable painting abilities, but he preferred that the painter remain in front of a canvas rather than speaking in front of a PCM meeting.

During the Party's Third Congress in April 1925, members of the National Executive Committee discussed their growing concerns with Rivera, Siqueiros, and Guerrero, and critically assessed their previous decision to name the three major artists to the National Committee.[78] Although Siqueiros and Guerrero appropriately assumed their leadership positions, committee members reported that their lack of experience led to certain problems. For example, economic difficulties as well as the Party's lack of knowledge over the country's agrarian issues prohibited Guerrero from adequately carrying out his job as secretary of agrarian issues. PCM officials expressed greater concern for Siqueiros, stating that he had "good will," and was "active and tenacious," but his inexperience still caused him to "suffer . . . certain bad prejudices, especially for a national leader."[79] Although the Executive Committee considered Guerrero's and Siqueiros's downfalls to be reparable with time, their report on Rivera revealed the beginnings of the muralist's troubled relationship with his fellow comrades that would last for years to come. Officials harshly criticized Rivera for his continued "slide down a reformist slope," arguing that he failed to "meet the most basic duties of members[,] criticize[d] secretly the acts of the Committee[,] and [did] not fulfill the tasks entrusted to him." Even worse, the committee determined that Rivera's position within the Party should be considered more as a supporter than as an active member, although they further suggested that a commission be named "to finalize this matter of the uncertain situation concerning Rivera."[80]

Despite such criticisms, the artists nonetheless continued their work for the Party and its increasingly popular propaganda organ, *El Machete*. Reflecting the Party's faith in the paper to reach a growing number of potential readers, the outgoing National Committee of the PCM's 1925 Third Congress decided to take a more formal stance toward *El Machete*. Although the paper operated as the PCM's unofficial publication for about a year, the PCM now declared that *El Machete* lacked any issues that could impede its adoption by the PCM, and committee members recommended that the Party recognize it as the PCM's *official* newspaper. Although Party officials expressed reservations regarding Siqueiros's, Guerrero's, and most especially Rivera's contributions to the PCM, the committee still applauded the artists' work in establishing *El Machete*. PCM members also noted that *El Machete* represented a "heroic" effort on the part of its collaborators, but most especially Siqueiros, Guerrero, and Graciela Amador. In fact, the PCM's report of the Third Congress noted with pride that *El Machete* boasted the largest circulation among Mexico's peasants and workers in comparison to other "proletarian" newspapers, and that it played an enormously important role in explaining the PCM's views and tactics to the workers and peasants.[81]

Even as the Executive Committee recognized the importance of the artists' "valuable" efforts with *El Machete*, they nonetheless discussed ways to strengthen their newspaper for future publications. Now that the paper acted as the Party's official organ, *El Machete*'s proper administration ranked high on the list of necessary improvements, especially in areas involving management and finances. According to the committee, although Siqueiros, Guerrero, and even Rivera on some occasions focused their efforts on the paper, "the comrades did not believe in a strict accounting of inputs and outputs." As a result, the artists were unable to supply a list of the amounts donated to the paper, which made it impossible to establish a precise and detailed accounting of the paper's finances. Additionally, the PCM recommended that in order to give the paper "a more proletarian character" in the future, *El Machete* should rely more on a collaboration of the peasants and workers with less writing done by the National Committee. Moreover, Party members hoped to expand the paper's radius of influence so that information on the PCM could reach a greater number of people.[82]

The driving motivation behind the PCM's move to assume leadership of *El Machete* originated from the "Bolshevization of the Party," the new direction adopted during the Fifth Congress of the Comintern, which took place a year earlier, June 1924, in Moscow. In Mexico Bolshevization reflected a move toward greater discipline and centralization within the PCM, and a sign that the Party no longer would support various factions among its members.[83] Under the Bolshevization reform process, *El Machete* converted from a paper by the artists to a publication "FOR the workers, BY and FROM the workers."[84] *El Machete* also played a role in the educational process of potential PCM members, and Party leadership required them to read the paper during their period of probation and undergo a simple test over the material covered throughout its pages.[85] In addition to the applicants' examination over *El Machete*, PCM leaders also requested that all workers who could write contribute to *El Machete*, and that each union, workshop, and farming community name a correspondent who would report on the activities or injustices in their area.[86]

It was in this era of Bolshevization that Rivera's unpredictable behavior as a PCM member raised even greater concerns among his colleagues. As a result of the growing chorus of criticism as well as pressure from Wolfe, Rivera resigned from the Party in April 1925. Arguing that he no longer could carry out his work as a painter alongside his requirements for the Party, Rivera asked that the PCM now consider him a "sympathizer" rather than an active member. Rivera justified his position, though, by arguing that his work as a painter influenced a greater number of people than his possible accomplishments as a "militant" member of the Party.[87] Although the Central Committee eventually readmitted him in 1926, and returned him to his official duties on the committee, at this point members of the PCM questioned Rivera's loyalty to the Party and his decision to elevate art above communism. Indeed, in response to Rivera's resignation, members of the local executive committee wrote, "We cannot understand how a man who considers himself a revolutionist and who is firmly identified with communist principles can desert the International for the love of painting, and how his work as an artist can exclude the more important work of revolutionary struggle." They continued that Rivera should no longer speak to the press as a representative of the PCM, or execute acts that characterized him as a "militant" member of the Party. In the end, they wished the artist luck that his "artistic work [would] be as profitable for the cause of the proletariat as you wish it to be."[88] Indeed, it would appear that the PCM valued Rivera's reputation as an artist of global stature, but of course the tensions between Rivera and Party members only intensified as the years passed.

The "Bolshevization of the Party," and *El Machete*'s adoption by the PCM, also instigated considerable alarm among Mexican officials. Indeed, almost immediately after the PCM recognized *El Machete* as the Party newspaper, Mexico's internal security agents opened an investigation to determine if any members of the federal or state government had offered monetary or moral help to the paper, especially because they maintained that the newspaper operated with meager economic backing.[89] Although officials soon ascertained that only "red" workers supported the PCM's publication, and not government employees, they still embarked upon a covert investigation of anyone associated with *El Machete*. To follow up on this line of inquiry, in late May 1925, Agent Number 8 stopped by the paper's administrative offices where he asked, without success, to speak with the director. Presenting himself as an "enthusiastic admirer . . . of communist ideology," the spy offered his unconditional help in whatever areas the publication might need.[90] Determined to carry out his duties, Agent Number 8 returned to *El Machete* the following day to interview Xavier Guerrero, only this time he was told that he would be able to meet with the artist between six and seven in the evening at a house located at 169 Ayuntamiento Street. Not surprisingly, although the agent arrived at the supposed meeting place, neighbors responded that they knew no one by the name of Guerrero.[91] Agent Number 8 would not wait much longer for his interview, however, as the elusive Guerrero arrived at the office the next day while the agent spoke with the "enthusiastic communist," María del Refugio García. According to the confidential report, although Guerrero said very little, he still discussed his obsession with *El Machete*'s financial difficulties and the losses the paper experienced on a regular basis. Moreover, when asked what the paper paid for articles, Guerrero replied that they customarily considered contributions as collaborations that were not subject to reimbursement.[92]

Over the next several years, artists and intellectuals continued to work for the Party, not only with their duties at *El Machete*, but also with a number of other commitments. For instance, Siqueiros moved toward union organizing and away from painting, but he still found time to create new—although short-lived—newspapers. Utilizing his innovative talents for graphic design, in 1926 he founded *El Martillo*, or The Hammer, and in 1927 he established *El 130*, which fought against the power of the Catholic Church.[93] Revealing the painter's continuing ability to push for controversial change, within days after *El 130* first appeared, a "Friend of the current Government" wrote to government officials to complain that the newspaper presented "intense Bolshevist propaganda" and seditious, disrespectful articles that promoted violence toward businesses and the federal government.[94]

A number of prominent transnational and Mexican artists and intellectuals also contributed to *Mexican Folkways* from its inception in 1925 to the final edition in 1937. Founded by Frances (Paca) Toor, who assumed the role of editor, the journal also enjoyed the creativity of Diego Rivera, who joined as its art editor by issue no. 5, as well as Manuel Álvarez Bravo, Anita Brenner, Pablo O'Higgins, Edward Westin, Tina Modotti, Concha Michel, Doctor Atl, Carlos Mérida, Manuel Gamio, Esperanza Veláquez Bringas, Carleton Beals, among others.[95] From its inception Toor dedicated *Mexican Folkways* to the study of Mexican folk art, music, poetry, traditions, festivals, archeology, literature, language, and clothing. Written in Spanish and English, and published in Mexico City, *Mexican Folkways* represented an innovative collaboration between artists and writers from several countries, as Toor gathered together an exciting group of her friends and acquaintances in the service of her journal. Even though Toor's interactions with the PCM revealed a rather ambivalent political position toward Marxist ideology, many of *Mexican Folkways*'s contributors, although not all, professed allegiance to the PCM, including Modotti, Kahlo, and Rivera. As much of the art and many of the articles published in the journal reflected the radical nature of their creators, *Mexican Folkways* exposed a largely non-communist readership to their radical ideas and art.

Besides their work on various journals and newspapers, the artists also represented Mexico's Communist Party at local and international conferences and demonstrations. Despite the PCM's reservations with Siqueiros and Rivera, they both enjoyed growing international reputations, and they also proved to be lively and charismatic speakers. In 1927, Rivera served as leader of the PCM's delegation to Moscow to mark the 10th anniversary of the Russian Revolution, with the Russia portion funded by the Soviet government. His trip coincided with Leon Trotsky's expulsion in January 1928, and after Rivera backed dissident artists and Trotsky supporters, his invitation to remain in the country came to an abrupt end, and he returned home in May 1928.[96] Just a few days later, *El Machete* proudly announced a talk on the "New Russia," given by the "great revolutionary painter," Diego Rivera. With excitement, the journal invited its readers to "come know what it's like in the country where the workers and peasants govern."[97]

During his time in Moscow, Rivera met with Siqueiros, who also had made the journey to the country along with a delegation of various laborers and union members, to attend the Fourth International Congress of Red Trade Unions.[98] His wife, Amador, joined him on the trip, and she later asserted that Siqueiros insisted that she accompany him because he felt her "humble presence" to be indispensable.[99] During their time in the Soviet Union, Rivera and Siqueiros took a side trip to Berlin, where they decided to visit a cabaret as a nighttime diversion. According to Siqueiros, Rivera instructed the taxi driver, in broken German, to take them to the "most interesting" nightclub possible. No sooner had they arrived at a richly decorated cabaret and began to drink, that the elegantly dressed owner took Siqueiros aside to warn him that the beautiful performers surrounding them were men rather than women. Both artists admitted to being "amazed," although once they left the club, Rivera argued that he knew their "true" sex from the beginning.[100] Eventually Rivera and Siqueiros shared a cabin on their return home to Mexico, although during their journey they disagreed bitterly over the significance of Trotsky.[101]

Rivera's and Siqueiros's views on art and politics grew increasingly disparate as the 1920s came to an end. Less concerned with painting at this point in his career, Siqueiros threw himself into his work with the labor movement.[102] Rivera took a different path and instead devoted his time to painting and art. Siqueiros also opposed working with government officials or accepting state funding, while Rivera received government backing for his paintings, seemingly with few qualms. Although they later would appear together at rallies and protests in support of radical causes, for the most part, their earlier political and cultural connections now came to an end. Coalitions, or the lack of them, proved to be especially important throughout the next few years as conservative government officials took a turn to the right and condemned PCM members and the artists associated with the Party. When communists faced jail time or expulsion from Mexico, loyalty to Party principles assumed a greater significance.

Suppression of Art and Radical Politics

Besides the internal dissension between Rivera and Siqueiros, conflicts also intensified between many of the radical artists and an increasingly oppressive government apparatus. Throughout much of the 1920s, representatives of the Mexican state and the artists associated with the PCM negotiated for the distribution of revolutionary ideals through culture, but by the late 1920s, this uneasy cooperation ended. Several issues led to the sharp break between the artists and the Mexican government at this point. For one, the PCM's hard turn to the left after the Sixth Congress of the Comintern in 1928 meant that the Party now disapproved of working with representatives of the Mexican government, and members even condemned more progressive reforms.[103] Moreover, the Party's new tactical position also created internal dissent within the PCM that resulted in the loss of many of its more moderate members, either through expulsions or by their own will, who would be more predisposed to cooperate with the government. Second, by the late 1920s conservative elements within the government, under President Emilio Portes Gil, expressed grave concerns with the growth of communism, both in Mexico and internationally.[104] As a consequence, members of Mexico's Communist Party, and even those suspected of maintaining ties to the PCM, experienced violent attacks as henchmen cracked down on the PCM. During the subsequent years of repression, the communists persisted with their work to organize workers and the popular groups, including the unemployed in Mexico City during the early 1930s, and their sustained efforts continued to alarm the ruling party.[105] PCM members paid a heavy price for their Party affiliation as state officials arrested numerous men and women throughout the country, sending some to the Islas Marías penitentiary, and deporting others.[106]

By the end of the 1920s, governmental repression toward the PCM increased almost monthly. In June 1929, the Mexican government closed *El Machete* and then destroyed the newspaper's presses on 29 August.[107] Rafael Carrillo, general secretary of the Party, appealed the closure of the periodical, asking that the secretary of the interior order the chief of police to reopen *El Machete*'s offices. A frustrated Carrillo noted the contradictions between the president of the republic's report to the district judge, which denied any blame with the paper's closure, and the chief of police's claim that he only followed higher orders from superiors.[108] Even after the shutdown of *El Machete*, internal security agents remained concerned that the PCM would continue printing the paper at another location.[109] Almost immediately, a number of spies investigated possible locales in the hopes of discovering *El Machete*'s new operations and inhibiting any renewed operations.[110] In September, Agent Number 12 thought he identified the new whereabouts of the printing press after talking with a fellow who sold newspapers in front of the post office. Although this informant revealed a possible address, he told the agent to wait until the next issue so that he could ask the deliveryman where he currently obtained *El Machete*. The tip revealed insufficient evidence, however, as the man never returned to deliver the papers.[111] Nearly a year later, in June 1930, Agent Number 13 continued the search for *El Machete*, only at this point he attempted—unsuccessfully—to track down a mimeograph machine that printed leaflets filled with communist ideology from the home of a sympathizer.[112] It was no accident that the PCM employed cat and mouse maneuvers to evade another closure of their paper. Members of the Central Committee understood the dangers they faced from the "counter-revolutionary government," and in response to the constant threats, they reorganized their distribution methods to avoid detection.[113] Although sustained government repression drove the PCM underground from 1930 until December 1934, the PCM newspaper continued to publish clandestinely during much of this time, just as the agents feared.

The suppression of suspected communists within Mexico reflected a broader, transnational crackdown on the growth of communism. Mexican officials, however, remained especially concerned about the relationship between the country's artists and the USSR. For instance, Agent Number 20's report on the "communist elements in Mexico," written in June 1929, asserted that the country's communists enjoyed the strong support of Russia's Third International. Even worse, according to the memo, high-level members of the Third International periodically had been sending "foreign elements" as well as large sums of money into Mexico with the help of false passports and aliases in order to create a base in Mexico City from which to spread out to the United States and all of Latin American. Although foreigners, including Tina Modotti, theoretically spearheaded this effort, the agent also singled out Mexican nationals, and especially Siqueiros, who led the organization of the workers.[114]

Of all the artists originally associated with the SOTPE, only Rivera maintained a working relationship with an increasingly repressive government apparatus. Not surprisingly, though, as he continued to paint state-sponsored murals, Rivera's work with the government caused considerable concern among PCM members. Even though Rivera persisted in attending Party-sponsored rallies, including the PCM's 1929 demonstration to honor the burial of the Cuban revolutionary Julio Mella, for the most part he focused his attention on painting rather than PCM work.[115] Given Mexico's climate of increasing government repression against PCM members, and Rivera's continued willingness throughout the 1920s to accept governmental commissions for his painting, his expulsion seemed only a matter of time.

And indeed, on 17 September 1929, the PCM's Central Committee finally agreed to expel one of their most widely known members.[116] Two months earlier, concerned Party members discussed Rivera's situation during a plenum of the PCM's Central Committee. Their argument against Rivera consisted of several points: (1) Most importantly, Rivera's actions undermined the very existence of the Party by refusing to cut ties with state officials and continuing to work with a "fascist" government that actively repressed the Party and outlawed its very existence. (2) Rivera failed to accept the decisions of the Sixth Congress of the Communist International that called for the bolshevization of the Party and its subsequent left turn. As a consequence, Rivera's work with the "bourgeois" government constituted "counter-revolutionary" and "treasonous" acts against the working class.[117] In other words, Rivera rejected the party line and preferred to continue to reap the benefits of government funding. Indeed, soon after his expulsion from the PCM, and only a month after marrying Frida Kahlo on 21 August 1929, Rivera and Kahlo left for Cuernavaca to paint a mural at the Palace of Cortés, a job commissioned by U.S. ambassador Dwight Morrow.[118] Certainly the fact that Rivera agreed to accept such a paid assignment provided even more evidence to Party members that the painter's loyalty aligned with both the Mexican and U.S. governments. And as a further confirmation of Rivera's allegiance, at least according the PCM, Rivera and Kahlo left for San Francisco a week after finishing the Cuernavaca fresco.[119]

The PCM's apprehensions with repressive government maneuvers and anticommunist rhetoric were justifiable as these tactics increased with the beginning of the 1930s. Just a few months following Rivera's expulsion from the Party, Mexico severed its diplomatic ties with the Soviet Union in January 1930, and the two countries would remain without relations until the middle of the 1940s.[120] Moreover, as the influence of anticommunist factions increased in the United States, Mexico also experienced growing pressure from U.S. interest groups and government officials to restrain the activities of those within the Mexican population who may be affiliated in some way to communism. Not surprisingly, members of the PCM denounced outside influences on internal Mexican affairs as imperialism and further condemned the right of U.S. reactionary groups to dictate Mexico's policies on left-wing activities within the country.

In 1930, the "Fish committee," with its multinational focus, especially caused grave concern for members of the PCM. U.S. congressman Hamilton Fish not only investigated supposed communist activities within the United States, but also scrutinized foreigners who possibly could import communist ideas into the country. While members of the Fish committee particularly sought out suspected communists within the borders of the United States, supporters of this right-wing body also feared "alien" radicals and the influence of international subversives, including Mexican leftist groups, and the possible danger such alliances posed to the United States.[121] According to *El Machete*, the Fish committee stated that it now would investigate the relationship between the U.S. Communist Party and the PCM, even directing the Mexican government to send PCM documents and propaganda to Washington via diplomatic means. Although the author expressed little doubt that Mexico's President Ortiz Rubio would provide the United States with all that it requested, they added that Mexican officials had collected nothing of importance to send.[122]

The Mexican state's assault on suspected communists and radical leftists not only applied to supposed national threats, but also to foreigners as well. As the next chapter discusses, Tina Modotti, the Italian photographer, fell victim to the roundup, and government officials detained and then expelled her in 1930. Modotti was not the only transnational artist to run afoul of the law for communist affiliation—real or imagined—while living in Mexico during this era. Much like Modotti, in late 1930, Mexican police monitored the movements of Soviet filmmaker Sergei Eisenstein and briefly detained him on suspicion of meddling in communist affairs.[123] Eisenstein only recently had arrived in the country to film *Que viva México*, originally funded by Upton Sinclair.[124] Indeed, according to Sinclair, the Russian filmmaker "had completely fallen in love with Mexico," and he most likely looked forward to working with like-minded Mexican artists.[125] Despite Eisenstein's excitement about his new film, Mexican officials scrutinized his movements for possible involvement in communist activities. And to be sure, many in the United States attempted to reinforce the suspicions of the Mexican government by instituting a letter-writing campaign against the filmmaker, accusing him of attempting to export communism disguised as art. The avowed anticommunist crusader, Major Frank Pease, president of the Hollywood Technical Director's Institute, led the attack against Eisenstein, both in the United States and in Mexico. Pease sent a number of letters directly to Mexico City's chief of police, stating that he had absolute proof that Eisenstein was a "notorious international communist and agitator," and also that the Hollywood Technical Director's Institute had been responsible for Eisenstein's deportation from the United States.[126] Eisenstein managed to remain in Mexico for a little over a year working on his film before he returned to the USSR.[127]

Along with the other intellectuals and artists, internal security agents targeted Siqueiros as a threat to the government. But by late 1929, however, the PCM also considered the painter to be a danger to the Party. Among other issues, Siqueiros's relationship with Blanca Luz Brum, his new lover, raised the greatest concern among PCM officials.[128] Because of the sharp tensions between the PCM and the Mexican government, Party members operated on heightened alert with increased security measures. In such an extreme political climate, suspicions ran high, and many comrades expressed grave concerns that Luz could divulge confidential PCM information, be a Trotsky supporter, or even secretly work for the Mexican government.[129] Additionally, after being married since 1918 to Graciela Amador, Siqueiros ended his relationship with this much-admired PCM member and original founder of *El Machete* to carry on with Brum, who he met in May 1929 while traveling to Montevideo to represent Mexico's PCM at the Congreso Latinoamericano.[130] Siqueiros's affair and the end of their marriage devastated Amador. Indeed, the destruction of her partnership with Siqueiros caused her to fall gravely ill. Deprived of sleep and unable to eat, Amador's mother sent her to a sanitarium to recover.[131] She described the pain of this period in her life when she wrote, "David broke that covenant [of marriage] and I had to leave, but our heart, that was one, was broken into pieces."[132]

Despite his wife's suffering, and the PCM's warnings to end his affair, Siqueiros continued to openly flaunt his new relationship. Members of the PCM's Central Committee maintained that Siqueiros strolled the streets with Luz on his arm, even though he told the Central Committee that he was under constant police surveillance and confined to his hotel. Even worse, the PCM argued that Siqueiros endangered their members by divulging to Brum the location of the Party's underground offices.[133] The seriousness of the situation resulted in a series of meetings throughout January 1930 to consider the painter's grave errors. In the first of the discussions on 5 January, the Central Committee met to hear a report given by members of the Special Commission appointed to consider Siqueiros's case, and ultimately to adopt a resolution that would decide his future within the Party. The report began with a few clarifications. Although the

Commission formed and members expressed a readiness to go forward during the previous November, Siqueiros's erratic attendance at the Central Committee meetings, combined with the new wave of government repression toward the PCM, resulted in a delay to discuss the artist's situation. Still, given that the PCM warned Siqueiros in the last session that they would discuss the matter "WITHOUT FAIL," the Commission now considered it impossible to the delay the hearings any longer.[134]

That said, the Commission proceeded with the following charges against Siqueiros: (1) He neglected his work at conferences in Montevideo and Buenos Aires and greatly damaged the prestige and international standing of the Party, all because of his relations with Blanca Luz Brum. (2) He spent the amount of his return ticket on enjoying his time with Brum. (3) He completely neglected his work in the Party upon his return to Mexico, to the extent that the Central Committee had to wait many days before Siqueiros gave his report on the Montevideo conference. (4) After having neglected all his work in the Party for several months, he justified his mistakes to the Central Committee and then compromised all union work entrusted to his direction by continuing to abandon his duties. (5) He caused, by his love for Brum, various public scandals that could discredit the Party. For example, according to the PCM's report, Brum and Amador insulted and even struck each other in the offices of the Unitary Labor Confederation of Mexico (CSUM), and in front of workers. (6) He allowed Brum to hold Party papers, where they possibly could fall into a stranger's hands. (7) He provided information to Brum, despite her suspicious behavior, on important and confidential Party issues. (8) Because of his relationship with Brum, he sabotaged all of his work in the CSUM and the Central Committee. (9) He persisted in his relations with Brum, even though she insulted the Party, the Central Committee, and other members in some of her letters.[135]

The Special Commission proposed to resolve the situation by requiring Siqueiros to pay back the monetary charges from Montevideo and to leave Mexico City to carry out his duties to the Party. The Central Committee unanimously removed Siqueiros from the Central Committee and his work with the CSUM and also demanded that he end his relationship with Brum. The Committee warned the painter that failure to abide by their orders in an absolute and unreserved manner would result in his expulsion from the Party.[136] Siqueiros agreed to accept the committee's decision, and he promised to comply with all his duties as a communist. Foreshadowing even greater differences between himself and Diego Rivera in the near future, Siqueiros also utilized his rebuttal to the committee as an opportunity to criticize his fellow expelled artist: "Rivera, like most artists of bourgeois extraction, is a buffoon of the bourgeoisie who pays him and whom he serves. He has not been nor will he ever be a communist." Siqueiros continued that Rivera acted as an instrument of the government, and that his prestige as a "revolutionary painter" gave him a "slight red varnish."[137]

Although Siqueiros swore to demonstrate his loyalty to the Party, he soon reneged on his vow to end his relationship with Brum. Under heightened political tensions, in which police arrested members of the PCM's Central Committee and other communists, police apprehended Brum "for her relationships with communists" and sent her to the Mexico City Penitentiary. They soon released her, however, on 3 March, a fact that the PCM's Central Committee viewed as suspicious, especially because "all of the other arrested foreigners up until this point, including those who had contact with the Party, had been invariably expelled from the country."[138] After Brum's release, Siqueiros covertly continued to visit her under cover of night, despite the obvious danger his amorous liaisons presented to himself and the Party. On 6 March, though, his secret liaisons came to an abrupt end when three members of the Central Committee surprised Siqueiros together with Brum. To assess such a serious offense, PCM members appointed a special committee to discuss the grave situation. Before the group met, however, government authorities also discovered Siqueiros in the company of Brum and the Uruguayan consul and promptly arrested him on 10 March. He only remained in jail for a week, and officials released Siqueiros on 17 March.[139]

The Party ultimately expelled Siqueiros at the end of the month for failing to understand the gravity of his situation, exhibiting an incapacity to subvert his emotional inclinations and personal issues to his duties as a communist, violating the Party discipline, and lying to the Central Committee. Most importantly, the PCM argued that Siqueiros represented in the Party "a rightist and opportunistic trend that in many key points coincides with the 'Communist Opposition' formed by agents of the bourgeoisie and the government."[140] His expulsion from the Party and his time spent in jail failed to stop him from participating in antigovernment rallies and PCM-sponsored events. Not surprisingly, security agents kept a close watch on his movements at the protests. For example, several internal security officials, including agents Number 5 and Number 1, diligently followed the painter's activities at the 1930 May Day demonstration in Mexico

City. Agent Number 5 reported that many in the crowd chanted "subversive phrases," such as "Down with politicians," and sang the *Internationale*. According to his report, although the May Day parade attracted different groups, the "thoughtful actions of the police" kept the groups apart and thus avoided possible "bloody clashes." Despite the heavy police presence, the communists still attempted to break through their barriers, although once again "energetic" intervention by the local authorities kept the peace.[141] Agent Number 1 also filed a report on the May Day protest, noting that Siqueiros led the large group of "subversives." According to the agent, after the protestors knocked a mounted officer off his horse, the police charged the group and confiscated their posters and propaganda leaflets.[142] Following the clash, police arrested many of the communists who attended the rally, including the "well-known leader," Siqueiros.[143]

Even as the police labeled Siqueiros the organizer of the May Day demonstration, the PCM also expressed grave misgivings concerning his actions during the event. After all, Siqueiros attended the May Day rally only a few weeks following his expulsion from the Party and also during a time of heightened danger for PCM members. At this point, *El Machete* even published a public notice to let its readers "know the truth about the Siqueiros case" and to announce his previous expulsion from the Party.[144] Additionally, at a special session of the PCM held on 2 May, the Party critically discussed Siqueiros's participation in the May Day ruckus. Siqueiros's former comrades argued that although the painter started out as a simple demonstrator, he soon took the initiative to act as a leader. Even worse, according to the PCM, Siqueiros also attempted to assume the leadership role at the very moment when the mounted police charged the demonstrators. Given the confusion over who was in charge, Siqueiros's actions resulted in mass confusion among the protestors and caused considerable problems for the marchers.[145] The muralist had played an important role within the Party structure throughout the previous decade, but many PCM members now questioned Siqueiros's current position as the 1920s came to an end. Certainly, many labeled his unwillingness to abide by PCM directives and his predisposition toward individualism as undisciplined behavior, especially during a time when the communists faced increased oppression by the Mexican government. Although the newly formed PCM previously relied on the painters to attract new members and bring attention to the young Party, by 1930, a number of fellow communists viewed their "artistic" natures as liabilities. Indeed, the PCM's Central Committee even considered Siqueiros's recent activities to be representative of the "opportunistic and rightest tendencies that crystalized in the small group headed by Diego Rivera," or put another way, "opposition communism."[146]

Conclusion

The 1920s started out with great hope for the artists who supported the PCM. Placing their art in the service of Mexico's Communist Party, they contributed seemingly endless energy and ideas to the creation of *El Machete* and other PCM undertakings. Art and politics merged during this era when so much seemed possible, and the murals of this time reflected Mexico's great historical themes of the rich versus the poor or the conquistadors versus the indigenous population. For Rivera and Siqueiros, culture played a key role in the movement to transform Mexican society from one controlled by bourgeois capitalists to a more equitable, socialist world. Much had changed, though, by the end of the decade. The PCM faced grave difficulties as the Mexican state enacted a policy of repression against those associated with communism and arrested a number of suspected radicals. By this point, the PCM's Central Committee also expelled Rivera and Siqueiros for behavior deemed inappropriate, and the artists' future within the Party structure appeared uncertain.

Although the two muralists both encountered grave difficulties with the PCM, by the late 1920s, Mexican state officials treated Rivera and Siqueiros in entirely different manners. Following Siqueiros's detention during the 1930 May Day demonstration, he remained locked away in Mexico City's penitentiary for months.[147] Released in November, authorities sent Siqueiros to Taxco, where they ordered him to remain throughout 1931 and only allowed him to leave the town with police permission.[148] After months of living in this difficult situation, Siqueiros finally left the country, first traveling to the United States in 1932 and Uruguay and Argentina in 1933.[149] It was during his trip to Argentina that Siqueiros's relationship with Brum ended amid scandal and heartache.[150] Despite Siqueiros's stormy affair and break with the Party, he continued to criticize Rivera's move toward Trotskyism and his close ties to the Mexican government. Ultimately, the ideological chasm between Siqueiros and Rivera only widened throughout the 1930s.

In contrast to Siqueiros's months of prison time, Rivera escaped the harsh measures of the Mexican government. Indeed, Rivera continued to receive public contracts to paint murals on government buildings, and he also traveled freely to the United States with Kahlo to paint murals and exhibit his work. For example, Rivera and Kahlo moved to San Francisco from November 1930 until June 1931, to New York in November 1931 for Rivera's MoMA retrospective, and on to Detroit in the spring of 1932. Almost a year later, in March 1933, Rivera completed the Detroit murals, and afterward, he and Kahlo journeyed back to New York City to work on the never-completed Rockefeller Center mural. Frustrated by the controversy surrounding his inclusion of Lenin in the mural, Rivera relocated back to Mexico in late December 1933.

Rivera and Siqueiros disagreed on a number of issues, but as the next chapter discusses, they still maintained similar, ambivalent positions toward the issue of women within the Party. Although married, Rivera carried on a number of affairs with women associated with the PCM, including Tina Modotti. Moreover, Frida Kahlo also joined the PCM, but Rivera's outsized personality meant she left the Party soon after her husband's expulsion. Siqueiros deserted his wife and PCM comrade Amador for another woman and even faced Party removal for his behavior. Although the artists' attitudes toward their female colleagues reflected larger, complex trends within the PCM and Mexican society as a whole, women fought back with tenacity as political and creative actors. Chapter 2 analyzes the ways in which PCM women negotiated the uneasy terrain between their political activism and traditional gendered roles to forge a space within the Party.

CHAPTER TWO

The Gendering of the Cultural Revolution, 1919–1934

In January 1942, Mexico's influential daily newspapers announced the strange news that Tina Modotti, the "notorious" Italian photographer, had died alone the previous evening in the backseat of a taxi on her way to a Mexico City hospital. The unusual details of Modotti's demise intrigued the city's population much in the same way as her politics, beauty, and multiple love affairs had during her time in Mexico from 1922 to 1930. Indeed, at the moment of her death, Modotti only recently had returned to Mexico after years of exile. Still, her period away from Mexico failed to diminish popular fascination with Modotti, and avid Mexico City readers devoured the front-page articles on her grim death with great interest. After all, sensational stories in *Excélsior* reported that even as she lay dying, the "well known photographer and political extremist" still carried a photo in her pocket of her former Cuban lover, Julio Antonio Mella, assassinated in 1929.[1] Besides Mella, though, *Excélsior* clearly pointed out that Modotti also had "united her destinies to those of Carlos Jiménez Contreras," who "was one of the principal agents" of Joseph Stalin's secret police.[2] In many ways *El Universal*'s coverage of Modotti's sudden death echoed that of *Excélsior*'s. The paper reported that, as a photographer, Modotti experienced success, but again it also clearly positioned Modotti as "a communist leader" although according to the newspaper she appeared to have severed her ties to communism in the months just before her death.[3]

The newspapers' discourse surrounding Modotti's life and death not only reflects many of the key elements most crucial to the relationship between Mexico's postrevolutionary state and radical artists, but an analysis of the articles also reveals much about the ways in which popular understandings of gender permeated Mexican society during this era. For one, the newspaper accounts of Modotti's death stressed the photographer's popularity, or even her notoriety, and the fact that she had been "well known" during her time in Mexico. Certainly, the newspapers displayed an obsession with her life and loves during her earlier years in Mexico. Modotti's escapades and unwillingness to abide by societal sexual norms created appealing copy, and the large number of articles printed about Modotti suggests that the public read the stories with great interest. Second, besides her lovers and personal life, the newspaper accounts recognized Modotti's importance as a photographer, or at least that she garnered some success in this career while in Mexico. Third, Modotti was a woman of the world, a political player who acted in Hollywood when she was young, moved to the Soviet Union, fought in the Spanish Civil War, and ultimately abandoned her photography, at least for many years, to devote her energies to the spread of international communism. Lastly, and perhaps more importantly, Modotti's affiliation with the *Partido Comunista Mexicano*, or Mexico's Communist Party (PCM), took center stage throughout the reports of her death, and also those written while she lived.

Even as the papers stressed Modotti's radical and dangerous ties to communism, they also fixated on her sexuality and her role as a sexual partner to several men. In this manner, the newspapers' statements reproduced contradictions inherent in official state rhetoric that originated during the Mexican Revolution. Revolutionary reforms promised to provide women with greater freedoms, but the laws also reflected liberal philosophy that stressed the inherent differences between men and women and their subsequent "natural" functions in society.[4] Accordingly, a woman's emotional temperament as a sensitive nurturer ensured her function as mother or wife within the home, while a man's rational thinking and inherent intelligence guaranteed an appropriate demeanor for public duty.[5] Certainly Modotti's radical political views, international lifestyle, multiple lovers, and her choice to remain childless positioned her as diametrically opposite from the traditional view of women who, according to liberal notions, should remain ensconced at home and in the kitchen, focused on family, and devoted to their husbands throughout their lives. As shared concepts of women's and men's distinct roles permeated through all levels of society, even freethinking women experienced the weight of patriarchal oppression, regardless of class and ethnicity.

Chapter 2 highlights the artistic and political contributions of Tina Modotti, while recognizing her ambivalent position within postrevolutionary society, and analyzes the complex and often contradictory gendered positions of women artists associated with Mexico's Communist Party during the first decades of the twentieth century. This chapter argues that even as the postrevolutionary state grew increasingly concerned with Modotti's communist leanings, Mexican officials nonetheless co-opted Modotti's image in several ways. Not only did her photographs help to shape an "authentic" Mexican identity, but her very presence, indeed her own body alone in death, provided a cautionary morality tale to all women as to the consequences of having "questionable" morals and, even worse, of adhering to communist principles. Modotti's influence far outweighed her lone photographic exhibition during her eight years in Mexico, partly because her work widely appeared in other outlets, including *Mexican Folkways*, but also because of her impact on fellow artists, including Diego Rivera. As a true transnational citizen, Modotti moved beyond the physical borders of the nation-state as well as the gendered social perimeters of the time to blur the boundaries that separated her art from her political commitments and to craft a legacy that helped define a vision of Mexico's revolutionary past and future place within a changing global modernity. Ultimately, as John Mraz points out, the photographs of this Italian communist figured most prominently within national discussions on "how best to photographically portray *mexicanidad*."[6]

Scholars traditionally have lauded the three great muralists, Diego Rivera, José Clemente Orozco, and David Alfaro Siqueiros as the principal leaders of Mexico's politically influential artistic movement, but they often diminish the revolutionary contributions of female artists by stressing their dramatic and unhappy love affairs or even their secondary standings within a patriarchal movement (and society).[7] And indeed, when examining the lives of many women artists and intellectuals of the era, including Antonieta Rivas Mercado, José Vasconcelos's abandoned lover who committed suicide in Notre Dame Cathedral, Modotti's romance with the strange and controlling Vittorio Vidali, or even Frida Kahlo's often anguished relationship with Rivera, it is clear that "thriving machismo took its toll on the modern woman," as Mary Kay Vaughan emphasizes.[8] While it can be argued that tragic affairs and marriages contributed to women's identity and art, narratives that focus primarily on their relationships with unfaithful men relegate the actions of vibrant postrevolutionary women to scorned lovers and bury the historical memory of the women's activism beneath the very patriarchal rhetoric that feminist scholars hope to eliminate. A close reading of a variety of historical sources moves the analysis beyond the traditional account of the long-suffering woman and places women's contributions squarely within Mexico's struggles for gender and class equality as well as the country's vibrant cultural scene. Moreover, the addition of original archival materials allows us to build upon more customary narratives to reread Modotti's contributions in novel ways and to delve more deeply into her roles as a revolutionary photographer and PCM member.

This chapter considers women's roles as prominent activists within postrevolutionary Mexico to analyze the ways in which artists, such as Modotti, moved beyond traditional gendered stereotypes and assumed positions within the vanguard of radical politics and revolutionary change. For these women, Mexico's postrevolutionary years provided a vibrant cultural and political environment to practice their art and their political principles. Indeed, during this era, the slogans of the Mexican and Russian revolutions still lingered on the lips of those committed to transformation, and, for many, communism offered the vehicle for fundamental change. Involvement in radical politics during the 1920s presented them with previously unknown options, and progressive women, including those from Mexico and other countries, seized upon the opportunities to be involved in international struggles.[9] In Mexico, as female activists broke new ground with their revolutionary views on the restructuring of society, they also refused to abide by the traditional sexual and gender norms of the times. In many ways, their radical political and social viewpoints allowed them to seize the unique intellectual and artistic openings created in the aftermath of the Mexican Revolution and to produce powerful images that reflected both the political and the personal.

Despite women's increased activism during the postrevolutionary era, their relationship with Mexico's Communist Party proved to be problematic. Concepts of essential differences between men and women permeated all sections of society, including those dedicated to radical change within the PCM. During the postrevolutionary years, many PCM members—both male and female—replicated notions of women's distinct roles in society and, more importantly, in the revolutionary struggle. As Jocelyn Olcott reveals in her study of Concha Michel, the singer and ardent PCM participant, even those dedicated to Party principles often upheld the notion of essential gender differences and the ensuing separate functions for women and men.[10] Several factors reinforced ambivalent attitudes toward notions of absolute equality between the sexes. First, while progressive women, such as Michel, agitated for women's rights, they nonetheless regarded feminism as an external, bourgeois ideology, foreign to a Mexican nation whose cultural foundations rested upon a proud, indigenous heritage.[11] Moreover, the Soviet example also served to provide a case against Western-style feminist principles. Indeed, the Soviet Communist Party condemned feminism as a bourgeois ideology that failed to understand the institution of private property as the tangible foundation of gender inequality—a gendered disparity that only a unified effort of both men and women could resolve (as opposed to women-only groups).[12] Accordingly, as a movement that promoted the right of women to achieve their separate goals, feminism missed the critical point that women and men should join together in the crucial revolutionary crusade that would free both sexes. By dividing the struggle of the working class into categories of sex, feminism not only was immaterial to the fall of capitalism, but it also weakened the possibilities for a united front.[13]

Second, the underlying ideological principles at the core of Marxist philosophy, especially during the first half of the twentieth century, also played a key role in the PCM's complex relationship regarding women and the "woman question." According to classic Marxist theory prevalent at the time, "the complete and real emancipation of women" would come about with the abolition of the private ownership of land and factories, and the "passing from petty, individual, domestic economy to large-scale social economy."[14] While women's economic independence within the means of production thus would ensure their equality, women's social and political emancipation could occur *only* after the fall of capitalism. Women would be equal to men following the proletarian revolution, but before that critical moment women's issues would have to wait; the struggle to overcome class disparities trumped the fight against gender inequalities. All things considered, men were not the source of women's oppression, but rather the capitalist system lay at the core of women's secondary position.[15]

The search for egalitarianism often frustrated women as they fought side by side with men for greater class equality, only to be literally and rhetorically relegated to the home or "women's" duties once off the battlefield. Women worked within the PCM as party members, but in the end, many desired to break free from core structural constraints that translated into gendered divisions of labor.[16] Not all women left the Party, however, and in Mexico, women artists especially found a place within the PCM to make a difference, if at least for a few years. Women's relationship with the Party may have been temporary and fraught with difficulties, but their contributions made a long-lasting impact, not only on the PCM, but also on post-revolutionary Mexican society and the arts.

The Woman Question and the PCM

Women contributed to the everyday affairs of the PCM from the year of the Party's inception in 1919. Although the PCM limited women's involvement in an official capacity throughout the 1920s, a variety of progressive female intellectuals and artists belonged to the PCM, or at least engaged in activities that involved the Party. For example, during the first few decades of the PCM's existence, women artists, including Modotti, participated in the routine activities of the Party, even as their contributions largely remained informal. For example, Graciela Amador, poet, actress, and first wife of David Siqueiros, selected the name—*El Machete*—for what became the official newspaper of the PCM in 1925, and several other women supplied art, photographs, and articles for the paper.[17] Indeed, Amador's work for the PCM caught the attention of internal government agents, who noted in a 1925 confidential memo that she regularly received communist correspondence.[18] Despite such official state-level concerns, few women assumed editorial roles with *El Machete*, even as they spent long hours providing artwork or editorial assistance.[19]

Although women occupied few official positions within the PCM, female members still displayed a tenacious capacity to put forward their demands, both within Party structures and beyond. During the same year as the Party's formation, PCM members and teachers María del Refugio García, or Cuca García, and Elena Torres cofounded the *Consejo Feminista Mexicano* (Mexican Feminist Council), whose members were dedicated to the emancipation of women.[20] The Consejo's biweekly newspaper, *La Mujer*, published news about the group, but it also acted as a conduit for general items of interest for women concerned with progressive issues. García acted as the paper's manager, and under her direction, *La Mujer* printed a variety of articles on women's issues from around the world. Moreover, the paper directly addressed matters relating to the "Mexican woman." In this capacity García and other contributors stressed the equality of women in all respects, the right of women to exercise the same legal rights as men, the importance of education, and the dangers of conservative forces. Those who worked for *La Mujer* also conceived of the paper as a propaganda tool to reach out to women not yet affiliated with any political party, including the PCM. For example, in January 1920, an article titled "To the Mexican Woman" clearly hoped to attract women to the PCM by stating "we would like to appeal to all women who are not organized, in order to unify their efforts with ours, to work selflessly for the dignity of our people . . . our homeland."[21] García's political activities, both for women's rights and in Party politics, even drew the attention of government officials. After a careful investigation of her activities, however, Agent Number 6 could only report back that García, along with another communist in question, were "friends of the government."[22]

When addressing the "woman question," the PCM looked beyond borders during the early years of the Party. Given the ties between the

Mexican and Russian revolutions as well as similarities concerning the issue of revolutionary reforms and women in both countries, the Soviet Union provided an ideological partnership of sorts. After all, following both revolutions, women sought to remove the barriers that limited their advancement in social and political arenas through their membership in their respective communist parties. Revolutionary rhetoric in Mexico and the USSR also explicitly challenged traditional ideas about women's secondary position within the family and endorsed a variety of new laws directed at women.[23] For example, officials promoted the idea of easily available divorces, in theory freeing women from unhappy and binding marriages and leaving them able to embrace marriage as a partnership of equals. Mexico allowed for divorce in 1914 and expanded the provisions with the 1917 Law on Family Relations, which allowed married women to draw up contracts, to participate in legal suits, to act as guardians, and to take custody of their children on an equal basis with men.[24] Soviet Russia soon followed with their own reforms in the area of the family and permitted divorce with the 1918 Bolshevik Code on Marriage, the Family, and Guardianship. Unlike Mexico, Soviet officials also legalized abortion in 1920, although the procedure was outlawed under Stalin in 1936, and at this point, divorce became far more difficult to obtain.[25] Despite the implementation of the new laws that appeared to support women, theoretical and even legal transformations proved difficult to translate into practice. As a result, women still experienced discrimination on a number of levels, including within the Party structures in Mexico and the USSR where women often worked as secretaries and rarely reached the upper levels of leadership.[26]

Arriving from the Soviet Union, Alexandra Kollontai, the internationally renowned women's rights advocate, author, and political leader, attempted to address these continuing issues of gender inequality during her short stay in Mexico. In September 1926, the USSR's Central Executive Committee sent Kollontai to act as the Soviet ambassador to Mexico, and although Kollontai only remained until June 1927, her brief presence in Mexico left a substantial legacy.[27] Tina Modotti visited the ambassador often, and they continued their friendship after Kollontai left the country.[28] The two comrades even shared a particularly harrowing episode the night before Kollontai's departure, as police raided her going-away party and detained many PCM members, including Modotti. The authorities almost arrested Kollontai herself and ordered her taxi driver to deliver her to the police station. Before the situation escalated further, though, government officials interceded at the last minute and demanded that Kollontai be freed due to her diplomatic status.[29] According to Modotti, the deputies later stated they believed the group was a political gathering after hearing the participants sing "red hymns," although most likely the songs provided a thinly veiled pretext to arrest supposed communists and troublemakers.[30] In addition to their comparable political views, Modotti and Kollontai also shared similar key positions on women's place in society. For years, the Soviet ambassador advocated for women's social and political equality, but most especially for women workers. Indeed, Kollontai considered the feminist movement of the West to be inherently bourgeois in nature, arguing that while feminists desired the same power as men within a capitalist society, women workers aimed to abolish all privileges of birth, regardless of whether the "master" was a man or a woman.[31] In the early 1920s, Kollontai also promoted "free love" and the right of women to enjoy sexual freedom, arguing that only a socialist society provided women with the necessary economic freedom to allow them to break free from dependent, damaging sexual relationships.[32]

But as Modotti suffered public criticism for her refusal to live within the gendered cultural norms of the time, Kollontai also faced political scorn for her ideas on sex.[33] Shortly before his death, Lenin warned against Kollontai's writings on sexual freedom, arguing that unbridled passions between men and women would be dangerous for the revolution. According to Lenin, promiscuous and narcissistic couples, obsessed with their own unrestrained sexual desires, lacked the discipline to carry forth their duties for the good of the whole. Even worse, Lenin and other Party leaders equated such individualism with bourgeois, decadent behavior that carried consequences destructive to the proletariat body—both rhetorically and physically.[34] Theoretically, women shouldered the greater burden, or even responsibility, for preventing the erosion of the working class by restraining female sexuality. In his 1920 interview with Clara Zetkin, the influential German Marxist, women's rights activist, and future member of the Presidium of the Executive Committee of the Communist International (1921–1933), a seemingly frustrated Lenin addressed Zetkin with his direct question: "I ask you, is this the time to keep working women busy for months at a stretch with such questions as how to love or be loved, how to woo or be wooed? . . . Nowadays all the thoughts of Communist women, of working women, should be centered on the proletarian revolution, which will lay the foundation, among other things, for the necessary revision of material and sexual relations."[35] Although Kollontai later defended her argument on free love, stating that she never conflated the concept with "immorality, promiscuity or loose living," perhaps her real offense had been to challenge prevailing Party ideology by insisting that solutions to the problem of sexual inequality should be solved alongside the reorganization of the economic structures of society.[36] In her essay "Sexual Relations and the Class Struggle," Kollontai clearly confronted such a viewpoint when she argued, "Doesn't this 'putting off of the problem until the future' suggest that we still haven't found that one and only 'magic thread'? . . . Shouldn't we find it now? At this very moment?"[37] In other words, according to Kollontai, gender equality, along with class, played a critical role within a revolutionary restructuring of society.

Even as Kollontai called for the importance of sexual equality, Mexico's Communist Party encountered formidable hurdles in overcoming commonly shared beliefs, held by many of its members, that women still occupied "helper" positions within the Party structure and in society more generally. For example, a 1927 *El Machete* article concerning Mexico's female population articulated just such a viewpoint. According to the newspaper, before the Russian Revolution, women lived in a "state of misery and humiliation" until they fought hand in hand with their Bolshevik comrades. Not only did women struggle as a group, but they also rose to the leadership level of the "glorious" revolutionary movement, "the largest of all recorded history." Today's Mexican women, the article explained, were much like Russian women prior to the revolution—in need of guidance by the Communist Party in order to improve their sad state of affairs. Indeed, the author lamented that comrades expressed concern that "everything already has been done that can be done" for the country's female population. Still, the example provided by the Russian women gave hope for Mexico, especially if women worked together with their male comrades to force the power from the hands of the bourgeoisie and deliver it to the workers and peasants. In other words, only the proletarian revolution would free women.[38]

Women's experiences within the revolutionary struggle reflected the burden of gender biases, but members of the PCM nonetheless understood the necessity of acknowledging the presence of women, especially those within the labor force. After all, Mexican women worked in a variety of jobs, and many within the Party argued that the emancipation of the proletariat could not occur if the large numbers of working women stayed out of the fight. By early 1931, however, the PCM had done very little specifically to organize women, and some within the Party even complained that such a failure was nothing less than "criminal neglect."[39] To address the "women's issue," in April 1931, the PCM announced the creation of a "Women's Department," or *Departamento Femenino*, within the Central Committee. Moreover, the PCM also suggested the formation of regional women's sections within Party cells around the country.[40] The PCM's push for greater women's participation resulted in the creation of various *Ligas Femeniles Campesinas*, or Leagues of Women Rural Workers, and *Centros Femeniles Revolucionarios*, or Revolutionary Women Centers, to "fight for the rights of women workers."[41] Party officials also advocated equal pay for equal work, land for female agricultural workers and poor women, and help for women without work. Moreover, members suggested additional reforms that uniquely addressed women in their roles as mothers, including eight weeks of rest with full wages before and after the delivery of their child, and the establishment of "*Casas Cuna*," or "Cradle Houses," where the workers' children would be "carefully attended" during the workday.[42]

Beyond the creation of the Women's Department, the PCM also pushed for women's involvement through social measures. For example, the Party endorsed the celebration of the "International Working Women's Day," held on 8 March to honor women workers who often earned salaries far below those of male workers.[43] Despite the PCM's active promotion of Women's Day, during the early 1930s, the event remained largely symbolic, attracting few women throughout the country. The government's refusal to provide permits for the event in many areas outside of the capital must have contributed to women's hesitation, but even in Mexico City total attendance remained low.[44]

In their efforts to involve more women in progressive issues, by the early 1930s, the PCM reluctantly agreed to collaborate with other national women's groups, including members of the Mexican government's *Partido Nacional Revolucionario*, or the National Revolutionary Party (PNR). From the beginning of this difficult alliance, however, members of the PCM and the PNR disagreed over a variety of issues. For one, PNR women argued for the necessity of single-sexed groups, while members of the PCM pushed for women's collaboration with existing labor and peasant groups. More importantly, many PCM women expressed grave apprehension over their collaboration with government-sponsored organizations.[45] High unemployment rates fueled the PCM's concerns, especially because many within the Party claimed that government officials and the *Confederación General de Trabajadores*, or the General Workers Confederation (CGT), sought to eliminate women workers from their positions and replace them with men who had lost their jobs due to the Depression-era economy.[46]

Despite their initial reluctance to align with noncommunist groups, PCM members still participated in the *Primer Congreso Nacional de Obreras y Campesinas* (First National Congress of Women Workers and Peasants). Held in Mexico City's Alvaro Obregón Civic Center in October 1931, the meeting brought together women from various political groups, but most specifically from the PCM and PNR. Even as participants discussed issues considered crucial for both groups, including women's citizenship rights, they nonetheless fiercely debated ideological matters throughout the congress. Moreover, some supporters of the PCM continued to question the wisdom of aligning with other noncommunist groups, especially those connected with the national government. An article covering the conference in *El Machete* specifically addressed this point, reporting that "a group of petit-bourgeois women at the service of the PNR had convened the meetings to create a political base among the country's women workers."[47] The same piece defended the PCM, though, stating that the Women's Department of the PCM's Central Committee had delivered a manifesto to the women workers and campesinas, informing them of the "criminal politics of the Fascist Government of [Mexico's President] Rubio" and calling them to fight for their most important immediate demands: equal salaries for women and men; annual paid vacations of fifteen days for women workers; land for campesinas; and a month paid leave before and after giving birth.[48] Although PCM members acknowledged the meetings as a tentative starting point for further work in the organization of women, they argued that future efforts only should take place under the direction of the Party.[49] For the next few years, and despite concerns over the First National Congress of Women Workers and Peasants, the communists clearly took a defining role in other women's meetings that followed, including the 1933 Second National Congress of Women Workers and Peasants.[50]

By 1934, PCM strategy highlighted an even greater need for cross-party alliances. The advance of fascism throughout Europe precipitated the shift in PCM policy that pushed for increased political coalitions, including women's organizations, in the international struggle against ultra right-wing groups. Responding to the heightened PCM concerns, in November, PCM activists, including Graciela Amador and Doctor Esther Chapa, invited "all organizations that have women in their ranks," regardless of political affiliation or philosophy, to an antiwar women's conference held in Mexico City.[51] Although a significant number of women, 18 percent of the total, had attended a previous meeting on fascism open to both sexes, women now organized separately against the growing threat of fascism.[52] The purpose of the all-women's meeting arranged by Amador and Chapa was to hear a talk by Consuelo Uranga, Mexico's delegate to the "World Congress of Women Against the War and Fascism," held in Paris just a few months earlier. The Paris meetings involved over one thousand women from over twenty-eight countries, including the Soviet Union, and Uranga's presentation shared the Paris Congress's resolutions with the women of Mexico City. Much like the participants of the earlier international symposium, the Mexico City organizers argued that women, as over half of the human population, shared in the duties and responsibilities to stop the advance of fascism and war. Even as an obligation to defend the lives of their children and their men formed the basis of their struggle, the discussion coordinators still stressed women's right to work and the "total emancipation of women."[53]

The PCM's efforts to set aside political differences and push for a united front against fascism reflected official international communist policy. Indeed, the Communist International's general secretary, Georgi Dimitrov, formally endorsed the Popular Front during the Seventh Congress on 2 August 1935, when he called for "a *common language* with the broadest masses for the purpose of struggling against the class enemy, to find ways of finally overcoming *the isolation of the revolutionary vanguard* from the masses of the proletariat and all other working people, as well as of overcoming the fatal *isolation of the working class itself* from its natural allies in the struggle against the bourgeoisie, against fascism."[54] In Mexico the PCM supported the Comintern's strategic position against fascism, and in response Mexico's Communist Party now promoted the need to alter its long-standing antagonistic position toward the ruling party and instead cooperate with President Lázaro Cárdenas and his mass organizations.[55] The PCM's shift in policy created mixed results. The ensuing alliance lifted the persecution of the communists for the most part, at least during Cárdenas's time in power, and also provided the Party with the opportunities to increase its influence within different government organizations, including women's groups. But as Barry Carr stresses, the PCM's recognition of Cárdenas's Popular Front credentials, and the Party's considerable drive toward unity with the national government, also weakened the PCM's "credibility and reputation for independence."[56] Women, who already experienced marginal status within the Party, soon found themselves particularly vulnerable to the PCM's decision to join a national framework.

The Comintern and PCM leadership argued that women, specifically, played a special role in the fight against fascism. According to the Communist International, fascism ruthlessly enslaved women with particular contempt, forcibly sending "needy girls into the country, dooming them to the positions of unpaid servants of rich farmers and landlords."[57] In an obvious break with previous mandates, during his speech at the Seventh Congress, Dimitrov highlighted the importance of drawing women into the struggle against fascism by promoting their participation in separate women's organizations within Party structures. In this vein, he argued that the "preconceived notion that the women's organizations under Communist party leadership in the capitalist countries should be abolished as part of the struggle against 'women's separatism' in the labor movement, has often done great harm." Dimitrov also elucidated the call for women's groups, including "revolutionary, Social-Democratic and progressive anti-war and anti-fascist" organizations, to align and create a united working-class front against fascism.[58]

Following official Comintern initiatives, women within Mexico's Communist Party now rallied around the goals of the Popular Front and promoted alliances with non-PCM women's groups. Indeed, it was in this brief moment of optimism in 1935 that PCM women, together with the Women's Section of the PNR, formed the *Frente Único Pro-Derechos de la Mujer*, or the Sole Front for Women's Rights (FUPDM).[59] *El Machete* proudly announced the birth of the FUPDM, reporting that after "great efforts," women put aside their differences to bring together various ideologies and religious creeds in the creation of the FUPDM. Participants elected longtime activist and PCM member, Cuca García, to act as secretary general and also instructed PCM cells to urge all women to support the FUPDM.[60] Although questionable, the PCM claimed that the number of women who joined this female-only organization reached almost sixty thousand, as women leaders from the PCM and the PNR attempted, with limited success, to ignore political and ideological differences and concentrate on improving women's place within society, promoting women's suffrage, and fighting against fascism.[61]

To celebrate the establishment of the FUPDM, women came together at the "First National Women's Congress" in the Theater Hidalgo in Mexico City in March 1936. During the final session, the communist and FUPDM's secretary of political action, Esther Chapa, gave her position paper titled, "Women's Right to Vote."[62] In her presentation, Chapa examined the various popular arguments against women's suffrage and eloquently identified the fallacy of each. For one, Chapa pointed out that while conservatives and religious authorities insisted on women's intellectual inferiority in comparison to men, recent scientific studies had shattered this myth. Second, Chapa asserted that women possessed the same preparedness to vote as many electoral males, and that they were sufficiently familiar with the mechanism of the elections. And lastly, addressing the favored argument of those who opposed women's right to vote, or the notion that women's "inherently" conservative nature would guarantee an equally conservative vote, Chapa contended that recent elections had proved otherwise.[63] Accordingly, women's increased opportunities for political inclusion, education, and civic rights led to a sophisticated female electorate who refused to follow religious or conservative authorities blindly and instead mobilized around a progressive front.

Chapas's impassioned plea for women's suffrage produced few concrete results. Moreover, even as the momentum for a united front grew stronger among PCM members, their commitment to women's rights weakened amid fears of fascism in the years following the creation of the FUPDM.[64] Still, PCM members continued their campaign to organize Mexico's women, even with attenuated dedication. To this end, in early 1938, PCM activist and former delegate to the World Congress of Women Against the War and Fascism, Consuelo Uranga, crafted a guide for female Party members to follow as they carried out their duties in small rural communities well outside of Mexico's capital. Upon arrival in a region, the PCM document directed its workers to obtain vital statistics concerning existing communist women from the area, and to ask each one to develop a specific task relating to the organization of women. Additionally, the PCM initiatives offered detailed instructions for working with the local trade unions. Here the memo stressed not only the need for unions to appoint an auxiliary committee specifically dedicated to the demands of the women workers, but also to provide maternity rooms and lessons for women that covered proper hygiene practices within the home.[65] Of course, in the process of emphasizing women's separate needs in the workplace, the PCM directive also positioned female workers as essentially different from their male colleagues and widened the gulf that hindered the ability of workers to unite as a whole.

Even as the PCM stressed women's distinct gendered positions, it nonetheless instructed members to "convince communist women that their role [wa]s to MAINTAIN UNITY AT ALL COSTS." In this same vein, Consuelo Uranga urged all PCM women to support the Cárdenas government to carry out PCM initiatives. Here Uranga's memo optimistically asserted that "if each communist man or women [*sic*], consumed with enthusiasm for the work of organizing women, enlisted all women, without distinction of creed or religion, in the struggle together with workers', campesinos', and soldiers' demands, then Mexico will be transformed in very little time."[66] At this point, what interested the PCM most was that passionate Mexican women "of all ideologies," even those not from the Party, were given the opportunity to experience greater advantages—but only by utilizing those reforms, such as maternity leave, schools, and hygiene issues, that reproduced traditional gender roles that related to women as mothers and not as equal citizens with a vote.

Ambitious goals often failed to materialize into concrete reforms for women throughout the 1940s, and "accord" among the women's groups resulted in the diluting of PCM ideals. As Carlos Monsiváis asserts, the PNR's "Stalinist internal structure" guaranteed that the ruling party disregarded other women's groups, eventually even co-opting the FUPDM within the structure of the government's insignificant "feminine sector."[67] Although members of the PCM continued to align with other women's groups, a fractured PCM produced an increasingly difficult environment for women activists within the Party organization. Moreover, as women's options narrowed within the PCM, they resorted to activism in more mainstream national organizations in order to maintain their grasp on the potential for influence within a power structure, especially in their struggle for the right to vote. Unfortunately for the female PCM members, incorporation within the national governmental party softened their more radical ideas and failed to provide the anticipated outlet for women's activism or improve political positions.[68]

Women Shape the PCM—Tina Modotti

Clearly, PCM women experienced setbacks on the road to change. Still, a conviction in the need for cultural and political transformation as well as a radical restructuring of society motivated women's activism, even as they often encountered obstacles within the Party structure. Despite the difficulties of such constraints, however, radical women dedicated to revolutionary change worked within the PCM to put forward their ideas and create a space for women's contributions. The work of Tina Modotti, for example, proved to be crucially important for the PCM, both through her photographs and with her political efforts. Modotti officially joined the Mexican Communist Party in 1927, although previously she had been politically active. She remained in the country only until 1930, but Modotti left an enormous artistic and political legacy that belies her limited days in Mexico. Indeed, this photographer and dedicated communist from Italy created the photographs of Mexican workers, indigenous women, and forceful still-lives that contributed significantly to the shaping of the popular image of a "true" Mexico.

Modotti first came to Mexico in 1922 to participate in Mexico's vibrant political and artistic scene. Her photographs reflected a national image of a country in revolution, and even her own body symbolized the very notion of fundamental beauty as numerous artists and photographers, including Diego Rivera and Edward Weston, immortalized her physical essence in murals and photos. The images of her exposed breasts and often-reclining figure, however, also portrayed a woman who deviated far from the standard norms of women's proper—and certainly more modest—roles in society. Moreover, Modotti refused to abide by local moral conventions, no matter the country, and in Mexico she took well-known artists and revolutionaries as her lovers. Not surprisingly, Modotti's rejection of traditional gender norms, both sexually and in her radical political principles, attracted considerable scrutiny. As a result, critics in Mexico and even her home country of Italy accentuated Modotti's "unbridled" sexuality in their attempts to undermine her political positions. For example, a memo from Italy's Prefecture of Udine to the Public Security Division of the Interior Ministry erroneously reported that Modotti practiced "clandestine prostitution" as a young woman in San Francisco.[69] According to Bertram Wolfe, even Mexico's secretary of education, José Vasconcelos, portrayed Modotti as "depraved," "insatiable," and even worse, as a "vampire" who "liquidated" her many husbands.[70] The vision of Modotti as a home wrecker, overflowing with unrestrained sexuality, would be one that her critics evoked repeatedly throughout her short stay in Mexico.

Modotti's path to Mexico was anything but direct. Although originally from Italy, she joined her family in San Francisco in 1913, where her free spirit and striking good looks led her to look for work as an actress.[71] After a few years, in 1918, Modotti hoped to improve her career by relocating to Los Angeles with her new husband, the painter Roubaix de l'Abrie (Robo) Richey, and to try her luck in Hollywood. While there she acted in silent movies, but more importantly, within a couple of years of her move to Los Angeles, she met numerous artists and photographers, including Edward Weston. Although Modotti and Weston became friends, their sexual and intellectual attraction soon transformed their companionship into a passionate love affair. Modotti often modeled for Weston, and in early 1922, she expressed her profound affection in a letter, writing "Oh, Edward, what beauty you have given my life!"[72] She continued, "Your last letter laid under my head till morning—Was it its faint fragrance that awoke me? Or the spirit of your desires and mine?"[73] Despite their strong mutual infatuation, both lovers remained married to other often-forgotten spouses. Modotti's husband, perhaps reacting to her growing disaffection as well as his own desire to expand his craft as an artist, decided to move to Mexico City to participate in the country's exciting cultural awakening.[74] His letters home must have intrigued Modotti, and she traveled to join her husband in Mexico shortly afterward. Before he could share his excitement in person, however, Modotti's husband contracted smallpox and died just a few days following her arrival.[75]

The allure of Mexico's vibrant cultural and political environment enticed Modotti, even as she made arrangements for her husband's burial. Indeed, after returning to the United States to wrap up the loose ends of both her husband's and father's deaths, in July 1923 she journeyed to Mexico, only this time with Weston and his thirteen-year-old son by her side.[76] In theory, Weston would teach Modotti the art of photography, and in exchange, she would act as his agent, translator, and assistant.[77] The three set up their household and quickly established their circle of friends among Mexico's radical intellectuals and artists, including Xavier Guerrero, Diego Rivera and his wife, Lupe Marín, Jean Charlot, David Alfaro Siqueiros, and José Vasconcelos.[78] Besides their active social life, the two photographers practiced their craft and found inspiration in Mexico's rich social and cultural landscapes where almost every corner provided an abundance of artistic inspiration. To cover their rent and other expenses, Weston took portraits of Mexico City's wealthy, and Modotti photographed the works of the muralists, including Rivera's murals in the Secretaría de Educación Pública and Chapingo.[79]

Although Weston and Modotti collaborated on a number of projects over the next couple of years, they slowly drifted apart. Their disenchantment stemmed from several sources: Modotti's developing interest in leftist politics, their desire to take on other lovers, and most importantly, Modotti's growth as a photographer in her own right. Not only did Modotti devote more time to her art, but her work also earned her an increasing number of accolades in return. Diego Rivera sang the praises of Modotti and Weston in *Mexican Folkways*, first writing that "Few are the modern plastic expressions that have given me purer and more intense joy than the master-pieces [*sic*] that are frequently produced in the work of Edward Weston, and I confess that I prefer the productions of this great artist to the majority of contemporary, significant, paintings."[80] In the same piece, though, Rivera also applauded Modotti, declaring that "Tina Modotti, [Weston's] pupil, has done marvels in sensibility on a plane, perhaps, more abstract, more aerial, even more intellectual, as is natural for an Italian temperament. Her work flowers perfectly in Mexico and harmonizes exactly with our passion."[81] Modotti would not remain Weston's "student" for long, as he returned to California and his family in late 1926. Even on the train home, though, Weston recorded his ambivalent feelings about leaving Mexico and Modotti in his notebook, "This time, Mexico, it must be adiós forever. And you, Tina? I feel it must be farewell forever too."[82]

Julio Antonio Mella and the PCM

After Weston left Mexico, Modotti lived a life divided between her love of photography and her growing interest in radical politics. As her reputation as a photographer grew, she collaborated with a number of artists and intellectuals on a variety of projects. For instance, she provided both photographs and ideas to the popular journal, *Mexican Folkways*, acting as the journal's premier photographer and contributing editor from 1927 to 1930. At this point in her career, Modotti also produced some of her most striking photographs that combined her passion for both artistic form and political meaning. For example, *Workers Parade*, taken in 1926, reveals a group of men from a top-down perspective; not only is the viewer aware of the circular shape of the men's sombreros repeated throughout the photo's frame in an abstract manner, but the photograph clearly portrays the political potential of the crowd. As captured by Modotti's camera, art merges with action within this revolutionary moment, and the observer witnesses the beauty of impending possibilities as expressed by the march of the collective will to some unknown destination. In some ways, the men's traditional hats hint at the essence of an "authentic" Mexican identity, but the men in *Workers Parade* also suggest something much more that transcends time and location—the need of all workers to unite in their desire to construct a better future. Besides the male worker, Modotti also focused her lens on Mexico's indigenous women, once again displaying an aptitude to merge both artistic form and radical political implications. In

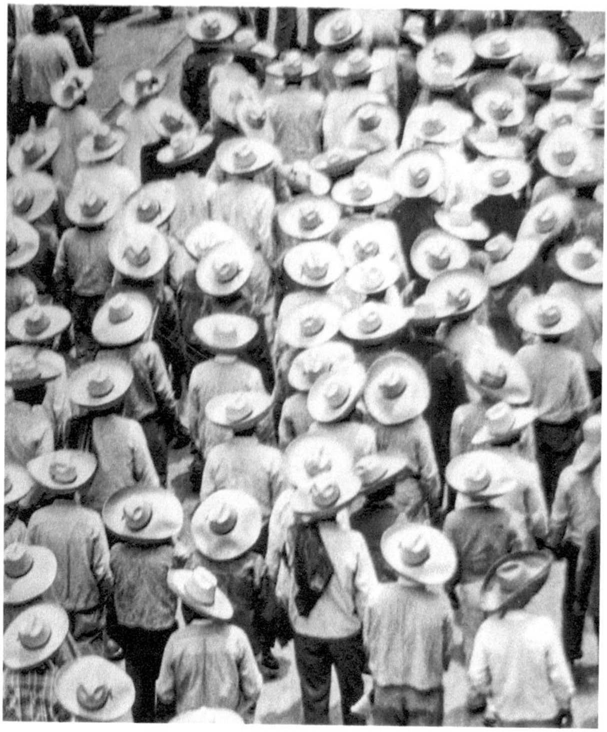

Tina Modotti, *Workers Parade*, 1926. Digital Image © The Museum of Modern Art/ Licensed by SCALA/Art Resource, New York.

Woman with Child, taken in 1929, a pregnant woman carries her naked baby who wraps his tiny arm around his mother's shoulder. As with *Workers Parade*, the viewer is denied a view of the subject's face, but the image of her sturdy grasp around her child suggests a certain timelessness. As a poor indigenous woman, she stands proudly, representing both strength and beauty of form.

Besides photography, Modotti also devoted increasing amounts of time to PCM-related activities. Revealing her commitment to social change, Modotti joined the Mexican Communist Party in late 1927.[83] Her decision represented a natural progression from her past—including the influence of her socialist father—but during this era, Modotti also surrounded herself with a close circle of Party members.[84] Moreover, during 1927, Modotti encountered several internationally active Party members who would figure prominently throughout her life. First, she became involved with the PCM revolutionary painter and cofounder of *El Machete*, Xavier Guerrero, and they remained together until the PCM's Central Committee sent Guerrero to Moscow for extended training.[85] Second, comrades introduced Modotti to Vittorio Vidali, an Italian communist who had recently arrived

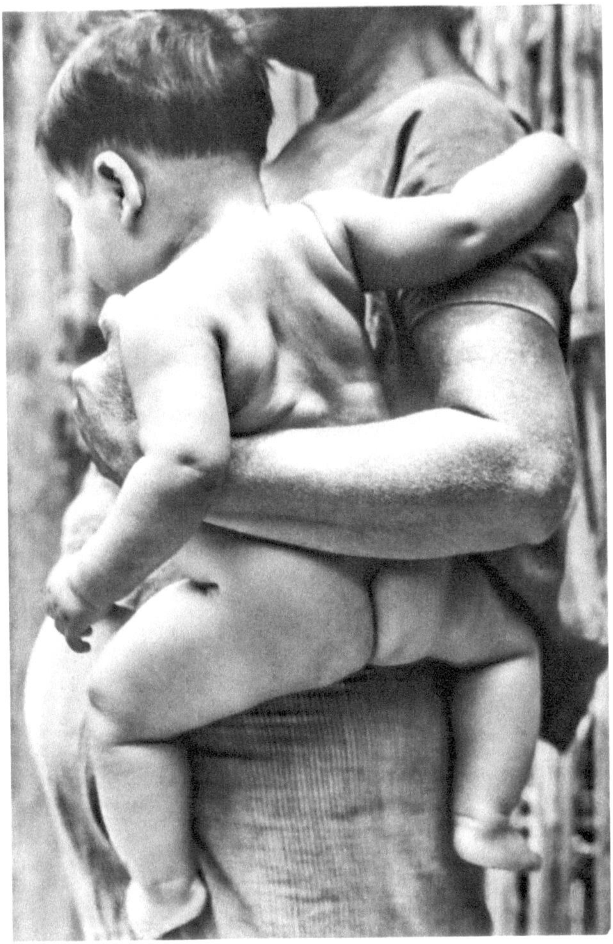

Tina Modotti, *Woman and Child, Tehuantepec, Oaxaca, Mexico*, 1929. Digital Image © The Museum of Modern Art/ Licensed by SCALA/Art Resource, New York.

in Mexico after the Comintern sent him there to help organize the fledging PCM.

Although Guerrero and Vidali played key roles in Modotti's life, in 1927 she met the man who most influenced her future path. Through her work for *El Machete* and the PCM, Modotti often consulted with Julio Antonio Mella, a young Cuban revolutionary and cofounder of the *Partido Comunista de Cuba*, or the Cuban Communist Party (PCC). Mella only recently had traveled to Mexico in 1926 after the PCC expelled him for a period of two years following his unauthorized hunger strike to protest the imprisonment of his companions.[86] Moreover, Cubans, and especially politically active citizens, experienced repression under President Gerardo Machado, and Mella faced recurring prison time.[87] After fleeing Cuba, Mella arrived in Mexico and soon joined the Mexican Communist Party, although at times he clashed with the PCM over ideological issues and worse, some even accused him of being a Trotsky supporter. Still, Mella quickly became an important element in Mexico's radical society, and by 1928, Modotti and Mella fell in love. Modotti's relationship with Mella marked her profoundly; not only did they share a deep emotional and physical love, but also a passion for changing society. The couple only enjoyed each other's company for a short while, however, as an assassin's bullets cut short Mella's life on 10 January 1929.[88] Certainly Mella knew that he faced imminent danger, and on the morning of his shooting, he told Modotti that two men had just arrived from Cuba with the purpose of attacking him.[89] Still, despite his growing sense of vulnerability, Mella continued his normal routine. Earlier in the evening, Modotti and Mella attended a meeting of the *Socorro Rojo Internacional*, or the International Red Aid, an organization established in 1922 by the Communist International to provide aid for communists and nonpartisan political prisoners around the world.[90] After the meeting, Modotti and Mella went their separate ways for a short time, only to meet up again for their walk home. It was at the corner of Abraham González and Morelos that Mella's killers caught up with their victim and shot him. Although authorities rushed him to the hospital, he died on the operating table.[91]

Almost immediately, police considered Modotti to be a prime suspect in her lover's murder, and the very next day police interrogated her for hours, searching her apartment for possible clues. Police finally released her in time to join Mella's funeral procession, which was in progress. Four government agents closely observed the large demonstration and diligently reported the details of the event in a confidential report. According to their description, the PCM organized the affair, and Diego Rivera, among others, headed the large gathering. Speaking before the group, Rafael Carrillo, the secretary general of the PCM, alternated between passionately praising Mella's contributions and fervently denouncing the Cuban government and Yankee imperialism. After the first round of fiery talks, the group began its march through the streets, stopping at various points, including in front of the National Palace and the site of Mella's death. Along the route, others gave energetic speeches "expressing more or less in the same terms what others already had spoken." What especially concerned the agents, though, was that several in the group denounced Mexico's President Emilio Portes Gil (1928–1930), stating that his was a "bourgeois government," that General Machado was nothing more than a "mannequin," and also that Mexico should break diplomatic relations with Cuba.[92]

Following the funeral, police continued to hound Modotti, although they eventually acquitted her of any responsibility in her lover's shooting. But even worse than the treatment Modotti received by the Mexico City police officers was her portrayal as little more than a prostitute by the local press. Splashing the lurid details of the crime in large, front-page headlines, the local newspapers described the many shocking rumors that circulated during the investigation on Mella's killers. For instance, *Excélsior* reported that police doubted Modotti's premise that Mella's death was a political crime, committed by Cuban henchmen. Instead, the paper pointed out that the chief of police, Valente Quintana, asserted that the motivation behind the "tragedy" was "passion" and not Cuban politics. Even worse, according to Quintana, Modotti knew the murderer's identity.[93] Modotti's friends, including Graciela Amador, Concha Michel, and Cuca García, vehemently protested against Modotti's portrayal in the press, and most especially in *Excélsior*. According to the women, *Excélsior* "defended Yaqui imperialism and the fascist tyranny" that dominated Cuba. They further argued that any amorality attributed to Modotti by the newspaper only existed in the "atrophied mind of the editorialist."[94]

Despite the arrest of several suspects, including the Cuban José Magriñat, over time, questions still persisted as to the identity of Mella's killers.[95] An article in *El Machete* even accused Mexico's president, along with Machado, of helping to organize Mella's assassination. *El Machete* stated that it managed to obtain an account of the events surrounding Mella's death from "the mouth" of someone who was entangled in the murder. According to the PCM newspaper, government officials from Cuba and Mexico planned the details of the assassination during several meetings at the Cuban embassy, and the Cuban dictator ordered two Machado loyalists to carry out the crime. Most importantly, *El Machete* insisted that Police Chief Quintana even attended the planning sessions, along with other high-level government representatives. Early in the evening, Quintana visited several police stations in order to establish an alibi and therefore his innocence, but at the time of the murder he personally met with the assassins and participated in the horrendous event. Immediately after the crime, the accomplices reconvened in the Cuban Embassy before the killers left for Veracruz to board a boat for their return to Cuba, substantially enriched by the money paid for their work.[96]

During the months that followed Mella's death, concerns surrounding Modotti's questionable morality and radical political affiliations continued, and government agents—both in Mexico and abroad—closely monitored her movements.[97] Indeed, internal security officials considered Modotti "dangerous" enough to list her with other nationally known Party members, including Siqueiros, "first leader and agitator in Mexico," and Valentín Campa and Hernán Laborde, both important in the Party and labor movements.[98] To reduce the constant harassment, Modotti now limited her friends to other PCM members, especially communist artists. Modotti's houseguest and Rivera's mural assistant at the time, Ione Robinson, stressed this detail in her letter home to her mother when she wrote, "A constant stream of people is coming to see Tina—writers, musicians, and painters who wear overalls with a red star pinned on the front. Everyone is a Communist . . . it is evident that one must take sides in Mexico, and the side that the painters are on is red."[99] During her short time living in Modotti's home, Robinson also noted the increased police surveillance around Modotti, writing, "Even the house where I live seems to be spotted by the police. It has to do with that trial involving Tina, which apparently has not finished yet."[100]

Memos from Italy's Public Security Division of the Interior Ministry reveal that Italian security agents also monitored Modotti, even in Mexico. A February 1929 report not only listed her personal relationships both past and present, but further commented on her current emotional state, noting that Modotti was deeply in love with Mella at the time she gave her deposition following his shooting. Expressing grave concern that Mella's death threatened to "compromise the good relations between Mexico and Cuba," the Italian agents clearly blamed Modotti for much of the resulting political fiasco. To the Italian security officials, Modotti represented an international danger and a "subversive element." Even worse, the report indicated that a "certain [José] Magriñat, the Cuban . . . implicated in Mella's death, declared that Tina Modotti [wa]s a 'fascist spy.'" Modotti's comrade and future lover Vittorio Vidali defended Modotti and denied such vicious charges, pointing out as proof that Modotti devoted her time and energy to Mexico's "Committee for the Defense of the Victims of Fascism," as well as contributed to the antifascism cause in numerous other capacities.[101]

Aware that Mella's murder brought her unwelcome public scrutiny and increased police surveillance, Modotti understood that little time remained for her in Mexico. In response to her increasing concern that Mexican officials soon would force her to leave the country, Modotti spent long hours on her political and artistic projects. In memory of her former lover, Modotti joined the editorial board of the International Red Aid's newspaper, *Mella*, which first appeared on 1 May 1929.[102] Not surprisingly, *Mella* sternly criticized Cuban foreign policy, and in response the Cuban embassy expressed grave concern that the paper contained political material that could cause serious problems for Cuba's president, General Machado.[103] In the first edition, the contributors wrote articles that denounced Mella's death, but also called for revolutionary action. Utilizing fiery rhetoric, one author demanded that all "vanguard parties, the union organizations, as well as the anti-imperialist organizations of whatever social character, should form a united front to fight against . . . the crimes of imperialism."[104] Besides their concern over the anti-Machado language found in *Mella*, officials at the Cuban embassy also complained bitterly about another radical newspaper, *Cuba Libre!* Originally founded by Mella and printed in Mexico City, the paper's articles opposed the tyranny of Machado and extolled the dedication of Cuba's workers.[105] Illustrating Mella's death, a cartoon titled "Geraldo Machado Morales: Assassin without Frontiers" appeared on the front page of the May edition of *Cuba Libre!* and depicted the long arm of Machado reaching across the Gulf of Mexico to stab Mella in Mexico. His other hand held a bag of money.[106]

In addition to her work with the International Red Aid and *Mella*, Modotti continued to practice her photography. Although at this point Modotti's political efforts began to supplant her artistic ambitions, her photography must have provided a welcomed counterpoint to the hardships she endured during the previous year. Moreover, as an increasingly conservative government apparatus intensified their surveillance of supposed radicals, including Modotti, certainly she understood that her life in Mexico would only become more precarious. It was in this era of political instability, in early December 1929, that Modotti and her friends organized the first (and only) major exhibition of her work in the *Biblioteca Nacional* (National Library) of Mexico City's great university, the *Universidad Nacional Autónoma de México*, or the National Autonomous University of Mexico (UNAM). For Modotti, the show represented a rare opportunity to display much of her impressive work, but it also carried the potential to command the respect that possibly would allow her to remain in the country. For the event, the organizers planned a series of activities for the opening day, including a reception in her honor, a lecture on photography, a speech by the university's rector, Ignacio García Téllez, and most importantly, revolutionary songs performed by Modotti's friend, Concha Michel. The university rector even invited Mexico's President Portes Gil to Modotti's show, although he "sadly" replied that his busy schedule kept him from attending.[107] To accompany her photographs, Modotti wrote a manifesto that organizers printed and provided to the attendees. In her statement, Modotti elucidated her position on photography and art, "I consider myself a photographer and nothing more, and if my photographs are different from those generally produced in this field, it is because I just try to produce, not art, but photographs, honored, without traces or manipulations." Strangely, Modotti also included a quote by Leon Trotsky, "Technique will become an inspiration much more powerful than artistic production."[108] Although Modotti may have shared Trotsky's sentiment on art, she also must have known that including a statement by an enemy of the Comintern would create immense controversy—both within the PCM but also with the national government. After all, the organizers reached out to President Portes Gill with their personal invitation, and his response indicated an awareness of the event, even if Modotti's radical politics precluded any possibility of his personal attendance. Regardless of Modotti's motivations in including Trotsky's quote, her 1929 exhibition included many iconic images later appropriated by Mexico's political elites as ideal representations of a national identity.

The Crackdown on Communists and Modotti's Expulsion from Mexico

By the late 1920s, political pressure to fight against the spread of global communism led to the arrest and expulsion of a number of high-profile radical artists who lived and worked in Mexico. It was within this increasingly hostile climate that police officials detained Tina Modotti on 7 February 1930, along with numerous suspected communists and other "unhealthy" international elements connected to the internal communist movement.[109] An attack on Mexico's new president, Pascual Ortiz Rubio, by an obsessive supporter of the Catholic Church supplied the pretext for the crackdown, but conservative government officials had carried out the suppression of the communists for months. Theoretically, Modotti's wrongdoing was her "participation in the last attempt to kill the recently elected president," but a confidential memo also revealed that government officials had grown concerned with Modotti's participation in the PCM as well as her involvement in the labor movement.[110] In his report to Mexico's secretary of state, Mexico City's chief of police stressed a similar point when he wrote, "Detailed investigations that have been practiced by this police headquarters have found fully that . . . Tina Modotti, who [is] detained in this municipal headquarters . . . developed a work that was frankly corrosive and that did

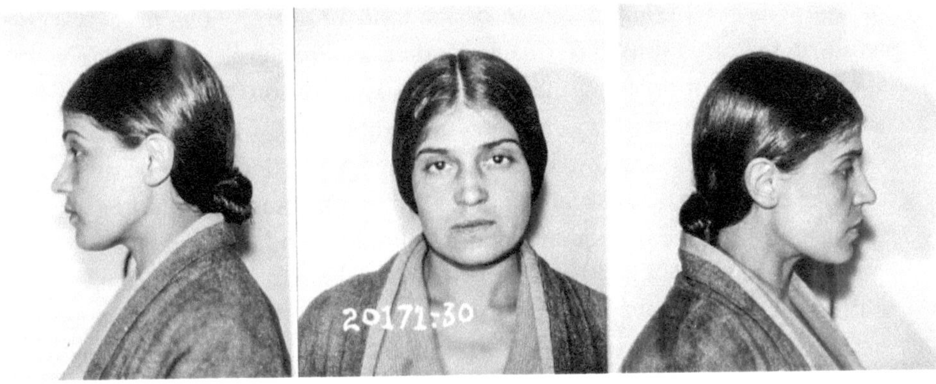

Tina Modotti, arrest photo, 1930. Archivo General de la Nación, Dirección General de Investigaciones Políticas y Sociales, caja 259, exp. 34.

not correspond to the hospitality that we protect in our country, [and] for that in my opinion . . . should be considered to be a pernicious foreigner."[111] Even Italy's Royal Legation in Mexico weighed in on Modotti's "traitorous" activities. In their report to Italian security officials dated 22 February 1930, they gravely declared that Modotti should be considered a "seriously dangerous agitator" based on her supposed connections with Ortiz Rubio's attempted assassination.[112]

Within hours of her arrest, members of the International Red Aid energetically protested the unfairness of Modotti's predicament. In a strongly worded letter to government officials, they objected to the detention of many high-ranking local communists, including Modotti and various union leaders, and pointed out that the government used the attack on the president as an "excuse for carrying out the unjust detentions" on the "revolutionary organizations."[113] Besides Red Aid, numerous unions also wrote to Mexico's president demanding justice and arguing that her apprehension, along with four other detainees, was unfounded. For example, the Workers Federation of Tamaulipas called for her immediate liberty, and the Bakers and Allied Workers Union forcefully objected to the communists' detention under false pretexts.[114] Despite such vigorous complaints, authorities held Modotti in various prison facilities until they finally ordered that the Italian revolutionary, along with two other "pernicious" foreigners—the German Hans Windisch and the Russian Isaak Rosenblum—"be deported from the country," to their respective homes.[115] After giving her only two days to pack her belongings, Mexican bureaucrats expelled Modotti from the country, along with Windisch and Rosenblum, on 24 February at a cost of 950 pesos, including fifteen pesos for food and cars.[116] The next day, while on the cargo ship to Germany, Modotti spelled out her unhappiness about the difficult ordeal in a letter to her friend Weston. "Only thanks to an enormous amount of will power," she wrote, "have I kept from going crazy at times, as for instance when they moved me around from one jail to another and when they made me enter a jail for the first time and I heard the slamming of the iron door and lock behind me and found myself in a small iron cell with a little barred skylight, too high to look out from."[117] Ultimately, Modotti would only remain in Berlin for a few short months before moving to Moscow with Vittorio Vidali in October 1930. Modotti and Vidali began their strained relationship in Germany, and although they never married officially, they soon lived together in Moscow.[118]

Tina Modotti was not the only foreign artist to run afoul of the law for their communist affiliations—real or imagined—while living or working in Mexico during this era. Much like Modotti, in late 1930, Mexican police also monitored the movements of Soviet filmmaker Sergei Eisenstein and briefly detained him on suspicion of meddling in communist affairs.[119] Modotti never met Eisenstein in Mexico, but instead encountered him in 1932 in Moscow, where both were living.[120] Eisenstein admired Modotti's photographs, but at this point in her career, as early as 1931, Modotti had distanced herself from her art. According to her friend Francis Toor, Modotti clearly expressed this point in a recent letter when she wrote that she had "given up photography for the present."[121] Instead of her art, she now devoted her time to the International Red Aid, an organization familiar to Modotti since she directed the Mexican section during her time in Mexico.[122] Although she contemplated such a move away from art even before she left Mexico, Modotti now passionately embraced communism as a revolutionary means to an end and dedicated her time to her work within the Party. Modotti was becoming more radical as the months went by, and even denounced her former friend, Diego Rivera, as a traitor following his expulsion from the PCM.[123]

Modotti's art reflected her devotion to political causes, and the loss of a pictorial outlet must have caused her considerable uneasiness. Indeed, it was only three years earlier, in 1929, that Modotti explained her personal views on photography as well as her determination to produce images for the collective good in *Mexican Folkways*: "Photography, precisely because it can only be produced in the present and because it is based on what exists objectively before the camera, takes its place as the most satisfactory medium for registering objective life in all its documentary value. If to this is added sensibility and understanding and, above all, a clear orientation as to the place it should have in the field of historical development, I believe that the result is something worthy of a place in social production, to which we should all contribute."[124] In other words, even at the height of Modotti's career as a photographer, she subscribed to the notion that her work served a social function. Moreover, Modotti applied a deliberate philosophical approach to her photography, eschewing manipulations to the medium, such as retouching, common to the more painterly approach practiced in Mexico during the 1920s.[125] For Modotti, it was an impression she attempted to capture, combined with her responsiveness to her subject matter, which portrayed a revolutionary moment and produced a visual record of an ideological movement.

If Modotti utilized photography as a political tool, the question still persists as to the motivations behind her decision to give up this aspect of her core identity. Contradictory accounts of Modotti's frame of mind during her early years in Moscow remain in the historical record. For example, Mildred Constantine notes in her biography of Modotti that when the film historian Jay Leyda visited Modotti in Moscow, he found her to be excited about her new life and at peace with her decision to choose the path of a revolutionary over that of a photographer.[126] In his memoirs, Pablo Neruda also recalls that Modotti threw her camera into the Moscow River as a symbol of her dedication to service (albeit tedious) to the Communist Party.[127] In her last letter to Weston, Modotti even confessed that she was "living a completely new life, so much so that I almost feel like a different person, but very interesting."[128] But Modotti's biographer, Margaret Hooks, questions Modotti's eagerness to sacrifice her art and photographs so easily. Instead, Hooks points to her interview with Modotti's friend, Concha Michel, who spoke of Modotti's unhappiness with the Soviet Party's lack of artistic appreciation and, in response, her unwillingness to sublimate her aesthetics to the service of Party business.[129]

Indeed, shortly before she left Mexico, Modotti expressed doubts about abandoning photography when she wrote Weston in April 1929, "Of course I have changed my convictions, of that there is no doubt in the least, but in regards to mode of living, tastes, new habits, etc., are they just a result of living in a certain environment, or have they really taken the place of the old life?"[130] Later that summer she also conveyed her uncertainties about her ability to devote her life to her political principles and her art simultaneously. In one of her last letters to Weston, Modotti worried, "You know Edward I still retain the good standard of photographic perfection, the trouble is that I have lacked the necessary leisure and peace to work satisfactorily. I had to take advantage of a few sporadic moments and interrupt my work constantly, and the final result suffers. At times I feel that it would be more honest on my part to give up all pretences [*sic*] and not do any-more photography, outside of the purely commercial and portraiture work. Yet it is a sacrifice and it hurts me to even think about it."[131]

Moreover, artists in the Soviet Union worked in a far different cultural environment than those practicing their craft in postrevolutionary Mexico. Whereas the arts blossomed within Mexico's atmosphere of artistic exuberance during the 1920s, government restrictions funneled artistic expression into politically sanctioned forms in the USSR of the 1930s. For example, in March 1931, the Central Committee of the Soviet Communist Party issued a resolution to promote political art, or visual propaganda, as a means to reach all people at their "deepest subrational level."[132] A year later, the Party decreed that all artists belong to a single union, thereby abolishing all other independent artist organizations and bringing artists under tight governmental control.[133] The resulting political posters presented vigorous men and women who carried out their tasks with great conviction and joy; in this manner the political art represented the "ideal," a projection of an idyllic and modern future as it already existed in the present—at least in the popular visual propaganda.[134] Much like her distaste for the painterly photos of the 1920s Mexico, Modotti must have shied away from producing images that presented a vision of a perfect imaginary future rather than a reality as she saw it. Although Modotti could have taken a position as the Party's official photographer, the resulting sanctioned portraits of bureaucrats would have differed in fundamental ways from her earlier documentary photos, and not surprisingly, she refused the offer.[135]

Ultimately, Modotti faced a decision: to continue her work as a photographer within the artistic confines of the 1930s Soviet Union or to devote herself to revolutionary change through direct action. Although her lover and ardent Stalinist supporter, Vittorio Vidali, later recalled that Modotti believed that she only could commit herself to one or the other—photography or politics—perhaps the issue was less black and white than Vidali understood.[136] By the early 1930s, Modotti lived the life of a dedicated revolutionary and communist, and at this point in her career, the vehicle to carry out her political objectives mattered less than her commitment to communist principles. For Modotti, *all* women, including herself, should throw themselves into the struggle against capitalism, a point of view she clearly explained in her 1932 pamphlet, *5,000,000 Widows, 10,000,000 Or-*

phans, Women! Do You Want That Again?: "We stand on the eve of events that will bring about the demise of the capitalist world, and that must liberate you women from capitalist exploitation and enslavement. And yet this will only be possible if you, working women of the entire world, invest all of your energy and your strength in this decisive battle. Each of your actions—at home, at work, on the street—must be a class conscious proletarian action that helps to weaken the power and the plans of the bourgeoisie."[137]

The Death of a Revolutionary Photographer

Over the next few years, Modotti served the Communist Party in a number of ways and places before Comintern officials first sent Vidali to Spain in late 1934, and Modotti followed a year later.[138] Both were in Spain in 1936 when the civil war erupted after fascist elements attempted to overthrow the elected Popular Front government. Revealing her belief in direct political action, Modotti fought against fascism on the ground in Spain, even as her former Mexico City comrades formed the FUPDM in their support of the Popular Front. To protect her identity during such dangerous assignments, Modotti assumed the name María del Carmen Ruíz for her work with the Popular Front and International Red Aid, and Vidali changed his name to Carlos Contreras. In Spain, Modotti took on a number of important tasks related to the war, even while she refused the suggestion of other photographers, including Robert Capa, that she return to her art and photographically document the fighting that surrounded her. Instead, Modotti devoted her time to her work for the International Red Aid until the advance of Francisco Franco's armies forced her to flee the country in February 1939. Joined by other artists and revolutionaries from Mexico, including Siqueiros, both she and Vidali remained in Paris while they regained their bearings. Fearing Stalin's wrath, partly because of Vidali's criticism of the Soviet Union's treatment of refugees and also due to the Comintern's growing criticism of Red Aid, Modotti and Vidali decided not to return to Moscow in order to avoid reprisals.[139]

In mid-1939, Modotti finally moved back to Mexico after being denied entry into New York. The Mexican government gave both Vidali and Modotti political asylum and allowed them to enter the country, at least temporarily, as long as they stayed clear of all subversive political activities.[140] Once again Modotti took several aliases, including Carmen Ruíz Sánchez and María Cortés, to avoid possible reprisals as a result of her work in Spain (or at least this was the reason she gave the Mexican government for her name change).[141] While in Mexico City, Modotti kept a low social and political profile, and by all accounts these months represented a difficult period in her life.[142] She refused to communicate with her previous friends, and even her old confidant, Weston, complained that he had not heard from her "in years."[143] Modotti and Vidali lived on little money, and to economize, they moved to a dismal apartment that leaked water when it rained and consisted of little more than an overflowing toilet and tiny bedroom. Vidali later reported that they occasionally skipped meals, even though they only paid a paltry fifty pesos a month in rent.[144]

Moreover, agents resumed their close watch on Modotti, carefully keeping track of the various addresses she reported to the government. What concerned the government officials most, however, was that when they snooped around Modotti's apartments, using "various pretexts," no one seemed to know who she was. The inspector in charge speculated in his 1941 report, "I think that if the woman whom I am talking about has actually lived in these homes, she has ordered that if someone asks for her, they always should say no." If this scenario was incorrect, according to the agent, then perhaps Modotti asked her friends to accept her letters at their residences while she lived in altogether different locations. Either possibility disturbed the agent, especially because when Modotti returned to Mexico, she obtained a letter of recommendation from Hernán Laborde, who at the time was secretary general of the Communist Party.[145] Even though immigration officials required Modotti to refrain from her previous activities related to the Communist Party, clearly, they suspected that she would return to her "seditious" pursuits.

Either way, Modotti's time in Mexico proved to be short. Soon after her return to Mexico, she died at the young age of forty-six from heart failure on 5 January 1942. Her supporters arranged her burial, and a crowd gathered to remember Modotti's accomplishments during her funeral. A close companion of Modotti's and a former colonel in the Spanish Republican Army, Pedro Martínez Cartón, not only spoke at her funeral, but soon afterward sent out letters to her friends in various countries to solicit funds for the construction of a monument in Modotti's honor.[146] The correspondence began by passionately asserting that Modotti's funeral was "an expression of the love and admiration of all the friends and artists who admired her revolutionary and artistic work." According to the note, Modotti's "companion," none other than Carlos Contreras, or Vittorio Vidali, provided the names of those who would be willing to give money. Besides a monument, Martínez Cartón also sought contributions for the publication of a pamphlet that would include a few of her photos, articles, a list of the names of those who provided donations to the monument fund, and Pablo Neruda's poem written in Modotti's honor.[147] Neruda's poem praised Modotti's work as he passionately promised, "You shall not sleep in vain, sister." Neruda also assured Modotti's mourners that her memory would live on:

> They are your people, sister: those who today speak your name,
> we who are from everywhere, from the water and the land,
> with your name leave unspoken and speak other names.
> Because fire does not die.[148]

After her death, many of Modotti's closest friends critically examined her long relationship with Vidali and accused him of causing her life to take a downward trajectory. Throughout her life, Vidali certainly played a role in many of Modotti's key moments—from the moment she left Mexico in exile, to her move to Moscow, to her involvement in the Spanish Civil War. But Vidali was an enigmatic man, and many even suspected his involvement in the deaths of not only Mella and Leon Trotsky, but even Modotti herself. Complicating the circumstances of Modotti's demise was the fact that Modotti's colleagues reported that the couple often quarreled after they returned to Mexico, with Vidali harshly criticizing Modotti for her decidedly "undisciplined" former sexual life.[149] Not surprisingly, Vidali later denied that he and Tina fought. To defend his version of events, Vidali pointed out that even though doctors discovered a "small defect in her heart," they assured him that it was nothing dangerous.[150] Modotti's former lover even was willing to expose their personal life together, writing that "Tina was a normal woman and she liked to make love; we both liked generous love, full of fantasy, complete. We were good together."[151] Perhaps Vidali's "generous" desires exceeded those he encountered at home, though, because it was at this point that he began a series of open affairs, something that even internal government sources noted. One agent reported just such circumstances in 1941 when he wrote that Constancia de la Mora recently divorced her husband and currently had "very intimate relations" with Carlos Contreres, or Vidali.[152] In fact, in the days following Modotti's death, the same de la Mora provided refuge for Vidali as he attempted to escape the Mexico City press and their accusations that he had orchestrated Modotti's demise through poisoning.[153]

Nonetheless, from the time Modotti joined the PCM, and especially during her years in Moscow, she increasingly grew more loyal to the Party. Vidali even claimed that when she lived in the Soviet Union, Modotti told other Party members that she agreed with the declaration that "The Party is always right."[154] Moreover, given the complex political climate in Mexico during the late 1930s, especially after the execution of Trotsky in 1940, it is no surprise that many suspected a Stalin supporter, such as Vidali, to be a Soviet agent or even worse—a murderer.[155]

As Modotti's complicated relationship with Vidali reveals, much of her life, and certainly her death, remain shrouded in mystery. And ultimately, perhaps the details of Modotti's life are less important than the photographic record that remains well after her death. In many ways, her vital body of art is her legacy, as are her political beliefs so apparent in her photographs. Ironically, today her original prints of poor Mexican men and women, their hands and faces wrinkled by sun and work, sell for many thousands of dollars and earn substantial profits for many. Even more paradoxical, perhaps, is that the memory of Modotti—the exiled communist from Italy—now has assumed a place as one of Mexico's most important photographers, who not only immortalized Mexico's revolutionary past but also contributed significantly to Mexico's postrevolutionary self-vision. Modotti only joined Mexico's Communist Party three years before she faced deportation orders, but the relevance of her efforts as a PCM member and artist endured for years to come.

Epilogue

At its November 1956 women's conference, the PCM roundly denounced its previous mistakes in minimizing the importance of women's contributions to the Party.[156] After much discussion members put forward a number of responses: (1) The liberation of the Mexican people and the defense of world peace only could be carried out with the active participation of women. (2) The Mexican Communist Party acknowledged and accepted Marxist-Leninism principles in its struggle to improve women's rights. (3) The PCM denounced its past errors and deficiencies in its political work with women. (4) The PCM acknowledged the necessity to discuss the ideological and political questions concerning its methods and other faults in relationship to women. (5) The PCM also recognized the necessity to discuss, at all levels, the revolutionary importance of women's work within the Party.[157]

The key points of the 1956 conference reflected the PCM's criticism of its historical lack of commitment to the incorporation of women at all levels of Party structures. Of course, at the time, women's efforts for inclusion within a revolutionary struggle had been decades in the making. Despite the PCM's ambivalent position toward women, their involvement with the PCM remained a complicated negotiation on many levels. The PCM provided space for radical women, and comrades such as Modotti supported the PCM in return. During her years in Mexico, this radical photographer became a public figure, for better or worse. Moreover, as awareness of her public persona grew, so did interest in her photographs. Modotti's impact on Mexico far outlasted her short time in the country, and her images of Mexico helped to define the country's postrevolutionary national identity in ways that few others have replicated. Modotti, the citizen of the world, uniquely captured and beautifully preserved the character of a postrevolutionary Mexico in images that even today resonate with significance.

Much like Diego Rivera and David Alfaro Siqueiros, Modotti's reputation grew, as an artist, radical thinker, and as an unorthodox woman. But as the subject of women's place within Mexico's Communist Party illustrates, not all PCM members agreed on the appropriate path forward concerning a number of issues. Although Rivera and Siqueiros experienced lingering disagreements over politics and the meaning of art, the most serious point of contention proved to be the arrival of Leon Trotsky in Mexico in January 1937. As the next chapter discusses, fierce public debates among PCM members accompanied Trotsky's time in Mexico, and his presence in the country resulted in violence, attempted assassination, and finally his death in 1940.

CHAPTER THREE

Trotsky in Mexico

Artists United, Artists Divided, 1930–1940

Toward the end of August 1935, Mexico City's newspapers splashed prominent, front-page headlines revealing the shocking news of a "scandalous" debate that took place between the "communists" David Alfaro Siqueiros and Diego Rivera.[1] Held in Mexico's most important cultural center, the grand *Palacio de Bellas Artes*, or the Palace of Fine Arts, the event packed at least a thousand viewers eager to witness the two great artists come to blows over their artistic and political differences.[2] Their most recent clash emerged during the previous two days after both artists delivered papers at a conference on education sponsored by Mexico's secretary of public education. Rivera first presented "The Arts and Their Revolutionary Role in Culture" on 27 August, followed by Siqueiros's talk, "Art," on the subsequent afternoon.[3] According to Emanuel Eisenberg, who reported on the spectacle for the *New Masses*, although Rivera gave a rather subdued speech, Siqueiros still planned to focus his presentation on his many criticisms of Rivera. Siqueiros spoke for only a few minutes, however, when "the victim himself unexpectedly entered—large, hippopotamus-like, grinning."[4] Emotions quickly escalated at this point, as Siqueiros leveled charges at Mexico's most successful muralist, and Rivera demanded time to defend his position in return. When Rivera supposedly "pulled out his pistol and waived it in the air," the conference chairman agreed to schedule an additional meeting for the artists to continue their heated discussions during the following afternoon.[5]

The next day crowds arrived at the *Palacio de Bellas Artes* to watch the next installment of the verbal match between the two popular public figures. Artists, teachers, union members, journalists, students, art critics, foreigners, members of LEAR (*Liga de Escritores y Artistas Revolucionarios*), and other interested parties packed the lobby.[6] Although Bellas Artes's officials first attempted to usher the large group into an inadequately small room, the masses soon pushed their way into the main hall. If the audience expected a continuation of the previous day's antics, Rivera and Siqueiros may have disappointed them with their rather subdued and measured responses. Siqueiros began by laying out his arguments against Rivera: his indoor murals were inaccessible to the general public; Rivera produced work based on the individual; he cooperated with reactionary governments; and in terms most damning to any serious artist, Rivera was an "opportunist, a sell-out and a painter for tourists."[7] Unwilling to let these points stand alone, Siqueiros further elaborated his disputes with Rivera the following day to the newspaper *El Universal Gráfico*: Rivera received official backing from the Mexican government, even during extreme counterrevolutionary periods; Rivera accepted commissions from North American capitalists; Rivera collaborated with the Mexican government on its educational curriculum; Rivera lived and worked in imperialist countries; among others.[8] For his part, Rivera defended his use of murals and even his collaborations with the Mexican government and foreign capitalists by noting that working from "within," as endorsed by Lenin, could be a subversive tactic.[9]

Although Siqueiros and Rivera agreed to continue with their discussions at Bellas Artes during the next few days, the museum's directors claimed that other groups already occupied all available meeting rooms. Not surprisingly, both artists protested this decision, with Rivera forcibly arguing that the *Palacio de Bellas Artes* failed to exist as a space for the Mexican people, although they paid for it at a great cost.[10] Despite Rivera's impassioned demand for a large room, museum officials refused to permit the continuation of the debate. The two artists and all interested parties nonetheless resumed their discussions on a smaller scale, meeting at the local headquarters of the bakers' union, the *Casa del Pueblo*. The talks lasted for a few days in the new location, with Rivera supported by those who admired Leon Trotsky, and Siqueiros backed by members of LEAR, including Pablo O'Higgins, Leopoldo Méndez, Luis Arenal, and others.[11] According to Eisenberg, who also attended these meetings, Siqueiros "tricked" Rivera into signing a nine-point agreement that, among others, sharply criticized mural painting.[12] For instance, Point Seven stressed the fact that Mexico's artists had concentrated excessively on the mural as an art form, while Point Eight argued for the inappropriateness of placing the murals almost exclusively inside large buildings and instead praised transportable graphic work.[13] Although Rivera's intent in agreeing to the document remains open to interpretation, the meetings dissolved after both artists gave excuses for not resuming the discussions.[14] Following the Bellas Artes event, Rivera continued to defend both his artistic and political positions against continued attacks. According to the muralist, however, his loyalty to Trotsky and the Fourth International sparked the intense animosity directed at him by the Stalinists associated with the PCM, but given his artistic success, professional jealously also played a role.[15]

An analysis of the Bellas Artes debate and the differences as articulated by the artists reveal the blurring of art and politics during Mexico's postrevolutionary years. Yet this "battle of the century," as labeled by journalists, represented only the latest chapter in the ongoing dispute between Rivera and Siqueiros over the meaning of art and its relationship to the Mexican state.[16] Their disagreements emerged wholeheartedly not long before Rivera's expulsion from Mexico's Communist Party in 1929, even though just a few years earlier, Rivera and Siqueiros shared similar artistic and political viewpoints.[17] Ideological comrades during the early 1920s, the young artists, both prominent members of the PCM, played key roles in the creation of *El Machete*, the official journal of the PCM.[18] Both also agreed on the importance of art presented in such a manner and location as would benefit the welfare of Mexico's popular groups. However, as Rivera accepted a number of government commissions for large-scale projects, and as the great muralist increasingly supported the exiled Trotsky, the two artists grew apart. As early as 1930, Siqueiros sharply criticized Rivera on both political and artistic fronts, including his critique of Rivera's cooperation with the government.

But even worse, according to Siqueiros, was Rivera's politically reckless—even counterrevolutionary—embrace of Trotsky, and his narrow focus on "Indianism" as a "Picasso in Aztecland." Siqueiros critiqued Rivera with obvious frustration, "He doesn't know even yet that revolutionary art is bound to reflect the international character of the revolution."[19] In a number of published venues, Rivera countered Siqueiros's harsh accusations, arguing that it was entirely possible to function as a revolutionary artist outside of the official Stalinist Party.[20] He also addressed the issue of "Indianism," asserting that foreigners appreciated his artworks because they reflected the authenticity and beauty of Mexico. It was his paintings' accurate portrayal of Mexican reality, Rivera argued, that provided "the basis of all painting that seeks to build a revolutionary content within a dialectical materialist ideology."[21] Ironically, even Mexico's internal security agents took note of the ideological split between Rivera and Siqueiros. As Inspector Number 12 explained, "Communism was divided in the wake of the events leading to the fall of Trotsky from Russian power and the exaltation of Stalin. . . . This phenomenon had repercussions in Mexico . . . [with] the controversial painter Diego Rivera on the one hand, and Hernán Laborde and Alfonso [*sic*] Siqueiros on the other."[22]

Deep political and creative differences between those who backed Stalin (led by Siqueiros) and those who sided with Leon Trotsky (headed by

Rivera) fractured Mexico's artistic community. Reflecting the divisive split, one Mexico City newspaper narrowed down Rivera's and Siqueiros's main areas of contention during their public deliberations, "Who of the two painters is the best communist; who interprets best the basic principles of historic materialism; and who adheres most loyally to the doctrine of the Party?"[23] In addition to his critique of Rivera's art and politics, Siqueiros also condemned Rivera's personal role in advocating for Trotsky's asylum in Mexico, for allowing Trotsky and his followers to "penetrate" Mexico's political activities, and, even worse, for facilitating a "counter-revolutionary offensive" that turned the government against the left.[24]After Rivera broke with Trotsky in 1939, and even after assassins achieved their goal of ending Trotsky's life in 1940, Siqueiros continued his campaign against Rivera for years to come.

With its focus on both art and politics, the implications of the Bellas Artes debates far exceeded the discussions that occurred during those few days in 1935. For one, the deliberations at the museum represented a milestone in the creation of a postrevolutionary identity for Mexican artists specifically, and for a shared notion of a greater national culture more generally. Not only did the artists battle among themselves over personal issues, but they also disputed the fundamental meaning of art and its relationship to the state and the general populace. Throughout Mexico City, newspapers catered to the public's seemingly endless desire to read about Rivera's wild gun-toting ways, but everyday people and politicians alike also contemplated the fundamental questions over the meaning of art and society that characterized the theoretical core at the center of the debates. Second, in this manner, the talks revealed that many in Mexico's capital followed the details of the artists' lives with avid interest, not only with the 1935 showy public event but also with the Trotsky matter and the artists' relationship to the Russian. According to Leandro A. Sánchez Salazar, then chief of the secret service of the Mexican police, "The newspapers gave up whole pages to the [Trotsky] affair. In political circles, cinemas, and cafés, all conversation hinged on this subject."[25] In other words, with their avant-garde lifestyles and unpredictable actions, the radical artists occupied a similar position as the celebrities of today, providing an endless stream of entertainment and escape from everyday routines.

Chapter 3 focuses on the ongoing disputes between Rivera and Siqueiros, including their central disagreements over Trotsky and his significance to global revolution, to analyze the multiple roles of culture within Mexican society and the profound connections between art and politics during the

1920s, 1930s, and 1940s. This chapter examines the importance of art and artists in Mexico's postrevolutionary state formation to argue that the radical artists and government officials utilized art and culture as a medium to negotiate larger issues whose general relevance fell well beyond art's more traditional influence. During this particular postrevolutionary moment, where almost anything seemed possible, art transcended abstract notions of beauty and concretely shaped many topics of political discussion, especially in areas such as education and foreign affairs. Artists and government officials alike recognized the importance of art and, despite their disparate political and artistic views, all argued that art could not be separated from politics and politics from art.[26] As a consequence, at times even the most radical artists influenced governmental policies, including those that involved public art projects and architecture, but also others that concerned high-level decisions as well.[27] Ultimately, this work seeks to avoid the more common but problematic historiographical discussions that merely evaluate the Trotsky situation through a political lens (i.e., debates for or against Trotsky vis-à-vis his relationship to Stalin). Instead, this chapter positions the controversial revolutionary within the unique historical framework of a remarkable time in Mexico's past, highlights the artists' complex associations with Trotsky and each other, and analyzes the negotiated nature of the artists' relationship with the Mexican state.

Rivera and the Push for Trotsky's Asylum

Siqueiros roundly condemned Rivera as Leon Trotsky's major supporter, but in reality, Rivera's relationship to the exiled former leader was fraught with difficulties. Indeed, at the time of their 1935 debate at Bellas Artes, Trotsky remained exiled in Norway, and Rivera and Trotsky had yet to meet in person. Questions exist as to when Rivera "officially" affiliated with Trotsky. In his biography of Rivera, Bertram Wolfe contends that Rivera moved closer to Trotskyism only after his expulsion from the PCM in 1929.[28] Still, Rivera did little to dispel the common notion that his "Trotskyist convictions" ranked high among the reasons that the PCM removed him from their ranks.[29] Moreover, both Wolfe and Rivera point out that "once he found himself cast out into the void" of life outside the Party, the muralist sought to fill the political emptiness by aligning himself, at least temporarily, with the exiled Russian.[30] Either way, Rivera argued that his first contact with the Trotskyites occurred in 1931 in New York City, and even these initial interactions remained minimal.[31] Trotsky originally communicated with Rivera by letter from his temporary home in Turkey in June 1933. Although at this point the exiled leader only encountered Rivera's paintings through reproductions in books, he nonetheless flattered Rivera, writing that his frescoes moved him with their "union of virility and the sweetness, almost of tenderness, through the internal dynamic and the peaceful balance of shapes." Trotsky closed his note by expressing his hope that one day he could view Rivera's paintings in person.[32] Ironically, Trotsky's wish would come to pass in less than three years.

Despite Trotsky's desire to visit the Americas, high-level Mexican immigration officials consistently expressed hesitation in granting him permission or providing the required documents to enter the country.[33] As early as February 1935, the secretary of the interior, Juan de Dios Bojórquez, answered President Cárdenas's request for information explaining the reasons why Trotsky "systematically" had been denied entrance into the country. Responding to the president's inquiry, the secretary answered that Trotsky's presence in Mexico posed major drawbacks for a number of reasons. For one, "the Russian" had accrued a list of serious offenses, including the fact that he assumed a wide variety of aliases, was accused of several crimes, including forgery and movement of vehicles across borders, and had fled Russia, evading federal justice. Moreover, according to the secretary, Trotsky had been sentenced to a trial in the United States, and as a consequence the United States requested that the Mexican Senate quickly deport the controversial figure if he entered the country. As a result of such grave charges, the secretariat sent a memo to all national branch offices prohibiting the "said alien" from entering the country.[34]

By refusing to provide asylum to Trotsky, Mexico shared a policy toward the controversial Russian similar to almost every other country. Expelled from the Soviet Union in 1929, Trotsky lived a nomadic life in Turkey, France, and finally, Norway for the next few years. Facing pressure from the Soviet Union and conservatives within their government, Norwegian officials apprehended the former revolutionary in late August/early September 1936 and prohibited him and his wife, Natalia, from communicating with his family and colleagues around the world.[35] Four months of house arrest followed Trotsky's detention, and his prospects for asylum on any foreign shore looked bleak.[36] Worried by the recent turn of events, Trotsky's advocates sought out a safe haven for him and his wife in a number of countries.

In Mexico, Rivera's direct involvement in the Trotsky situation began after Anita Brenner, acting on behalf of the U.S. Committee for Asylum for Trotsky, sent the painter a telegram toward the end of November 1936, asking him to intervene in this "life and death" matter.[37] Rivera responded quickly by contacting high-level political officials, including Mexico's President Cárdenas, for help. In his autobiography Rivera assumed much of the credit for Trotsky's safe passage to the country, writing that it "was I who had been instrumental in securing Trotsky's admittance into Mexico," but only after "pleas by his supporters."[38] According to the painter, once he accepted the complete responsibility of procuring Trotsky's legal asylum in Mexico, he then requested and received an audience with President Cárdenas, who granted Rivera's appeal on behalf of Trotsky.[39] Thus, according to Rivera, with a mere meeting, he accomplished what no other country was able to achieve in years—to provide at least a temporary refuge for Trotsky. Rivera offered two reasons behind his willingness to support Trotsky: (1) his belief that a country should provide sanctuary to those suffering from political persecution, and (2) his certainty that his actions did not constitute a betrayal to the Mexican Communist Party because of his earlier expulsion from the PCM in 1929.[40]

Rivera may have exaggerated his claim that he easily facilitated Trotsky's asylum in Mexico through his pressure on the president, but clearly Cárdenas listened to the painter. Still, the matter of Trotsky's asylum took more time and effort than Rivera admitted. Only five days after he received Brenner's telegram, on 26 November 1936, the muralist personally paid a visit to Mexico's secretary of foreign relations, General Eduardo Hay. Rivera informed the secretary that, due to the pressure exerted on the Norwegian government by Russia and Germany, the Russian only had until 18 December before being expelled. Even worse, if no other country accepted him, Norway would turn the aging revolutionary over to the Soviet Union, where, according to Rivera, he faced certain assassination. Because of this immediate danger, Rivera pressed the high-ranking official to sanction Trotsky's residency in Mexico. Without doubt, however, Rivera did not agree with the secretary's response. Although General Hay pointed out that the decision of Trotsky's asylum did not lie within his jurisdiction, he nonetheless felt obliged to express his opinion that Trotsky's admission to Mexico would be interpreted as a demonstration that the Mexican government shared Trotsky's "radical" theories. Even worse, the secretary continued that many unjustly labeled the Mexican government as "communist," and that Trotsky's presence only would serve to cause even greater alarm for other Latin American countries and for the United States.[41]

General Hay's carefully crafted arguments against granting Trotsky asylum failed to achieve its goal. Cárdenas overruled Hay's recommendations, and on 7 December 1936, he officially announced his decision to welcome Trotsky into the country. President Cárdenas's response to General Hay's concerns provides insight into the president's reasoning behind his decision. Although Cárdenas pointed out that he carefully considered the secretary's suggestions, he nonetheless agreed to Rivera's request on the grounds that the current government of Mexico refused to acquiesce to fear-mongering caused by the presence of Trotsky or any other citizen regardless of their country of origin, beliefs, or political affiliation.[42] In this vein, Bertrand Patenaude, the scholar of Trotsky's time in Mexico, argues that the Mexican president extended his invitation to Trotsky "because he believed it was the proper thing to do."[43] Cárdenas's determination that Mexico would not succumb to outside pressure in the matter of whom they allowed within their borders reinforces Patenaude's hypothesis that Cárdenas followed his own path. As Patenaude points out, however, Cárdenas's decision to welcome Trotsky also confirmed the president's "independence vis-à-vis the Stalinist left."[44] Certainly the PCM opposed Trotsky's arrival in the country, but Cárdenas also faced external pressure to align with forces that would fight against the growing international fascist threat. The secretary of foreign relations specifically addressed this concern in his letter opposing Trotsky, stating that within a short time, Mexico likely would encounter "fascist and reactionary governments joining in a single block" to place political and economic pressure on countries like Mexico.[45] Cárdenas risked alienating possible allies with his controversial decision, but apparently, his conviction in the right of asylum for political exiles superseded all else.[46]

Even with the support of Mexico's president, Trotsky still encountered a number of divergent internal political forces that fiercely opposed his entry. Without doubt, Mexico's Communist Party, the *Confederación de Trabajadores de México*, or the Confederation of Mexican Workers (CTM), and the painter Siqueiros ranked high among those who vocally protested all discussion of granting the exiled Russian asylum in Mexico.[47] Although the PCM and CTM actively led the opposition to Trotsky during the later months of 1936 and early 1937, factional infighting between the two groups weakened the possibility of a united front against Trotsky during the subsequent months.[48] Nonetheless, in late 1936, Trotsky's potential arrival in Mexico provoked outrage among members of the PCM and the CTM, and they showered the president with telegrams and letters asserting their position. For example, on 9 December 1936, the prominent communists, Valentín Campa and Manuel Díaz Ramírez, wrote President Cárdenas in their capacity as members of the PCM's Central Committee to register their disapproval over the president's pronouncement about Trotsky. The two high-level Party members not only labeled Trotsky a traitor, but they also considered the fact that Diego Rivera acted in the capacity of Trotsky's representative in Mexico as irrefutable proof of Trotsky's counterrevolutionary character. According to Campa and Díaz Ramírez, the PCM expelled Rivera after he attained a government contract, worth tens of thousands of dollars, to paint President Calles "as a savior of Mexico." In this vein, the PCM leaders considered Trotsky's ties to the muralist—and Rivera's ties to Trotsky—as nothing less than an insult to the memory of the great Russian and Mexican revolutions. Even worse, Campa and Díaz Ramírez argued that despite any promises to the contrary, Trotsky would not refrain from politics while in Mexico, and as a consequence, his presence would present a danger for the country.[49]

In many respects the CTM's arguments against Trotsky reflected similar concerns to those of the communists. Created in 1936 under Cárdenas, within two years the CTM claimed nearly one million members under thirty-six hundred umbrella organizations.[50] Over the years, differences plagued the CTM's relationship with the PCM, but from the Confederation's inception, the Party still played an important role in the workers' organization.[51] Indeed, the CTM leadership resolutely detailed their position against Trotsky, arguing that although their organization favored the right of asylum in theory, Trotsky and his followers opposed the goals of the CTM and, consequently, the vast majority of the "Mexican proletariat." The question of whether labor should align with other "exploited" groups lay at the heart of this dispute; Trotsky advocated self-sufficiency for the working class while the CTM supported the building of a broad, popular front with other groups as a protection against fascism and other threats, both internal and external.[52] Additionally, the CTM outlined several other devastating charges against Trotsky, including the allegation that he acted as an enemy of the working class, historically and in Mexico.[53]

Siqueiros would play an outsized role in organizing armed opposition against the Russian's presence in Mexico, but in these early phases, the painter protested Trotsky's asylum from his temporary residence in Spain. Joining numerous other artists and writers, and drawing upon his experience during the Mexican Revolution, Siqueiros traveled to Spain in late 1936 to fight against the fascist forces during the Spanish Civil War. The revolutionary painter remained for the most part until 1939, first serving in the Fifth Regiment with Vittorio Vidali, Tina Modotti's lover, and then rising to the rank of Lieutenant Colonel of the Twenty-Ninth Division.[54] Even from outside of his home country, Siqueiros registered his disapproval of Trotsky in a number of ways. First, Siqueiros sent several strongly worded protest letters and telegrams from Spain to old friends and acquaintances asking for their help in this issue. The painter next struggled to discuss the matter directly with President Cárdenas, with whom, according to Siqueiros, he maintained a friendship that developed from their time spent together as drinking companions during the revolution. Because the president already understood that Siqueiros only wanted to pressure him into revoking Trotsky's asylum agreement, he refused to speak on the issue. After his unsuccessful attempt to sway the president, Siqueiros next contacted the secretary of the interior. Although Siqueiros's demands also failed to influence the minister, he still consented to pass along the painter's concerns to Cárdenas, especially after Siqueiros threatened "to solve the problem by force." Unfortunately for Siqueiros, his warnings of violence did little to persuade the president, although in an attempt to assuage Siqueiros's anger, he ordered the Treasury Department to pay five hundred pesos to each veteran who fought in Spain. Ironically, Siqueiros reported that he spent his bonus on sending telegrams to Cárdenas in an unsuccessful attempt to demand that he close the "counterrevolutionary headquarters of Trotsky in Mexico."[55]

Trotsky's First Days in Mexico

In December 1936 Trotsky and his wife boarded the Norwegian oil tanker, *Ruth*, on their way to Mexico. After a relatively uneventful trip, the couple arrived in Tampico barely over a month from the date that Cárdenas officially announced his decision that Mexico would offer them asylum.[56] Immediately after stepping foot on Mexican soil, Trotsky assured his host government that he would comply with the wishes of the president and others not to interfere in national politics and abstain from "actions that might prejudice the relations between Mexico and other countries."[57] Trotsky had little choice in his declaration of neutrality, as his immigration papers specifically required him to respect Mexico's laws and refrain from producing political propaganda.[58] Trotsky's noninvolvement promise proved to be an empty one, as his mere presence in the country polarized Mexico's politics and immediately sparked a firestorm of controversy within the artistic community. Even as the exiled Russian made his way to Mexico's capital on the railway car, *El Hidalgo*, specially sent by President Cárdenas, surely Trotsky understood that he faced an uncertain future in his newly adopted country.[59]

Frida Kahlo and other supporters greeted Trotsky and his wife upon their arrival in the country, although illness prevented Rivera from making the trip to Tampico. Still, the muralist proved well enough to leave the hospital, albeit briefly, to welcome the exiles to Mexico City.[60] Surprising even to Rivera, Trotsky first addressed the painter with the following question: "What happened to your beard?" Because Rivera sported facial hair during his Paris years, especially from 1917 to 1921, he assumed that Trotsky hoped to imply, through his "joke," that Rivera was not a stranger to him.[61] Kahlo and Rivera offered the couple the use of the Kahlo family home in Coyoacán, a suburb of Mexico City, and Trotsky, his wife, and various assistants moved in on 11 January. As Natalia later described the experience, "We arrived . . . at a low house painted blue; it had a patio filled with plants, fresh, airy rooms, a collection of pre-Columbian objets d'art and a vast number of pictures. . . . We had come to a different world, the house of Frida Kahlo and Diego Rivera."[62] The very next day, Trotsky met with journalists to declare "I think I am in full accord with you in thinking that neither you nor I have reason to occupy the public opinion of this country too long with myself."[63] Trotsky's pronouncement proved to be at least partly correct, but for reasons not yet clear. Although the Mexican people never tired of reading about Trotsky's life and politics, the exiled revolutionary would not live but for a few short years more.

The Blue House provided the Russians and their assistants with a comfortable reprieve from their years of exile, but the issue of safety still remained the number one priority. Even high-level bureaucrats, including President Cárdenas himself, stressed the importance of protecting Trotsky while he lived within the country.[64] Not only did Trotsky's safekeeping represent—at least symbolically—Mexico's ability to protect international political figures within its borders, but it also signified the capabilities of law enforcement agents to effectively monitor their own citizens at home. After all, Trotsky's external enemies from the USSR and other countries presented serious risks, but so did PCM members within Mexico City. Only a few months after his arrival, Trotsky wrote the president a letter addressing just such security issues. Arguing that he was a victim of the Soviet secret police and "their agents in Mexico," Trotsky insisted that the PCM was plotting his expulsion from the country by publicly accusing him of participation in counterrevolutionary plots against the government.[65] In response to increasing threats against Trotsky and his family, Mexican officials positioned six police officers outside of his home, although Trotsky's secretaries quickly arranged for additional recruits, including young members of the Mexican Trotskyite group, to help protect the property.[66] Trotsky ordered his personal guards to collaborate with the police and maintain a cordial relationship with the local patrols at all times. Friendship between the two groups, however, had its limits. As an extra layer of precaution, Trotsky insisted that one of his personal guards accompany a policeman whenever he entered the property for water or for any other purpose.[67]

Security measures—and concerns—increased considerably during the spring with the Joint Commission of Inquiry into the Moscow Trials, or the Dewey Commission. Theoretically, the purpose of the hearings was to determine Trotsky's innocence or guilt in the serious charges, including that of sabotage, brought against him in absentia by Stalin.[68] Because the American Committee for the Defense of Leon Trotsky first initiated the commission, detractors questioned its neutrality from its inception and throughout the hearings.[69] Still, in his speech prepared for a large gathering organized by the committee, Trotsky promised, "If this commission decides that I am guilty in the slightest degree of the crimes which Stalin imputes to me, I pledge in advance to place myself voluntarily in the hands of the executioners of the GPU."[70] Once John Dewey reluctantly agreed to act as chair, the commission went forward as planned, even authorizing a small group to travel to Mexico with the purpose of obtaining Trotsky's testimony.[71] According to the ensuing report, written by Dewey, the subcommission took Trotsky's testimony over a period of thirteen hearings from 10 April to 17 April. Instead of a public forum, the group met in a large room of Rivera and Kahlo's Blue House with about fifty people, half of whom participated as journalists, in attendance.[72] Never shy of publicity, Rivera and Kahlo, both dressed in their finest, also listened to the proceedings.[73] To prepare for the event, Trotsky and his assistants not only compiled thousands of documents, but Trotsky also ordered the removal of a painting of a nude from the house. Kahlo originally placed the art in the house's sole bathroom as decoration, but Trotsky feared possible criticism from the members of the press who attended the meetings.[74] The commission returned home to New York to deliberate and ultimately delivered their "not guilty" verdict on 14 December 1937.[75]

Despite the commission's declaration on Trotsky's innocence, he still faced sustained hostility by those, including Siqueiros, who adamantly disapproved of his presence in the country. Time failed to lessen Siqueiros's antagonism toward Trotsky, and if anything, the painter grew increasingly opposed to Trotsky's existence in Mexico during the months he lived in the Blue House. Mexico's internal security agents also noted the widening ideological split between Rivera and Siqueiros when they reported on the factious divide within the country's communists "in the wake of the events that caused the fall of Leon Trotsky." As the security official explained, Rivera and Siqueiros operated in an environment of powerful, opposing political sectors. Those who supported Stalin had triggered a fierce struggle to achieve the expulsion of Trotsky, while the Russian exile attempted to maintain a defensive response. Even worse, according the agent, the artists' split resulted in a number of embarrassing situations—"pseudo assaults" and "boisterous rallies" filled with insults—all orchestrated by the leaders of the PCM in order to oust Trotsky from the country at all costs.[76]

The Trotsky-Rivera Split

Rivera facilitated Trotsky's existence in Mexico, but within a few short months of his arrival the muralist's relationship with the exiled Russian soured over a number of issues. According to the painter, their differences of opinion seemed virtually "impassable" from practically their first conversations.[77] Certainly Rivera's political inconsistencies led to many of the conflicts between the painter and Trotsky, but the additional causes that precipitated their break remain disputed—much as they did during the 1930s and early 1940s—depending upon the political sympathies of those assessing the situation.[78] Trotsky reported that Rivera first became dissatisfied during the autumn months of 1938 after he limited the painter's administrative positions within the Mexican League and suggested that Rivera concentrate on his painting instead.[79] Even worse, Rivera contended that several of Trotsky's personal guards had advocated for his expulsion from the Fourth International.[80] Long active in radical politics, Rivera understood well the divisions that often developed over complex issues, large and small. But what likely proved most difficult for the painter was Trotsky's inability to censure his remarks toward those who surrounded him. Rivera illustrated this point by relating a conversation in which Trotsky grew visibly irritated with Rivera and publicly chastised him for his supposedly naïve political viewpoints. According to Rivera, Trotsky disagreed with the painter's assessment of a relatively small political issue involving the Soviet ambassador, arguing "Your response is stupid. . . . Your views are completely out of place . . . you are a very talented painter, but in politics, a completely childish character." At another point, Trotsky repeated the same assertion as before, stating "My friend Diego Rivera . . . is a great painter, a mature artist, but to the contrary, is entirely childish in politics."[81]

As their disagreements deepened, Trotsky remained convinced that Rivera orchestrated and even heightened their political differences in order to lessen his ties to the Fourth International.[82] In a sense, Trotsky may have understood the situation correctly. To be sure, Rivera—intentionally or even unintentionally—hastened the breakdown of their relationship in December 1938 with the matter of a letter written to his colleague André Breton in Paris. According to Rivera, he asked Trotsky's personal aid and secretary, Jean van Heijenoort, to write his correspondence to Breton in French, but evidently when Rivera spoke poorly of Trotsky, his secretary refused to continue. After Rivera promised to show the message to Trotsky himself, however, van Heijenoort brought the letter home to the Trotsky compound to type at a later point. Natalia's discovery of this damning piece of evidence, compounded by Rivera's refusal to remove his criticism of Trotsky, significantly alarmed the Russian.[83] Concerned that Rivera's provocative behavior represented a growing disillusionment, Trotsky dolefully commented that Rivera's actions signified a "moral break with the Fourth International, and, I have every reason to fear, his preparation for breaking personal relations with me."[84] Even while Trotsky criticized Rivera on a rather consistent basis for his "political ambiguity," he nonetheless hesitated to end their relationship.[85]

Those close to Trotsky confirmed his growing exasperation with Rivera's somewhat unorthodox and inconsistent political views. Trotsky's wife, Natalia, recounted that her husband insisted that Rivera "lacked the firmness or lucidity of mind that went with serious political activity," although his "best" work expressed a feeling for the "social struggle," albeit naïvely.[86] Criticizing the painter even more, Natalia wrote that Rivera was their only friend or comrade who "later made a noisy conversion to Stalinism."[87] Charles Curtiss, the dedicated U.S. Trotskyist who worked in the exile's compound with his wife during the year before Trotsky's death, further elaborated on the Trotsky-Rivera disagreement.[88] Commenting that their dispute began over the role of the artist in the revolutionary workers movement, Curtiss argued that their differences came to a head after Rivera backed General Francisco Múgica in the controversial presidential campaign to replace Cárdenas. According to Curtiss, Trotsky labeled Rivera's support of Múgica as nothing more than "opportunism" and "unprincipled adventurism," especially considering Trotsky's position that a Marxist should not support a "bourgeois" candidate.[89] For his part, Rivera denied such charges and instead argued that, historically, Marxists have shown "examples of support, making compromises with the most favorably inclined candidates" in the absence of an appropriate Marxist contender. Providing insight to Rivera's view of politics, he further clarified his position, "one has to be a dialectician; that a person [Múgica] can be a friend at the one time and act as an enemy at another."[90]

Despite Rivera's political inconsistencies, Trotsky proved surprisingly reluctant to abandon his alliance with Rivera. More than once he attempted to repair the damage between himself and the painter, but Rivera refused, "stating that the break was final and irrevocable."[91] No longer committed to the Fourth International, Rivera officially resigned on 7 January 1939.[92] Just two days later, Trotsky expressed clear concern, once again stressing their friendship: "Truly, one can hardly believe one's ears. When there are differences within an organization, and when both sides remain loyal to the fundamental principles, an open discussion can have a completely friendly character, without in any way poisoning personal relationships."[93] On 12 January, Trotsky contacted Frida Kahlo in New York, requesting her help in resolving the dispute between him and Rivera. Trotsky appeared to be baffled by Rivera's refusal to continue with the Fourth International, writing that Rivera refused to reveal the "real source" of his "discontent." Still, Trotsky listed a number of plausible reasons, including Rivera's letter to Breton, that possibly led Rivera to make his break, but he added that "the idea of my wanting to be rid of Diego is so incredible, so absurd, permit me to say, so mad, that I can only shrug my shoulders helplessly." He concluded his letter by reassuring Kahlo that he would refuse to abandon his friendship and political union with Rivera.[94]

Within a few days, however, Trotsky's tone changed, especially after he heard that Rivera accused him of carrying out "intrigues behind the scenes." Responding to these serious charges, Trotsky asked Curtiss to meet with Rivera to discuss the painter's intentions in going forward.[95] The resulting conversation, on 20 January 1939, reflected Rivera's utter exasperation with Trotsky, and his desire to end all alliances with the exile. According to Curtiss, Rivera resolutely declared that he planned to retire from politics and instead dedicate himself to his art. He continued that, although he would not pursue his accusations toward Trotsky, he still found it impossible to work with him and that he did not feel comfortable in his presence. What seemed to bother Rivera most was the fact that Trotsky read his letter to Breton, an act that "if revealed publicly, would result in the condemnation of these actions by all workers." The painter practically threatened Trotsky and his affiliates, declaring that if Trotsky continued to "bother" him, he would talk about the issue that previously he had "considered his duty to keep quiet."[96] Although Rivera remained mum on the specifics of this supposed secret, he concluded their talk by once again emphasizing the point that "he wanted only to be left alone to work on his art."[97]

There is some question as to the role that Kahlo's brief affair with Trotsky played in Rivera's break with the Russian exile. Patenaude argues that "there is no hint that Diego's new willfulness was brought on by a discovery of his wife's affair with Trotsky."[98] Van Heijenoort also reported that Kahlo specifically told him that Rivera knew "nothing of what had happened" between her and Trotsky. Although van Heijenoort speculated that Rivera might have learned of their relationship a few years after Trotsky's death, he argued that Rivera's extreme jealously would have led him to take a radically different, and possibly violent, path when ending his ties with Trotsky.[99] Still, the possibility exists that Rivera knew of his wife's romantic trysts with the Russian even before his friendship with Trotsky ended. In fact, Rivera later wrote that he was sick with an eye issue that confined him to his darkened room when Trotsky came by his house in San Angel and "asked my compañera Frida for the return of a number of love letters that he had written her."[100]

Even if the timing of Rivera's knowledge of Kahlo's affair with Trotsky remains uncertain, there is little doubt that his passion for making art precipitated the breakdown of his short-lived relationship with the Russian. As with Tina Modotti in the Soviet Union, at this point in his career, Rivera faced a decision: to continue his association with Trotsky or devote more time to painting. Unlike Modotti, however, Rivera argued for the relevance of an artistic existence rather than one solely comprised of politics. Clearly Rivera's decision to forgo politics proved to be short-lived, as he continued to infuse his art with provocative images until his death. Still, the matter of art's place in revolution played a role in the termination of Trotsky and Rivera's friendship.[101] As an example of their artistic differences, van Heijenoort related a conversation between Trotsky, Breton, Rivera, and others that took place during a trip to the small town of Pátzcuaro. Evidently Trotsky described his thesis on art, explaining that "art would dissolve into life" in a future communist society. Revealing his dismissal of traditional art forms, Trotsky argued that in this same socialist civilization, paintings no longer would exist, although people would decorate their houses.[102] Clearly, Rivera placed greater emphasis on the importance of the artist in a revolutionary world. As Rivera explained, "The role of the artist in the revolution . . . is not that of a sympathizer, is not that of the servant of the revolution; the function of the artist is that of a soldier of the revolution." In other words, art occupied a central, indispensable place in revolution, without which people could not survive.[103]

The Hunt for Trotsky's Head: Siqueiros and the First Attempt on Trotsky's Life

Trotsky's situation in Mexico grew more precarious by the day, especially in regard to his safety. Soon after his break with Rivera, in March 1939, Trotsky moved out of the Blue House and into a new home just a few blocks away.[104] Although a number of teams, including Trotsky's personal guards and the local police, patrolled the perimeters of the Blue House from his first days in Mexico, the security measures surrounding the exile and his staff, especially at the new Calle Viena headquarters, remained elemental at best.[105] The rather primitive nature of the alarm system particularly concerned many within the household, especially given the fact that almost daily Trotsky received reports of Soviet secret agents who lurked dangerously nearby. Even worse, Stalin's show trials forced a number of high-ranking Soviet spies to flee to the West, and Trotsky's supporters understood that many of these defectors died sooner rather than later under suspicious circumstances.

In response to such potential dire threats—from within and outside of Mexico—Trotsky and his assistants issued intricate orders in the hopes of improving security. Specific instructions ordered the guards to keep the patio as light as possible at night, while making sure to darken the guardhouse. The directive also required the guards to keep their guns fully loaded and to carry them on their person "whether on or off duty" when on the premises. This order applied to all members of the household since the guidelines required everyone to become familiar with all aspects of handling a weapon. Special provisions applied to guards on night duty, with the admonishment to stay awake at all times and to refrain from typing or carrying out other chores that could distract the lookouts. The gate to the grounds was to be kept locked, and guards could not open this entry for any reason between 10:00 P.M. and 7:00 A.M. unless they personally knew the caller. To protect the Trotsky compound, the patrols had at their disposal five .38 caliber Colt revolvers, one Venus Automatic pistol, one .22

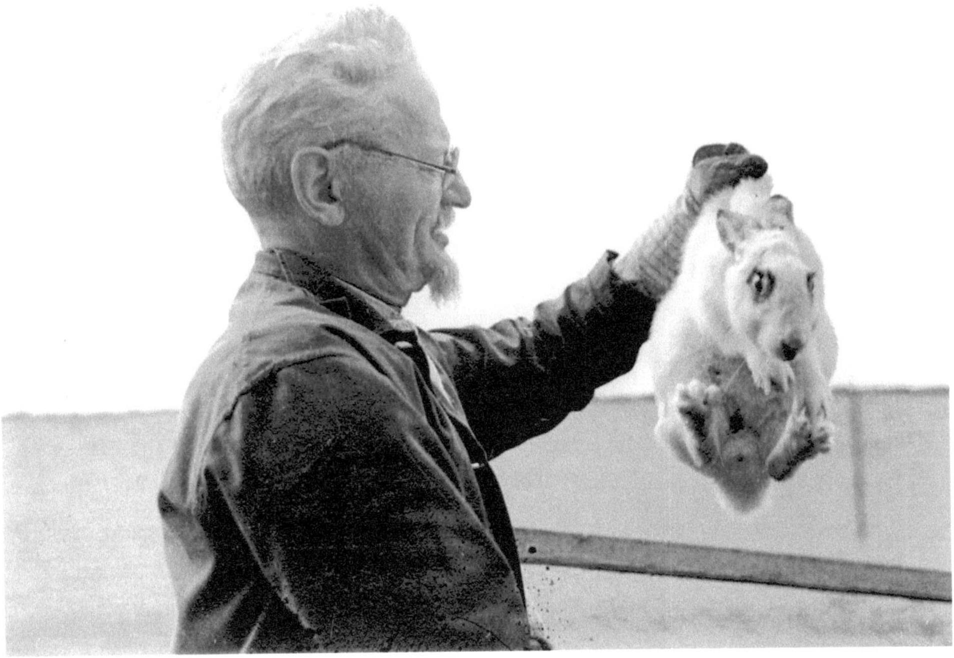

Leon Trotksy with rabbit. Alexander Buchman Papers, envelope E. Courtesy of the Hoover Institution Library & Archives, Stanford University.

caliber Colt revolver, one single shot target pistol, one Remington rifle, one Winchester carbine, one Thompson submachine gun, and one Winchester shotgun. In addition to their regular duties, the regulations required the second shift sentries to spend two hours cleaning Trotsky's beloved rabbit pens and the chicken coops.[106]

Reports from Mexico's internal security agents confirm many of Trotsky's principal safety concerns. For example, in a 1938 memo on the activity of Soviet secret police (or the NKVD, formerly the GPU) in Mexico, agents reported on two "extremely important" Soviet defectors: Walter Krivitsky and Ignace (or Ignaz as listed on the document) Reiss. According to the report, Krivitsky, who previously directed the Soviet military espionage in Germany, met with Trotsky's son in Paris to warn of preparations "on a very large scale" against Trotsky that were already underway in Mexico. Even more alarming, the same document also provided details on Reiss's death at the hands of Soviet agents in Switzerland on 3 September 1937.

Although the assassins initially avoided capture, police questioned their two female accomplices—Renata Steiner and Helena Hessen—who later divulged that one of Reiss's killers lived next door to Trotsky's son in Paris and the other recently had visited Mexico City.[107] Not surprisingly, the Mexico connections particularly concerned the Mexican officials, especially because police detained three other coconspirators in France who revealed that the Soviet agent who murdered Reiss lived in Switzerland and Holland under false identities and had worked in the service of the GPU for quite some time. Although the suspect, who assumed numerous aliases, including Roland Abbiate, had since escaped, Swiss police searched his apartment and found: (1) a Mexico City street map; (2) a map of the republic of Mexico; (3) Air France information; and (4) three applications to enter Mexico signed by "Carrol Georges Quinn," another alias. Given such disquieting evidence, Mexico's agents concluded that the Soviet operatives moved from one country to another by airplanes, and thus avoided arrest.[108]

Soviet plans to eliminate their greatest enemy began to solidify, as a number of NKVD operatives arrived in Mexico to carry out Trotsky's assassination. For the most part the various anti-Trotsky plots involved NKVD agents from around the world; but ironically, none other than the country's most illustrious painter, Siqueiros, would assume a leading role in one of the principal groups to rid the country of its most notorious exile. As an avowed enemy of Trotsky, Siqueiros elevated direct action ahead of words or even the paintbrush and willingly devoted himself to the task at hand after being contacted by representatives of the NKVD in Mexico.[109] Siqueiros later remarked that he and his small group of anti-Trotsky comrades, including the artists Luis Arenal and Antonio Pujol, asked each other if they could "permit Trotsky to continue in Mexico, protected by the government," to which they responded with a pledge to end the "disgrace."[110]

After Siqueiros and his comrades united in the promise to take matters into their own hands, they next had to determine the best means to carry out their objectives. Almost all had attained experience during their shared experiences in the Spanish Civil War. According to the radical painter, Trotsky's orders to improve the compound's security resulted in creating a "fortress" of sorts, with high walls and electrified fences surrounding the area. The Mexican police who guarded the Trotsky home, however, represented a more serious obstacle for Siqueiros and his group, especially with the officers who manned a surveillance booth located in the eastern corner of the residence. Still, Siqueiros later noted in his memoirs that he believed that several Mexican police officers revealed crucial information to "female hooks" during the days before their attack.[111] In his investigation of the plot against Trotsky, Colonel Sánchez Salazar, then chief of the secret service of the Mexican police and investigator in charge of researching the incident, confirmed the identities of the women as Ana López Chávez and Julia Barradas Hernández, who was the wife of another member of the conspiracy.[112] Such inside tips provided by the women allowed Siqueiros to penetrate a few of Trotsky's most critical security measures. For example, the group learned the system for entering the building, the interior layout of the house, and the approximate placement of defenses.[113] Siqueiros admitted that his personal task in the attack was to immobilize the external defense surrounding Trotsky's house, and that he "complied adequately with this objective."[114] United in their objective to eliminate their enemy, and seemingly well prepared for their mission, Siqueiros and his cohort agreed that the time had come to launch their offensive against the Trotsky headquarters.

Trotsky's account to the authorities immediately following the assault on his home provides an intriguing narrative of the events that took place, although at this point Siqueiros's involvement remained unknown. At around four in the morning on 24 May 1940, he awoke to the sound of gunfire that, at first, he mistook for firecrackers from a neighborhood celebration. Part of his initial confusion, and his grogginess, may have resulted from the sleeping pill he took earlier in the evening after a long day of work. But because the explosions sounded too close, and the room filled with the pervasive smell of gunpowder, Trotsky and his wife soon understood the dire reality of the long-feared attack. At the sound of the first shots, Trotsky's wife jumped out of bed, and her husband soon followed, sliding to the ground in a place between the bed and the wall. She stood for a few seconds, leaning against the wall with her body protecting Trotsky, but he soon gestured for her to get down. The shots came from all over, and chips and particles of the doorframes scattered around the couple. Trotsky's wife later recalled that she clearly could see the flashes of the guns in the room, although the faces of the gunmen remained obscure by the dark. After the shooting stopped, Trotsky heard his grandson, Seva, cry out "Grandfather!" from the next room. In a panic at the sound of the first shot, the child hid under his bed, although a bullet went through the mattress and injured Seva's big toe. After throwing incendiary devices, the assailments finally left the house. When questioned later about the near impossibility of surviving

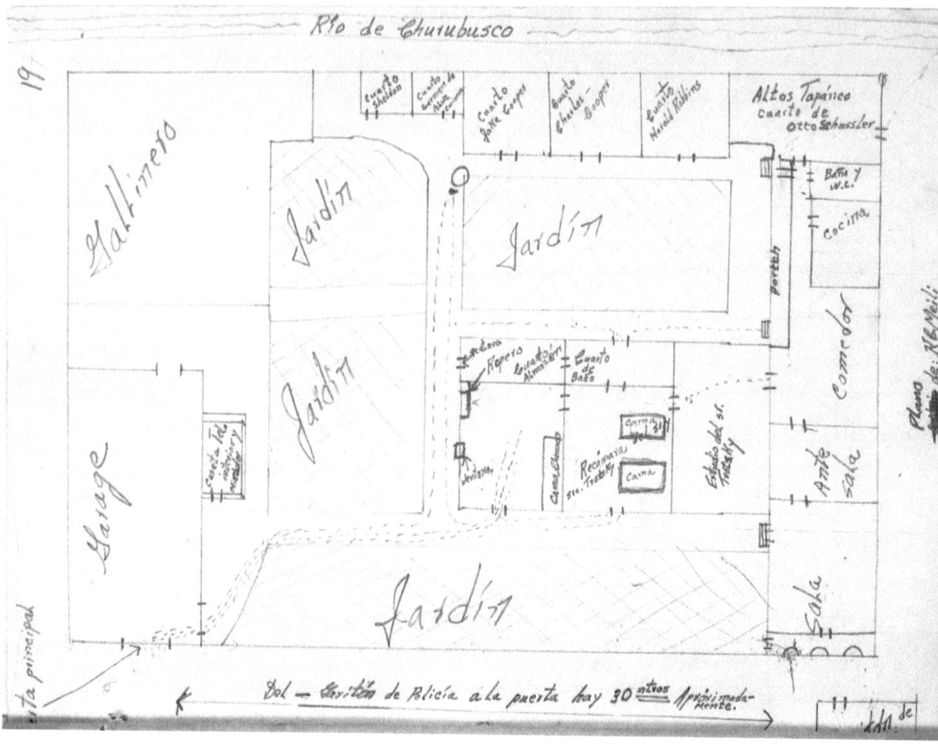

Map of Trotsky's home soon after the May 1940 attack. Archivo General de la Nación, Dirección General de Investigaciones Políticas y Sociales, caja 126, exp. 28.

such an aggressive offensive, Trotsky speculated that the attackers possibly feared killing each other, and instinctively shot higher or lower than necessary. In addition to bad luck on the part of the shooters, Trotsky also credited his family's survival to their capacity to stay calm, remain quiet, and essentially to play dead in the face of sustained gunfire.[115]

Immediately following the assault on Trotsky's life, representatives from Mexico's various police and intelligence services began the process of investigating those who instigated the attack against the country's most controversial exile. Colonel Sánchez Salazar was first on the scene but agents from Mexico's intelligence services also arrived within hours. Even members of the United States' Federal Bureau of Investigation (FBI) took an active interest in the crime, noting with displeasure that Sánchez Salazar, who "had no police experience whatever," insisted on personally taking charge of the case "much to the disgust of one or two men in the Department who are really good officers."[116] Despite the FBI's seemingly lack of confidence in Sánchez Salazar's ability to uncover the identity of the assailants, the colonel and a number of internal security agents soon questioned witnesses to piece together their version of events. Many of their conclusions confirmed Trotsky's description, but they also supplied new evidence as well. For example, detectives surmised that gunmen simultaneously attacked Trotsky's bedroom from three sides: (1) from the balcony to the garden; (2) from the opposite side of the yard through an open window; and (3) from the office or dining room through the closed door that connected Trotsky's bedroom. When the shooting first started, Trotsky and his wife fell to the ground, an act that Trotsky attributed to saving their lives. None of Trotsky's staff members sustained any injuries, although one assistant recounted that a bullet barely missed him as he stood in a window. The memo further noted that Trotsky's grandson, "a smart boy 14 years old," stated that he received an abrasion on one foot, although the police doubted its likelihood. A number of additional issues also puzzled the investigators, including the fact that three of the assailants remained in the child's bedroom for quite some time, but they failed to look into the room where Trotsky and his wife slept, located just a few feet away, to confirm "the success of the shooting" and if necessary "to finish his work." Moreover, Seva stated he crawled under his bed, even while the three individuals stood in his room, without them noticing his presence. The child also refused to reveal his injury because he said it was bandaged, although the police failed to see a trace of the wrapping or even a "patch" through his socks.[117]

A few days after the attack, Mexican intelligence officials again visited the Trotsky house to continue with their questioning of the witnesses. According to their confidential report, before they could even knock on the door, several other agents joined them to discuss the possibility that Trotsky had faked the assault on his compound. Their discussion centered on Trotsky's outwardly calm demeanor so soon after the violent event, and the seemingly contradictory evidence involved in the case. After their conversation, the agents proceeded to the garden in the compound's interior, where they encountered Trotsky together with his grandson near the henhouse. Following formal introductions, the group walked to Trotsky's office where he readily addressed all questions, but also insisted that the NKVD initiated the attack on his home.[118] Inspectors interrogated the guards in charge of protecting the Trotsky compound the night of the incident, and after noting several contradictions in their stories, they ordered the sentries to provide a written declaration of their testimonies.[119] Not surprisingly, Trotsky fiercely denied the "auto-assault" theory that he staged his own attack to discredit Stalin and the GPU and attract greater attention to his difficulties. Refuting the idea that he could pursue "an act so monstrous, repugnant and dangerous," Trotsky questioned how the assault against his home could harm the reputation of the man who "exterminated all the old generation of the Bolshevik Party." Insisting that while Stalin risked nothing in organizing from afar the attack "to exterminate his number one enemy," to the contrary Trotsky would have endangered his and his family's life, his fate, his reputation, and the political movement that he served.[120]

Besides their "auto-assault" hypothesis, police also suspected Rivera's involvement in the attack on Trotsky's compound, or at the minimum, that of his drivers. Despite his earlier dispute with the painter, Trotsky vehemently denounced the possibility of Rivera's participation in the violent act. Writing to Colonel Sánchez Salazar, Trotsky clearly stated that any attempt to involve the "great painter" in the conspiracy would be an "absolutely absurd fantasy." He continued that although he no longer maintained a relationship with Rivera, either political or personal, efforts to link Rivera with the recent attack on his home would lead to a dead end. The termination of their association, according to Trotsky, nonetheless failed to prevent the newspapers from speculating on the relevance of his disagreements with Rivera as well as the circumstances surrounding the painter's "disputes with his wife Frida Kahlo, that culminated in divorce."[121] When further interrogated by two government security agents, Trotsky repeated his regret that newspapers and authorities would tie his name with Rivera's and stated that he always had admired his murals.[122]

Given Rivera's previous ties to Trotsky, the PCM's Central Committee also viewed the possibility of Rivera's involvement in the assault on Trotsky with skepticism. Nonetheless, the manifesto put forward by the PCM's Central Committee soon after the attack clearly illustrated the Party's exasperation with the painter when they wrote that Rivera was "fulfilling the task entrusted by his henchmen, the traitors and enemies of Mexico."[123] Even worse, the PCM also accused Rivera of calling for the immediate intervention of "Yankee imperialism" and the overthrow of President Cárdenas in his recent letter published in the *New York Times*.[124] In the days following Trotsky's assault, Rivera remained doubtful that Trotsky would exonerate him, even reporting in his biography that, after the attempt on his life, Trotsky suggested to police they should investigate a car "belonging to a well-known local painter."[125] Following this lead, a few days later, police surrounded Rivera's home, although he managed to go into hiding and avoid capture.[126] Rivera argued that the instructions for his arrest order originated from no less than President Cárdenas, although he insisted the warrant was unconstitutional.[127] Still, Mexico's internal security officials denied having issued an "order of apprehension," or an arrest order against Rivera.[128] Regardless of such disclaimers, at least the local police considered Rivera to be a suspect, and he fled rather than face arrest. Even the FBI noted that Rivera "quietly left Mexico via Pan-American plane at 7:45" in the morning on his way to the United States. The FBI memo also added that Rivera planned to remain away from Mexico for quite some time, which, according to the agent, was fortunate because "his life was really in danger . . . from more than one direction."[129]

Although authorities initially identified Rivera as Trotsky's attempted assassin, they soon focused their attention on another of Mexico's great muralists—Siqueiros. In his letter to the attorney general and the chief of police dated 27 May, even Trotsky recommended that authorities question Siqueiros in order to "throw light on the instigators of the assassination attempt."[130] Just a few days later, on 18 June, General José Manuel Núñez, chief of the Mexico City police, announced a break in the case and the subsequent arrest of twenty-one people believed to be involved in the attack. According the report, Siqueiros personally participated in the offensive, disguised with a fake mustache and a uniform.[131] News of the plot against Trotsky's life spread far and wide, but Siqueiros, Luis Arenal, and the others involved in the act continued to elude capture.

Trotsky soon voiced frustration that those who led the attack on his house escaped arrest, and even worse, possibly had left the country. Within a few days, though, rumors began to circulate that Siqueiros had fled to New York City. For example, on 6 July, Inspector Number PS-24 addressed this issue when he reported the existence of a letter sent to Trotsky's lawyer. Alarmed that Siqueiros and Arenal might be hiding in New York, the author of the correspondence, or "Al," promised to "do [his] best through Anita Brenner to trace the whereabouts of [Luis] Arenal."[132] At the time, the Museum of Modern Art was displaying five paintings by Siqueiros as part of a larger exhibition of Mexican Art, and a number of people described seeing Arenal and his brother at the show.[133] By 15 July, Colonel Sánchez Salazar reported that Trotsky wrote him to discuss the return of Luis Arenal from New York, and more importantly to advise him that a "reliable" source notified him that the Soviets had sent a boat to pick up Siqueiros, the Arenal brothers, and "other G. P. U. agents" from their secret location in Manzanillo.[134] Even the

New York Times printed similar information, reporting that the Mexican police maintained a close watch on the Russian ship, *Severski*, which had arrived in Manzanillo a month earlier under the pretense of carrying metals back to Vladivostok. Given the fact that the local population saw little activity around the boat, the police feared that Siqueiros, his wife, and the Arenal brothers planned to use the *Severski* as their means of escape.[135] Little did the police know, however, that Siqueiros remained hidden in the Mexican countryside, where he would continue to elude police until others succeeded in assassinating his sworn enemy, Trotsky.

Trotsky's Death and the End of an Era

After the first attempt on his life, Sánchez Salazar heard the exiled leader lament, "Fate has granted me a reprieve. It will be of short duration."[136] And indeed Trotsky foretold his future, for less than three months later, on 21 August, he died from an icepick blow to the skull.[137] Once again, Sánchez Salazar took the lead in the investigation, along with General José Manuel Núñez, chief of police.[138] A Soviet operative named Ramón Mercader, alias "Jacques Mornard," "Raymond," and "Frank Jacson," killed Trotsky with the inadvertent help of Sylvia Ageloff, an avid Trotsky supporter. Mercader befriended Ageloff during a trip to Europe and he soon seduced her with the intent of entering the close circle of confidents who surrounded the old Russian. The Trotsky household had entrusted Ageloff's sister, Ruth, who lived in Mexico City during the Dewey hearings, and who had offered her translating and clerical skills as the Trotsky supporters prepared his case. As a result of his warm relationship with Ruth, Trotsky also welcomed Sylvia Ageloff as a trusted friend when she traveled to Mexico City and invited her to the compound in January 1940.[139] Mercader, who already had arrived in Mexico City the previous October, now had an insider within the Trotsky complex, and he quickly took advantage of his position to become friends with Trotsky's closest advisors.[140] Just a few days after the first assault on the Trotsky house, Mercader even met Trotsky himself, and over the next few weeks, his presence among the Trotsky comrades became more commonplace.[141] When he arrived at the Trotsky compound on 20 August, invited in by the guards without hesitation, Trotsky greeted him near the rabbit hutches before leading him back to the library, in theory to discuss an article. Within minutes, Mercader attacked Trotsky, and he died the following day.[142]

Reflecting on Trotsky's death, a *Washington Post* piece drew an alarming connection between "left wing art groups" in the United States and Mexico and the international flow of communist ideology. As evidence of an artist network of "fellow travelers," the author erroneously pointed out that soon after leading the attack on Trotsky, Siqueiros arrived in New York City, where he hobnobbed with other artists and traveled the streets with impunity. Moreover, police first searched the studio of the Taller de Gráfica Popular, or the Popular Graphic Art Workshop (TGP) for "propaganda posters" and for the uniforms used by those who carried out the first assault on Trotsky. The article emphasized the international nature of a global communist circle, focusing on the Trotsky affair to expose the links between Mexico's artists and the Communist Party.[143] Such bonds clearly existed between many of Mexico's radical artists and international communism, but a closer analysis underscores the complexity of their situation and impossibility of simple categorizations. For one, following Siqueiros's assault on the Trotsky compound, the PCM refused to acknowledge a tie between the Party and those who carried out the attack, although they later supported Siqueiros during his time in prison.[144] Second, not all artists agreed with Siqueiros and his tactics. The printmakers associated with the TGP especially voiced their concern when Siqueiros and his group, including Arenal and Pujol, changed into their uniforms in the Taller before their attack on Trotsky—without the consent of its members. As a result, the following day, police arrested key figures in the artist group, including Leopoldo Méndez, and hauled them off to jail.[145] According to the local newspaper *El Nacional*, Siqueiros deceived Méndez, borrowing the key to the workshop in theory to paint but instead using the offices as launching pad for their assault.[146] Not surprisingly, Méndez's time in prison left bitter feelings between the printmaker and Siqueiros that would last for years to come.

Even though the author of the *Washington Post* article raised grave concerns about radical artists and Trotsky's death, Siqueiros played no role in the Russian's ultimate assassination.[147] Indeed, in his court testimony, Mercader readily admitted to stabbing Trotsky, but he denied having connections to Siqueiros. Throughout their questioning, court officials kept insisting that Mercader must have received pertinent information about Trotsky and his house from the artist, or in the very least, that he met Siqueiros previously. Indignantly responding to repeated questioning about his political links to Mexico's artists, Mercader replied that he did not know

Siqueiros, that he only knew *about* him, that he was a painter like Diego Rivera.[148] To a similar query about his ties to Siqueiros, and the possibility that Mercader had kept an office in an apartment once inhabited by the muralist, Mercader replied for the second time "that if it turns out . . . that the apartment in the building 'Ermita,' is the same apartment that David Alfaro Siqueiros occupied within the building, that this can be explained as a mere coincidence; that I have never seen Siquerios."[149] The questioning brought to light an interesting point, though. When Sylvia Ageloff returned alone to the United States during the spring of 1940, Mercader testified that he gave her a false apartment number in the Ermita building, "being the apartment number 800 and something," after she begged him to give her his address. He continued that although the building actually existed, he simply gave her the name of the property because he drove by it often, although he never had stepped foot inside.[150]

Mercader also refused to confess to his ties to Stalin and the GPU. Testifying about his motivations for killing Trotsky, Mercader related a fictional account of his life, describing himself as a disillusioned Trotsky devotee who resented Trotsky's orders that he leave his girlfriend and travel to the Soviet Union to make contact with supporters of the Fourth International. According to Mercader, after this conversation he felt immense hatred for Trotsky and even considered suicide. Instead, however, he "decided to kill [Trotsky] and not kill [him]self." Describing the scene of the crime, Mercader stated that upon entering Trotsky's office he took an "ice ax" hidden in his raincoat and then closed his eyes before striking the Russian's skull. Mercader also carried a gun, which he bought from a fellow named Bartolo Pérez with a "wad of cash." According to Mercader, he met Pérez in the "Kit-Kat-Club," and he immediately recognized him "as one of those guys" who lives in every major city and who is "willing to do all kinds of operations." After Mercader slammed the pick into Trotsky's head, the Russian let out a "mournful cry," even while attempting to defend himself by biting his attacker's left hand. Hearing the commotion, Trotsky's aids rushed in the office and began to beat Mercader, although police soon arrested him and took him to the station.[151]

Within hours of the assault, Ageloff arrived at the Trotsky house, where police promptly arrested her, in theory for her participation in Trotsky's death. Describing her in unflattering terms, with small eyes and thick glasses, Sánchez Salazer made the following observations about the distraught Trotsky supporter, "Extremely nervous and inclined to histrionics she wept constantly and assured us that 'Jacson' had used her as a means of getting into Trotsky's house to assassinate him."[152] Four days after her imprisonment, reporters from the *Novedades* newspaper interviewed Ageloff in her small prison cell at the Green Cross. They described her environment as a dark room, lit only by a skylight. Because she suffered from a nervous condition, Ageloff remained bedridden, looking much like a pale wax figure between very white sheets. Although she appeared afraid to talk, Ageloff became more animated when she insisted that she would never forgive her former lover, who promised her the world. Pointing out Ageloff's sad deception, the writers of the *Novedades* article presented her as a morality tale of what could happen to all women, not just inexperienced girls, because "they were born to love." Reflecting on women's intrinsic nature and their vulnerability in the matters of love, the article asked "all women to ponder for a moment what this means, and then return to [Sylvia's] eyes now consumed in despair and disillusionment."[153]

During Ageloff's trial, she denied ever being involved with the GPU, having only interacted with members of the Fourth International while in Mexico. She also denied knowing that Mercader, whom she understood to be "Jacques Mornard," maintained connections with the GPU. She testified that he only spoke highly about Trotsky in terms that he was a great man, and as far as she knew, he never changed his mind.[154] After Trotsky's death, though, Ageloff now believed that her former lover only met her to gain intimate access to Trotsky.[155] Even Trotsky's widow testified that the assassin "used Sylvia as a tool," uniting with her only as a strategy to reach her husband, and she even inadvertently provided the assassin with information on their home.[156] Eventually, toward the end of 1940, a Mexico City judge ordered Ageloff's release for insufficient evidence in her role as an accomplice in Trotsky's slaying.[157]

Putting the case of Trotsky's death to bed, the police now resumed the hunt for Siqueiros, who still remained at large. Following a series of similar leads concerning Siqueiros's location, Colonel Sánchez Salazar finally discovered the fugitive painter in Guadalajara in early October.[158] According to Sánchez Salazar's confidential report from the secret service of the chief of police for Mexico City, in late September, Sánchez Salazar and six agents drove to Guadalajara to obtain information on the whereabouts of the fugitive and, ultimately, to capture the painter. After arriving in the area, the agents bought traditional regional clothing and various goods so that they could pass as street vendors, and they also traveled the final distance into town as passengers aboard area buses so as to blend into the local population. To further avoid appearing suspicious, one agent dressed as a buyer of fibers and another passed himself off as a trader looking for flint used in ornamental ceramic flowerpots. The agents then fanned out to several locations, talking with the various people and following rumors of Siqueiros's location. After making a number of contacts, the mayor of the small town of Hostotipaquillo eventually revealed that Siqueiros had hidden in the area, and another resident—Cristóbal Rodríguez Castillo, the miner and longtime friend of the painter—revealed his exact location under threat of prison time. After receiving this final tip, Sánchez Salazar and several groups of agents and soldiers traveled throughout the night to arrive at San Blasito, a small ranch. There they "energetically" questioned a farmer who confessed to knowing Siqueiros, but by his alias "Hagario," and to giving him food. Soon afterward, and after dodging the police for four and half months, the agents captured the exhausted Siqueiros without a fight.[159]

After spending several months in jail, the court acquitted Siqueiros of "directing" the unsuccessful machine-gun attack on the Trotsky compound earlier in May 1940.[160] Although he still faced charges of trespassing and breaking and entering, President Camacho allowed him to go free, but only on the promise that he would leave the country.[161] Agreeing to this ultimatum, Siqueiros attained his freedom without a trial, but only after a judge required a payment of four thousand pesos as a deposit, or bail, for his liberty. At ten in the morning in the spring of 1941, numerous reporters and photographers waited for Siqueiros to emerge from the main entrance of the *Palacio de Lecumberri*, although to avoid the crowd, the painter left from another door a little over an hour later. When one of the guards who accompanied Siqueiros from his cell asked the painter about his future plans, he replied, "to paint." The same guard then asked if Siqueiros would leave politics, to which his wife, Angélica Arenal, answered before her husband had a chance, "Forever! To paint, to paint, that is what makes it great!"[162]After experiencing their recent difficulties, clearly Arenal wished her husband would abandon his previous radical existence, although for Siqueiros, a life—and painting—devoid of a political purpose would prove to be impossible. With the help of Pablo Neruda, Siqueiros accepted the president's proposal to leave the country. And in April 1941 he and his family traveled to Chile, only to return again to Mexico in November 1943.[163]

Conclusion: Art Trumps Politics

Rivera and Siqueiros slowly overcame many of their differences in the years following Trotsky's assassination. Although the PCM readmitted Kahlo in

1949, they only allowed Rivera's return in 1954.[164] Despite the Party's continued reluctance to admit Rivera, the grand muralist repeatedly attempted to repair damages with the Party. During the 1940s, Rivera cooperated with the PCM on several occasions in his effort to win back his comrades' support, and Siqueiros occasionally even defended his old enemy, at least when discussing Rivera's art. After all, at various times Siqueiros also had experienced differences with the PCM, and the recent circumstances surrounding the Trotsky affair forced his exile from 1941 to 1943. But back in the country, the painter once again played an active role in the PCM.[165]

As an illustration of the healing powers of time, in 1948, Rivera and Siqueiros joined forces over the events surrounding Rivera's controversial mural, *Dream of a Sunday Afternoon in Alameda Park*. Located in the Hotel del Prado, the painting depicted an imaginary scene in Mexico City's Alameda Park and included key political figures and a young Rivera as a boy of ten holding the hand of a skeleton. What outraged the public and many representatives of the Catholic Church was the inclusion of the slogan, "God does not exist," painted as a notation on a scrap of paper held by Ignacio Ramírez, the noted nineteenth-century poet, political activist, and atheist. Those who opposed the mural organized demonstrations, and on 4 June, religious supporters even vandalized the painting by scratching out the supposedly offensive quotation. After Rivera repaired the damage, the hotel covered the mural with a removable, white nylon screen.[166]

Siqueiros and the PCM fiercely supported Rivera and his freedom to depict political ideas in his art. In early June, Siqueiros even gave a fiery defense of Rivera's mural at a PCM-sponsored rally held at the Union of Newspaper Workers. The PCM organized the meetings to hear Siqueiros's lecture on the evolution of revolutionary painting in Mexico, but he also utilized his time to discuss Rivera's mural in the Hotel del Prado.[167] The popular newspaper *Excélsior* covered the event, although with moralistic disapproval. Writing that Siqueiros arrived accompanied by Rivera, the paper reported that a large crowd of PCM members enthusiastically greeted the two painters with applause. The reporter also noted with concern the large number of communist women who attended the meeting, especially because they rejected the "absolutely justified" attitude of Mexico's archbishop and his refusal to bless the Hotel del Prado mural. Although the women critiqued the Church, a "humble but courageous worker" who was among the listeners got up from his seat and yelled: "God exists! . . . God exists!" Not surprisingly, the crowd responded to the young man's shouts with their own demands to "Get out!"[168]

Internal security inspectors Number 20 and Number 58 even offered their version of the PCM-sponsored rally in favor of Siqueiros. With his long-time comrades, Rivera and Xavier Guerrero, by his side, Siqueiros's lecture first stressed the links between culture and politics before moving on to the issue of Rivera's painting. Addressing the audience, the muralist presented the audience with a series of questions and answers. "What has Diego painted in the Hotel del Prado? He has painted the history of Mexico, the patriotic figures and progressive men of the fatherland, the heroes of the revolution." As with *Excélsior*, the agents also reported the disruptive youth who insisted on the existence of God, as well as the outraged audience reaction, "Crazy, crazy paid for by the Clergy!" After PCM members removed the young man from the room, Siqueiros told the audience that the question of whether or not God exists was not the problem; rather the issue was freedom of expression. After a long discussion of painting and imperialism, the conference concluded with "Viva Mexico" and a request to help with the Party expenses.[169]

In the end art trumped politics. Siqueiros came to the aid of his old friend and in defense of Rivera's right to paint as he pleased, even after years of bitter disputes. As the next chapter discusses, women such as Frida Kahlo, Francis Toor, Aurora Reyes, Anita Brenner, and others also forged deep friendships based on their art and political connections. Creative women, dedicated to their craft, joined the PCM and worked assiduously to advance both their careers and Party ideals. They also provided support for each other and often shared meals or even homes. But unlike their male counterparts, women encountered a multitude of issues that hindered their abilities to achieve equal status, both with their art and the PCM. Women joined Mexico's Communist Party hoping to make a difference within Mexico's political system, but the seemingly never-ending obstacles often led them to abandon their original goals. Still, most remained artists throughout their lives, and as PCM members or sympathizers, they impacted Mexico's cultural and political landscapes in significant ways.

CHAPTER FOUR

Revolutionary Women in the New Society, 1930–1954

In 1940, Frida Kahlo testified in a $200,000 lawsuit brought by Diego Rivera's former wife, Lupe Marín, against the publisher Alfred A. Knopf, Alfred A. Knopf, Inc., and Bertram Wolfe.[1] Marín, who first initiated the legal process in 1940, sued Wolfe, author of the biography *Diego Rivera: His Life and Times*, for injuring "her good name, fame and reputation" at various points throughout the manuscript.[2] According to the court papers, Wolfe's book stated that when Marín first agreed to model in the nude for Rivera's mural, she understood it meant "yielding her body, as well as posing."[3] Wolfe also wrote that Rivera became obsessed with Marín "not as a mere object of sexual passion, for he had already possessed her and she was beginning to live with him as his wife."[4] The legality of Lupe and Diego's marriage, or lack of, appeared to be an especially contentious issue in the case. In this regard, Wolfe asserted that Rivera insisted he never legally married Marín and even left a handwritten note for Wolfe and his wife, Ella, to say that any mention of a church wedding would be a lie. Wolfe also noted, however, that Rivera's sister contradicted her brother's statement by arguing that the painter and Marín wed in person in a Mexico City church, and the final court papers confirmed the date of their Roman Catholic matrimonial rites as 20 July 1922, with the Roman Catholic curate officiating.[5]

For both sides of the lawsuit the question of Marín's "morality," sexuality, and a woman's proper behavior, both in and out of marriage, ostensibly resided at the heart of the matter.[6] Wolfe questioned Marín's "true" intent in bringing forward her lawsuit, even insisting that she sought his money based on his status as a wealthy "gringo," or that she desired revenge against Kahlo.[7] But even though deciphering historical motives often results in philosophical quagmires of the most basic sort, Marín's legal actions certainly challenged Wolfe's implicit criticism of her behavior. Wolfe's inclusion in his biography of Marín's supposed affairs, for example, with a "street cleaner" and a "reputed mail [*sic*] homosexualist [*sic*]" meant to imply that Rivera's ex-wife's conduct carried the power to humiliate the painter, even long after their marriage ended.[8] Additionally, Marín's lawsuit against Wolfe noted the "false and malicious words" in his book that argued she operated in Mexico's "magic circle," which, according to Wolfe, was "a euphemism for the homosexuals who play a surprisingly large part in the group of painters, critics, journalists, novelists, and poets in Mexico, especially the last."[9] Here Wolfe apparently referenced Marín's ties with Mexico City's *Los Contemporáneos*, a writers and poets group that contained several openly gay members (including Salvador Novo), and her short-lived marriage to a *Contemporáneos* writer, Jorge Cuesta.[10] Marín, whose legal bonds to Rivera ended in 1927, married Cuesta in 1929, although they subsequently separated in 1932 and divorced two years later.[11]

Marín must have understood the subversive nature of her relationship with Cuesta. In many ways the *Contemporáneos*, who promoted modern and formal notions of "pure" art, functioned in opposition to the self-described revolutionary, Rivera, whose murals represented the embodiment of political art.[12] Moreover, as Rivera presented a "masculine" story of Mexico's history through his images of powerful soldiers, workers, and agrarian laborers, he also openly ridiculed what he perceived as the "effeminate" sexuality of Salvador Novo and other *Contemporáneos* members.[13] As an artist, Rivera symbolically positioned both women and the gay members of the *Contemporáneos* as the antitheses of the "virility" so central to the Mexican Revolution, but his ideas also reflected a generalized culture within Mexican society that sought to control women's sexuality and homoerotic desires.[14] Gay men and female artists, especially those who divorced or took on multiple lovers, fell outside of the traditional definitions of family life, and as Adriana Zavala argues, both groups "found themselves at the margins of the 'true' (nationalist, patriarchal) Mexican nation."[15] This sense of difference, however, could create bonds between the female artists and male writers. By enjoying friendships with gay men who openly relished the masculine embrace, Marín, for example, both rejected traditional patriarchal conventions of the era and reclaimed a space where she assumed a measure of control.

Kahlo's testimony during the Marín trial fueled the fires of controversy surrounding Rivera's ex-wife. At this point in their relationship, Kahlo and Marín openly disagreed on a number of issues, but their mutual loyalty toward Rivera also guaranteed their lives often intersected. Regardless of her motives, Kahlo's statements concerning Marín reveal a few of the deeper, more complicated events surrounding her lawsuit against Wolfe. Almost all questions concerned Marín, and similar to the marriage issue, most focused on the appropriateness of her behavior and reputation. However, two specific issues guided Kahlo's interrogation: Marín's sexual freedom and her association with "homosexuals." For example, when pressed for information about Marín's friendships with male "homosexuals," Frida replied that men often visited Marín's house, and she also enjoyed meeting them at Mexico City's Café Paris Express.[16] Besides the issue of Marín's friends, Kahlo also provided an answer concerning Marín's various lovers. When questioned if Marín ever talked about her sexual activities, Kahlo replied, "She spoke freely and boisterously about her sexual freedom at parties at which a large number of people were present, just as often as she did when there were few people present." When asked if Marín ever discussed a specific affair, Kahlo testified, "She told me and other people in my presence what she thought were amusing stories about [an engineer], concerning his stinginess, that he never gave her any gifts, and concerning the unusually small size of his sexual organ. That was the chief theme of her conversation concerning him, and she thought that a very amusing thing." According to Frida, Marín also spoke of a certain bullfighter, boasting that "she was very eager to sleep with him, and that she was determined to do so whether he liked it or not." And when questioned whether Marín ever discussed her sexual independence in public, Frida responded, "She said that she was glad that she was not married to anybody, because it gave her freedom, in sexual as well as in other matters."[17]

Ironically, at the time Kahlo provided her testimony for the trial of Rivera's ex-wife, she and Rivera recently had ended their own marriage.[18] Separated for only a short time after their divorce at the end of 1939 and subsequent remarriage on 8 December 1940, the couple remained close.[19] Still, for Kahlo, the difficulties of her relationship with Rivera continued to trouble her, and she sought out and received both advice and gossip from well-meaning friends. For example, Anita Brenner wrote to warn Kahlo against reconciliation with her ex-husband and ardently recommended that Kahlo remain independent.[20] Besides Brenner's words of wisdom, others cautioned Kahlo that Marín had moved back into Rivera's home. Whether true or not, Wolfe reported the same stories to his lawyers, speculating that, as the mother of his children, Marín sought to reclaim her rightful place as the most important woman in Rivera's life.[21] Another close confidant and editor of *Mexican Folkways*, Frances (Paca) Toor, contended that Marín at least partially instigated Kahlo and Rivera's divorce by relating stories to Rivera that caused him to respond with jealously.[22] According to Kahlo, though, Marín first became furious when she learned of Kahlo and Rivera's plans to remarry. Moreover, she also labeled Marín's drive to seek attention as the major incentive in her lawsuit against Wolfe. Kahlo argued, "She divorced me from Diego just in the same dirty way she is trying to get some dough from . . . Wolfe."[23]

Ultimately, the judgment in Marín's lawsuit against Wolfe and Knopf favored Marín, but she obtained only six cents in damages.[24] Even though Marín received a paltry sum, the final ruling still concluded that, at the time of the lawsuit "and at all times thereafter," the plaintiff displayed good moral character and reputation, and, as such, any printed matter that implied otherwise could be considered libelous. To buttress this point, the ruling pointed out the defamatory nature of Wolfe's depiction of Marín as "yielding her body as well as posing." The judgment further criticized (and labeled defamatory) Wolfe's contention that Marín married Rivera by proxy after Rivera claimed he was too busy for "such nonsense," by which he meant to appear personally at his wedding. Despite Marín's apparent "decent" behavior, the court nonetheless also concluded that Marín failed to suffer "substantial damage by reason of said publication"; hence the award of six cents. The point in question remained the lack of proof that Wolfe's book, *Diego Rivera: His Life and Times*, produced sales beyond the United States. Moreover, the court also noted that Marín taught a drawing class as well as a dressmaking class in order to maintain an appropriate home for her family. Here the findings stressed that Marín took care of her children "at all times" by providing for their education and paying their support beyond the two hundred pesos that Rivera contributed for his daughters.[25] Although clearly Marín failed to receive the dollar judgment she desired, and despite her supposed unruly behavior in the bedroom, the judge determined that her adequate mothering equaled good moral character.

Marín's trial against Wolfe provides insight into the contradictions at the core of commonly shared values concerning women's proper place during Mexico's postrevolutionary era. Kahlo's and Marín's visions of a normative family life and women's sexuality may have positioned them at the far end of the cultural spectrum during the postrevolutionary years, but their seemingly conflicting views on the right of women to experience sexual freedom while remaining "a respectable Mexican woman" still reflected current gendered assumptions about women's proper place within the family, the workplace, and politics. In this respect Marín's court case against Wolfe in defense of her unspoiled reputation paradoxically juxtaposed two creative and talented women who insisted on their right for sexual freedoms, but the subtext also positioned Marín as a "respectful" mother beside Kahlo, who never gave birth to children of her own.[26] Moreover, although both Marín and Kahlo pushed at the boundaries of society's normative sexual roles, Kahlo's passion for leftist (and often conflicting) ideologies meant that she presented an even greater threat to those who sought to maintain traditional cultural, gendered, and political conventions within Mexico City and beyond. Indeed, through her refusal to adhere to sexual categories, her paintings, and her political actions, Kahlo subverted traditional ideals of women's place—both within the family household and the political family. And if we return to the trial, Kahlo's testimony failed to alter the judge's opinion concerning Marín's role as a mother and her subsequent moral reputation.

Chapter 4 analyzes the roles of women to locate their contributions squarely within Mexico's vibrant cultural and radical political scenes during the 1930s and 1940s. To insert the crucial work of women artists into Mexico's history of radical politics, and to understand better how women practiced their art while participating in revolutionary change throughout the postrevolutionary era, this chapter focuses on Frida Kahlo, Paca Toor, Aurora Reyes, and Anita Brenner, among others.[27] The remarkable art produced by these women left indelible marks on Mexico's history: Kahlo's self-portraits offer a powerful legacy that lives well beyond Kahlo's short life; Reyes painted as well, and she also penned poetry; and Brenner focused on journalism and Mexican history. Besides her publications devoted to popular art and tourism in Mexico, Toor founded *Mexican Folkways*, a key journal devoted to the study of culture and Mexico's indigenous population. Brenner, especially, provided articles for *Mexican Folkways*, but Kahlo contributed as well.[28] The women also developed deep personal bonds that lasted for years, and their interactions significantly impacted the development of their ideas on art and leftist ideology.[29] Reyes and Kahlo even met in childhood. From their early years, the two adventurous young women broke gendered barriers by enrolling in the prestigious National Preparatory School, Reyes in 1921 and Kahlo in 1922, as two of the remarkably few women allowed to attend.[30]

Thus art took center stage in the women's lives, but so did radical politics. Either as members of Mexico's Communist Party or as close personal and/or professional friends to their colleagues in the PCM, these creative women often immersed themselves in leftist work.[31] For Kahlo, Reyes, and certainly the photographer Tina Modotti (as discussed in chapter 2), at different points in their careers, participation in Party politics represented a crucial aspect of their life and work. Indeed, with their dedication to the Party, much of Reyes's and Modotti's art reflected their commitment to Marxist ideology, but also a deep exploration of women's roles in Mexican society. As with many of their friends, Toor and Brenner never officially joined the Party themselves, although they maintained close friendships with

Mexico City's inner circle of international communists.[32] Thus, as members or as sympathizers, the women experienced the excitement of the 1920s, a time when the artists powerfully influenced politics, and Marxist ideology impacted the artists' images. The women reflected on their varied backgrounds, including both poverty but also privilege, to imagine—and implement—a better future. Regardless of the women's official affiliation with Mexico's Communist Party, the mere act of rubbing shoulders with other communists, as formal card-carrying PCM members or not, often led internal security agents to consider them as security threats.

Women often struggled to solidify their positions within the PCM, but the Party also questioned the role of women in return. As this chapter discusses, women faced the same entrenched prejudices when challenging political boundaries as they did when confronting the rhetorical walls that defined them as proper mothers and wives. Indeed, certain comrades belittled the importance of female Party members or at least argued that women's participation within the Party remained solely a "women's issue."[33] In this respect, Reyes characterized both the gratifications and difficulties of female PCM members when she stressed the rare "purity" of "leftist activism" during the early years of the PCM, but also the "male chauvinism, which was at its peak, and which was responsible for many of the era's mistakes."[34] Women's art disrupted political customs, revealing a revolutionary future through powerful images, but their personal lives reflected the continued efforts they waged to have their voices heard on an equal basis.

The Building of Revolutionary Coalitions among Women

Beyond the differences in their artistic mediums and their willingness to join the Communist Party, all women discussed in this chapter shared elements in common. As Olivier Debroise notes in his analysis of the photographer Lola Álvarez Bravo, some creative women during the early twentieth century avoided the trap of traditional marriage by assuming the supportive role of "artistic muse," or even more importantly by creating their own art.[35] Kahlo, Toor, Reyes, and Brenner all resisted conventional gender roles within a family structure, and they insisted on creating their own path in their relationships with men (and women). As reluctant as they were to allow customary marriage norms to constrain their lives, they also rejected a life limited to the geographical and cultural space as defined by national boundaries. All four women traversed national borders throughout their lives, and in a number of ways they also experienced the pleasure and pain associated with being an outsider.[36] For example, as a child of immigrants originally from Latvia, Brenner's family first traveled to various cities throughout the United States before finally settling in Aguascalientes, Mexico, where Brenner was born in 1905.[37] After her family moved to Texas in 1916, Brenner returned to Mexico City in 1923 to enroll in the National University.[38] Writing in the capacity of Brenner's biographer, Susannah Joel Glusker, Brenner's daughter, points out that "Anita was both a Mexican and American citizen during her lifetime, legally and figuratively."[39]

Regardless of their origins, all four women embraced life with all its complexities in postrevolutionary Mexico City.[40] And for many, the gifted Jewish folklorist and writer, Paca Toor, symbolized the heart of Mexico City's cultural vortex.[41] Toor maintained a great number of friendships with many of the creative intellectuals who lived in Mexico City, and she delighted in connecting people, including those from the capital's Jewish community. Originally from the United States, in 1922 Toor traveled to Mexico to attend summer school classes at the National University, and within months she decided to remain in the country.[42] Although Toor ignores any mention of a spouse when writing about her early days in Mexico City, most scholars acknowledge that her husband, "Dr. Joseph L. Weinberger," accompanied her.[43] Either way, clearly the marriage was short-lived, and Toor quickly moved into Mexico City's artistic circles, soon counting some of the city's most celebrated artists and writers as her close friends. Joseph Freeman, a member of the U.S. Communist Party and cofounder of the *New Masses*, recalled his impressions of Toor when he first arrived in Mexico City in 1929 as a correspondent for the Telegraph Agency of the Soviet Union, or TASS. Because of her position as editor of *Mexican Folkways*, Freeman made Toor's home his first stop in the country. Toor invited Freeman inside and, after a few moments of talking, she even agreed to introduce him to her personal friends, including Diego Rivera, who could help him as a journalist. As Freeman explained, Toor knew many of Mexico's top artists, officials, and scholars, thus making her home the nexus for anyone who wished to be involved in Mexico's cultural scene.[44]

Although Anita Brenner and Toor grew apart by 1927, it was Toor who originally introduced Brenner to the world of Mexico City's artists, including Lupe Marín, Tina Modotti, Concepción (Concha) Michel, and eventually Frida Kahlo.[45] As with the other exceptional women who traveled in Toor's inner circle, Carlos Monsiváis describes Brenner as a writer who took "full advantage" of a 1920s Mexico where many women exhibited a determination to live "in a different way."[46] Certainly Brenner welcomed the companionship of strong-minded women, especially as she expressed feelings of being the perpetual outsider—as a woman who traversed national and class borders. Like Toor, Brenner also was Jewish, and, during her early days in the capital, Brenner met a wide variety of women and men through her friendship with Toor and Weinberger, who directed Mexico City's B'nai B'rith office.[47] At this point in her life, Brenner sought to learn more about Judaism, and she also studied Hebrew. Indeed, Rick López's analysis of Brenner locates her Jewish heritage as a motivational factor behind Brenner's keen interest in Mexico's indigenous population and an inspiration in her desire to illuminate their traditions.[48] Throughout her career Brenner wrote a number of articles on Jews in Mexico, and she assisted Jewish refugees as they established their new life in Mexico.[49]

Toor first published *Mexican Folkways* in June 1925, and throughout its existence, the Mexico City journal included an impressive roster of Mexican and transnational intellectuals and artists among its collaborators.[50] As López notes, *Mexican Folkways* was the "first comprehensive cross-disciplinary journal to promote rural aesthetics as part of the nation's proud heritage rather than as embarrassing evidence of backwardness."[51] From 1925 to 1937, Toor completed nine total volumes, although the final three appeared only sporadically after 1930.[52] Women brought significant artistic and conceptual direction to *Mexican Folkways*'s intellectual life. Besides Toor's position as founder and editor, *Mexican Folkways* utilized the talents of a diverse group of female artists and writers, including the musician and PCM member Concha Michel. Contrary to the popular journals of the era, including even *El Machete*, the official newspaper of Mexico's Communist Party, *Mexican Folkways* placed female contributors in prominent positions. Toor worked in her job as editor and writer; Modotti as the journal's premier photographer and contributing editor (1927 to 1930); anthropologist and feminist Elsie Clews Parsons offered insights on the customs of Mexico's indigenous populations; Brenner wrote numerous articles, which appeared in the early editions; and many others, such as Margaret Park Redfield, anthropologist and wife of Robert Redfield, provided occasional pieces.[53] Brenner showed particular interest in *Mexican Folkways* during the early years, writing that the journal was "noted for its charm, its accuracy, its simplicity, sincerity, and beauty."[54] Besides her position as editor, Toor also provided articles for each edition of *Mexican Folkways*, and her works significantly shaped the publication overall.

Throughout the life of the journal, Toor called upon her deep personal friendships with many of the PCM artists and writers, and several of *Mexican Folkways*'s contributors, although not all, professed allegiance to Mexico's Communist Party.[55] Besides Rivera (before his expulsion from the PCM in 1929), Toor also included the creative works of a number of PCM artists and writers, including Leopoldo Méndez, Pablo O'Higgins, and Modotti, among others.[56] Toor developed professional and personal ties to artists with close, official connections to the Party, but she herself never joined the PCM. In fact, according to Margaret Hooks's account of Tina Modotti, "Paca was more than simply averse to the Party." However, Hooks also notes that Modotti visited Toor upon her return to Mexico City in 1939, although she assiduously avoided Rivera and Kahlo for their roles in sheltering Trotsky.[57] In 1927, the Mexico City newspaper, *Excélsior*, even linked Toor's name with that of her friend Ella Wolfe, the U.S. communist and wife of Bertram Wolfe, and claimed the communist activities of the two women were "well-known in the workers' centers."[58] Anita Brenner took note of the article and recorded in her diary that *Excélsior* described Toor as "the most dangerous woman in Mexico, whose notorious Communist activities are well known. . . . Poor *Folkways*!"[59] Most likely the piece meant to discredit Toor, but it nonetheless revealed popular assumptions about the *Mexican Folkways* editor based on her close association with noted communists.[60]

Even though Toor avoided direct contact with Mexico's Communist Party, Mexico's intelligence services still considered the editor an internal security threat. After she leased a post office box in her name in October 1925, concerns surrounding Toor only increased when the agents determined that she had falsified her home address on her postal forms. In response to growing suspicions, the security officials monitored the various people who retrieved Toor's mail and observed their movements as they left the building. One particular spy followed an "American" about twenty-five years old, with a "medium height" and "regular build," throughout the day after he picked up Toor's mail at the post office. After meeting with several others, eventually the "man in question" returned to his presumed home around five.[61] The official report never revealed the original motivations for monitoring Toor's postal box, but home addresses that received communist literature or other kinds of suspected "anti-government" materials caused concern among the internal security community. The fact that Toor arrived in Mexico from the United States and befriended known communists must have triggered apprehension among some Mexican officials.

Regardless of their political links, many of the women involved with *Mexican Folkways* maintained especially close friendships. Modotti and Toor even lived on the fifth floor of the *Edificio Zamora*, the same Mexico City building where *Mexican Folkways* retained its offices.[62] Work carried over into play, as contributors to *Mexican Folkways* also enjoyed lively parties where they wore colorful clothing and discussed the political events of the day.[63] Anita Brenner recorded her stories of such occasions in her diary, including an account of a 1927 dinner party hosted by Modotti and attended by a "gang of people," including Toor, who "dressed up in a Oaxaca costume."[64] Besides politics, the women also participated in discussions on a number of current topics, including art and artists, with their creative colleagues.[65] Indeed, the building's get-togethers could present opportunities to meet other like-minded friends, with some encounters leading to romance. Joseph Freeman, for example, met his future wife, Ione Robinson, while visiting Modotti's apartment. Nineteen-year-old Robinson only recently arrived in Mexico City to work as Rivera's painting assistant, and Rivera quickly arranged for her to live with Modotti.[66] Although Freeman and Robinson's marriage lasted only a few short years, the relationship still illustrates the passions, politics, and art that circulated throughout the lively group.

Radical politics also assumed a central role in the lives of the creative women, even solidifying their friendships in certain cases. Much like Modotti, who joined Mexico's Communist Party in 1927, Reyes and Kahlo soon followed suit. Reyes officially joined the PCM in 1927 and she remained in the Party for the next thirteen years.[67] As a member of the Young Communist League, Kahlo previously had participated in Party work by attending meetings and contributing to various PCM activities.[68] During these lively years Kahlo grew especially close to Modotti, and by 1928, Kahlo herself became an official member of the PCM.[69] In 1928, Kahlo met her other great passion, the painter Diego Rivera, through Modotti.[70] Before Kahlo's devotion to Rivera consumed much of her time, though, the two women enjoyed getting together for various occasions. For example, Modotti threw parties for her friends, including Kahlo, Toor, and even Marín. As Modotti wrote to Kahlo: "Because tomorrow is my birthday I have invited Paca, Maria and Lupe to an Italian dinner that my brother promised to prepare. I would very much like if you also could come and I beg you . . . [to ask] your mommy to let you. After dinner we will accompany you to your home or if you prefer you could stay here. . . . I hope to see you there!"[71]

Rivera illustrated Kahlo's and Modotti's commitment to communist ideology, or perhaps more appropriately his gendered vision, by portraying both women in his mural series in the Ministry of Public Education building.[72] In the third-floor *En el Arsenal* panel, completed in 1928, Rivera positioned Kahlo in the middle of the painting, dressed in a red shirt embellished with a star and dutifully distributing weapons to workers. To her right stands Tina Modotti, who looks up at Julio Antonio Mella, the Cuban revolutionary and her lover at the time, while also dressed in a red shirt and holding a bandoleer. A worker proudly displays the red flag emblazoned with a hammer and sickle at the top of the mural, while both women appear attentive to the male popular classes, in the form of agrarian workers, who surround them. Indeed, their roles appear to be as able assistants, even if communists, rather than soldiers in their own right. In this manner, Rivera positioned the women as literal and symbolic helpers of the communist revolution, a striking reflection of Rivera's assumptions for the roles his future wife would play after their marriage in August 1929.[73] Kahlo, however, left the PCM not long after she joined. Although she would return to the PCM in 1948, Rivera's 1929 expulsion from the Party just a few months after the couple married resulted in Kahlo leaving the PCM as well, a decision she later defined as a "political error" due to her relative inexperience.[74]

After Kahlo and Rivera left the Party, their ties to other communists unraveled. For example, Modotti resolved that she could not maintain her connections with a PCM "traitor," and her friendship with Rivera and Kahlo effectively ended. Toor, as an outsider to internal Party politics, continued her close friendships with Rivera and Kahlo throughout their political firestorm of controversy. After the newly married couple moved to their first house, Toor provided the furniture for the dining room, and the two women maintained their bond for years to come.[75] Despite Kahlo and Toor's friendship, Kahlo rarely provided work to *Mexican Folkways*. Still, in 1929, *Mexican Folkways* reproduced (in black and white) Kahlo's painting, *Two Women*, that accompanied Elsie Clews Parsons's article, "On the Travels of Folk Tales and One Tale from the State of Puebla."[76] Painted in 1928, *Two Women* depicted indigenous women, one sitting behind the other, with a close background of lush leaves and fruit. Although completed early in Kahlo's career, her painting revealed many of the pictorial elements that marked her later work, including the tropical backdrop, attention to textual details, and a focus on female beauty (most often represented by Kahlo herself). Additionally, the same issue included the full-page photograph, *AN 'ARTISTIC' PHOTOGRAPH OF DIEGO RIVERA AND HIS BRIDE FRIEDA KAHLO ON THEIR WEDDING DAY, AUGUST 19TH, 1929.*[77] In the photo, Kahlo, wearing a flowing dress and rebozo, sits while Rivera stands behind her. Rivera's hand

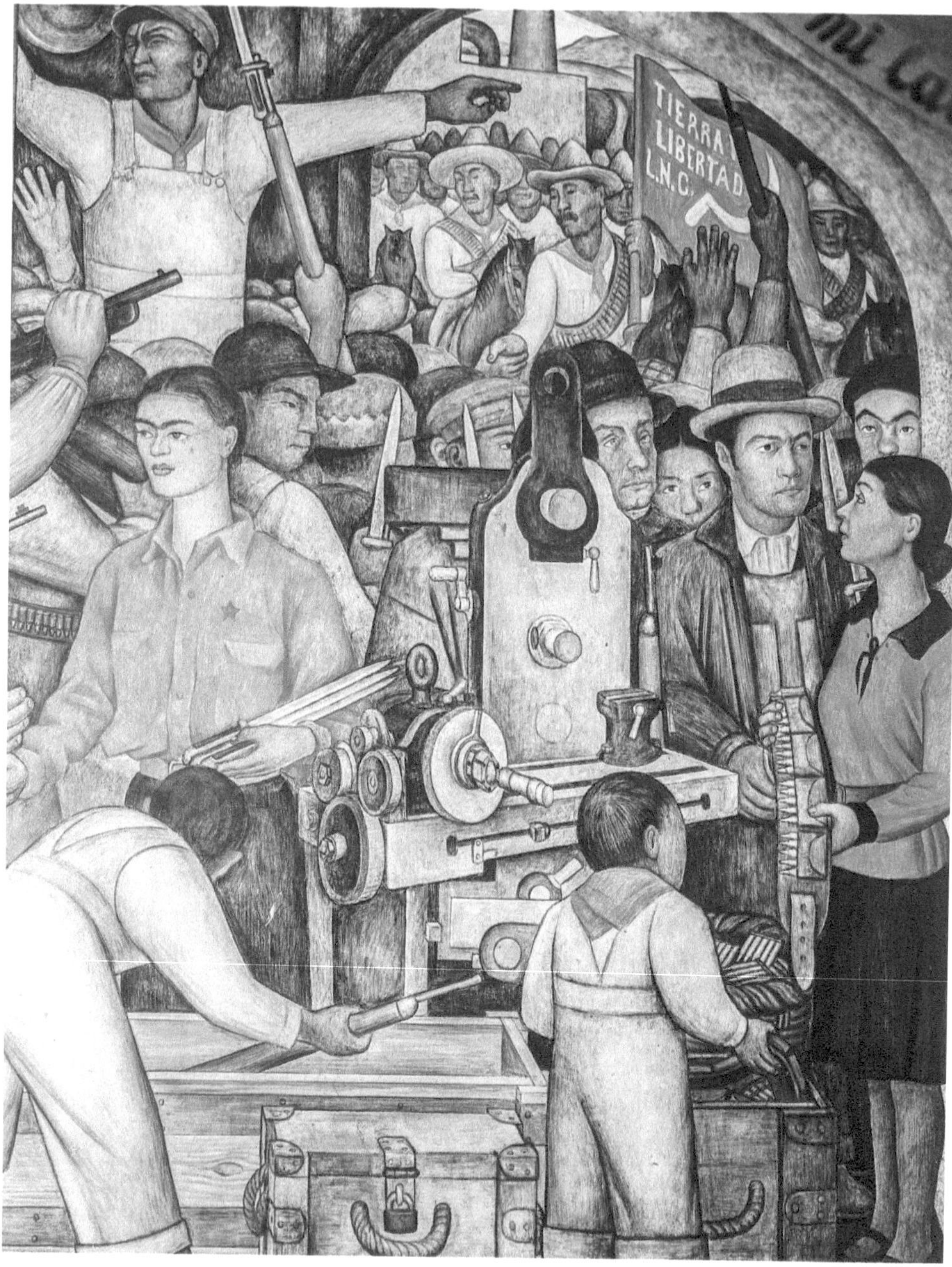

Diego Rivera, *En el Arsenal*, 1928 or *The Distribution of Arms*. Fresco in the Ministry of Education (Court of the Fiestas), Mexico City. Photo by Gianni Dagli Orti/ The Art Archive at Art Resource, New York. © 2015 Banco de México Diego Rivera Frida Kahlo Museums Trust, Mexico, DF/Artists Rights Society (ARS), New York.

rests on Kahlo's shoulder, appearing to hold her close, while her head noticeably tilts away from her new husband.

The Conservative Backlash into the Cárdenas Years

The end of the 1920s and the early 1930s brought great transformation to the country and huge changes to the lives of Kahlo, Toor, Brenner, and Reyes. By 1929, an increasingly conservative government apparatus turned against the PCM and anyone suspected of having ties to communism, and at this point police officials detained Modotti on 7 February 1930.[78] Toor understood that the photographer's time in Mexico was limited, and she expressed marked unhappiness concerning her friend's upcoming absence from the country.[79] After government officials expelled Modotti, Toor even moved into Modotti's vacant apartment.[80] During the subsequent months, Toor would continue to worry about Modotti, who was living in Berlin, especially because her letters expressed profound loneliness for Mexico and depression about working in Germany.[81] Brenner would visit Modotti during a trip to Hamburg, although she said that Modotti's airs of secrecy gave her "the willies."[82]

Kahlo, Toor, and Brenner also left Mexico at various points in their careers, although under clearly different circumstances. Following a similar pattern for the rest of her life, Brenner frequently traveled back and forth between Mexico and the United States. After leaving Mexico in 1927 and returning to New York, Brenner enrolled at Columbia University, also in 1927, and published *Idols behind Altars* in 1929. Modotti and Edward Weston provided the photographs, taken in 1926, for *Idols behind Altars*, although the hardships and lack of money encountered during the photographic expeditions created a deep rift in the two photographers' relationship.[83] Brenner ultimately completed her PhD in anthropology from Columbia and received the Guggenheim in 1930, and in the subsequent years she contributed numerous articles on a number of topics, including art and politics, for several newspapers and journals.[84] After marrying David Glusker, the couple returned to Mexico in 1930, although Brenner once again departed for New York in 1932. Still, Brenner would visit Mexico in 1935 and again in 1938 to update *Your Mexican Holiday* and cover the Cárdenas presidency.[85]

In late 1930, Kahlo and Rivera temporarily moved to San Francisco so Rivera could complete his mural commissions. Although they returned to Mexico City in June 1931 to allow Rivera the time to continue his work at the National Palace, within a few weeks, they again left for New York City and Rivera's retrospective at the Museum of Modern Art, which opened on 22 December.[86] While in New York, Kahlo expressed her dislike of "high society" and the difficulties of living in the crowded city to her close confidant and trusted doctor, Leo Eloesser. Noting the abject misery of the large number of homeless people during the height of the Depression, Kahlo wrote, "It's horrible to see the rich having parties day and night, while thousands upon thousands of people are starving to death."[87] In April 1932, Kahlo and Rivera arrived in Detroit so Rivera could paint the Ford commission at the Detroit Institute of Arts. Almost a year later, in March 1933, the couple once again returned to New York for Rivera's Nelson Rockefeller commission. By May, political controversy effectively halted the completion of Rivera's mural, but Lupe Marín still found time to visit her ex-husband and Kahlo in New York. According to Kahlo, as she gave Marín a tour around the city, Rivera's former wife continually attracted attention by falling down the escalators at Macy's and yelling in Spanish to all the women who worked in the stores.[88] By December 1933, the couple returned to Mexico City.

During the early 1930s, Toor also traveled to the United States, giving talks and catching up with old friends. In addition to Los Angeles, Toor often frequented New York City. During a 1930 winter trip to give a series of talks on Mexico's art and artists, Toor invited Kahlo to join her for the Christmas and New Year holidays, although she expressed doubt that Rivera would allow her friend to travel alone.[89] Upon her return to Mexico, Toor continued with *Mexican Folkways*, but not with the same intensity as before. Toor completed three final volumes of the journal—Volume 7 in 1932, Volume 8 in 1933, and Volume 9 in 1937—but health issues, financial concerns, and growing interests elsewhere took their toll on the normally energetic Toor.[90] In 1931, Toor suffered from "inflammation of the liver" and was unable to work for about six months.[91] At this point, Toor also tired of the constant pressure required in producing the multilingual publication.[92] Indeed, by 1933, Toor expressed her desire to explore new creative opportunities besides her work with *Mexican Folkways*. Publishing and managing the journal consumed much of her time, and when she completed Volume 8 in 1933, Toor looked forward to future writing opportunities.[93] Still, Toor pushed forward with *Mexican Folkways* in order to complete the final 1937 Volume 9, which was composed of two special numbers, "The Popular Plastic Arts" and "Customs, Music, and Dances."

Even as the government's crackdown on the PCM altered the lives of the artists associated with the Party, Mexico City's lively cultural scene persevered. Still, politics continued to play a central role in the artists' gatherings, and Siqueiros's ideological split with Rivera loomed large as a focus of discussion. Siqueiros's January 1932 exhibit at the *El Casino Español* proved to be a theatre of sorts where the audience largely supported either Siqueiros or Rivera. Siqueiros, who lived in exile in Taxco following his 1930 May Day arrest, received permission to attend his first one-man art exhibit of more than one hundred pieces produced during his time away from Mexico City.[94] Brenner, along with others, organized the show, although Kahlo remained away from Mexico City and Toor refused to go to the opening. Not surprisingly, Toor and Brenner took radically different positions toward Siqueiros's paintings with Toor defending Rivera and Brenner backing Siqueiros's art.[95] Along with the usual crowd of artists, the Soviet filmmaker Sergei Eisenstein, who would leave Mexico under pressure from the government in less than a month, also attended the grand opening. Assessing the split between Siqueiros and Rivera, Eisenstein explained to Toor that male Mexican artists were like revolutionary soldiers; each had their own *soldaderas* (female combatants and camp followers) to support them.[96]

Brenner's defense of Siqueiros reflected her admiration for the painter. Her 1932 article, "Siqueiros Is the Aesthetic Revelation of the Greatest Importance in the Artistic Movement of Mexico," clearly presented her thesis on the importance of Siqueiros and his current work exhibited at *El Casino Español*. Here Brenner discussed Siqueiros and his historical significance to Mexico, arguing that the true aesthetic worth of Siqueiros's art far exceeded that of Rivera's in several aspects. For one, according to Brenner, although Siqueiros influenced all aspects of the "modern Mexican pictorial art," the "superficial propaganda" as published by newspapers and critics erroneously gave Rivera credit for creating Mexico's most important art movement. Second, Brenner positioned Siqueiros as Mexico's most noteworthy painter "because he was the first one to produce an aesthetic closely bound to the social, geographical and traditional conditions of Mexico." Brenner also claimed Siqueiros to be free of both "folkloric influences" and contemporary European influences, while still representing an "ethnological type" in his paintings. Brenner closed her favorable assessment of Siqueiros's work with the bold assertion that the muralist represented Mexico's greatest achievement in the area of modern painting.[97]

Given Brenner's arguments in favor of Siqueiros's art during the 1932 exhibit at the *El Casino Español*, she ironically supported Trotsky's asylum in Mexico, even before his arrival in 1937. Still, Brenner's daughter notes that, early on, Brenner expressed an interest in Marxism, socialism, and communism, although she avoided joining the Communist Party. According to Glusker, Brenner grew attracted to Trotsky's political theories after reading his autobiography, and she contributed an article on Trotsky to the *New York Times Magazine*.[98] Although Brenner originally supported Siqueiros and his artistic achievements, even helping him sell his paintings in New York, Glusker mentions that Brenner ended their friendship after Siqueiros's attack on the Trotsky compound on 24 May 1940.[99] Moreover, Brenner's support for Trotsky, and her work in favor of Trotsky's asylum in Mexico, guaranteed that Modotti refused to see her old friend after her return to Mexico City during the previous year, in 1939.[100] Even though Modotti agreed to visit another former colleague, Paca Toor, the two women argued, supposedly after Toor insisted that communists had destroyed the photographer's life.[101]

Cárdenas's presidency particularly fascinated Brenner, and after difficulties, she obtained an interview with him to discuss his 1938 expropriation of the oil industry. According to Brenner's daughter, however, although Brenner wrote a positive article in praise of Mexico's revolutionary reforms for *Fortune*, the journal edited her piece to reflect a more critical approach. Brenner attempted to apologize to the president several times, although without much success.[102] Even as Brenner researched her piece, though, security agents carefully tracked her movements as she traveled in Tampico with a friend of "Mexican nationality." On 1 July 1938, Agent Number 14 followed orders from his superiors to uncover the activities and whereabouts of Anita "Bremenn" [*sic*]. Agent Number 14 understood that Brenner should be arriving that day by airplane to Mexico City from the port of Tampico. However, after Brenner failed to appear on any of the airlines, the agent discovered that the "señorita" and a female friend already had arrived from Tampico a couple of days earlier. Additionally, his report noted that Brenner had flown on the same plane as an official of the Sinclair Petroleum Company, which Agent Number 14 thought might somehow be related to Brenner's activities.[103] An additional memo sent by Agent José Clavé declared that the two women merited close surveillance, especially due to the fact that Brenner was a well-known journalist and correspondent. The informant recounted that Brenner devoted her time to photographing the refineries and oil fields, and also awaiting the return of the president, whom she hoped to interview. Moreover, Clavé reported that the U.S. Consulate in Tampico supplied Brenner with reports on local issues and even money "that she spent freely."[104]

According to the agents, Brenner and her friend posed a possible threat to national security. Several factors, however, especially alarmed Clavé. For one, Brenner acted outside of traditional gendered norms. During her time in Mexico, she refused to demurely wait for permission to interview President Cárdenas, and she boldly took photographs of the Mexican countryside in her role as a journalist. Clearly Brenner acted as an independent agent, traveling alone or with another woman rather than in the company of her husband. Eventually Brenner completed her interview with President Cárdenas, and more importantly, she remained active throughout the 1930s, writing a number of articles for the *Nation*, *New Masses*, the *New York Times*, and other outlets. Besides *Mexican Holiday*, published in 1932, and *The Wind That Swept Mexico*, in 1943, Brenner submitted a number of pieces on art, the artists, and politics to journals and newspapers throughout the 1930s and 1940s.

As Brenner maneuvered national borders seemingly with ease, negotiating family life and work created challenges for the writer. After Brenner gave birth to her son, Peter, and her daughter, Susannah, the competent and prolific writer quickly encountered the difficulties associated with raising children and maintaining a productive career. In 1941, Brenner discussed her frustrations with her friend, the composer Carlos Chávez, concerning the complexities of combining a career with family life. "I am starting to understand why so few women have done something worthwhile in the arts, sciences, and etc. That to combine serious work with attending to home and kids is something that is driving me to . . . despair. What is needed is the willingness of all the demons, and [the] soul of friar or something similar."[105] Late in her career, Brenner recalled that she never experienced professional discriminations as a female writer or journalist. Juggling her responsibilities as a mother and "housewife" while making her deadlines, however, proved more difficult. According to Brenner, carving out time for home and writing could be a "real problem" and an ongoing issue for Brenner and her female colleagues.[106]

Aurora Reyes also traveled for shows and conferences, but unlike Brenner, for the most part, Reyes concentrated her efforts to make a difference through art, activism, and feminism in Mexico. Reyes married young and gave birth to two sons, the first born in 1926 and the second in 1931. When her last child was still a baby, however, Reyes divorced her husband and began teaching art.[107] In order to avoid intellectual frustration, Reyes well understood the importance of not sacrificing her art, even for a cause as "noble as motherhood and family duty."[108] As a result, Reyes continued to work on a number of fronts throughout the decade. Combining her passion for both painting and politics, in 1936, Reyes joined the *Liga de Escritores y Artistas Revolucionarios* (LEAR).[109] As a member of the PCM, Reyes fit well with LEAR's ideological commitment to leftist politics, and she enjoyed her work for the organization. In 1936, LEAR arranged a competition to offer painters the opportunity to create a mural in Mexico City's *Centro Escolar Revolución*; Reyes succeeded in obtaining the commission for one of only six spaces.[110] Her subsequent *Ataque a la Maestra Rural*, or *Attack on the Rural Teacher*, resulted in the first mural painted by a Mexican woman.[111] In this deeply political work, Reyes depicted a female teacher during the Cristero Revolt struggling to fight off an attack by two armed male campesinos while three small children look on in fear.[112] To illustrate the violence many women faced while in the rural classrooms, Reyes painted one of the men dragging the teacher by her hair as he ripped up her books, while the other man slammed his rifle against her distraught face. Given the mural's location in a school, the work must have acted as a warning to protect public education for those who served on the front lines of the educational battles.

As demonstrated with her powerful mural, Reyes remained committed to women's issues and her painting reflected the difficulties women faced every day. Even as Reyes argued for the effectiveness of art as a powerful weapon, she also understood that the patriarchy of the times, even within the radical leftist movements, simultaneously constrained women's possibilities for advancement.[113] Still, Reyes combated women's oppression on a number of fronts. In 1938, as a delegate from the *Sindicato de Trabajadores de la Enseñanza de la República Mexicana*, or the Mexican Republic Teachers' Union (STERM), Reyes traveled to the National Women's Congress held in Havana, Cuba. While there, Reyes presented her paper, "Women and Culture," to great acclaim.[114] Here Reyes argued that women's status as "protected beings" resulted in their exploitation by men. Moreover, Reyes analyzed the inadequacy of culture—throughout history—created by men and solely for men's needs.[115] Throughout her life, Reyes championed women's right to vote, as well the importance of women obtaining government positions, as vital elements of her work.[116] Even as Reyes agitated for improved political and working conditions for women, though, she continued to paint and exhibit her artwork. In 1940, the Galería Romano in

Mexico City arranged a one-person exhibit of her paintings, and in addition, she organized a number of shows throughout the city.[117] By the late 1940s, Reyes's poetry also earned her high praise.[118]

Women and the PCM: Negotiation and Power from the Late 1930s through the 1940s

As creative individuals, art assumed a key place in women's personal connections at all levels. And as progressive women, well-versed in the discourse of leftist or socialist ideology, they also either belonged to the PCM or else maintained close friendships with Party members. From the initial moments of the PCM's creation in 1919, women played crucial, although often unrecognized roles within the Party's structure. Even though PCM members addressed the issue of women during numerous subsequent meetings, many years later, Mexico's Communist Party still continued to struggle with the question of how to incorporate women most effectively. Women's art disrupted political customs, revealing a revolutionary future through powerful images, but their personal lives reflected the continued struggle they waged to have their voices heard on an equal basis, even among fellow Party colleagues.

As discussed in chapter 2, from the mid-1930s, the PCM promoted the need for cross-party alliances, including ties with women's organizations outside of the Party. The momentum for greater unity only increased after the Communist International sanctioned the Popular Front on 2 August 1935.[119] At this point, comrades within the PCM called for increased political coalitions to join together in the struggle against a growing fascist threat, even if it meant overcoming their previously antagonistic relationship with President Lázaro Cárdenas and his administration.[120] Following the unity mandate, in 1935, PCM women, together with those from the Mexican government's *Partido Nacional Revolucionario*, or the National Revolutionary Party (PNR), formed the *Frente Único Pro-Derechos de la Mujer*, or Sole Front for Women's Rights (FUPDM).[121] The "First National Women's Congress" followed soon afterward in March 1936. Held in the Theater Hidalgo in Mexico City, the PCM member and FUPDM's secretary of political action, Esther Chapa, gave her position paper titled, "Women's Right to Vote."[122] Still, as Concha Michel would recall, the organized women remained divided over the best path forward to implement women's reforms. Additionally, according to Michel, PCM members split on the issue of women's key positions. While some agreed on the importance of women as mothers and workers, others insisted that their role of worker trumped that of mother.[123]

Even as Chapa argued that women possessed the appropriate intellectual and political readiness to vote intelligently and free from religious or conservative influences, the PCM's commitment to women's rights weakened amid calls for unity across party lines. Mexico's Communist Party, led by the feminist and communist Consuelo Uranga, put together a series of working points to address specifically the issue of women within the Party in January 1938. Chief among the topics was the mandate to "maintain unity at all costs" as well as the support of the Cárdenas government.[124] The plan further considered the upcoming Mother's Day, insisting that all communists, female or male, should mark the event with rallies, parties, and celebrations in each and every town. In the manner in which the PCM guidelines for women's inclusion stressed motherhood, they also promoted the importance of lectures to guide women, "alongside men," in their responsibilities as defenders of the revolution.[125]

In February 1938, only a month after PCM released its instructions to fellow comrades, women came together in the Hidalgo Theater for the "Special Women's Conference."[126] Held during the period of lively debates by lawmakers and activists over the issue of women's suffrage, the invited guests spoke on a variety of controversial topics concerning women's rights in Mexican society.[127] Illustrating the PCM's call for organizational unity, the women represented a number of different organizations, including the Communist Party, the FUPDM, various government groups, and many more. Over three hundred women "of different social classes" attended the conference, as did many of Mexico's top women activists. Besides the female delegates, internal security Agent Number 5 also visited the meetings, and faithfully reported on the proceedings in his neatly typed account of the conference's activities.[128] The presence of an agent within the large crowd illustrates the concerns held by some government officials with organized women's political action in general.

Although PCM members occupied leading roles during the conference meetings, so did representatives of the Cárdenas administration. While some women harshly criticized government policies toward women, others defended Cárdenas's recent positive reforms in this area. PCM member María del Refugio García, or Cuca García, gave the opening speech. Particularly critical of the hypocrisies embedded within Mexico's popular revolutionary discourses, García argued that the Mexican Revolution had conceded nothing to women and also had failed to establish justice in the home, the office, the field, the school, or the factory. García continued by describing the difficult lives of market women, whose children rested in filthy drawers full of trash and microbes while their mothers sold their merchandise, and those who lived in shantytowns alongside dogs and pigs. García next moved to the labor issue, stating that because businesses refused to pay minimum wage to women, they had no choice but to work in one of the countless clandestine workshops earning a mere thirty pesos a day. She finished by stressing the importance of motherhood and the need to improve wages for women in general.[129] In many ways, García echoed the criticism articulated by the singer and former PCM member Concha Michel toward the Party when she insisted that the elimination of patriarchy could, in fact, be separated from the eradication of capitalism.[130] In other words, for both Michel, who also spoke during the meetings, and García, revolutionary change should include women's issues as an integral part of the revolutionary process instead of waiting for the fall of capitalism to confront the problems that challenged women on an everyday basis.

Not all the participants expressed displeasure with the current government's reforms toward women. Indeed, some adamantly endorsed working with President Cárdenas to achieve greater gender equality, especially during the time of increasing global threats. To this end Señora Balmaceda, an employee of the Ministry of the Interior, followed García's talk with her own warm assessment of Cárdenas. In her presentation, Balmaceda contended that Cárdenas's work toward granting women a role in the formation of the new Popular Front should earn him the title of "Second Father of the Americas." Even though Balmaceda emphasized the importance of cooperating with Cárdenas in order to achieve a more just society and to fight against the growing fascist danger, at the end of the conference, the women remained divided over the role of the Cárdenas government with regard to women's reforms. Internal security Agent Number 5, who remained throughout the heated discussions, carefully noted the dissension between the women, writing the conference ended with a "big fuss and shouting that finally resulted with the meeting being adjourned, without reaching any agreement." Before signing his report, though, the security agent reported that delegates formed a new committee that promised to continue the discussion of women's participation in the Popular Front.[131]

Less than a year later, Cuca García spoke in favor of women's reforms during the PCM's Seventh National Congress, held in Mexico City early in 1939. Overall, thirty-eight women delegates representing many states attended the meetings, including Esther Chapa from Mexico City.[132]

García first called for the creation of more jobs for women through increased industrialization, especially by utilizing Mexico's abundant raw materials "that have until now been the source of wealth for imperialist companies." More importantly, though, García called upon all Party members to help with the organization of the women's movement in Mexico and within the PCM. Here she stressed the need for a sustained push for women's specific and immediate demands in the hopes of recruiting active, determined, and revolutionary women. Referencing her previous theme of women in revolution during the 1938 "Special Women's Conference," García insisted that her fellow PCM members often failed to understand Lenin's great maxim that revolution would not be possible without women. Moreover, without the Party's leadership, women faced the danger of falling into the hands of reactionaries. Therefore, García requested that Congress members officially support the organization and recruitment of women in order to create a stronger party, "such as Comrade Lenin wished."[133]

With the advent of World War II, the PCM continued to place concrete reforms for women on the back burner while the country dealt with the immediate concerns of war. Once again drawing upon women's gendered position within society, the PCM's rhetoric emphasized the significance of women's proper roles in the fight to defend the homeland. Esther Chapa, writing in the PCM's newspaper, *La Voz de México*, raised this concern in 1942 when she argued that Mexican women faced a great danger—one that surpassed all others of the past centuries. According to Chapa, all Mexican women understood, cherished, and respected the "Fatherland" and would defend it to the death if necessary. Indeed, women would work for the good of their country, even serving in the field if called upon, to protect their homes and their children. Chapa listed the various positions women could fulfill in the struggle, including forming first aid groups, assisting firefighters, helping law enforcement, and providing emergency food and shelter.[134]

Soon after Chapa's article, in late 1942, *La Voz de México* once again highlighted women's roles during times of conflict with "La mujer y la Revolución." In this piece, the journalist, feminist, and communist Adelina Zendejas Gómez stressed women's historical experience, arguing that from the colonial era to the present, Mexican women understood the insignificance of gender in the matter of defending the "Fatherland." According to Zendejas Gómez, with the spread of fascism, Mexico faced a particularly serious internal and global state of affairs. Zendejas Gómez continued that Mexican women should be attentive to the tragic lives of women and men who lived in countries invaded by the Nazi fascists and commanded by Hitler. Here Zendejas Gómez harked back to the Mexican Revolution, arguing that women realized the importance of the "unity" of Mexican women to defend their country and their rights to work, for culture, for peace, and for the safety of their homes. After all, during the struggle against the dictatorship of Porfirio Díaz and the subsequent revolution, women fought for similar concerns: "freedom and justice, bread for their children, equal education for men and women; ownership of the land they worked . . . ; fair wages for women and men; maternity protection; labor protection for minors; equality and new rights in the various codes."[135] Clearly, in both *La Voz de México* articles, women's duty to defend their children and country came first, superseding other issues; equal pay for women, for example, remained on the back burner.

But even as the war neared its conclusion, women's specific matters remained low on the PCM's hierarchy of priority. During PCM meetings, members often lumped the discussion of women together with the organization of communist youth, thus suggesting that both groups needed guidance and education. Party leadership also continued to promote the involvement of PCM women in a national women's movement, including the *Bloque Nacional de Mujeres Revolucionarias*, originally the *Frente Único Pro-Derechos de la Mujer*.[136] According to the PCM, the *Bloque Nacional de Mujeres Revolucionarias* provided an appropriate venue for a women's organization, at least partly because its leadership incorporated Party members, including Esther Chapa.[137] As a women's group, the *Bloque* promised to fight for women's rights in their various roles as mothers, workers, and citizens. To achieve its goals, the *Bloque* leadership declared it would tackle women's issues by promoting: (1) women's participation in the process of industrialization; (2) women's technical, professional, and artistic training; (3) expansion of social welfare institutions for the mother and the child in the cities and in the countryside; (4) women's full citizenship rights; (5) an increased number of women's jobs, "according to their ability and physical strength;" and (6) Mexican women's participation in all activities of Mexico's economic, social, cultural, and political life.[138]

The reports of the Tenth Congress of the Communist Party, held from 24 November to 1 December 1947, only briefly discussed the subject of women, but the minutes nonetheless stressed the importance of developing a revolutionary organization of women that could forge links to broader groups, including the proletariat and peasantry, in the struggle for their common and specific interests. Here PCM members insisted that the Party needed to convince women that it would be in their best interest to unite their forces, especially in the fight for women's issues. To assist women in their duties, the Party promised to assume the crucial task of organizing women in the countryside and factories, "putting [women] at the forefront of the defense of their specific interests and thus creating the conditions of a national women's movement, having as a base the *Bloque Nacional de Mujeres Revolucionarias*." Comrades also emphasized the importance of raising male members' awareness concerning the need to attract women to the revolutionary struggle, because, as the participants argued, "without the existence of a women's movement it will not be possible to develop our revolution."[139] Even as the reports stressed the need to consider matters relating to women, though, PCM members still argued that women should work within the *Bloque Nacional de Mujeres Revolucionarias*. Indeed, according to the Congress, as "the only national organization to organize and mobilize the broad masses of women, to fight for their specific demands," the *Bloque* represented the appropriate path to women's full political rights.[140]

Throughout the late 1930s and 1940s, the PCM emphasized women's theoretical importance, even while many within the Party still questioned whether women could make equal comrades. In December 1949, Mexico City's PCM members discussed just this issue during the Fifth Congress of the Committee of the Party. Throughout the meetings, comrades expressed concern that very few women belonged to the Party, and even worse, the fact that certain Party members resisted the recruitment of compañeras. To help solve the matter, the congress recommended that each and every PCM member should focus their attention on factories as an appropriate location to recruit women, and also that they organize working women at these centers. As an example of the Party's development on the issue of women, representatives now argued that comrades should not consider the efforts to involve more women as a problem exclusive to women, or that only women could address the gender matter. Instead, congress delegates urged *all* Party members to consider women's recruitment a priority, and they set a target of one hundred new female members for the month of January.[141]

The Long Road Home

Unfortunately for Reyes, the PCM's renewed commitment toward a greater inclusion of women came too late. Indeed, on 1 June 1940, *La Voz de México* published the names of eight comrades recently expelled from the Party—seven men and one woman. The Communist Party's paper listed Aurora Reyes among the former PCM members removed for currently having "links with Trotskyist groups, always working without connection with the Party's higher organizations and base, and receiving influences from people foreign to the political line of the PCM."[142] Reyes's removal from the Party in some ways mirrored Concha Michel's previous experience in late 1933 and 1934. As Jocelyn Olcott notes, Michel left the PCM after the Party's newspaper published notice in November 1933 of the Central Committee's decision to expel her. Long active in the PCM, Michel refused to conform to the Party's position that characterized "women's issues" as secondary, an interpretation labeled as "antimarxist" by the Central Committee.[143] Although *La Voz de México* failed to provide the specifics underlying Reyes's own expulsion, much like Michel, Reyes promoted women's positions within the PCM but also expressed criticism with many of her male comrades' decisions to treat women differently from themselves.[144] After she left the PCM, Reyes continued her work as an artist and a poet. Kahlo and Reyes also remained close, even through the twists and turns of their respective careers and relationships. Demonstrating the eloquent words of a poet, Reyes wrote to her friend from Oaxaca, "From this other land, from this other country, or more accurately from another planet, I remember you, Frida, now more intimately and closer than ever."[145] After a long career, Reyes died on 26 April 1985, in Mexico City.[146]

Lying in a Paris hospital bed in February 1939, Kahlo clearly found herself in another world of sorts. Following her November 1938 New York show, held at the Julien Levy Gallery, Kahlo traveled to Paris in January 1939 to participate in an exhibit organized by the surrealist and Trotskyite André Breton.[147] Breton wrote the preface for her New York exhibition, and theoretically had arranged for Kahlo to show many of the same art pieces in Paris. Upon her arrival, however, Kahlo found her paintings still in customs and the supposed show in disarray. To make matters even worse, her stay with Breton and his wife resulted in an exceptionally disagreeable experience for Kahlo.[148] Very quickly, Kahlo became ill with a serious kidney infection, and after over two weeks in the American Hospital, she refused to return to the Breton home. As she wrote her intimate friend and portrait photographer, Nickolas Muray, Kahlo remained convinced she caught her infection from food served during her time at Breton's residence.[149] Eventually the promised show came to pass, but not without additional

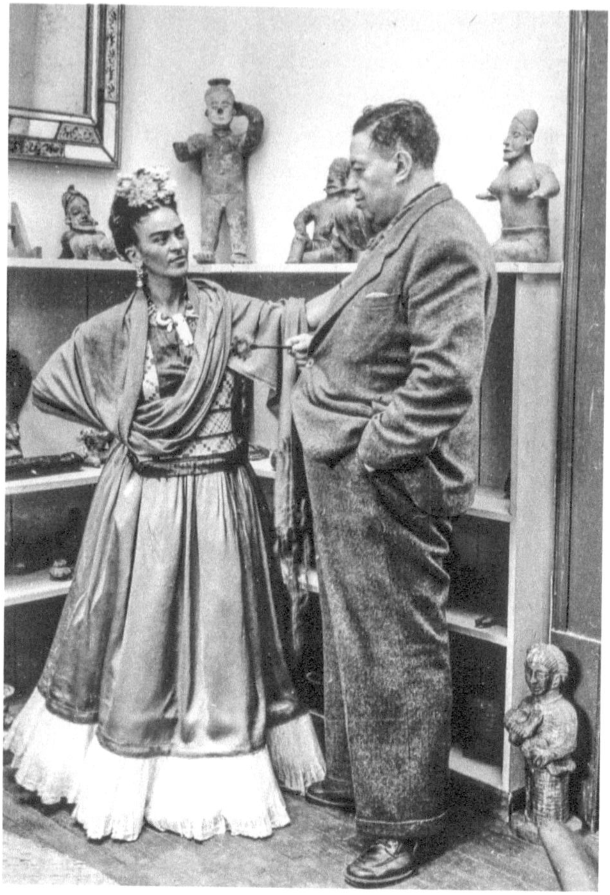

Frida Kahlo with her husband, the Mexican artist Diego Rivera, in her studio in Mexico City, 1945. Photo credit: Album/Art Resource, New York.

conflict. Kahlo furiously reported to Muray that the gallery only would include two of the paintings because the subject matter of her other art could disturb the public.[150] According to the catalog, however, Kahlo ultimately exhibited eighteen of her works at the Renou & Colle Gallery from 10 March to 25 March.[151] Appropriately titled *Mexique*, the show also included photographs by Manuel Álvarez Bravo, nineteenth-century portrait paintings from Mexico, pre-Colombian art, and a hodgepodge of "popular art" pieces that Breton discovered in Mexico's markets.[152] Besides her Paris show, in 1953, Lola Álvarez Bravo also organized a one-person show of Kahlo's paintings at her Mexico City gallery, the *Galería de Arte Contemporáneo*.[153]

In her own way, Kahlo discovered her path back home when she returned to the PCM in 1948. Over the next few years, from 1948 until her death in 1954, Kahlo grew increasingly impassioned by Marxist ideology and the

Communist Party.[154] Toward the end of her life, Kahlo boasted that she joined the PCM before she met Rivera, and throughout her years, her devotion to communism surpassed that of her husband's. And even though she grew too ill to participate fully in the PCM, she dutifully paid her dues, attended Party events when she could, and kept abreast of current, internal deliberations.[155] For instance, the Silvestre Revueltas cell of the PCM sent Kahlo an "urgent summons" to attend a meeting of painters "in order to discuss the position, duties and responsibilities of the Communist Party painters." Also on the agenda was the consideration whether to create a Revolutionary Painters Front to help promote Mexico's artists and to fight against reactionary infiltrators. The PCM secretary ended his note with the stern warning: "We are sure you will not miss this important meeting, [thus] complying with your duty."[156] Besides her dues, Kahlo also contributed funding to other areas of the Party, including the Communist Youth.[157]

An historical analysis of Kahlo's relationship with Mexico's Communist Party and the question of her loyalties provokes debate.[158] In a similar vein, considerations of Kahlo's reliance on Rivera and his ever-shifting political interests also generate controversy. Certainly, Kahlo and Rivera made decisions, with the Trotsky affair at the top of the list, which theoretically should have resulted in irreparable ruptures with the PCM. But Kahlo also displayed a fierce independence, especially after she returned to the Party.[159] At this point, she obsessed less about Rivera's affairs or at least claimed that she and Rivera enjoyed a "mutual understanding" that provided for freedom of action without jealousies or misunderstandings.[160] With her anxieties over matters of the heart diminished, Kahlo still worried that her health impeded her from devoting more time to revolutionary causes. More importantly, though, she expressed concerns that her paintings, and the self-expressions as portrayed in her art, lacked a certain kind of usefulness that could "help the Party."[161] Despite Kahlo's self-doubt, members of PCM's Central Committee recognized the importance of Kahlo's artistic contributions. A mere six days before her death, the PCM's secretary general, Dionisio Encina, sent Kahlo a note to express warm birthday greetings and the hope that she enjoyed many more years "for the good of the revolutionary cause of our people." Before signing their correspondence with a "communist embrace," the leadership applauded Kahlo for her work to promote the sovereignty of the Mexican people.[162] As Kahlo's life came to an end, she returned to what provided meaning to her existence. Ever complex and fraught with complications, the PCM nonetheless occupied a central position, separate from Rivera, within Kahlo's self-identity.

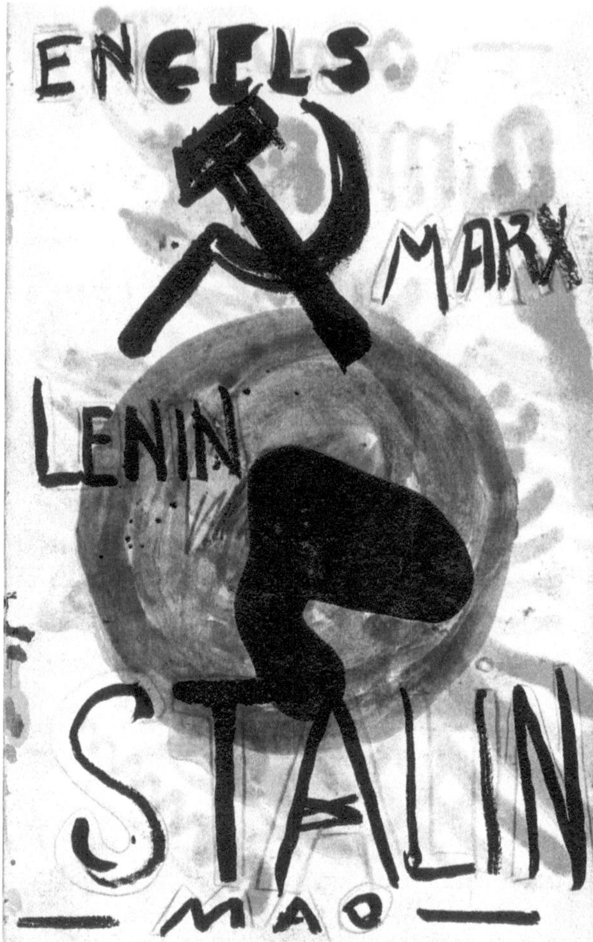

Frida Kahlo, ENGELS, MARX, LENIN, STALIN, MAO. Page 114 from the Frida Kahlo diaries, 1944–1954. Frida Kahlo Museum (Casa Azul), Coyoacán. Photo by Schalkwijk/Art Resource, New York. © 2015 Banco de México Diego Rivera Frida Kahlo Museums Trust, Mexico, DF/Artists Rights Society (ARS), New York.

Frida Kahlo died on 13 July 1954. Andrés Iduarte, Kahlo's longtime friend from the preparatory school and the general director of Mexico's *Instituto Nacional de Bellas Artes*, or the National Institute of Fine Arts (INBA), agreed to place Kahlo's coffin in the lobby of the *Palacio de Bellas Artes* on the condition that politics would remain separate from the formalities. Although Rivera approved these terms, a former student of Kahlo ignored the warnings and placed a flag with a hammer and sickle on the casket.[163] According to Iduarte, he repeatedly asked for the removal of the flag bearing the hammer and sickle from Kahlo's coffin. When he confronted her relatives, however, they refused, arguing that the flag was Kahlo's last wish. At this point, Iduarte reluctantly accepted the situation and chose to respect "Death."[164] Among others, Kahlo's longtime friends, Lola Álvarez

Bravo and Aurora Reyes, stood next to her coffin in respect.[165] A little after noon the following day, Kahlo's body was moved to the crematorium at the Mexico City cemetery, the Panteón de Dolores. Rivera, Siqueiros, Iduarte, Mexico's former president Cárdenas, and others formed Kahlo's final honor guard. Once her body reached its destination, accompanied by over five hundred mourners, various guests gave their final respects to Mexico's memorable artist.[166] With Rivera by his side, Iduarte spoke first, sadly pronouncing, "Frida has died. Frida Kahlo has died." He continued, "Friend, sister of the people, grand daughter of Mexico, continues to live."[167] Among others, PCM representative Juan Pablo Sáinz offered a tribute that moved well beyond a discussion of the painter's life.[168] Indeed, according to a critical editorial in the newspaper *Excélsior*, the remembrances given at Kahlo's funeral praised communist ideas even more than they celebrated the dead artist.[169]

Within days of Kahlo's funeral, Iduarte lost his position at the INBA. Dismissed for permitting the hammer and sickle flag to drape Kahlo's coffin, the former director of the INBA faced an outcry from those who demanded his resignation. Iduarte, who previously held a longtime position as a Spanish professor at Columbia University, responded to his termination with a defense of his actions.[170] According to Iduarte's rebuttal, his job permitted him to make the kinds of decisions that would allow the public to view Kahlo's body at Bellas Artes. Furthermore, although his critics questioned whether Kahlo's "work was of sufficient merit to justify her body being brought to Bellas Artes," Iduarte pointed out that even Kahlo's politically antagonistic detractors still recognized the merits of her paintings. Given the political climate, though, Iduarte considered the ideological charges to be the most serious. Here he responded to the accusations of communist sympathies by pointing out that, although throughout his life he held dear to the ideas of liberty and social justice, he was not and had never been a communist. He boldly asserted, "If I had been or were now, I would have said so, and would now say it frankly, as is my custom."[171] Clearly Iduarte paid a price for his loyalties to the artists.

Kahlo's friend, Paca Toor, died on 16 June 1956. Throughout her life, Toor's accomplishments attracted the attention of many of the world's noted scholars and artists.[172] For example, in her transplanted home, the Mexican government awarded her the Order of the Aztec Eagle in 1949, the highest honor given to a foreign citizen for their services given to Mexico.[173] Although she had planned to return to Mexico City and her teaching position at the National Autonomous University of Mexico (UNAM) on 3 July 1956,

Toor fell ill in the United States, after living in Italy for two years, and died before returning to her adopted country.[174] Perhaps Diego Rivera best captured Toor's spirit—as well as the complexity of their longtime relationship—when he remembered his "Yankee friend" in a 1956 tribute published by the Mexico City newspaper, *Novedades*. Honoring Toor as a true supporter of Mexico, Rivera stressed her tenacity, patience, and deep love for the Mexican people. Rivera also highlighted Toor's studies of Mexico, asserting, "her work, difficult to define, especially positively influenced what is now Mexico's cultural life, namely that part of the cultural life that does not work with imported materials." Here, Rivera clearly referenced *Mexican Folkways* and the broader debates of the late 1920s and 1930s that discussed and deliberated on the "purity" of Mexico's indigenous population. Ultimately, Rivera credited Toor with spreading the word about Mexican art and creating a true global appreciation of Mexico's culture from 1921 to World War II. Rivera bid good-bye to Toor by predicting that the entire Mexican people would share his high opinion of his friend and understand the role she played in Mexico's history as one of the country's great supporters.[175]

Much like Kahlo and Toor, Brenner continued to work throughout her life, and she also negotiated national borders. In 1944, Brenner moved back to Mexico City with her two children. The official paperwork from the secretary of the interior recorded Brenner's nationality as "North American" and admitted her with the status of "immigrant" for one year, renewable up to five years.[176] During the subsequent three years, Brenner dutifully renewed her application for herself and children, which the Mexican government approved.[177] Although born in Mexico, Brenner also identified with the United States. Her dual identity clearly brought her some sense of conflict, as she expressed in 1943, "I would like to say, sometime, somewhere, that being an American brought up in Mexico gives one an obsession to reconcile two ways of life, two almost opposed points of view, two sets of emotions and interests."[178]

Over the years, Brenner continued to write. In addition to her many articles, in 1955, Brenner founded *Mexico/This Month*, a journal she produced into the early 1970s. She also published a number of children's books and continued exercising her passion for writing. During the last years of her life she returned to Aguascalientes and her parent's farm, where she enjoyed the challenges of managing a large, working agriculture operation. Still, Brenner remembered fondly the exciting early years of her career. In an interview soon before her death, Brenner recalled the time in

Mexico City when anything seemed possible. As Brenner explained: "You know, the generation of the 20's lived through a great moment in national life, a time when the world was beginning, and we were creating it, we were making it in terms of 'Here at last, something can be done, and we can do it.' And it was a very beautiful moment and a very vigorous one. . . . Revolution was still real in the world."[179] Brenner's musings captured a rare period in Mexico's history, but according to Brenner, one that soon lost its momentum. Although Brenner had delighted in the world of Mexico City's cultural and political scene during the early twentieth century, by her later years she experienced a growing sense of skepticism in regard to the realities of political transformation.[180] In 1974 Anita Brenner died in a car accident while driving home to her farm in Aguascalientes.[181] Although she traveled throughout the world and lived as a true transnational citizen, Brenner's life ended where it started.

Conclusion

The legacies left by Kahlo, Toor, Reyes, and Brenner offer much to those who study art and postrevolutionary Mexico. Easily traversing national borders, both in geographical space and friendships, these women's histories also provides an example of boldness in moments of great political excitement and turmoil. At a time when women faced tremendous obstacles in their personal and private lives, Kahlo, Toor, Reyes, and Brenner not only placed women front and center in creative production, but their lives also provided an example of women who refused to abide by contemporary gendered norms. Outspoken and assertive, Kahlo, Toor, Reyes, and Brenner operated firmly at the center of Mexico's intense postrevolutionary artistic scene, and they aptly circulated within a lively social and political environment composed of artists, political actors, and intellectuals. They assumed oversized roles in Mexico's postrevolutionary cultural life, and their influence in the establishment of an "authentic" Mexican identity will last for many years to come.

Chapter 5 continues the discussion of women, but as members of LEAR and the Taller de Gráfica Popular (TGP). Here again, women from Mexico and other countries contributed much to the artists' organizations, and within the collective nature of the groups, their art offered powerful images that revealed the horrors of fascism and war. An analysis of the issues facing PCM women and artists during the era of the Popular Front, however, provides salient points of comparison. As the PCM women found their specific needs diluted during the Popular Front, the LEAR artists also softened their powerful political critiques during this time of national unity. The following chapter discusses just such issues to advance the examination of the interactions of radical artists with state officials and locate Mexico's printmakers as important players in the international fight against fascism.

CHAPTER FIVE

Revolutionary Printmakers

LEAR and the TGP, 1934–1957

In 1957, the Taller de Gráfica Popular, or the Popular Graphic Art Workshop (TGP), celebrated its twenty-year anniversary. Created in 1937 by former members of the short-lived *Liga de Escritores y Artistas Revolucionarios*, or the League of Revolutionary Writers and Artists (LEAR—established in early 1934), the TGP represented an extraordinary group of radical artists whose cultural and political work contributed significantly to the international struggle against the spread of fascism. Artists associated with Mexico's Communist Party played key roles in the formation and everyday affairs of LEAR and the TGP, and the alliances between the PCM and the two artists' groups remained strong.[1] Although tensions eventually developed between individual TGP printmakers and the PCM, the distinctive union of politics and art resulted in the creation of two of Mexico's most significant creative movements of the twentieth century. Indeed, the artists mirrored their ideologies in the powerful images they produced, and as a result, their work both represented—and influenced—the changing political environment in which they operated.

To mark the TGP's twentieth birthday, artists and artists' organizations from all over the world sent hearty congratulations to the Taller.[2] Stressing the importance of the TGP for the international working class, David Alfaro Siqueiros highlighted the TGP's defense of the Mexican Revolution, and the "Marxist-Leninist principles that look to make [the working] class their indispensable vanguard."[3] Another of the grand muralists, Diego Rivera, sent his greetings to the TGP as well, writing that the "twentieth anniversary of the founding of the Taller de Gráfica Popular of Mexico is a date that should be commemorated with enthusiasm, not only for Mexico but for artists all over the world."[4] Besides Mexico's artists, transnational groups also offered their good wishes to the TGP. For example, Li Hua, representing the Graphic Art Group of the Union of Chinese Artists, wrote, "Now on the occasion of the 20th anniversary of the founding of [the] Taller de Grafica [*sic*] Popular, allow us, from this far country, [to] offer you our hearty congratulation[s]." Hua emphasized the TGP's use of striking art as a "powerful weapon," thus praising their unique combination of revolutionary graphics that garnered the "high esteem from the progressive people all over the world."[5] The Union of Czechoslovakian Artists offered their salutations, friendship, and admiration, while also expressing hope for the TGP's future success.[6] Uri Baer, from the Wilfrid Israel House for Oriental Art and Studies in the Kibbutz HaZore'a, also wrote to convey proletarian solidarity, as did the Artistic Youth of Moscow.[7]

The letters from Mexico's prominent artists and other activist groups from around the world reflected the TGP's emphasis on a global membership roster. During the late 1930s and 1940s, many of the world's top writers and artists moved to Mexico to escape the horrors of fascism. Mexico not only provided a shelter for this notable population, but also a creative space to collaborate with Mexico's finest printmakers and artists. Together they produced compelling drawings, prints, books, and posters that detailed fascism's atrocities. The 1956 Statutes of the Taller even included two types of TGP membership: those who lived and worked in the country and guests from outside of Mexico.[8] Despite separate membership categories, Mexican and transnational artists worked together as a unified group to produce work that reflected both national and global political currents. Indeed, it was not uncommon for those from outside Mexico to assimilate so fully as to never leave the Taller or their adopted country.

Over time, LEAR and TGP artists negotiated with intellectuals and government representatives on a number of issues. Artists from Mexico and other countries created global partnerships, and they also worked with high-level bureaucrats to produce images that illustrated the dangers of fascism through books and posters. As this chapter discusses, however, although the art produced through the temporary partnership of Mexico's radical artists and government officials retained much of its initial revolutionary character, many of the artists nonetheless argued that ties to the state authorities constrained their abilities to affect radical change. Moreover, according to LEAR and TGP members, art created in the service of the people—with topics understood by the popular classes—still represented work of the highest quality. In this respect, the artists argued that art should reflect the social reality of the times, but as David Craven points out, they did a great deal more than simply mirror reality. Instead, those who contributed to LEAR and the TGP also attempted to alter social and political structures through their use of culture, and in the process, they left a significant legacy of art and print production that resonates today.[9]

Liga de Escritores y Artistas Revolucionarios (LEAR)

The artists and PCM members Leopoldo Méndez, David Alfaro Siqueiros, Pablo O'Higgins, Luis Arenal, and the writer Juan de la Cabada were among the founding members of the League of Revolutionary Writers and Artists in early 1934.[10] From the beginning, LEAR closely aligned with Mexico's Communist Party, especially since its leadership as well as its most prominent members all belonged to the PCM (although LEAR leadership did not require members to join the Party).[11] Following the directives as established by the Sixth Congress of the Communist International, LEAR came together as an organization in support of the working class against the dominant elite and the current government.[12] In this manner, the artists' creation of LEAR dovetailed nicely with their individual ideological beliefs, and the original members remained close to the PCM and loyal to Party directives.[13] Among the visual artists, Siqueiros, of course, long had been a member of the PCM, despite his contentious relationship with the Party. Méndez joined the PCM in 1929, and he soon locked arms with other Mexico City artists and intellectuals who advocated the use of art for political purposes in the fight against tyranny.[14] O'Higgins, originally from the United States, arrived in Mexico in 1924, and within six months, he began his work as Diego Rivera's assistant on the murals at the Secretaría de Educación Pública building. By 1927, the PCM accepted O'Higgins into their ranks, and he remained loyal to the Party for the next twenty years.[15] As a PCM member and Siqueiros's brother-in-law, Arenal was active in LEAR, and he also participated, along with Siqueiros, in the 1940 Trotsky attack.[16]

LEAR's predecessor, the 1931 *Lucha Intelectual Proletaria*, or the Intellectual Proletarian Struggle (LIP), provided the ideological foundation for LEAR.[17] The LIP Declaration of Principles included four points, including the promise to bring together artists and intellectuals who would dedicate their work to the service of the proletariat in the class struggle; the assurance that each member would advocate for intense intellectual activity; the knowledge that the proletarian struggle would demand that members reflect the objective reality of the conditions of the proletariat and the historical role of their struggle against the capitalist class; and the agreement that all members should refuse to satisfy—and instead combat—the political demands of the bourgeoisie.[18] Ultimately, LIP survived only two months and produced one issue of its journal, *Llamada*.[19] Despite its short life, the group provided a blueprint of sorts for the same artists who would assume the leadership of LEAR just a couple of years later.

In the early years, LEAR positioned itself as an organization of intellectuals and artists that specifically avoided electoral politics. Instead, LEAR's founders conceived of their association as one that would advance the arts and sciences to envision a better future for artists and writers. In this regard, LEAR members sought to create and then strengthen a broad cultural front composed of individuals or groups in Mexico and other countries.[20] Siqueiros, O'Higgins, Méndez, and other members promoted culture as the tool that would free Mexico's workers from a lifetime of economic subjugation. According to LEAR's founding declarations, which they published in their journal *Frente a Frente*, LEAR would serve the working class in its struggle against capitalism, fascism, imperialism, and war. LEAR members also swore to oppose the institutions and corrupting currents of the bourgeois arts and sciences, while defining reactionary artists and writers as those who served the clergy and the exploiting class.[21]

Six sections represented the various cultural categories within LEAR: fine arts; literature; theatre and film; music; pedagogy; and science.[22] Through literature, painting, music, theatre, and other expressions of intellectual work, LEAR members promised to constantly demonstrate unfailing class content in their art. To become and remain a member of LEAR, all participants agreed to specific procedures and obligations. First, the applicant applied formally, with their membership sponsored by an existing member. Afterward, the appropriate section would approve the potential candidate. After acceptance into LEAR, members could vote in the general assembly and within their particular section. LEAR also obliged all artists to pay the fee approved by the general assembly, with exceptions for those who lacked the funds. LEAR rules required the larger general assembly to meet approximately every two weeks and the individual section assemblies as well as executive committee to convene at least once a week. Members of the executive committee served for six months, but they could be reelected if they carried out their duties efficiently. In addition to the full members, LEAR also permitted others to form groups, categorized as "Friends of the LEAR," which lacked specific functions except to help with the program development.[23]

In the early months, LEAR lacked formal space to meet. Indeed, during the first year of LEAR's existence, the Party and the PCM's official paper, *El Machete*, remained outlawed after the Mexican government forced the PCM underground.[24] Thus, with their close ties to the PCM, LEAR members originally met secretly in cafes until they finally rented a space.[25] One of LEAR's early members, Angelina Beloff, the Russian artist and Rivera's first wife, described LEAR's headquarters as a large, sparse room in an old, dismal building. Furnished only with a table, some benches, and a few boards, LEAR members plastered the walls with posters and proclamations. According to Beloff, to arrive at LEAR's office, members had to walk through several corridors and little patios where children played. Beloff nonetheless was able to utilize the area to teach Russian to workers. Given the difficulties in learning this language, Beloff soon abandoned Russian to offer lessons in English, which she considered more practical. Still, she continued to share her skills with artists and musicians who needed to learn Russian, and she also noted that eventually LEAR was able to obtain a more pleasant operating environment.[26]

Despite their initial difficulties, by April 1934, thirty members participated in LEAR, including painters, writers, musicians, playwrights, educators, architects, photographers, and filmmakers.[27] Soon others joined the group, bringing the number of those belonging to LEAR to eighty by January 1935, with an additional section in Puebla.[28] Over the four years of LEAR's existence, the membership grew to include more than five hundred notable artists and intellectuals in all fields represented.[29] Indeed, soon LEAR's roster of artists contained many of Mexico's and Latin America's finest painters, photographers, and sculptors, including Siqueiros, Méndez, O'Higgins, Arenal, Alfredo Zalce, Ignacio Aguirre, Rufino Tamayo, Carlos Mérida, Antonio Pujol, Ángel Bracho, Fernando Gamboa, Xavier Guerrero, Fernando Castro Pacheco, José Clemente Orozco, Manuel Álvarez Bravo, Juan O'Gorman, and others.[30] Women such as María Izquierdo, Aurora Reyes, Clara Porset, Marion y Grace Greenwood, Angelina Beloff, and Lola Álvarez Bravo also assumed active roles in LEAR.[31]

According to LEAR's executive committee, within a few months of its formation the artist organization offered lectures, art exhibitions, plays, as well as a school for workers and correspondence classes.[32] Of course, such ambitious programs cost quite a bit, and from the beginning, LEAR persistently searched for international connections as possible sources of assistance and funding. For example, in 1935, LEAR members reached out to Joseph Freeman, the national secretary of the John Reed Club, to establish a working relationship for future artist exchanges and to request aid to help alleviate their dismal financial circumstances.[33] Throughout the year LEAR officials continued with their outreach activities, contacting the *New Masses* in New York City to ask for copies of the journal; additionally, they sent their own *Frente a Frente* to international organizations in France and the USSR.[34] Despite the lofty educational aspirations of the LEAR leadership, a lack of operating capital hindered the organization's ability to carry out many of its potential projects.

Still, with its stark art and hard-hitting articles, the journal *Frente a Frente* effectively served as LEAR's mouthpiece. Operating intermittently from November 1934 to 1938 (with sixteen total issues), *Frente a Frente* averaged from two to ten thousand copies and appeared in Mexico and other countries, including the United States and Panama.[35] LEAR adopted its title from the slogan of the 1928 Sixth Congress of the Communist International, or class against class (or head to head).[36] But *Frente a Frente* also reflected LEAR's original intent as a united proletarian revolutionary front.[37] The first issue of *Frente a Frente* listed Siqueiros, Méndez, de la Cabada, and Arenal as members of the editorial committee, but also "Rab-Kor." According to Deborah Caplow, Rab-Kor was a pseudonym for "Rabochii Korrespondient," or "worker correspondent," an unidentified Moscow contributor.[38] The editors changed throughout the issues, as did the contributors, illustrators, and even the format size. For example, Siqueiros remained as an editor for the first two issues, but not from the third onward. After the first three copies, the numbers of *Frente a Frente* also reverted to "Number One" to delineate the first phase of LEAR, or the "proletarian front" that stressed revolutionary changes and ties with the Soviet Union, with the second phase that reflected the beginnings of increased political opportunities and greater unity with the Cárdenas government.[39] Within its richly illustrated pages, *Frente a Frente* demonstrated a number of objectives.[40] First, articles often presented discussions on the role of art in promoting revolutionary ideology, and the best ways to reach the masses through the style and content of various images. Stark black-and-white graphics, including woodprints and photographs, also depicted the proletariat workers, the horrors of fascism, and the corrupt bourgeoisie. In this manner, *Frente a Frente* demonstrated LEAR's position that art should reflect social issues with an easily accessible narrative.

Frente a Frente essays also criticized Leon Trotsky, the Fourth International, and those who supported the Russian revolutionary.[41] Many LEAR members considered Diego Rivera, as Trotsky's advocate, to be the most notorious traitor to their cause, and they looked to Siqueiros to lead the LEAR attack against the painter within the journal's pages. Focusing on Rivera's recently completed mural, "Man, Controller of the Universe," located in the *Palacio de Bellas Artes*, Siqueiros analyzed Rivera's work in the

May 1935 edition of *Frente a Frente*. As a re-creation of the original Rockefeller Center fresco, destroyed in 1934 for its supposed anticapitalist symbolism and portrait of Lenin, Rivera's new mural included similar images but with several additions, including Leon Trotsky's portrait and a banner of the Fourth International. Rivera's inclusion of Trotsky's image insured political backlash, and Siqueiros utilized his *Frente a Frente* piece to attack Rivera not only on an artistic front, but also politically. Arguing that Rivera utilized archaic individualistic techniques when painting his murals, Siqueiros also effectively parodied his enemy's politics by labeling him "the head and supporter of the Fourth International in Mexico," and even worse, the "Communist terror of the U.S. tourists in Mexico."[42] Siqueiros thus branded Rivera a fake revolutionary whose fabricated ideology concerned only those foreigners who misunderstood Mexico's political terrain.

Frente a Frente's denunciation of Rivera reflected contemporary divisions between Siqueiros and Rivera. As discussed in chapter 3, LEAR artists ranked high among the crowds who attended the great public debate on the role of Trotsky and the meaning of art between Siqueiros and Rivera that took place at the Bellas Artes in 1935.[43] Moreover, representatives of LEAR and the PCM frequently pursued similar objectives, including the reestablishment of Mexico's diplomatic ties with the Soviet Union, the advancement of the welfare of the working class, and the struggle against fascism.[44] Even as LEAR's goals shifted over the few years of its existence, LEAR and PCM delegates continued to work hand in hand to advance parallel objectives. For example, during its initial months, LEAR members focused on class struggle as promoted at the 1928 Sixth Congress of the Communist International. After President Cárdenas assumed office in December 1934, though, LEAR artists slowly moved toward a position that called for cross organizational unity in the fight against fascism.[45] Still, it would take some time before LEAR members perceived the new Cárdenas administration as anything other than a reincarnation of corrupt past presidents. Indeed, LEAR's early motto revealed this viewpoint: "Neither with Calles, nor with Cárdenas."[46]

During the early years, LEAR members played a critical role in advocating for the reinstitution of previously closed political outlets. For example, LEAR adopted a resolution that promoted the reopening of *El Machete*, the PCM newspaper closed since June 1929. Although the paper continued to publish illegally, various LEAR members created a commission to meet with the president directly, demanding the legalization of the PCM and its press. After sustained agitation by LEAR and other organizations, President

Cárdenas permitted the PCM and *El Machete* to function once again, as announced in the circular dated 22 February 1935.[47] At this point, PCM members were able to dispatch two issues of the paper, at least provisionally, to be sold in the factories.[48]

The wheels of change nonetheless moved slowly, a fact duly noted by various LEAR and PCM members in their letters to Cárdenas.[49] As one disgruntled comrade from Veracruz wrote in April 1935, "As to date *El Machete* and the legality of our Communist Party of Mexico has experienced obstruction, and you have not complied with the offering you made to the commission of 'LEAR' in relation to the free movement of our revolutionary paper and the legality of our Party."[50] Several unhappy members from Puebla also wrote to complain in March of the same year, saying that while the "bourgeois" newspapers enjoyed the open circulation of their papers, *El Machete* operated under different circumstances.[51] In the same vein, Coahuila members reminded the president of his promise to LEAR representatives to allow the paper to operate without restrictions, and other groups reported that the postal service would not deliver *El Machete* due to prejudice against the communist paper and orders by the previous presidential regimes.[52] The administration of *El Machete* even reported that Veracruz military police arrested a paper vendor for the "crime" of selling the PCM's paper to the workers in a factory.[53] LEAR and PCM comrades bitterly protested, but by 1935, the PCM once again distributed *El Machete*, even if slowly at first.

LEAR encompassed not only those who worked in the visual arts, but also those from other creative disciplines, including music, theatre, architecture, and photography.[54] Even though LEAR included a variety of fields, the visual artists assumed the lead in the direction of the group. Still, all members remained dedicated to the notion that their work must serve the Mexican popular classes. In this manner, the architects promoted improved living conditions for workers, and the painters attacked the notion of "pure painting." Even as LEAR artists advocated for the Mexican people, they, themselves, often struggled to make a living. Many taught art or illustrated children's books to supplement the meager earnings from their creative work, but most held government positions for Mexico's secretary of education.[55] Government employment allowed for time off, though, and the artists utilized their May and November vacations to share LEAR's artistic endeavors with laborers. For example, LEAR's "cultural brigades" promoted the various arts outside of Mexico City, which, according to LEAR leadership, represented the center of the country's intellectual life. To carry out their objective, in May 1936, LEAR artists traveled to an agricultural exposition in Morelia, Michoacán, where they painted murals depicting local heroes in the Central Union meeting hall. Other members gave lectures on education and revolutionary literature, and they also showed Russian films.[56]

LEAR's creative ventures also included art shows, and the editors even published an open call for artists in the first issue of *Frente a Frente*. Reflecting their position that *all* artists should be allowed to exhibit their work, LEAR invited women and men, including nonprofessional artists, to submit their paintings, sculptures, drawings, and prints for a series of revolutionary exhibitions. The LEAR announcement clearly specified their only requirement: the artworks should "express a living protest against the current capitalist system."[57] In this manner, LEAR's proposed art shows reflected their emphasis on class struggle, artists' key place within revolutionary engagements, and the importance that members placed on paintings, drawings, novels, poems, and all other art forms whose content could be utilized as weapons in their struggles to liberate workers from oppression.[58] LEAR membership rolls contained a number of accomplished artists, but at this point, members emphasized equal opportunity among the group as well as the importance of art that reflected class struggle. As Francisco Reyes Palma points out, LEAR thus elevated the "collective interest" above the "mystique of the individual."[59]

Although the resulting art shows promised inclusion by unknown artists, they also could invite criticism for their nonprofessional quality. For example, LEAR's opening exhibit, which took place on 1 May 1936, in the former Santa Clara Church in Mexico City, elicited heated discussion. Sixty artists participated, the majority of whom displayed paintings rather than sculpture.[60] Although the exhibit attracted a large number of viewers, the art polarized Mexico City's intellectuals. Reflecting arguments over the meaning of art and revolution, detractors and supporters aired their views in public forums. Luis Cardoza y Aragón, the Guatemalan writer, essayist, poet, art critic, and LEAR member, offered a scathing review of the LEAR show in *El Machete*. Cardoza, who lived in Mexico City at the time, expressed serious concerns with the fact that the exhibit included a large number of inferior artworks that compromised not only the overall artistic integrity of the show, but also the capacity of the exhibit to be revolutionary in nature. Cardoza argued against an approach that included many artists by writing "The banality in art, in revolutionary literature, is one of the biggest enemies, and is true counter-revolution." Labeling the exhibition a mess, with only four to six worthy paintings, Cardoza complained that LEAR had accepted too many mundane works under the policy of "frente único." To counter this concept, the writer argued, "In art there is no united front, nor extenuating circumstances whatsoever." Cardoza further claimed that many LEAR leaders possessed a simple narrow-mindedness and childishness that was the enemy "not only of art but of revolutionary doctrine itself."[61]

Not surprisingly, other LEAR members argued against Cardoza's position. While admitting to certain weaknesses of the show, they still defended LEAR's inclusion of amateur artists. Just a week after Cardoza's critique appeared, Juan de la Cabada responded with a defense of the LEAR show. Also writing in *El Machete*, De la Cabada argued that even as Cardoza accused LEAR of being against art, LEAR membership included many of Mexico's most prominent artists, including, among others, Alfredo Zalce, José Clemente Orozco, Rufino Tamayo, David A. Siqueiros, Antonio Pujol, Carlos Mérida, and "Cardoza's best friend: Cardoza." While supporting the concept of "frente único," De la Cabada still suggested a number of possible changes: include more works by established artists; reject the worst paintings of any particular artist and incorporate only their strongest works; improve the placement of the art; and others. Despite these proposals, De la Cabada nonetheless argued that future shows should include only one work—the artists' best example—by "each one of the bad artists, and all the best of the good."[62] Additionally, an anonymous writer in *Frente a Frente* avidly defended the LEAR art show, especially because the "exhibition was visited by more than seven thousand workers," a fact that demonstrated "the real interest of the workers in the artistic work." Furthermore, the unnamed commenter noted that the quality of the art improved considerably after this first exhibit.[63] In another review of the exhibit, Chano Urueta specifically singled out José Clemente Orozco's "formidable lithographs" and the three engravings by Leopoldo Méndez, the "great artist and indisputably a connoisseur, like no one else, of the technique and craft of engraving."[64]

Although LEAR members fiercely defended the collective ideology behind their first show, their second considered the previous debates. Held in the lobby of the National Library during the summer of 1936, the exhibit showcased fewer pieces, all of which were prints, created by many of Mexico's finest artists, including Siqueiros, Orozco, O'Higgins, Méndez, Arenal, Angelina Beloff, Jean Charlot, María Izquierdo, and others.[65] In this way, LEAR presented a collective show that still represented the ideology of their members, but it also considered the quality of the art. In the August 1936 issue of *Frente a Frente*, the anthropologist, photographer, graphic artist, and current *Frente a Frente* editor, Julio de la Fuente, discussed the need to learn from the many discussions surrounding LEAR's first show. To illustrate the article, *Frente a Frente* utilized the engravings from the National Library exhibit, including prints depicting an attack against monopolies in the shape of a grimacing skeleton by Méndez, a workers' parade by Orozco, and a scathing indictment of academic artists by Gabriel Fernández Ledesma. De la Fuente pointed out that novice artists frequently included an "essential repertoire" of symbols, including hammers and sickles, red flags, and raised fists, in their attempts to create revolutionary metaphors. Much of the problem, according to De la Fuente, was that the artists lacked both the necessary training in political theory and the financial means to be able to produce appropriate revolutionary art. To remedy the situation, De la Fuente suggested greater discussion about technique and even content in order to elevate the quality of the art to a level understandable by the "masses."[66]

The Popular Front

During mid-1935 and into the summer of 1936, LEAR members transitioned from a position that criticized President Cárdenas's reforms to one that backed the new president and his governmental policies.[67] Supporting the Communist International's endorsement of the Popular Front on 2 August 1935 to fight against the growing fascist threat, the LEAR artists and the PCM now promoted a greater alliance with Cárdenas and his mass organizations.[68] LEAR's shift to back the president was part of a larger movement within the PCM to support a Popular Front position. On 6 September 1935, via "Circular No. 82," the Mexican Communist Party announced their Politburo's decision, based on the resolutions from the Seventh Congress of the Comintern, to approve the "urgent task" of forming an antifascist Popular Front. As announced in *El Machete*, and publicized in widely distributed memos, revolutionary organizations were to organize Popular Front groups immediately in all parts of the country.[69]

To mark the swing toward a Popular Front alliance, in March 1936, *Frente a Frente* increased its format size and reverted to number 1 of the "second epoch." As illustrated by the May Day edition's articles titled, "What is fascism?" "Fascism from within," and "The fascist threat in literature," LEAR's journal now devoted more space to this growing global threat.[70] The same

May Day issue also included an article that discussed the dire circumstances of Germany's women under Hitler. According to the author, Hitler's regime had stripped away all of the advances made by Germany's women during the previous decades of struggle. Indeed, the *Frente a Frente* piece pointed out that the only difference between Germany's modern women and the women of the Middle Ages was that Hitler forced single women to pay a tax penalty for not producing sons who could perform as future soldiers for the Nazi armies.[71]

As part of its commitment to forge greater links with President Cárdenas and the Mexican government, in January 1937, members of LEAR organized a transnational conference, the *Congreso Nacional de Escritores y Artistas* (National Congress of Writers and Artists), partly modeled on the U.S.-based American Artists' Congress.[72] Indeed, some delegates to the LEAR congress claimed that President Cárdenas considered LEAR to be the "spearhead of the cultural movement to establish the Popular Front in Mexico."[73] *Frente a Frente* even described the conference as the third transformation of LEAR: from an organization that united during an atmosphere of hostility, to one that operated within the regime of a progressive government, and finally, to a group that took the lead in organizing an event that brought together the vanguard of the Mexican intelligentsia.[74] Opening at the *Palacio de Bellas Artes* in Mexico City on 17 January and lasting until 24 January, over five hundred delegates attended in person.[75] Members of LEAR welcomed an international group, including representatives from Peru, Cuba, and the United States, to speak at the meetings. Both hailing from the United States, the editor of the *New Masses*, Joseph Freeman, and the radical St. Louis painter, Joe Jones, made key presentations and played active roles throughout the meetings. Representatives of LEAR's executive committee also invited President Cárdenas to attend the inaugural session of the congress, although he declined the invitation.[76] Still, as an indication of LEAR's commitment to the Popular Front, and Mexican officials' recognition of the importance of LEAR, President Cárdenas sent his representative, Luis I. Rodríguez, to give the inaugural talk. Other high-level Mexican dignitaries also attended, including undersecretary of education, Luis Chávez Orozco, several state governors, and even Hernán Laborde, secretary of the Mexican Communist Party.[77]

During the congress, the delegates split into six groups: the fine arts, sciences, literature, music, education, and theatre and film. For the fine arts section, Méndez, O'Higgins, Alfredo Zalce, Fernado Gamboa, and the photographer Julio de la Fuente presented their collectively written paper, which attacked the concept of "pure painting."[78] Given the importance of the arts, LEAR further divided this section into submeetings that focused on murals, the graphic arts, caricature, photography, and architecture.[79] Toward the end of the conference members of the fine arts section reunited to produce five resolutions that clarified their positions on the purpose of art and artists' obligations: (1) artists should create art that serves the interests of the working masses; (2) artists must strengthen the ties between themselves and workers through their various trade unions; (3) in order to better integrate art into the services of the revolutionary struggle, artists should generate a scientific analysis of the technical and formal procedures employed by the fine arts, both historically and in the modern era; (4) artists should be aware of the revolutionary ideological principles of the current struggle mainly against fascism, imperialism, and war, and with their professional interests defended by a union; and finally, (5) artists in Mexico must stand in solidarity with the struggles of artists abroad.[80]

To accompany the conference, the artists organized an exhibit held in the *Palacio de Bellas Artes*. Both Méndez and Joe Jones addressed visitors at the opening of the show. As a representative of two U.S. organizations, the American Artists' Congress and the American Friends of the Mexican People, Jones acknowledged the political and artistic links between the two countries. Speaking before the group, Jones explained, "No artist in the United States . . . is ignorant of the tremendous influence which the artists of Mexico have had in the development of present-day culture and the fight against reaction." Reflecting broad themes of the congress, Jones then appealed to the artists to "rediscover the social functions of art, [and] to organize themselves with the progressive forces of the world" in their fight against fascism, imperialism, and war.[81]

Excitement built throughout the week of the congress. For the final day of festivities, artists, intellectuals, and workers packed the main theater at Bella Artes for the congress's last session. Speakers included Julio de la Fuente, Leopoldo Méndez, Martín Luis Guzmán, author of *The Eagle and the Serpent*, and others from Mexico, Cuba, Spain, and the United States.[82] At the end of the meetings, members unanimously adopted four general recommendations: (1) the organization of a unified trade union of intellectual workers affiliated with the *Confederación de Trabajadores de México*, or the Confederation of the Workers of Mexico (CTM); (2) the building of a cultural center to be called the House of Intellectuals with living quarters for members of LEAR; (3) the creation of a publishing house, called New Mexico, based on the LEAR program; and (4) the creation of an international congress of intellectuals to meet in Mexico City in November 1937.[83] In addition to these specific internal LEAR proposals, members ultimately reiterated their connections to the Mexican government and the Popular Front ideals. And in return, LEAR received some government funding to help finance their projects following the congress.[84]

Although LEAR endured as an organized group for only about a year after the congress, LEAR members continued to support the Popular Front throughout their final months. A radical perspective initially motivated LEAR members, but after a few short years, the artists' politics endured, but in an essentially diluted form, as members upheld the Popular Front policies. Moreover, at this point, LEAR artists began to leave the group for a variety of reasons. In April 1937, many key members, including Antonio Pujol, Fernando Gamboa, José Chávez Morado, and others, accepted Pablo Neruda's invitation to attend the Congress of Writers in Valencia, Spain.[85] By May 1937, additional influential members, including Méndez, left the artists' league amid growing internal conflicts.[86] Still, other LEAR affiliates continued to seek support from the government just months before the group ceased to exist. In June 1937, Luis Sandi Meneses, LEAR president, wrote to Mexico's President Cárdenas to request permission to use the Bellas Artes Theater for a rally to commemorate the beginning the Spanish struggle, or the Spanish Civil War.[87] Government officials responded positively, and LEAR organized their rally on 18 July 1937 to demonstrate solidarity with the people and the legitimate government of Spain.[88]

Even as some LEAR members made plans for upcoming events, arguments over LEAR's and *Frente a Frente*'s future direction led to its eventual dissolution sometime between late 1937 or early 1938.[89] A number of reasons precipitated the LEAR's demise and subsequent creation of the TGP. According to the artist Raúl Anguiano, the TGP founders, all originally members of LEAR, created the new group at least partly out of frustration over LEAR's ideological path. As Anguiano described the situation, although LEAR members originally took a revolutionary, even "combative" approach to art and politics, they eventually "absorbed intellectuals of varying types and tendencies, so that it became bureaucratized and took on an opportunist hue, lining itself up in one form or another with each reigning government." Pablo O'Higgins described the later years of LEAR in similar tones, asserting that LEAR became so stagnant, so "lost in internecine discussions," that he had no choice but to break away and create a new art group that could help solve Mexico's problems.[90] Still, as Anguiano explained, even after LEAR experienced its "death throes," the artists and engravers remained committed to the idea of carrying out "work with a real social significance linked to the people of Mexico."[91]

Much like the women's arm of the PCM during the Popular Front, the LEAR artists softened their formerly sharp political edge to focus instead on the greater needs of the Mexican nation and to fight against global fascism. Méndez later described LEAR's demise in even harsher terms, "LEAR died of the worst disease: opportunism . . . But some of us didn't want to attend LEAR's funerals and we founded the *Taller de Gráfica Popular*."[92] Although the former LEAR artists maintained their devotion to Mexico's Communist Party, they nonetheless argued that social change could be attained most efficiently with fewer ties to government organizations. As Méndez eloquently illustrated with his funeral analogy, this group of talented artists ultimately resurrected the initial excitement and political dedication of LEAR's early days. By adopting the art of printmaking, they led the way to the creation in 1937 of the immensely influential Taller de Gráfica Popular.

El Taller de Gráfica Popular (TGP)

In June 1937, the former LEAR artists, and members of its fine arts section, formed their new artists' collective, the TGP. Although Leopoldo Méndez initially conceived of the TGP, soon additional artists joined.[93] Scholars offer slightly different accounts of the original, founding members, but according to Hannes Meyer, the TGP historian, Leopoldo Méndez, Pablo O'Higgins, and Luis Arenal led the group with backing from David Alfaro Siqueiros and Ignacio Aguirre, Raúl Anguiano, Ángel Bracho, Jesús Escobedo, Everardo Ramírez, Antonio Pujol, and Gonzalo de la Paz Pérez as early participants.[94] According to O'Higgins, though, because Siqueiros fought in Spain during the time of the TGP's formation, Meyer mistakenly included him among the founders.[95] In early 1938, Alfredo Zalce, Xavier Guerrero, José Chávez Morado, and Fernando Castro Pacheco also joined the TGP, and, over time, additional printmakers, including Alberto Beltrán, became part of the printmakers workshop while others left on good terms.[96] On average, around fifteen artists belonged to the TGP during any given year.[97]

Throughout the subsequent thirty years, many of Mexico's finest printmakers and artists would participate in the TGP. Women's representation within the TGP also continued to grow, and by 1957, the TGP's ranks included Celia Calderón, Andrea Gómez, Elena Huerta, Sarah Jiménez, María

Luisa Martín, Fanny Rabel, Elizabeth Catlett, and Mariana Yampolsky.[98] Two of the women, Yampolsky and Catlett, arrived from the United States and assumed important roles within the TGP, although neither joined the PCM.[99] A student at the University of Chicago, Yampolsky came to Mexico City at the age of nineteen and soon joined the TGP. Although she originally intended to return to the United States, Yampolsky remained with the printmakers' organization and became an integral member.[100] As with Yampolsky, Catlett knew of the TGP before her 1947 move from New York to Mexico, and she soon joined the printmakers' studio. Until her resignation from the TGP in 1966, Catlett created a series of prints that critically explored the difficulties experienced by black women in the United States.[101] As Yampolsky and Catlett's careers demonstrate, and despite internal disagreements, both male and female members remained loyal to the Taller for many years.[102]

As with LEAR, the founding members of the TGP, including Méndez, O'Higgins, and Arenal, belonged to the Mexican Communist Party, and members often discussed ways to formalize the relationship between the PCM and the TGP.[103] The artists incorporated ideas from the Party into their art, and their discussions of the role of national culture permeated PCM dialogue in return. In addition to graphics that portrayed the struggle against fascism, certainly the TGP images promoted the unity of the proletariat, dangers of war, and the foolishness of the rich. Moreover, given that the Taller formed during the Cárdenas era, with its stress on organizational unity and a move toward leftist policies, TPG members lacked the ardent opposition to the Mexican government as displayed by LEAR during its early days.[104] Although the relationship between the PCM and the TGP artists would reveal ideological cracks following Siqueiros's attack on the Trotsky compound, during these early years the artists remained loyal to the revolutionary ideals that lay at the core of the Party.[105] Indeed, to most TGP artists, meaningful, high quality art reflected the principles of the PCM.[106]

The TGP's 1937 Declaration of Principles represented the group's positions pertaining to art and Mexico's social issues. Although the main points discussed topics relative to the artists themselves, the principles also argued in favor of art that reproduced "social reality," as well as the need for the printmakers to align with other groups. The TGP's initial articles read as follows:

Article 1

The People's Graphics Workshop [Taller de Gráfica Popular] is a collective work centre for functional promotion, and for studying different branches of engraving and painting and different methods of reproduction.

Article 2

The T. G. P. will strive to ensure that its work helps the Mexican people defend and enrich their national culture. This can be achieved only if Mexico is an independent country in a peaceful world.

Article 3

The T. G. P. believes that, in order to serve the people, art must reflect the social reality of the times and have unity of content and form. By applying this principle, the T.G.P. will strive to raise the artistic standards of its members, in the belief that art can only truly serve the people if it is of the very highest plastic quality.

Article 4

The T. G. P. will co-operate professionally with other cultural workshops and institutions, workers' organizations, and progressive movements and institutions in general.

Article 5

The T. G. P. will defend freedom of expression and artists' professional interests.[107]

The Declaration of Principles clearly laid out the TGP's current positions and future goals. Arguing against the concept of individualism, TGP artists promoted collective work, an idea put forward originally by LEAR. As PCM members, the notion of a unified vision resonated among the founding members, even while they supported individual artistic styles, at least within certain parameters.[108] They also maintained that all contributors must remain true to their responsibilities to the Mexican people. According to TGP guidelines, art should reflect people's reality. Rather than abstract metaphors, the artists argued for the representation of political and social commentary in easily comprehensible images. Still, even socially motivated artwork could reflect high artistic standards, and throughout its existence, the TGP produced artistically impressive prints. Although the artists promised to promote a uniquely national culture within an anti-imperialist framework, they also advocated for cooperation with other groups in the struggle against fascism. The TGP quickly expanded its scope beyond a national approach to identify the ways in which engraving could be utilized in such a manner as would engage not only with Mexico's pressing issues, but also with shared struggles on an international scale.[109] And indeed, over the next twenty-five years, the TGP created more than ten thousand artworks and inspired similar groups throughout the United States.[110]

In the early years, the artists moved often from space to space, although they rarely could afford more than a few small rooms. During their first months, until July 1938, the TGP even utilized LEAR's facilities until they could find their own suitable creative workplace.[111] Early on, they bought a bulky lithographic proof press, which could run up to fifty thousand issues. Because the larger editions required a technical operator, and because the TGP constantly lacked money for rent, the members eventually sold the machine as scrap.[112] Still, they continued to own smaller mechanical presses and additional handpresses for lithographs. Even with their downsizing, the group often operated out of cramped, less-than-ideal spaces. For example, at one of their early locations situated at 69 Belisario Domínguez, the artists rented three rooms divided into an exhibition and sales area, a studio with desks, and the machine room for the presses. Even with a paltry monthly rent of fifty pesos, or fourteen U.S. dollars a month, the landlady regularly yelled insults at the artists from the patio when she failed to receive her payment.[113] Construction on their street forced the printmakers from even this dismal space. When proper new facilities failed to materialize quickly, the group had no choice but to place their materials in a storage space, where leaks in the roof allowed rain to ruin most of the items.[114] Their next workshop on Regina Street was hardly better. Once again, they rented three dark rooms illuminated by electric lights, but this time the ventilation was so poor that the artists' cigarettes often filled the studio with smoke so dense that "it was impossible to see who was talking."[115]

To cover the basic expenses, including its meager rent, the TGP required a registration fee of fifteen pesos. Still, in order to remain independent and avoid the previous pitfalls that confronted LEAR, TGP members also rejected government funding or private subsidies, at least during the early years.[116] The lack of available financial support also meant that many of the artists also took outside teaching positions to pay for their everyday expenses. Despite constant economic concerns, TGP artists nonetheless sought to distribute their work at prices that others could afford. They also gave away prints to organizations that lacked the funds to pay for TGP work.[117] Under the direction of its secretary general, labor leader Vicente Lombardo Toledano, the CTM ordered posters, flyers, and other printed materials from the TGP, and additional groups commissioned various graphics, often at a reduced rate. For instance, the TGP charged unions from ten to twenty pesos for a print, and by the late 1950s, they only minimally raised their price to fifty pesos. In addition to the unions, the TGP also printed items for the PCM.[118] To save on costs, members resorted to the use of inexpensive linoleum rather than wood or a metal blank for their engraving plates. For the most part, the TGP produced work in black and white rather than color, with its higher associated expenses, and they also bought mass-produced inks rather than making their own.[119]

The TGP focused on engraving and printmaking, but the artists evolved from a painting tradition.[120] According to O'Higgins, all TGP members had been painters before taking up the printmaking methods practiced by the TGP, and only Méndez, Arenal, Chávez Morado, and Zalce previously worked with engraving. Certain TGP artists thus required a steep learning curve when mastering this new medium. After they conquered the techniques, though, many members continued to practice both engraving and printmaking. Artists even favorably compared the similarities between muralists who painted on public spaces, and TGP members who plastered walls with posters and handbills for widespread public consumption.[121] To improve their work, the TGP artists practiced "collective criticism," a technique that aligned well with their Declaration of Principles. Collective criticism involved group discussions from beginning to end of a print, including the initial idea, the form, and the technique to be used in carrying out the original concept.[122] At times these group conversations proved difficult for some artists, and the members occasionally expressed discomfort with hearing the negative points about their art or even with the possibility of hurting others' feelings; still, it remained an important tool in developing new work and in creating a sense of comradeship.[123]

Taller members also agreed that within this collective environment they would produce realistic images that reflected essential social problems. In this manner, they promised to present key issues in such a way as to not only educate the popular classes but stir them to action as well.[124] The Taller's preference for realism thus firmly situated them in opposition to abstract art, which they viewed as individualistic and lacking all social meaning. According to the TGP's artistic philosophy, easily shared reproducible art would spread revolutionary political concepts in an accessible format. Beyond the TGP's self-defined objective of public service, Taller artists also revealed a high level of artistic accomplishment. Indeed, members argued that the "wedding of form and social content" furthered the development of Mexico's graphic art while elevating the work of individual members.[125] Throughout the next few years, the Taller produced a number of striking portfolios for sale and also exhibited their work at several key venues in Mexico and the United States, including the Museum of Modern Art in 1940.[126]

On 17 March 1938, the General Assembly of the Taller de Gráfica Popular approved a series of bylaws that meticulously laid out the guidelines by which Taller artists should abide. To be accepted into the TGP, for example, the organization required potential members to agree to the principles and rules of this constitution; pay the entry fee determined by the General Assembly; and be recommended by two current members. TGP artists also consented to the concept of collective, graphic production "for the benefit of the interests of the Mexican people," and that all individual and collective work should fight fascism.[127] General TGP statutes established the everyday business of the workshop as follows:

1. All work executed in the workshop must be signed by the author, and also must include the TGP symbol.
2. The Workshop is entitled to ten percent, and a maximum of ten copies of the best proofs of each individual work, intended for the TGP archive. Additionally, the Workshop Steering Committee can reserve any other proofs they deem necessary.
3. The Workshop has the right to request and obtain the collaboration of its members in its exhibitions and also those organized by popular or educational institutions.
4. All individual work will compensate the Workshop for expenses related to labor and materials, without prejudice to the other obligations contained in these bylaws.
5. For the improved organization of the Workshop, its administration shall establish internal rules, which the members are obliged to follow.
6. The general direction of the Workshop is entrusted to an organization called the Workshop Steering Committee, composed of three productive members, the administrator, and the head of exhibitions and publicity.
7. The Workshop Steering Committee shall be elected for one year in the members' General Assembly, but the Committee may be changed at any time—wholly or partially—by the majority of the Assembly. They also may be re-elected by a majority.
8. It is the duty of the Workshop Steering Committee to yield to the General Assembly every three months, or sooner if the majority

requires, an explanatory report on the general operation of the workshop.

9. It is the duty of the Workshop Steering Committee to submit the Workshop's plans for the General Assembly's approval, which will suit their purposes and conveniences. These work plans invariably will include, except in cases of force majeure, a monthly or bimonthly collective work in which all members should collaborate.
10. The Workshop Steering Committee may alter work plans when extraordinary circumstances sufficiently justify it, and they must promptly inform the General Assembly when this happens.
11. The three productive members of the Workshop's Steering Committee constitute the Technical Committee. It will review and give approval to the visual content of the work contracted by the Workshop.
12. The organizations will determine their own internal rules of procedure.[128]

Besides the Taller's overall guidelines, the TGP also instituted rules covering the rights and duties of its members. These included:

1. The members of the Workshop are those who signed the charter, which subjects them to the same rights and duties of the others.
2. Members must attend meetings when summoned, accepting the decisions of the majority, which are then required for all.
3. Members have the right to be called to their organizations at least twenty-four hours in advance, except when duly justified in cases of force majeure.
4. Each member is responsible for the loss or breakage of the Workshop materials while using them, and returning them as soon as they finish their work. The Workshop is not responsible for workers' own materials.
5. It is the obligation of all members to pay their dues in a timely manner.
6. Failure to pay two consecutive months warrants the suspension of rights as a member of the Workshop, unless otherwise agreed upon by the majority.
7. Workshop members are entitled to perform the work that they want to do, whenever permitted by the state of the materials and the workshop schedule as set by the administration.

8. Those who do not comply with their agreed-upon commitments of productive work and cooperation, and those who do not abide to the provisions of these bylaws, will no longer be members of the Workshop.
9. In order to retain the same rights as others in the Workshop, those members who are not able to pay their full dues must give special collaborative artwork that is equal to the difference between the required quota and the amount that a worker can pay. The Technical Commission will determine the collaboration.
10. The administration is responsible for internal discipline and the smooth running of the workshop.[129]

In May 1939, the TGP organized its first exhibit in Mexico City. Held in the gallery of Mexico's National University, eleven members of the TGP, including Méndez, O'Higgins, Arenal, Chávez Morado, Bracho, and others, participated in the show of twenty lithographs.[130] The invitation described the TGP as a "workshop of Mexico's young painters that has been formed with the cooperation and efforts of each of its members." The card also explained the TGP's economic circumstances, stating that work commissioned by various workers' organizations, as well as works sold directly to the public though exhibitions, provided financial support.[131] In the months following the show at the National University, the Taller remained actively involved in organizing expositions and produced a number of antifascist posters and illustrations.[132]

Soon after its first exhibition, though, the TPG experienced deep internal discord related to León Trotsky's presence in Mexico. Siqueiros especially protested the exile's presence in Mexico after he returned from his service in the Spanish Civil War. However, because many of the TGP artists belonged to the Communist Party, they also aligned with the movement to remove Trotsky from the country through any possible means. In the middle of May 1940, Siqueiros, two other TGP members—Luis Arenal and Antonio Pujol—and others attacked Trotsky's compound in a failed assassination attempt. In an incident that led to increased disagreement between Méndez and other TGP artists, Siqueiros and his group used the TGP's offices to make their final arrangements and change clothes before the assault. Afterward, police searched the TPG studio, interrogated members, and even detained Méndez and José Sánchez, a newly arrived printmaker. Tensions remained long after Arenal fled to the United States, Pujol to Argentina, and Siqueiros to Chile.[133]

As the TGP's director at the time, Méndez harbored deep resentment against both Siqueiros and the Party. Although the acrimony between the two artists would lessen somewhat once Siqueiros returned to Mexico in 1944, and even though Méndez remained in the PCM until his expulsion in 1946, Siqueiros and Méndez would continue to disagree about a number of concerns.[134] Most notably, the issue of acquiring a "modern" offset press proved to be especially contentious. In this respect, Siqueiros not only advocated seeking financial support from the Mexican government to buy the machines, but he also criticized the TGP for being mired in the past in its views toward printmaking. For their part, Méndez and other members, including Mariana Yampolsky, adopted a tough stance against the "mechanization of the Taller," arguing that the TGP should not increase its production and number of prints, nor should it employ workers who could maintain more complicated presses. According to Helga Prignitz-Poda, the TGP preferred to avoid state subsidies and, in the process, prevent a repeat of LEAR's previous economic and professional problems.[135] No matter how adamant the TGP proved to be on the issue of an offset press and government support, in the coming years, the TGP would reverse its positions on both. Even more importantly, over the following decade, the tensions created by the Trotsky affair eventually eroded the ties between the PCM and the TGP and created a number of growing problems, both financial and political, that festered throughout the 1940s.

The Struggle against Fascism during the War Years

By 1940, TGP members grew increasingly concerned with the growing Nazi terror and the spread of fascism. Even though World War II's bloodshed remained geographically removed from Mexico, the country still experienced the effects of war as European refugees found safety in Mexico. In addition to the thousands of Spanish Civil War refugees who fled to Mexico, approximately three thousand German-speaking people also sought protection in the country during the 1930s and 1940s.[136] Within this era of international tensions and heightened security concerns, government officials feared that an internal Nazi presence operated within the country. And indeed, at this point, Mexico was, in fact, home to a wide variety of organizations sympathetic to the Nazis.[137] Internal security agents from the Dirección General de Investigaciones Políticas y Sociales reportedly maintained files on more than four hundred "Nazi militants," and they even identified a "center of oppositionists to the national government" with links to militant Nazis and fascists located on Madero Street in Mexico City's center. According to these reports, Germans living in Mexico's capital, including a possible Nazi spy, met every day at the Hotel Isabel, where they talked for hours.[138] Besides the agents from the DGIPS, though, other agencies, including the *Policía del Distrito Federal* or the Mexico City police, also monitored alleged Nazi activity operating in Mexico City. DGIPS representatives bitterly complained that the two organizations often worked against each other or provided identical surveillance results. As one particularly disgruntled agent described the situation, "the 'Nazism' Section of the Mexico City Police is a headless centipede; our Section 'Nazism' is a head without feet."[139]

Investigative work at the bureaucratic governmental level occupied a place within Mexico's war against fascism, but culture did as well. And even as the internal security agents fought against the spread of fascism through their use of internal espionage, many of the world's artists also contributed to the ongoing struggle through their art. In Mexico, the prospect of World War II spurred the TGP artists to action as they discussed the various ways they could donate to the cause. But as the artists increased their output of illustrations, exhibitions, and other artworks in the fight against the Nazi terror, funding continued to be a critical issue. To generate additional revenues, in December 1940, Méndez and the TGP's executive committee proposed a new plan that would increase the number of required copies each TGP artist donated to the Taller's general upkeep from ten to twenty-five. Méndez further set the prices for each print at such a low figure that most artists left the group in anger, and only Méndez, O'Higgins, Aguirre, Bracho, Zalce, and Francisco Mora remained. According to Méndez, though, providing low-cost art to the popular classes remained a major point of the TGP's existence.[140] At this point, the TGP faced a crossroads: either they created a plan for the future or else dissolve their group, much as LEAR did before them.

Eventually the TGP came to terms with a financially feasible way forward, at least partially, with the creation of *La Estampa Mexicana*, a printing shop organized by Hannes Meyer. Meyer, the former Bauhaus director, arrived in Mexico in 1939, where he soon met Méndez in 1941 through their mutual work for *Alemania Libre*, a publication directed at exiles in Mexico.[141] In 1942, Meyer also assumed the role of the Taller's business manager in order to assist with the publication of the TGP's albums and the distribution of other work.[142] As an avowed Marxist and firm believer in the importance of art as a political weapon, Meyer's leftist ideology dovetailed

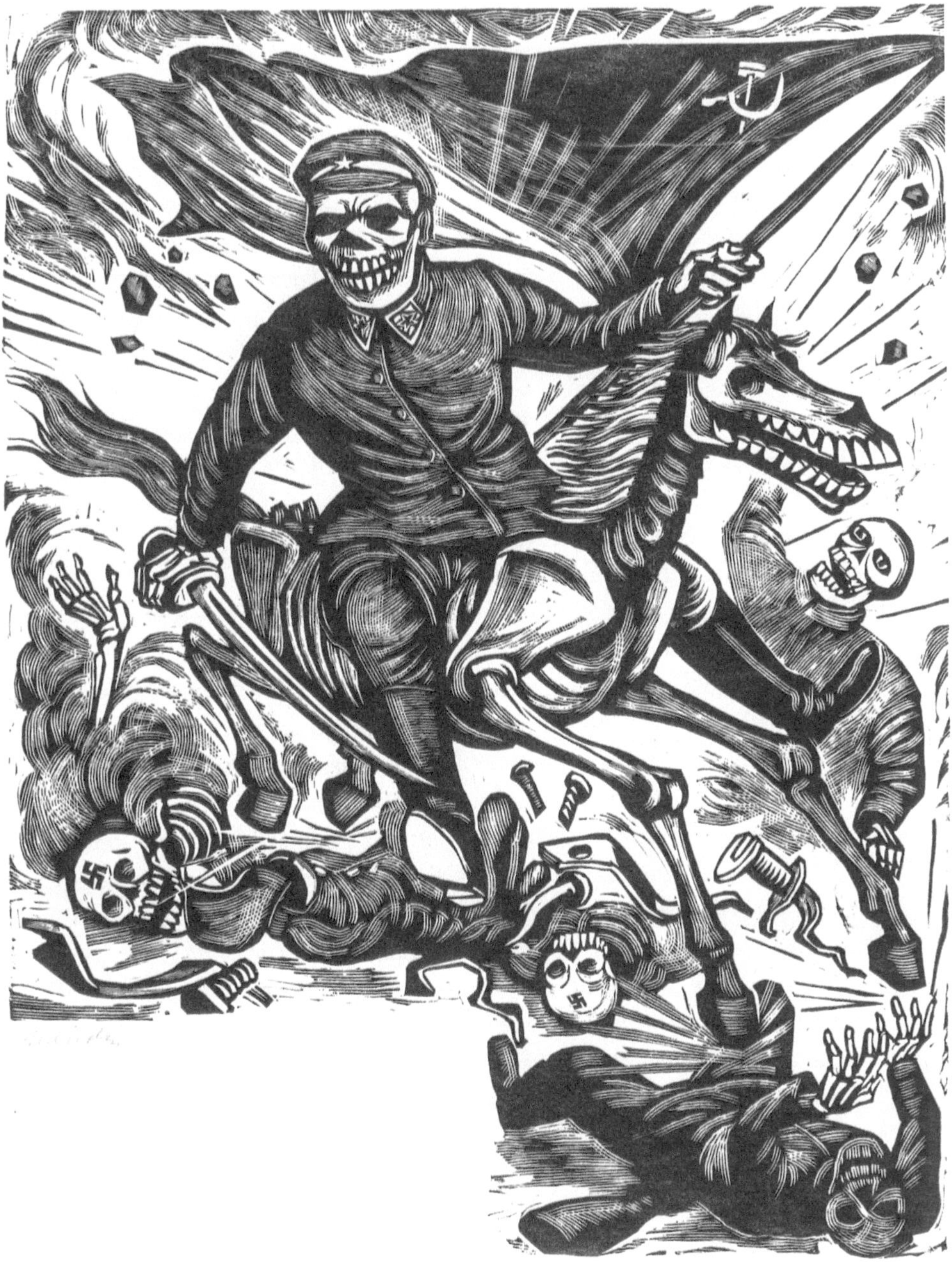

Leopoldo Méndez, *Corrido of Stalingrad*, 1942. Skeleton on horseback trampling skeletons beneath him. Art Resource, New York. © 2015 Artists Rights Society (ARS), New York/SOMAAP, Mexico City.

nicely with that of TGP members.[143] Moreover, Meyer also understood the group's precarious economic situation. What caused the greatest financial burden to TGP artists was the fact that members often relied on commercial publishing houses to print their art. To help rectify the financial situation, in 1942, Meyer organized an "independent cooperative," or *La Estampa Mexicana*.[144] Although not "entirely connected" to the TGP, *La Estampa Mexicana* still edited, printed, and distributed the Taller's prints as a noncommercial operation.[145] Twenty-five reproductions of Posada's prints provided the material for *La Estampa Mexicana*'s first portfolio, and the positive financial results helped to revitalize the Taller. Following the Posada prints, *La Estampa Mexicana* next produced a series composed of twenty-five pieces by Méndez, which succeeded in raising international awareness of the TGP as well as revenue flow.[146] In 1943, Georg Stibi, the German exile and member of the German Communist Party, assumed the duties as the TGP administrator (although Meyer would return to his position in 1947).[147] Over the next few years *La Estampa Mexicana* continued to create several other portfolios, including those by Bracho, Zalce, and others, as well as the *Estampas de la Revolución Mexicana* in 1947.

In addition to his work for *La Estampa Mexicana*, Meyer played a central role in organizing the production of *El Libro Negro del Terror Nazi en Europa: Testimonios de escritores y artistas de 16 naciones*. Published in 1943, the book brought together the work of fifty-six writers and twenty-three artists from sixteen countries, including their 164 photographs and 50 drawings.[148] Meyer solicited the help of TGP members for illustrations in *El Libro Negro*, and the radical outlook of the European contributors, most of who were communists, fit well with Taller philosophy.[149] Given the TGP's long-active dedication to the promotion of antifascist graphics, the group's involvement in *El Libro Negro* further aligned with its original goal to fight against fascism.[150] On a page at the front of *El Libro Negro*, the publication prominently announced the sponsorship of Mexico's President Manuel Ávila Camacho. The following page also noted that the president of Peru, Dr. Manuel Prado, and Czechoslovakia's exiled president, Dr. Eduardo Benes, endorsed the work.[151] With its shocking photos of Nazi crimes and its victims, *El Libro Negro del Terror Nazi en Europa* presented the horrifying truth of Nazi atrocities to the world. Moreover, the essays also covered Nazi terrors as well as resistance.

As the TGP solidified its ties with the exile community in Mexico, it also sought out international connections in the hopes of distributing its work to a greater number of potential buyers. To help with sales, early on, the TGP secured the Bonestell Gallery in New York City.[152] Unfortunately, the arrangement with the gallery proved far from financially beneficial for the TGP, and in response, in autumn 1943, members of the group retained the services of Edwin Mayer, who was to act as their agent in New York. According to Mayer, he visited the Bonaschell [*sic*] Galleries only to be told that they would be delighted to sell even one TGP piece per month. After learning of this dismal situation, Mayer asked the gallery to return the prints so he could deliver them elsewhere. Oddly, Mayer next offered the work through department stores, although he also suggested alternative shows outside of New York. Mayer remained most concerned, though, that the TGP prints arrived from Mexico signed and without creases. Regarding this issue, Mayer informed the TGP that the U.S. public insisted on signed lithographs, but if the original artist was not available then another could "duplicate" the signature instead.[153] Not surprisingly, the TGP's relationship with Mayer proved to be brief, and the artists soon sought other means to distribute their work.

By the mid-1940s, the TGP's continued lack of consistent funding forced the printmakers to make difficult choices. Although its membership increased, the TGP still experienced grave economic problems. The revenues produced by *La Estampa Mexicana* provided the TGP with financial support to locate to a larger space in August, but the expenses incurred during the move as well as everyday operating costs obliged the TGP to seek other means to stay afloat. As a result of their difficult monetary situation and weakening ties to the PCM, the printmakers revised their previous stance toward receiving state support.[154] Accordingly, although the group collaborated with the Cárdenas administration, it now pursued funding from an increasingly conservative Camacho administration.[155] In March 1945, the TGP even revised its original 1937 Declaration of Principles to reflect the Taller's struggle against fascism, and it also confirmed the TGP's aim to work with other progressive institutions.[156]

Still, funding played only a partial role in the TGP's move toward state support, as the struggle against the growing fascist threat resulted in closer connections between the Mexican government and the TGP artists. But the wheels of negotiation turned both ways, and Mexico's central government also pursued the artists in return, especially when their ideological visions aligned with state policy. For example, in 1944, Méndez created a controversial print that depicted the attempted assassination of President Ávila Camacho by a conservative military officer in April of the same year.[157] Although far from one of Méndez's best pieces, his work received praise and commendation for both his artistic presentation as well as his depiction of the *Partido de Acción Nacional*, or the National Action Party (PAN) as the brains behind the attack. Clearly Ávila Camacho sided with those who supported Méndez, including Orozco, Rivera, Siqueiros, and others, because he personally bought the print for the rather substantial sum of five hundred pesos.[158]

In solidifying its connections with the Ávila Camacho government, the TGP followed the Party's lead. Indeed, just a month earlier, in March 1944, the Central Committee of Mexico's Communist Party wrote the president seeking permission to hold the inaugural meeting of their Ninth National Congress in the Bellas Artes Theater. Stressing the PCM's intent to strengthen national unity, the Committee further emphasized the importance of the congress and the relevance of the speakers, including Earl Browder, secretary general of the U.S. Communist Party.[159] Even more notable, though, the Party's Central Committee also invited Mexico's president to attend the congress's opening ceremony. According to the Central Committee, conference members planned to discuss organizational and tactical changes to the Party that would interest the national government and the country's popular classes, especially in the struggle against Adolf Hitler, "the foremost enemy of Mexico and all the peoples of the earth."[160] The president not only agreed to the PCM's request to utilize Bellas Artes's theatre space, but he also instructed Bellas Artes's officials to provide the PCM with sufficient space.[161]

The end of World War II brought changes to the TGP. Although the Taller continued with their work in support of unions and the exile community, the number of immigrants living in Mexico decreased as many returned to Europe.[162] Moreover, during 1946, various members of the TGP stopped attending meetings, citing both poor leadership and a lack of group unity, and even Alfredo Zalce resigned from the group at the beginning of 1947. At this point, the PCM already had expelled Méndez in 1946, and O'Higgins left in 1947.[163] No longer members of the PCM, Méndez and O'Higgins actively participated in the newly formed *Partido Popular*, or the Popular Party (PP), as did other TGP members, including Beltrán and Bracho.[164] Founded by Lombardo Toledano, the PP attempted to bring together various progressive leftist groups, although it ultimately proved ineffective in attaining this goal.[165] Still, in the excitement generated during these early days, the TGP readily supplied artwork for the PP's constitutive assembly, held in November 1947.[166] Moreover, throughout 1947, the TGP provided the PP with a number of additional works, such as drawings and posters, either for free or at a discounted rate.[167]

In addition, the TGP continued to obtain occasional commissions from the Mexican government.[168] In this respect, Taller officials wrote President Miguel Alemán to thank him for the funding and provide an account of their resultant projects. First, the artists utilized the money to move to a more suitable location, and afterward, they acquired a special press for engravings.[169] Ironically, Méndez and other members had resisted the acquisition of this type of equipment for years. Indeed, as David Craven notes, the Taller's preference for woodcuts and linocuts originated from a political position to reject more "modern" print methods and instead employ a "*campesino*" cultural form.[170] Second, in 1948, the group also began work on the publication of *T.G.P México: El Taller de Gráfica Popular, doce años de obra artística colectiva/The Workshop for Popular Graphic Art, a Record of Twelve Years of Collective Work*. Published in 1949, and written in both Spanish and English, the eighteen hundred total copies included nearly two hundred pages covering over four hundred prints completed in the TGP workshop during its twelve years of existence. Third, financial support also underwrote the dissemination of the engravings, *Estampas de la Revolución Mexicana*, released in 1947 as part of the TGP's "La Estampa Mexicana," throughout the Americas, Europe, the Philippines, and South Africa. And last, the printmakers organized traveling art exhibits to help spread the word about the high quality of Mexican graphics.[171]

Even as Méndez previously criticized LEAR's opportunism, the TPG now faced a similar situation. As Taller members drifted toward tighter alliances with conservative government officials, they also moved away from their earlier, more radical stances. Growing tensions between the TGP and the PCM further contributed to the weakening of the Taller, as underlying divisions between the two groups only widened during the decade following Trotsky's stay in Mexico. Moreover, in reaction to the early years of the Cold War anticommunist anxiety, by the late 1940s, the Alemán government intensified its persecution of suspected communists and arrests of noted PCM members. After reassessing an increasingly oppressive Alemán presidency, in December 1949, the PCM condemned the government as reactionary in return.[172] As a result of the sustained oppression and internal dissension, longtime PCM members became less active within the Party or diverted their energies to the PP or other political outlets.

The early 1950s witnessed a marked increase in the internal disagreements over the role of the PCM and the question of its importance within the printmakers' group. The ideological differences between those who still supported the Communist Party, most notably the younger members of the TGP, and those who left or had been expelled, led to serious rifts between workshop members.[173] Méndez, no longer a member of the PCM, found himself mired in conflicts with several loyal Party members within the Taller who questioned his revolutionary commitment. The split between those loyal to the Party and those behind Méndez led to increasingly bitter struggles within the once cohesive group, and in 1952 the TGP removed Méndez as its director.[174] The disputes within the TGP represented both personal issues and larger, national themes. Great or small, though, such ideological clashes created rifts that would be difficult to repair.[175]

Conclusion

Although the TGP continues to operate even today, between 1957 and 1960, many of the original participants, including Méndez and O'Higgins in 1960, left the printmakers group.[176] Money, or the lack of funding, continued to be an issue, even though as late as 1957, Méndez argued that the members should maintain the Taller without subsidies. At this point, as interest in formalism grew, representational art that portrayed revolutionary images lost its popularity among artists, and those just out of art school preferred a different path.[177] The split between the TGP members who remained in Mexico's Communist Party and those who left voluntarily or by force also left a legacy of mistrust that weakened the group's cohesiveness.

Still, the artists overcame their differences to promote causes important to them. After all, most retained their core faith that art inspired radical change, even as they disagreed on the morality of assisting the current government. Throughout the 1950s, the printmakers supported a wide variety of global causes, including the push for peace and the campaign against the atomic bomb. For example, in June 1950, Siqueiros, Rivera, Xavier Guerrero, and José Chávez Morado signed a document, "Answer of the Artists to the Call of the Mexican Communist Party," in which they responded positively to the PCM's request to participate in an exhibition that would accompany the Eleventh Congress of PCM. In their reply, the old friends and enemies reiterated their original determination from the 1920s to direct their "actions and expressions on the path of socialist realism" and to reject the "formalist routines of the decadent bourgeoisie."[178]

In a similar vein, in April 1955, Rivera, Siqueiros, and Méndez once again lent their signatures to a "Call to the People of the World," and especially to the artists as the creators of beauty, to take up the struggle against nuclear weapons.[179] Although the causes that sparked the artists' actions evolved from their initial years of their involvement in the PCM, their passion for revolutionary transformation, and their belief in the power of art to motivate the popular classes, clearly remained. Much had changed, but even more remained the same.

Epilogue

Returning Home, 1952–1974

On 16 November 1952, Diego Rivera petitioned Mexico's Communist Party to consider his readmission to the Party. But after two previous unsuccessful requests, Rivera now promised to follow the party line and reiterated his earlier statement acknowledging his political errors from the time of his exclusion from the Party in 1929. Rivera and Frida Kahlo both applied for readmittance in 1946, but by 1948, the Party only approved Kahlo's application and not Rivera's. Despite this disappointing news, Rivera continued to appear at PCM meetings and agitate for Party acceptance. In 1948, Rivera even attended a Mexico City PCM meeting where Siqueiros served as the first secretary. Upon Rivera's arrival at the meeting, and amid a crowd of more than eight hundred people, a Party official announced that Rivera had submitted his application for readmission to the PCM, thus "correcting past mistakes." Rivera, however, seemed skeptical of any possible positive decision on his behalf, even arguing that the "enemies" of the PCM surely would oppose his request, especially since he also was a member of the Popular Party.[1]

In the following months and even years, Rivera refused to give up on his aspiration to return to Mexico's Communist Party. Indeed, his final request in 1952 revealed a particularly emotional apology for past errors. Of course, Party culture would expect no less than a complete confession, and the truth of the matter was that Rivera had, in fact, committed serious transgressions, most especially by supporting the PCM's enemy, Leon Trotsky. Although Rivera acknowledged his disloyalty to the Party by joining the Fourth International, he partially blamed his situation on being expelled from the PCM in the first place. According to the muralist, although he failed to fully recognize the mistakes that led to his removal in 1929, he immediately attempted to rectify them and even followed the Party's politics as closely as possible in order to repair "deviations." However, given his precarious position from outside the Party, he lost his direction, yielded "to the solicitations of [Trotsky's] gang," and slid into betrayal and counterrevolution. Rivera claimed he soon realized the depth of his mistakes once inside the inner Trotsky circle, and in response, laboriously created the conditions that resulted in his exit from the group. Still, the damage already had been done.[2]

Even as Rivera carefully constructed his argument to return to the PCM, he blurred the line between art and politics. Throughout his long career, Rivera embraced the position that art played a key role in politics and politics in art, whether as a member of the Party (or adherent) or as a Trotsky supporter. Of course, the images that emanated from Rivera's different political connections reflected these radically different positions. In his petition for readmittance, Rivera offered up his demolished Rockefeller Center mural as an example of his ideological relevance, and then its reconstruction at the Bellas Artes as an example of political disintegration. Here, Rivera made his point that his art reflected his politics—for good or evil. In the original New York version, Rivera included a portrait of Lenin, leading to a passionate debate, the ensuing controversy over the appropriateness of the content, and ultimately the work's destruction in February 1934. However, when Rivera recreated the mural in Mexico City, he also included an image of Trotsky holding the red banner of the Fourth International.[3] Addressing this unfortunate situation, Rivera argued that his Rockefeller Center images reflected "combative and correct political content," while his subsequent Mexico City re-creation instead revealed an "unclean example" of Trotskyism.[4] Further clarifying the relationship between politics and the quality of art, Rivera put forward his position, "This phenomenon concerning the content of my work could not stop affecting harmfully the form of it, because one and the other are always inseparable in its forms and distinctive characters."[5] For Rivera, then, his least impressive artwork corresponded to this time of corrupt politics within the Fourth International.[6] Thus, "recognizing the accuracy and correctness of the criticism as a generous and fraternal gift that has been made by the Communist Party, which I receive as an outstretched hand," Rivera acknowledged the support of the PCM and promised to follow the Party line from this point forward.[7]

Following this impassioned appeal, the Central Committee of Mexico's Communist Party still waited over a year and a half before they considered Rivera's request to return to the PCM. On 11 March 1954, PCM officials sent Rivera a memo asking to meet with him in order "to discuss some problems related to the readmission request you made to our Party."[8] And just a few days later, Rivera answered specific questions concerning his relationship with Trotsky. For example, the PCM grilled Rivera on how the painter first met Trotsky and if he continued to maintain links with Trotskyists. Even though Rivera desperately sought to reenter the Party, his answer nonetheless appears almost confrontational when he replied: "In regard to the subjective situation that made me go to Trotskyism, I said everything in my request for readmission to the Party and I have nothing to add or revise. . . . Instead, I will use the occasion of this questionnaire to clarify a number of objectives and concrete facts." Rivera continued that his first contact with the Trotskyists took place in New York in 1931, during his stay for a painting exhibition at the Museum of Modern Art. Prior to this time, either in Mexico or in the USSR, Germany, Belgium, Italy, or France, he never interacted with Trotskyists. However, he had attained a "certain notoriety" after his presentation and discussion of his position in the John Reed Club. At this point, certain Trotskyites contacted him, "especially the most active within the group."[9]

In his response, Rivera clearly emphasized the point that he met representatives of the Fourth International *after* his expulsion from the Party in 1929. Here Rivera mirrored his 1952 petition to return to the PCM when he stressed once again that his most serious errors occurred only after the PCM forced him to leave the political environment so necessary to his very existence. Moreover, when asked about morals, Rivera replied that his concept of morality certainly did not equal that of priests, "highbrow hypocrites," or even political progressives; instead, morality resulted from one's class position. Moreover, Rivera cautioned revolutionary parties operating in capitalist countries to prevent the bourgeoisie's use of ethics as a weapon in their arsenal to discredit the Party in the eyes of the workers, farmers, and "intellectuals still not sufficiently politicized."[10]

In September 1954, the PCM finally welcomed Rivera back into the Party.[11] However, even as the PCM readmitted Rivera on this, his final application, they did so with some reservations.[12] On 8 September, a PCM committee, including Rivera's old friend Xavier Guerrero, issued an opinion concerning Rivera's readmission. According to their report, Rivera had not yet made sufficient effort to overcome his many weaknesses or correct his previous mistakes. Even worse, the PCM described Rivera as having a keen "individualist" sense and a "marked tendency to replace reality with fantasy"—aberrations only a militant life of collective work and an emphasis on working-class interests rather than the personal could overcome. Despite this harsh evaluation, the study nonetheless concluded that Rivera had made positive changes in his political life, especially by breaking with Trotskyism and seeking reconciliation with the Communist Party leadership. As a result, the PCM officially ratified Rivera's return to the Party on 25 September.[13]

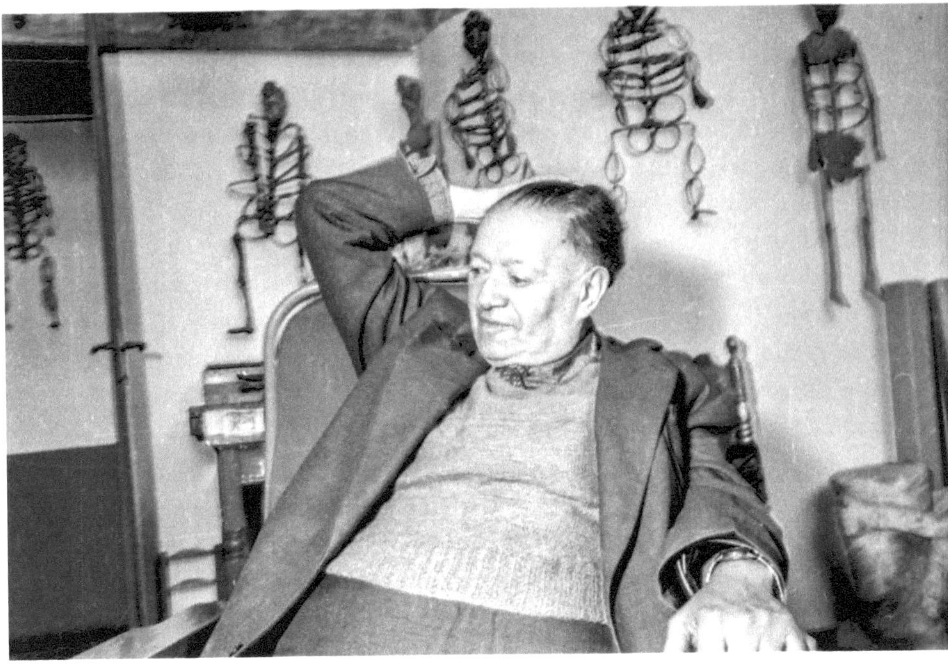

Diego Rivera. Archivo General de la Nación, Alfabético pintores, Fotográfico Hermanos Mayo, HM/AP/118-2A (Rivera), paquete 6.

Completing the Circle

Following so closely after Kahlo's funeral in July 1954, Rivera's return to the PCM proved to be bittersweet for Rivera. In the years prior to Kahlo's death, Rivera confronted the fact that while he remained active outside the official Party circle, his longtime partner increasingly embraced the PCM. In many ways, Rivera's loss of his great love, even with their stormy relationship, represented a passing of much of his life's meaning. For Rivera, renewed membership within the Party must have represented both a direction for conceiving a future without Kahlo, but also a return to his political purpose, an aspiration he now pursued with even greater determination. Even as Rivera continued to paint, his return to the PCM harked back to a more romantic time in their lives, when the revolution still seemed possible and before the many political intrigues and complexities.[14] The Party's "forgiveness," though complicated with his comrades' continued misgivings, must have brought some degree of relief to the painter as he increasingly faced health issues and the difficulties of becoming older.[15]

Despite his status as an "outsider," Rivera still actively participated in PCM events, although unofficially, in the years between his request for readmittance in 1946 and his official return in 1954. Alongside Siqueiros, Rivera attended PCM rallies and protests throughout the late 1940s and early 1950s, and both artists figured prominently in Party politics. Once again illustrating the historically close ties between the PCM and the artists, in 1950, Rivera, Siqueiros, Guerrero, and other artists, writers, musicians, and architects supported the PCM's request for artists to participate in the exhibition, "Art in Mexico in Favor of National Independence, Against Poverty and in Favor of Peace," which would take place alongside the Eleventh Congress of the Mexican Communist Party in November 1950. According to the Rivera and Siqueiros, the artists backed the Party's position concerning the current division of the world into two camps: one of imperialism and war as led by the United States, and the opposing democratic and peaceful one as led by the Soviet Union. Moreover, the artists also agreed with the PCM that only artists who acted in solidarity with the Mexican working class could transform their art into an instrument of social progress and in defense of women.[16] In addition to the artists' participation in the PCM's Eleventh Congress in November 1950, Siqueiros, along with Esther Chapa, also remained members of the Executive Commitee.[17]

The exhibit accompanying the Eleventh Congress moved forward as planned. However, not only did the art attract PCM members who came to view it, but internal security agents also took careful note of the various pieces. According to their report, the exposition first opened to PCM delegates on 21 November, and then the following day to the public, free of charge. Many people attended the show, which consisted of twenty oil paintings and two lithographs; each of the works presented themes that reflected the artists' "communist ideology," portrayals of the national and international situation, and critiques of Mexico's President Miguel Alemán and the U.S. president Harry S. Truman.[18] This particular DGIPS representative, who signed his document with the initials "J. N. M.," provided several colorful descriptions of the art, complete with his own opinions. Reporting on one particular piece, "The Smile" by a painter identified as C. Guadiana, the agent dutifully noted that the artist depicted Mexico's President Alemán as a "ridiculous figure, with an enormous and grotesque smile" and a "demonic" head. He continued that insects and parasites surrounded Alemán, which, according to the agent, represented the president's friends and collaborators. Juan O'Gorman also submitted a painting that included a cross with "arms" formed by a sword, and Raúl Anguiano depicted a farmer driving his team of oxen that pulled a plow with a canon attached to the back. The agent reported that although the normally left-leaning Siqueiros supplied a mural, "Cuauhtémoc against the Myth," this particular contribution lacked the "harsh criticism" of the others in the exhibit. After listing the additional donors, including José Chávez Morado, Arturo G. Bustos, and others, he promised to send a description of Rivera's painting the following day.[19]

As illustrated by the internal security agents' attendance at the Eleventh Party Congress art exhibit, the artists often found themselves the focus of government surveillance, especially during the PCM-related activities. From the early 1920s onward, Rivera and most especially Siqueiros often experienced state opposition to their political endeavors. Indeed, during the 1940s and 1950s, many radical artists and activists faced governmental coercion and even jail time for their activities. And much as they had during the previous decades, spies continued to keep a close watch on these leftists. As a result, during these Cold War years, Party members expressed fear of being subjected to monitoring and possible arrest by the police simply for attending communist meetings or events.

Larger PCM protests provoked even greater scrutiny and intimidation by government officials. In 1952, security officials reported on a May Day rally led by Siqueiros, Rivera, and other "recognized" communists. This group of about five hundred union and PCM members first gathered near the Central Alameda to protest President Alemán, and then began their march toward the Zocolo. Many carried signs that opposed the high cost of living, demanded workers' rights or higher wages, and other members passed out leaflets and distributed the PCM's newspaper, *La Voz de México*. Despite an initial festive atmosphere, the group soon encountered trouble that abruptly changed the tone of the protest. Along their route, about twenty-five members of "Los Dorados," a right-wing fascist and anticommunist group led by Coronel Aniceto López Salazar, physically confronted the marchers and yelled at them to throw down their "insulting" posters and "propaganda." Clearly revealing a remarkable bias against the demonstrators, one agent reported, "the communist group, egged on by the painter Siqueiros, launched an attack against the Dorados, who had to defend themselves, so a shootout ensued." Afterward, the anticommunists ran to the *Palacio de Bellas Artes* with the crowd following on their heels. Finding the doors locked, the group torched a truck to throw against the Museum's entrance, although the police soon intervened to prevent further damage to the building. According to the memo, the violent skirmishes resulted in the injury of the secret agent Carlos Pueblo, and afterward, the "communists dragged him through the streets," insulting and taunting him along the way. Eventually the Red Cross, as well as the police, intervened to "rescue" the fellow. Ultimately, the document dutifully reported that the coronel received a wound on his chin, but a PCM member and student died, and eight communists were hurt, including a woman, Elena Domínguez Anaya. The rally finally moved to its original destination, the Zocalo, where another, yet smaller, altercation occurred.[20]

No longer young men, Rivera's and Siqueiros's political activities—real or imagined—clearly still aroused governmental ire and suspicion. But on a personal level, at this point in their political careers, the two artists finally reached a mutual agreement of sorts and put the past behind them.[21] Reaching back to the 1920s, Rivera and Siqueiros shared an historical memory of the Party's early days, the establishment of the PCM's paper, *El Machete*, and the government's sustained attacks against communists, both those from Mexico and the transnational comrades who lived in the country during this era. Of course, their ideological positions diverged markedly during the 1930s and much of the 1940s as they took radically different political stances, especially concerning the Trotsky affair. But by the late 1940s and early 1950s, their paths once again converged on many issues. Indeed, the two artists often spoke at protests and appeared together at the same meetings.

Rivera and Siqueiros also continued to travel and paint, although Rivera's health issues hindered his ability to work on the larger paintings. Just a year following the May Day protest, Rivera completed his final mural in the Hospital de la Raza. Rivera still created smaller pieces, however, and produced a variety of paintings, including commissions, during the last years of his life. Both artists also returned to the Soviet Union in 1955—Rivera for medical treatment and Siqueiros to speak at the Soviet Academy of Art.[22] Despite seeing numerous doctors, in 1957, Diego Rivera died. Admirers from all parts of the world mourned his death, but certainly Mexico's radical artists understood the importance of his passing. TGP members put past differences behind them when they sent a letter signed by most members, including Leopoldo Méndez, Elizabeth Catlett, Pablo O'Higgins, Marianne (Mariana) Yampolsky, Elena Huerta, and others, to express their sorrow. The group pointed out that Rivera represented one of the most important founders of Mexico's art movement, and as such, his work constituted a national legacy. According to the artists, with his extraordinarily gifted and powerful mind, Rivera's death represented a great loss to Mexico

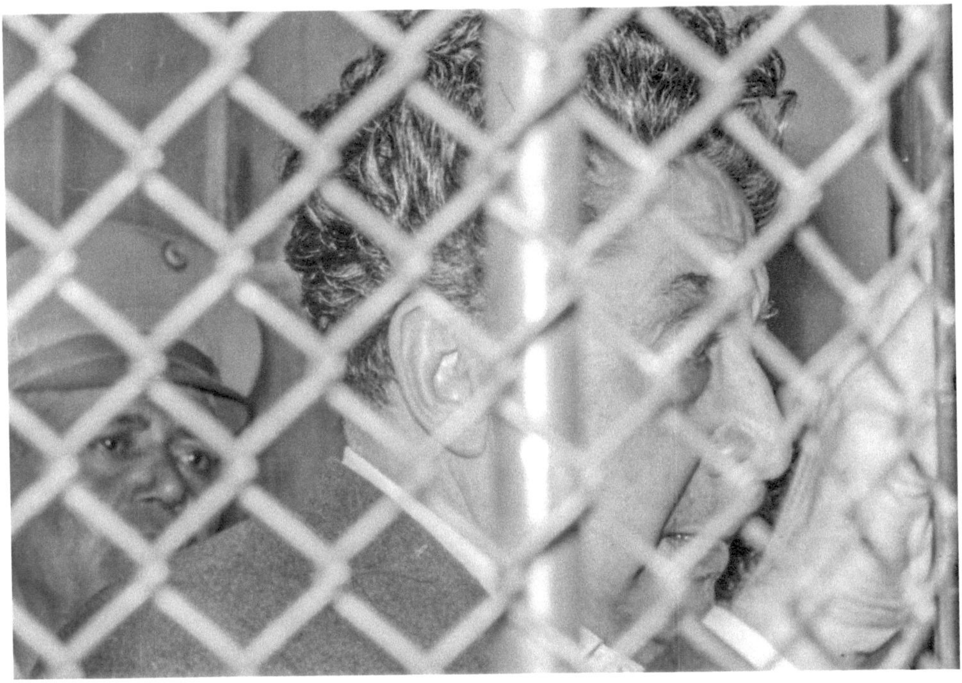

Siqueiros's release from Mexico City's Lecumberri penitentiary, 13 July 1964. Archivo General de la Nación, Alfabético pintores, Fotográfico Hermanos Mayo, HM/AP/132-1A (David Alfaro Siqueiros), paquete 3.

and to the world.[23] Rivera's commitment to Mexico's Communist Party wavered throughout his life, but his death represented a significant loss to those who understood the importance of his early politics and the legacy of his art.

Following Rivera's death, Siqueiros continued to be active in art and politics. In 1958, he contributed to the reorganization of the PCM, and in 1960, the members of the Mexican Communist Party elected him to the position of secretary general.[24] During the late 1950s and 1960s, Siqueiros also painted many of his most important works, including *The Revolution Against the Porfirian Dictatorship* (started in 1957) in Mexico City's Chapultepec Castle. Moreover, he experienced time in prison for his political activities. Indeed, in 1960, authorities locked Siqueiros in jail for nearly four years of an eight-year sentence based on the false charge of social dissolution, or more specifically, that he provoked yet another May Day riot during the same year.[25] Upon his release, Siqueiros spoke to the crowd that gathered in front of his home, saying, "I am happy to be free again for my party and my politics."[26] But Siqueiros also moved forward with his art projects, finishing the Chapultepec Castle paintings and working on his mural, *The March of Humanity on Earth and Toward the Cosmos*, finally inaugurated in 1971 in the Polyforum. Even as *The March of Humanity* marked a high point in his career, the painter suffered from health issues that meant his life was reaching its end. Just three years later, Siqueiros died in 1974 at the age of seventy-seven. Upon hearing of the muralist's death, Mexico's President Luis Echeverría Álvarez, who visited Siqueiros just a week before, released a message that said, "in his work Siqueiros collected . . . the dynamic currents of revolutionary thought, nourished with the advanced social thought of our revolution."[27]

Echeverría's supportive words for Siqueiros at the time of his death suggest a détente of sorts between the painter and the Mexican government. Indeed, Siqueiros's obituary in the *New York Times* echoed this assessment, reporting that his "status for the last three years has been that of a national institution, the object of frequent official praise. It was a status the old revolutionary obviously enjoyed."[28] Siqueiros's increasingly friendly relationship with the government, and especially with Mexico's President Echeverría, created tensions between the muralist and Mexico's Communist Party. Significantly, Siqueiros's association with the president occurred at a time when government forces only recently had countered student unrest and protest with military force, resulting in the deaths of hundreds at Tlatelolco in October 1968. Moreover, during 1971, the muralist openly criticized the Party, culminating in a rupture between Siqueiros and the PCM and the artist's suspension from his position on the Party's Central Committee.[29] As a result of ideological differences between Siqueiros and the PCM, a Party organ, OPOSICIÓN, printed the news that the PCM once again had expelled the muralist from their ranks in July of the same year.[30] Even Siqueiros's burial arrangements continued to provoke controversy and did little to diminish the resentment of many members of the PCM. Although his coffin rested for twenty-four hours in Bellas Artes, where Kahlo's coffin lay in state almost twenty years before, a Mexican flag draped his coffin rather than that of the Mexican Communist Party, as with Kahlo. Even worse, President Echeverría participated as an honor guard during the period of mourning at Bellas Artes, and he also appeared the following day at the gravesite in Mexico City's Rotunda of Illustrious Men. Indeed, Siqueiros's widow later remembered that Echeverría handed her the folded flag, at which point, with a dry throat, she barely could utter, "Muchas gracias señor president."[31]

An historical analysis of the relationship between radical artists, Mexico's Communist Party, and the Mexican state from the early days of the PCM in the 1920s until Siqueiros's death in the 1970s reveals a complex relationship in constant flux. As the final years of Rivera's and Siqueiros's careers illustrate, with Rivera's return to the PCM and Siqueiros's apparent working relationship with high-level government officials, artists alternately compromised with the government, especially during the Popular Front, and at other times, fiercely waged war against conservative policies. Certainly, the Mexican government also cycled through years of artists' support followed by times of oppression and the arrest or expulsion of those deemed to be subversive. As this book has argued throughout its pages, though, government sponsorship came at a high price, as art produced during the times of state endorsement often lost the sharp edge that delineated visionary art from work more modest in intent and outcome.

The artists' evolving relationships with Mexico's Communist Party, and the pivotal role of the PCM in their lives, significantly impacted the issue of art within revolutionary transformation. Clearly for many artists, their commitment to the PCM influenced their life choices, their politics, the images incorporated within their art, and even how they structured their lives. Creating art and the difficulties of earning a living consumed much of the day. But the duties associated with the PCM also demanded a hefty time commitment and stole hours away from painting.[32] Besides the issue of ongoing obligations, belonging to the PCM also could bring harsh governmental repercussions and even time in prison, and many artists paid a heavy price for their involvement. Toward the end of his career, Siqueiros even questioned the lifelong consequences of his Party activities, especially in terms of his "freedom" and time to paint.[33] But ultimately, for the artists discussed throughout the pages of this book, including those from Mexico and the intellectuals who arrived from all parts of the world, their sacrifices signified Mexico's best path forward for the future. For these radical artists, their work for the Mexican Communist Party and their art represented two sides of the same coin; politics shaped their artistic work and, in return, their art shaped politics. In the end, a deeper understanding of the ideological and political context in which the artists worked not only expands our knowledge of the contingencies that influenced the art of the era, but also the very nature of Mexico's postrevolutionary history.

Notes

Abbreviations

Amsterdam

IISG — Internationaal Instituut voor Sociale Geschiedenis
- PCMA — Partido Comunista Mexicano Archives

Mexico City

ADRFK — Archivo Diego Rivera y Frida Kahlo, Museo Frida Kahlo

AGN — Archivo General de la Nación
- PLCR — Archivo Particular de Lázaro Cárdenas del Río
- EPG — Archivos Presidenciales, Emilio Portes Gil
- LCR — Archivos Presidenciales, Lázaro Cárdenas del Río
- MAC — Archivos Presidenciales, Manuel Ávila Camacho
- DFS — Dirección Federal de Seguridad
- DGIPS — Dirección General de Investigaciones Políticas y Sociales
- CC — Fondo Carlos Chávez
- DGG — Fondo Dirección General de Gobierno
- GSM — Fondo Gobernación Siglo XX, Departamento de Migración
- TSJ — Fondo Tribunal Superior de Justicia del D.F.

CEMOS — Centro de Estudios del Movimiento Obrero y Socialista
- AMV — Fondo Arnoldo Martínez Verdugo
- PCM — Fondo Partido Comunista Mexicano

CENIDIAP — Centro Nacional de Investigación, Documentación e Información de Artes Plásticas
- FR — Fondo Reservado
  - DR — Archivo Diego Rivera
  - LM — Fondo Documental Leopoldo Méndez

MUAC — Centro de Documentación, Información e Investigación Arkheia, Museo Universitario Arte Contemporáneo de la Universidad Nacional Autónoma de México
- OD — Fondo Olivier Debroise

SAPS — Sala de Arte Público Siqueiros, Acervo Documental

Paris

PCBK	Pompidou Center, Bibliothèque Kandinsky AD Archives et dossiers

Rome

ACS	Archivio Centrale dello Stato

The United States

CCP	Center of Creative Photography, University of Arizona	
	LAB	Lola Álvarez Bravo Archive
CA	The Comintern Archives: Files of the Communist Party of Mexico, 1919–1940 (Microfilm)	
GRI	The Getty Research Institute, Special Collections	
	DAS	David Alfaro Siqueiros Papers, 1920–1991
HIA	The Hoover Institution Library and Archives, Stanford University	
	ABP	Alexander H. Buchman Papers, 1920–2003
	BW	Bertram D. Wolfe Papers, 1903–2000
	CNPC	Congreso Nacional del Partido Comunista, 1939
	JF	Joseph Freeman Papers, 1904–1966
	REM	Rodolfo Echeverría Martínez Collection, 1911–1986
	TC	Leon Trotsky Collection, 1917–1995
HL	The Houghton Library, Harvard University	
	TEP	Leon Trotsky Exile Papers
TGP	Taller de Gráfica Popular Records, Mexico City, 1937–1960 (Microfilm)	
TLRW	Tamiment Library and Robert F. Wagner Labor Archives	
	CPA	Communist Party of America Records

Introduction

1. Held on 3 June, *El Machete*, the official newspaper of the PCM, announced the rally the day before. The PCM Silvestre Revueltas cell sponsored the event. *El Machete*, 2 June 1948, 4. In addition to the history of the Mexican painters, Siqueiros also spoke in defense of Diego Rivera's mural, *Dream of a Sunday Afternoon in Alameda Park*, commissioned by the Hotel del Prado. In 1947, Rivera experienced criticism after he refused to remove the words, "God does not exist." Marnham, *Dreaming with His Eyes Open*, 314–16.

2. The inspectors' names were Jesús González Valencia and Fernando López Portillo. "ASUNTO: Informan sobre el 'mitin' auspiciado por el 'Partido Comunista de México,' en favor del pintor David Alfaro Siqueiros," AGN, DGIPS, caja 80, exp. 1, 4 June 1948; "ASUNTO-Informan sobre el 'mitin' auspiciado por el 'Partido Comunista de México,' a favor del pintor David Alfaro Siqueiros," AGN, DGIPS, caja 20, exp. 3, 4 June 1948; Gustavo Castañares, "Alfaro Habló de Arte y del Mural que Pintó Rivera," *Excélsior*, 4 June 1948, 3.

3. "¡6 DE JUNIO!" *El Machete*, 2 June 1948, 1.

4. "C. Lamberto Ortega Peregrina," AGN, DGIPS, caja 20, exp. 3, 7 June 1948.

5. "ASUNTO: Informan sobre el 'mitin' auspiciado por el 'Partido Comunista de México,' en favor del pintor David Alfaro Siqueiros," AGN, DGIPS, caja 80, exp. 1, 4 June 1948.

6. Although Alan Knight argues that Mexico's "cultural revolution" was "characterized by nationalism, anticlericalism, agrarian reforms, labor mobilization, educational programs, artistic projects, and party formation," this book focuses on the artists and their visual creations. Knight, "Weapons and Arches in the Mexican Revolutionary Landscape," 56–57.

7. Starn, "Seeing Culture in a Room for a Renaissance Prince," 205.

8. Put another way, culture during the postrevolutionary era consisted of meanings, ideologies, and symbols encoded in art and "read" by audiences through a "dialectic of cultural struggle." Stewart Hall, as cited in Joseph and Nugent, "Popular Culture and State Formation in Revolutionary Mexico," 17.

9. Letter dated 30 November 1922 from Rosendo Gómez Lorenzo to Alfred Stirner, CA, Fond 495, Opis' 108, reel 2, file 24, 21.

10. Carr, *Marxism and Communism in Twentieth-Century Mexico*, 28, 35, 36.

11. Letter dated 21 April 1923 to Alfred Stirner, CA, Fond 495, Opis' 108, reel 2, file 33, 20; Partido Comunista de México, Sección de la Internacional Comunista, *III Congreso Celebrado en la Ciudad de México del 7 al 12 de abril de 1925*, 2. Located in IISH, PCMA, box 1–13, document 2.

12. Partido Comunista de México, *III Congreso*, IISH, PCMA, box 1–13, document 2, 19–22.

13. Barry Carr explains that the PCM's members rose from "less than a hundred in 1920 to about fifteen hundred by 1929." Carr, *Marxism and Communism in Twentieth-Century Mexico*, 37.

14. For Reyes see Cano, "Las mujeres en el México del siglo XX," 33.

15. "Aurora Reyes: 1908–1985, Mexico," 150.

16. Tibol, *Frida Kahlo*, 30–31. According to Hayden Herrera, Kahlo even changed the date of her birth from 6 July 1907 to 7 July 1910 in order to reflect the beginning of the Mexican Revolution in 1910. Herrera, *Frida*, 4.

17. Folgarait, *So Far from Heaven*, 41.

18. Ibid., 40–41. Siqueiros and many of the other artists espoused Marxist ideology while simultaneously demonstrating an uneven loyalty to the PCM; at times Siqueiros and Rivera even exhibited erratic behavior that almost guaranteed their expulsion from the Party.

19. López, *Crafting Mexico*, 6.

20. Lenin, "On Proletarian Culture," 675–76.

21. Richardson, "The Dilemmas of a Communist Artist," 53–54. Mexico severed its diplomatic ties with the Soviet Union in January 1930, and the two countries would remain without relations until the middle of the 1940s. Carr, *Marxism and Communism in Twentieth-Century Mexico*, 45.

22. Richardson, "The Dilemmas of a Communist Artist," 54–55.

23. Bartelik, "Concerning Socialist Realism," 91.

24. Bown, *Art under Stalin*, 65.

25. Azuela, "Rivera and the Concept of Proletarian Art," 125.

26. Bown, *Art under Stalin*, 65. According to Masha Salazkina, Eisenstein first became interested in Mexico after meeting Diego Rivera in Moscow. Salazkina, *In Excess*, 22.

27. Bown, *Socialist Realist Painting*, 114; Bernard Smith, *Modernism's History*, 206.

28. Andrei Zhdanov at the 1934 First Congress of Soviet Writers, as quoted by Caplow, *Leopoldo Méndez*, 264, n. 14. Bown prefers the painter Aleksandr Gerasimov's definition of socialist realism as "an art 'realistic in form and socialist in content.'" Gerasimov's 1939 speech, *Iskusstvo*, no. 4 (1939): 150. As quoted in Bown, *Socialist Realist Painting*, 141.

29. Bown, *Socialist Realist Painting*, 141.

30. Hemingway, "Introduction," 7; Bartelik, "Concerning Socialist Realism," 90; Smith, *Modernism's History*, 206; Bown, *Socialist Realist Painting*, 134–35.

31. The writers' constitution as quoted in Bown, *Art under Stalin*, 90.

32. Ibid., 91.

33. Bown, *Socialist Realist Painting*, 123–24.

34. Ibid., 124.

35. Ibid., 137–38.

36. Ibid., 208.

37. Bryant Foundation Brochure, CENIDIAP, FR, LM, caja 29, exp. 1852, Sección Taller de Gráfica Popular, Subsección Publicaciones, 1, dated 2 December 1947; Caplow, *Leopoldo Méndez*, 127–29.

38. "Síntesis De Los Principios Declarativos De La LEAR," *Frente a Frente*, no. 1 (November 1934): 3. Edición facsimilar.

39. The inclusion of unskilled artists, however, could attract criticism. For example, LEAR's 1936 Mexico City show in the former Santa Clara church received harsh reviews in the local newspapers over its inclusion of "inferior" artworks. Luis Cardoza y Aragón, "Exposición de pintura organizada por la LEAR: Divagaciones y pretextos" *El Machete*, 23 May 1936, 3–4. Found online at the Documents of 20th-century Latin American and Latino Art: A Digital Archive and Publications Project at the Museum of Fine Arts, Houston, Registration ICAA: 779286. Accessed 7 February 2015.

40. Anreus, "Los Tres Grandes," 46. Moreover, Che Guevara also criticized socialist realism as backward and restrictive to creative expression. Craven, *Art and Revolution in Latin America*, 13–14, 45; Richardson, "The Dilemmas of a Communist Artist," 50.

41. Craven, *Art and Revolution in Latin America*, 17. A possible exception could be the TGP's representation of President Cárdenas.

42. Caplow, *Leopoldo Méndez*, 100–101.

43. This study references a number of important art histories in Spanish and English; the following represent only a few of the fine works. For example, see Tibol, *Palabras de Siqueiros*; Tibol, *Siqueiros, Introductor de realidades*, 69–71; Mraz, *Looking for Mexico*; Folgarait, *So Far from Heaven*; Folgarait, *Seeing Mexico Photographed*; Debroise, "Like Cut Glass"; Debroise, *Mexican Suite*; Reyes Palma, *Leopoldo Méndez*, 15; Prignitz-Poda, *El Taller de Gráfica Popular en México*; among others.

44. For example, in *The Eagle and the Virgin: Nation and Cultural Revolution in Mexico, 1920–1940*, editors Mary Kay Vaughan and Stephen E. Lewis offer path-breaking insights into the study of nation building and cultural politics, and Rick López's recent book, *Crafting Mexico: Intellectuals, Artisans, and the State after the Revolution*, presents an especially relevant analysis on the role of popular arts and the production of crafts in Mexico's transformation into a modern nation-state. Jocelyn Olcott's innovative article on Concha Michel includes an important examination of culture and the contributions of artists and, most especially, creative women. Olcott, "'Take Off That Streetwalker's Dress.'" Also see the historian John Lear's astute examination of the artists' involvement with the PCM, their artistic representation of work and workers, and also their work with *El Machete*. Lear, "La revolución en blanco, negro y rojo." Additionally, the art historian Mary Coffey's new work, *How a Revolutionary Art Became Official Culture: Murals, Museums, and the Mexican State*, examines the relationships between muralism and nationalist political culture between 1934 and the late 1960s within the framework of three Mexico City museums—the Palace of Fine Arts, the National History Museum, and the National Anthropology Museum. Coffey, *How a Revolutionary Art Became Official Culture*. Through her examination of images of Mexican womanhood in beauty pageant advertisements, art, films, and photos, the art historian Adriana Zavala considers the role played by visual culture during the late nineteenth and early twentieth century. Zavala, *Becoming Modern, Becoming Tradition*. Beyond Mexico's borders, Daryle Williams's *Culture Wars in Brazil: The First Vargas Regime, 1930–1945* examines the contentious nature and meaning of Brazilian national culture during the middle decades of the twentieth century, and the struggle for control of "Brazilianness" by artists, state officials, and ordinary citizens.

45. Vaughan and Lewis refer to national identity as "the symbols, icons, discourses, and places created, disseminated, celebrated, and appropriated as national." Vaughan and Lewis, "Introduction," 2. Scholars generally date the armed stage of the Mexican Revolution from 1910 to 1920. For a discussion on the history of the term "revolution," see Craven, *Art and Revolution in Latin America*, 6–14.

46. Vaughan, *Cultural Politics in Revolution*, 4.

47. Mraz, *Looking for Mexico*, 4.

48. Ibid., 2.

49. Because of Mexico's low literacy rates, Mraz states that "identity construction in Mexico has been carried out largely through the modern visual cultures of photography, cinema, and picture histories." Mraz, *Looking for Mexico*, 2.

50. Carr, "The Fate of the Vanguard under a Revolutionary State," 345.

51. López, "The Noche Mexicana and the Exhibition of Popular Arts," 29.

52. López, *Crafting Mexico*, 48; Vaughan and Lewis, "Introduction," 4.

53. Karttunen, *Between Worlds*, 195–202. Even as Jiménez served as the symbolic indigenous woman, Modotti's 1926 photo of the model and her daughter captured the confident gaze of a woman who looked to the future. After modeling, Jiménez worked as a writer.

54. Coffey, *How a Revolutionary Art Became Official Culture*, 6–7.

55. López, *Crafting Mexico*, 134–35. In brief, *indigenismo* was an influential ideology/movement in Latin America that celebrated or valorized the indigenous

population as an integral element of national identity. For more see Vaughan and Lewis, "Introduction," 4–5. By combining the "modern" scientific methods of the era with culture and activism, *indigenistas* reflected on Mexico's glorious indigenous past in their efforts to create a modern future. Dawson, "From Models for the Nation to Model Citizens," 279–81. Also see Dawson, *Indian and Nation in Revolutionary Mexico.*

56. Siqueiros's position is not particularly surprising given that those who supported the Soviet Union often did not demonstrate an equal enthusiasm toward *indigenismo* ideology during the 1920s and the early 1930s. Under the Cárdenas presidency (1934–40), however, the rhetoric shifted with a greater emphasis on the indigenous population in an international context, or at least until the president left power in 1940. Cárdenas's opening statement at the first Inter-American Indigenous Congress in Pátzcuaro in April 1940 linked the proletariat with the indigenous population. Kaltmeier, "Mexican *Indigenismo* in a Hemispheric Context," 287; Rupprecht, *Soviet Internationalism after Stalin*, 165.

57. Bruce-Novoa, "Offshoring the American Dream," 128–29. Ironically, Craven notes that by 1926, Vasconcelos disliked the "Bolshevism" in Rivera's murals. Craven, *Art and Revolution in Latin America*, 38. In the way he knew best, Rivera responded to such growing disagreements by painting a derisive image of Vasconcelos in a panel of his murals in the Ministry of Education. López, *Crafting Mexico*, 134–35.

58. Carr, *Marxism and Communism in Twentieth-Century Mexico*, 45.

59. As Carr also argues, "Some of the muralists' work also tended to mimic, and be mimicked by, the official artistic view of the Mexican revolution." Carr, "The Fate of the Vanguard under a Revolutionary State," 343, 345.

60. Joseph and Nugent, "Popular Culture and State Formation in Revolutionary Mexico," 17.

61. I argue that Octovio Paz's conflation of Mexican revolutionary art as "official art," as Mary Coffey analyzes in her fine study on Mexico's murals and museums, exposes only a small part of the complex history. Coffey, *How a Revolutionary Art Became Official Culture*, 1–6. As Coffey notes, Paz's critical assessment of Mexican mural painting as official art arose from the ashes of the 1968 Tlatelolco student massacre and his condemnation of Mexico's authoritarian one-party state that produced the state apparatus capable of cracking down on dissent in such a brutal fashion. But Coffey rightly complicates Paz's stance by looking to Roger Barta's notion of nationalism as "neither an authentic culture emanating from below nor an 'invented tradition' orchestrated from above. Rather it is something between." Ibid., 1, 4.

62. John Lear effectively delineates the debate among art historians in "Representing Workers, the Workers Represented," 236. According to Lear, David Craven argues for the possibilities of revolutionary art in *Art and Revolution* while Leonard Folgarait, in *Mural Painting and Social Revolution*, contends that postrevolutionary artists contributed to the "myth-making process of hegemonic institutionalization." For Folgarait, see *Mural Painting and Social Revolution in Mexico, 1920–1940s.*

63. While this study focuses on Modotti, Reyes, Toor, Kahlo, Brenner, and to a lesser extent Álvarez Bravo, many other women—from Mexico and other countries—also made a significant impact on Mexico's art world. For example, see Lola Cueto, María Izquierdo, Nahui Olin (Carmen Mondragón), Leonora Carrington (born in England),

Angelina Beloff (born in Russia), Elizabeth Catlett (born in the United States), Kati Horna (born in Hungary), Fanny Rabel (born in Poland), Remedios Varo (born in Spain), Mariana Yampolsky (born in the United States), and many others. Although she spent much of her life in the United States, Anita Brenner was born in Aguascalientes, Mexico. For an overview of women artists who lived in Mexico, see Mercado, *Women Artists of Modern Mexico*.

64. Here, the two sisters displayed their leftist politics with their murals (painted both separately and together) on the oppression of capitalism, workers and farmers at work, and the dangers of fascism. James Oles has written one of the few studies of Grace and Marion Greenwood in James Oles, "The Mexican Murals of Marion and Grace Greenwood."

65. For more see Hemingway, *Artists on the Left*.

66. See Yankelevich, *México, país refugio*; Fattal and Salus, *Out of Context*; Oles, *South of the Border*; Delpar, *The Enormous Vogue of Things Mexican*.

67. López, *Crafting Mexico*, 18.

68. Tibol, *Palabras de Siqueiros*, 509–10. Kati Horna offers an example of a notable photographer of the Spanish Civil War. Originally from Hungary, Horna moved to Mexico following her time covering the effects of the war on everyday people, most especially women and children, in Valencia, Barcelona, Madrid, and smaller villages. See Baki, Chévrier, and de Diego, *Kati Horna*.

69. López Guzmán, Espinosa Spínola, and Suárez Molina, "La oposición artística desde México al régimen franquista," 627.

70. From Mexico: the painters Dr. Atl, Diego Rivera, José Clemente Orozco, Carlos Mérida; photographer Manuel Álvarez Bravo; musician Concepción (Concha) Michel; anthropologist Manuel Gamio; the printmaker Leopoldo Méndez; and others supplied art and articles. Foreign contributors included the art historian Anita Brenner; artists Pablo O'Higgins and Jean Charlot; photographers Edward Weston and Tina Modotti; journalist Carleton Beals; and others.

71. Joseph Freeman, "Mexico: first week (1929)," HIA, JF, box 71, folder 12, 2. Also see "Mexico: first week," MUAC, OD, caja 34.4, folder Mexico: First Week (1929), dated 1935. MUAC is located on the Universidad Nacional Autónoma de México (UNAM) campus.

72. Robinson, *A Wall to Paint On*, 84–85.

73. Constantine, *Tina Modotti*, 61–62.

74. Hooks, *Tina Modotti: Photographer and Revolutionary*, 131; Folgarait, *Seeing Mexico Photographed*, 89.

75. Salazkina, *In Excess*, 1; Letter from Frank Pease and the Instituto de Directores Técnicos de Hollywood to the Jefe de Policía in Mexico City, AGN, DGIPS, caja 273, exp. 6, 26 December 1930; "Eisenstein Under New Suspicion: Russian Film Director Again Watched by Police in Mexico as Red Suspect," *Los Angeles Times*, 24 December 1920, 1; O'Mahony, *Sergei Eisenstein*, 135.

76. Eisenstein would be refused entry for at least four weeks. Bergan, *Eisenstein*, 229. "Eisenstein Is Barred under the Alien Law," *New York Times*, 22 February 1932, 15. According to O'Mahony, U.S. authorities denied entry to Eisenstein because they discovered his homoerotic drawings in his trunks. O'Mahony, *Sergei Eisenstein*, 139.

Bergan, however, argues that U.S. Customs agents discovered the erotic drawings and photographs of male nudes after Eisenstein was on the ship home. Bergan, *Eisenstein*, 232–33.

77. Vaughan and Lewis note that "transnational processes empowered national identity formation in Mexico as much as they encouraged new forms of international domination and global interdependence." Vaughan and Lewis, "Introduction," 2.

78. See chapter 5.

79. Herzog, *Elizabeth Catlett*, 5, 110–11.

80. Gall, *Trotsky en México y la vida política en el periodo de Cárdenas*, 20.

81. Letter from Leon Trotsky to Frida Kahlo, HIA, TC, box 11, folder 27, 12 January 1939.

82. Copies of Telegrams and Letters Received by Natalia Trotsky after Murder of Leon Trotsky, 1940, HIA, TC, box 24, folder 8, 1940.

83. Navarro, *Political Intelligence and the Creation of Modern Mexico.*

84. This book cites the documents from this particular group of intelligence documents as DGIPS for consistency reasons, but also because the AGN utilizes the label "DGIPS" to classify these papers. Navarro explains the shift in names over time in *Political Intelligence and the Creation of Modern Mexico*, 152.

85. Aguayo Quezada, *La charola.* Also see Aguayo Quezada, "Intelligence Services and the Transition to Democracy in Mexico"; Aguayo Quezada, *1968: Los Archivos de la Violencia.*

86. In particular, see Padilla and Walker, "In the Archives," 1–10.

87. In this respect, the reports must be read with care and with the understanding that they reflect the conservative biases of the agents.

88. While Trotsky's time in Mexico figures prominently in this chapter, and even though it would be naïve to argue that history can be apolitical, this work attempts to avoid the contemporary political debates that surround this controversial figure. For a fascinating discussion on the controversy surrounding the recent historiography on Trotsky see Patenaude's balanced review of Robert Service's and David North's recent books on Trotsky in "Trotsky: A Biography. In Defense of Leon Trotsky," 900–902; and McLemee, "The Re-Assassination of Leon Trotsky," http://www.insidehighered.com.

89. "Solicitud de reingreso al Partido Comunista," CEMOS, PCM, caja 24, folder 5, Diego Rivera, 16 November 1952.

Chapter One

1. Raquel Tibol, "Datos biográficos," 454–55; Marnham, *Dreaming with His Eyes Open*, 311. According to Marnham, in 1925, Rivera resigned from the Party under pressure from Bertram Wolfe. Marnham, *Dreaming with His Eyes Open*, 184–86.

2. "Solicitud de reingreso al Partido Comunista," CEMOS, PCM, caja 24, folder 5, Diego Rivera, 16 November 1952.

3. Siqueiros, *Me llamaban el Coronelazo*, 282–83; Stein, *Siqueiros*, 66–70; Tibol, *Palabras de Siqueiros*, 508; "David A. Siqueiros Expulsado del Partido Comunista," *El Machete*, (no day) April 1930, 2, 4.

4. Siqueiros, *Me llamaban el Coronelazo*, 283. Late in his career, Siqueiros stated that "As is well-known, I never consider it unnecessary to repeat that I have my Party, the Communist Party of Mexico, of which I have been a member for more than half a century." *Tiempo*, 14 January 1974, 9. As cited in Stern, *Siqueiros: His Life and Works*, 374. Other accounts support Siqueiros's assertions. For example, Debroise notes that although the PCM disavowed any ties to Siqueiros after the Trotsky attack, Siqueiros's relative, Ramón López Quiroga, possesses a 1939 PCM membership card with Siqueiros's name. Debroise, "Action Art: David Alfaro Siqueiros and the Artistic and Ideological Strategies of the 1930s," 65, n. 133. Still, other scholars conclude that the PCM did not readmit Siqueiros until years later. According to White's biography on the painter, Siqueiros was not a member of the PCM during Trotsky's time in Mexico. White, *Siqueiros*, 226. Tibol also states that the PCM only readmitted Siqueiros in 1946 after his initial expulsion in 1930. Tibol, *Palabras de Siqueiros*, 508. Even the FBI noted that although the PCM expelled Siqueiros before the Trotsky attack, he remained in close contact with the Party. Still, according to the FBI, Siqueiros only officially returned to the PCM during the summer of 1946. U.S. Federal Bureau of Investigation, FBI Records, "Special Intelligence Service History," Part 4 of 8, 25–26, https://vault.fbi.gov/special-intelligence-service/SIS%20History%20Part%2004%20of%2008/view. Indeed, Siqueiros and the PCM disagreed about the appropriate response to Trotsky's presence in Mexico. As related in the memoirs of the labor leader and PCM Central Committee member, Valentín Campa, Siqueiros claimed that the PCM and Hernán Laborde, the PCM's secretary general, were reluctant to support Stalin's orders to liquidate Trotsky and "in practice refused to help." The Trotsky assassination caused considerable disagreement within the Party leadership. In March 1940, the PCM expelled both Campa and Laborde, whose absences, according to Siqueiros, left "the Party under our control." Campa, *Mi testimonio*, 165.

5. *La Voz de México*, 23 June 1940; *Excélsior*, 20 September 1953, 2, cited in Stein, *Siqueiros*, 120.

6. Carr, *Marxism and Communism in Twentieth-Century Mexico*, 37.

7. Carr, "The Fate of the Vanguard under a Revolutionary State," 327.

8. Rochfort, "The Sickle, the Serpent, and the Soil," 43.

9. Spenser, *Stumbling Its Way through Mexico*, 153. The expelled PCM member was José C. Valadés.

10. Barry Carr estimates the Socialist Party membership in 1918 at around twenty-four active members. Carr, *Marxism and Communism in Twentieth-Century Mexico*, 20. For a history of the early days of the PCM, see Taibo II, *Los Bolshevikis*.

11. Reports dated 8 December 1919, CA, Fond 495, Opis' 108, reel 1, file 1, 6–10; Carr, *Marxism and Communism*, 22.

12. "Programa de Acción Adoptado por el Primer Congreso Nacional Socialista," 4 September 1919, CA, Fond 495, Opis' 108, reel 1, file 8.

13. "El Partido Socialista Mexicano tratará de unificar su actuación con los Partidos Comunistas de otras regiones," IISH, PCMA, box 1–13, document 1, 10.

14. Spenser, *Stumbling Its Way through Mexico*, 50–51.

15. Ibid., 53.

16. Carr, *Marxism and Communism in Twentieth-Century Mexico*, 25.

17. "El Partido Socialista Mexicano tratará de unificar su actuación con los Partidos Comunistas de otras regiones," IISH, PCMA, box 1–13, document 1, 10.

18. Report dated 8 December 1919, CA, Fond 495, Opis' 108, reel 1, file 1, 6. Also, see Carr, *Marxism and Communism in Twentieth-Century Mexico*, 27.

19. Letter dated 29 November 1919 to the Secretary of the Third International, CA, Fond 495, Opis' 108, reel 1, file 3, 1–2.

20. An alternative communist party (Partido Comunista de México) existed for about a year in Mexico. Linn Gale founded the party in 1919, soon before his expulsion from the then Mexican Socialist Party. Not surprisingly, Gale became the scorn of the official PCM, which sent out statements denouncing his actions. "Statement for the Executive Committee of the Third International by the Delegates of the Mexican Communist Party" dated 7 September 1920, CA, Fond 495, Opis' 108, reel 1, file 2, 4–10. Also see Spenser, *Stumbling Its Way through Mexico*, 53, 57, 64.

21. Letter from José Allen dated 9 September 1920, CA, Fond 495, Opis' 108, reel 1, file 3, 11–12.

22. "Report of the American Agency," no date but received in Moscow on 15 July 1921, CA, Fond 495, Opis' 108, reel 1, file 11, 36–41.

23. Mikhail Borodin arrived in late 1919. Carr, *Marxism and Communism in Twentieth-Century Mexico*, 19; Spenser, *Stumbling Its Way through Mexico*, 44.

24. Spenser, *Stumbling Its Way through Mexico*, 64–88.

25. Ibid., 80–88.

26. Letter from Sen Katayama dated 12 April 1921, CA, Fond 495, Opis' 108, reel 1, file 11, 5–10.

27. Letter from Sen Katayama dated 22 March 1921, CA, Fond 495, Opis' 108, reel 1, file 11, 4.

28. Ibid., 11; Letter from Sen Katayama dated 28 April 1921, CA, Fond 495, Opis' 108, reel 1, file 11, 22–23.

29. "Report of the American Agency," no date, but received in Moscow on 15 July 1921, CA, Fond 495, Opis' 108, reel 1, file 11, 36–41.

30. Spenser, *Stumbling Its Way through Mexico*, 99–100.

31. Letter from "Yavki" dated 26 May 1921, CA, Fond 495, Opis' 108, reel 1, file 11, 25; Carr, *Marxism and Communism in Twentieth-Century Mexico*, 29.

32. Letter from "Yavki" dated 5 June 1921, CA, Fond 495, Opis' 108, reel 1, file 11, 25; Carr, *Marxism and Communism in Twentieth-Century Mexico*, 24.

33. Letter from Sen Katayama dated 5 July 1921, CA, Fond 495, Opis' 108, reel 1, file 11, 26–28. Katayama estimated that Mexico City contained only one hundred fifty to two hundred Japanese people in 1921. Soon after leaving Mexico, Katayama helped to found the Japan Communist Party in 1922, and he remained politically active for the rest of his life.

34. The dates of the congress were 25 December to 30 December. Spenser, *Stumbling Its Way through Mexico*, 131.

35. Ibid., 132–33.

36. Report to the Small Bureau from Louis Fraina dated 2 January 1922, CA, Fond 495, Opis' 108, reel 2, file 22, 1–4.

37. Ibid.

38. Stein, *Siqueiros*, 34.

39. Ibid.

40. Siqueiros, "Tres llamamientos de orientación actual a los pintores y escultores de la nueva generación americana," 2.

41. Tibol states that Siqueiros entered the PCM in 1923. Tibol, *Palabras de Siqueiros*, 507–8; also see Stein, *Siqueiros*, 40. On Rivera see Wolfe, *Diego Rivera*, 166; Marnham, *Dreaming with His Eyes Open*, 165.

42. Letter dated 30 November 1922 from Rosendo Gómez Lorenzo to Alfred Stirner, CA, Fond 495, Opis' 108, reel 2, file 24, 21.

43. Letter dated 3 May 1923 from María del Refugio García, CA, Fond 495, Opis' 108, reel 2, file 33, 27–29.

44. Letter dated 21 April 1923 to Alfred Stirner, CA, Fond 495, Opis' 108, reel 2, file 33, 20. On the *Plebe*, see Spenser, *Stumbling Its Way through Mexico*, 153.

45. Partido Comunista de México, Sección de la Internacional Comunista, *III Congreso Celebrado en la Ciudad de México del 7 al 12 de abril de 1925*, 2. Located in the IISH, PCMA, box 1–13, document 2.

46. Letter dated 21 April 1923, CA, Fond 495, Opis' 108, reel 2, file 33, 20, 22.

47. Azuela places the date of the founding of the SOTPE on 9 December 1923 in Azuela, "*El Machete* and *Frente a Frente*," 82; Additionally, Caplow locates the date in December 1923 in Caplow, *Leopold Méndez*, 29. For additional information on the artists' union see Carr, *Marxism and Communism in Twentieth-Century Mexico*, 36; Lear, "La revolución en blanco, negro y rojo," 116. Both Carr and Lear place the date of the founding of the Union in December 1922. The artists also referred to the Union as the Syndicate of Revolutionary Painters, Sculptors, and Printmakers, or the *Sindicato de Pintores, Escultores y Grabadores Revolucionarios*. Caplow, *Leopold Méndez*, 29. Also see Siqueiros, *Art and Revolution*, 13.

48. Siqueiros, *Me llamaban el Coronelazo*, 214.

49. Azuela, "*El Machete* and *Frente a Frente*," 82.

50. Wolfe, *Diego Rivera*, 172–73.

51. Azuela, "*El Machete* and *Frente a Frente*," 85.

52. The manifesto later was published in June 1924 in *El Machete*, a newspaper also formed by the artists.

53. Siqueiros, *Art and Revolution*, 24.

54. Ibid. Italics in the original.

55. Ibid.

56. *El Machete*, no. 9, 10 August 1924, 3. Located in SAPS.

57. Siqueiros, *Art and Revolution*, 13; Carr, *Marxism and Communism in Twentieth-Century Mexico*, 36; Lear, "La revolución en blanco, negro y rojo," 118.

58. Ibid., 119.

59. Ibid., 121; Carr, *Marxism and Communism in Twentieth-Century Mexico*, 37. *El Machete*'s circulation increased even more during the next few years, growing to 11,500 in November 1928. Carr, *Marxism and Communism in Twentieth-Century Mexico*, 38.

60. Lear, "La revolución en blanco, negro y rojo," 120.

61. Partido Comunista de México, *III Congreso*, 64. IISH, PCMA, box 1–13, document 2.

62. Xavier Guerrero, "Propósitos," *El Machete*, no. 1, Primera Quincena de March 1924, 2. Located in SAPS.

63. David Alfaro Siqueiros, "Al margen del manifiesto del Sindicato de Pintores y Escultores," *El Machete*, no. 1, Primera Quincena de March 1924, 3. Located in SAPS.

64. Ibid.

65. D. Alfaro Siqueiros, "En el Orden Burgués Reinante hay que Buscar la Causa de la Decadencia Arquitectónica Contemporánea," *El Machete*, no. 5, Primera Quincena de May 1924, 6. Located in SAPS.

66. David Alfaro Siqueiros, "Si los Trabajadores no ponen el remedio, seguirán despilfarrando los Diputados seis millones de pesos al año, en automóviles, en gasolina, en coñac, en prostitutas y en tiros disparados al aire," *El Machete*, no. 6, Primera Quincena de June 1924, 1. Located in SAPS.

67. Azuela, "*El Machete* and *Frente a Frente*," 83.

68. *El Machete* attributed the play to "Por D. y G. Alfaro Siqueiros."

69. Siqueiros and Graciela Amador, "A los Soldados, a los Obreros y a los Campesinos: Farsa en Varios Actos," *El Machete*, no. 3, Primera Quincena de April 1924, 5. Located in SAPS.

70. *El Machete*, no. 5, Primera Quincena de May 1924, 6. Although Siqueiros's signature is missing under the print, Azuela attributes the work to Siqueiros while providing an astute analysis of the art in Azuela, "*El Machete* and *Frente a Frente*," 83.

71. See D. Alfaro Siqueiros, "Si los Trabajadores no ponen el remedio, seguirán despilfarrando los Diputados seis millones de pesos al año, en automóviles, en gasolina, en coñac, en prostitutas y en tiros disparados el aire," *El Machete*, no. 6, Primera Quincena de June 1924, 1–2. Located in SAPS.

72. "Los murciélagos y las Momias Pretenden Impedir el Desarrollo de las Pinturas Revolucionarias," *El Machete*, no. 8, Segunda Quincena de July 1924, 2. Located in SAPS.

73. Siqueiros, *Art and Revolution*, 13; Azuela, "*El Machete* and *Frente a Frente*," 85; White, *Siqueiros*, 83.

74. Stein, *Siqueiros*, 52–53.

75. Wolfe, *Diego Rivera*, 167.

76. Ibid., 249.

77. Ibid., 251.

78. The Third Congress was held in early April 1925. Partido Comunista de México, *III Congreso*, IISH, PCMA, box 1–13, document 2, title page.

79. Ibid., 2.

80. Ibid., 5.

81. Ibid., 19–22.

82. Ibid.

83. "INFORME DEL DELEGADO DEL P.C. MEXICANO AL QUINTO CONGRESO DE LA INTERNACIONAL COMUNISTA," Partido Comunista de México, *III Congreso*, IISH, PCMA, box 1–13, document 2, 61–63. Caps in original title.

84. Ibid., 66. Caps in original quotation.

85. To insure the understanding of the Bolshevization process, the PCM suggested that various sections hold classes covering the theories of Marx and Lenin for potential new comrades. Additionally, each applicant to the Party underwent a period of probation and education before being admitted as a regular member. During this phase, the potential PCM supporter appeared before a committee of three at least once, not only to ascertain details of their past, but also to receive instructions in the basic principles of the PCM, its structure, discipline, and even the dangers and sacrifices of being associated with the Party. Ibid., 68–69.

86. Ibid., 65–66.

87. "Diego Rivera to the National Executive Committee of the Communist Party of Mexico." HIA, JF, box 180, folder 3, 26 April 1925. This document was translated into English and appeared in English. For the date of Rivera's return to the PCM, see Wolfe, *Diego Rivera*, 252.

88. "The National Executive Committee of the Communist Party of Mexico to Diego Rivera." HIA, JF, box 180, folder 3, 7 June 1925.

89. "Al C. Agente de Primera #8," AGN, DGIPS, caja 34, exp. 3, May 1925. Document torn so exact date is unknown.

90. "Asunto: Investigación sobre qué elementos del Gobierno Federal o de los Estados prestan ayuda al periódico 'El Machete,'" AGN, DGIPS, caja 34, exp. 3, 20 May 1925.

91. Ibid.

92. Ibid.

93. Stein, *Siqueiros*, 57–58.

94. To illustrate the complexities of reading internal security documents, the author of the document also suggested that government officials inquire whether Siqueiros was a Mexican or a foreigner, since many locals (Jalisco, Guadalajara) believed him to be from another country. "Al C. Secretario de Gobierno," AGN, DGIPS, caja 33, exp. 33, 5 June 1927.

95. López, *Crafting Mexico*, 100–105. For the first four issues, Jean Charlot was art editor, but by issue no. 5, Diego Rivera took on the role. He remained the art editor until the journal's demise in 1937.

96. Marnham, *Dreaming with His Eyes Open*, 199–203; Wolfe, *Diego Rivera*, 244; Richardson, "The Dilemmas of a Communist Artist," 54, 63.

97. The participants were invited to hear the revolutionary songs of Conchita Michel as well. "Conferencia sobre la Rusia Soviética," *El Machete*, 23 June 1928, announcement on front page.

98. Siqueiros, *Me llamaban el Coronelazo*, 236. Agent Number 6 also reported on Siqueiros's attendance at the Fourth International Congress of Red Trade Unions, noting that his wife also participated. "Asunto: Agitadores rusos de la III Internacional," AGN, DGIPS, caja 260, exp. 6, 22 August 1928.

99. Amador, "Gachita Amador, la fiel y la extraña," Parte 2 de 2, 93–94.

100. Siqueiros, *Me llamaban el Coronelazo*, 237–38.

101. Stein, *Siqueiros*, 59–60; Siqueiros, *Me llamaban el Coronelazo*, 238–39.

102. Stein, *Siqueiros*, 59.

103. Carr, *Marxism and Communism in Twentieth-Century Mexico*, 43–46.

104. Garrido, *El partido de la revolución institucionalizada*, 104–5. Garrido locates the sustained crackdown on the PCM as beginning in May 1929.

105. Vázquez Ramírez, *Organización y resistencia popular en la ciudad de México durante la crisis de 1929–1932*, 138–39, 177–78.

106. "Decenas de Comunistas Aprehendidos," *El Machete*, (no day) March 1930, 1.

107. A little over a week before the destruction of the press, *El Machete* published a scathing critique of the government in a letter to fellow comrades on the front page. "EL GOBIERNO DE PORTES GIL PREPARA UNA NUEVA OLEADA DE REACCIÓN," *El Machete*, 17 August 1929, 1. Caps in original title. Marnham states that the government outlawed the Party in March 1929. *Dreaming with His Eyes Open*, 213.

108. "Memorándum: Clausura de 'El Machete,'" AGN, DGIPS, caja 34, exp. 3, 12 July 1929.

109. In fact, the newspaper continued under the name *El Machete Ilegal* until 1934. See *El Machete Ilegal: 1929–1934*, Edición Facsimilar.

110. "Memorándum del Dept. Confidencial al C. Agente número 12," AGN, DGIPS, caja 34, exp. 3, 9 August 1929.

111. "ASUNTO: Informar la Imprenta donde se publica el 'Matechete' [*sic*] y proceder a su clausura," AGN, DGIPS, caja 34, exp. 3, 3 September 1929.

112. "ASUNTO: Se informa sobre el periódico 'El Machete,'" AGN, DGIPS, caja 34, exp. 3, 13 June 1930.

113. "Al compaño," AGN, DGIPS, caja 34, exp. 3, (no day) April 1930.

114. "ASUNTO: Informa sobre de los elementos comunistas en México," AGN, DGIPS, caja 61, exp. 15, 22 August 1929.

115. Given the high national profile of the artists, their presence at the various events in Mexico also attracted the attention of Mexico's internal security agents. For example, no less than four agents attended the PCM's 1929 demonstration to observe the burial of the Cuban revolutionary, Julio Mella, and agents noted Diego Rivera's presence, among many others. "Asunto: Informan sobre la manifestación llevado a cabo por elementos del Partido Comunista de México con motivo de sepelio del cadáver de Julio Antonio Mella," AGN, DGIPS, caja 59, exp. 45, 12 January 1929. Even more than Rivera, though, officials feared that Siqueiros, and his fiery public speeches, would incite popular rebellion. Just a few months after the Mella march, Agent Number 14 duly reported the details of Siqueiros's speech at a PCM gathering, held in Mexico City, in honor of the twelfth anniversary of the Russian Revolution. The agent noted with obvious irritation that the proceedings began at 8:30 instead of 7:30 as announced, after which the attendants sang the *Internationale*. According to the official report, Siqueiros presented the audience with a fiery attack on the current president, labeling him a capitalist. Siqueiros particularly criticized Mexico's high-level generals, contending that they earned hundreds of pesos daily in addition to what they stole, in comparison to the common soldiers' lowly pay. "Asunto: Conmemoración del duodécimo aniversario de la revolución Rusa en el Frontón Hispano-Mexicano, Calle Balderas y Colón," AGN, DGIPS, caja 61, exp. 31, 8 November 1929.

116. Marnham, *Dreaming with His Eyes Open*, 216.

117. "Resolution Adoptée par le Comité Central du Parti Communiste de Mexique," CA, Fond 495, Opis' 108, reel 13, file 102, 138–42. Report dated 27 September 1929. Luis C. Monzón, Roberto Reyes Pérez, and Fritz Bach were the other ex-comrades mentioned in the memo who were expelled along with Rivera. According to Dawn Adès, Vittorio Vidali and his "henchmen" planned Rivera's expulsion in order to "purge the Party of unreliable elements," but Vidali's actions also were based in part on "more personal motives." Ades, "The Many Revolutions of Rivera," 17.

118. Marnham, *Dreaming with His Eyes Open*, 218, 225.

119. Ibid., 231–34.

120. Carr, *Marxism and Communism in Twentieth-Century Mexico*, 45.

121. Heale, *American Anti-Communism*, 102–3.

122. "Las Investigación de las 'Actividades Comunistas' en México y EE. UU.," *El Machete*, October 1930, 3.

123. Letter from Frank Pease and the Instituto de Directores Técnicos de Hollywood to the Jefe de Policía in Mexico City, AGN, DGIPS, caja 273, exp. 6, 26 December 1930; "Eisenstein Under New Suspicion: Russian Film Director Again Watched by Police in Mexico as Red Suspect," *Los Angeles Times*, 24 December 1920, 1.

124. Salazkina, *In Excess*, 22. Much like Frances Toor, Eisenstein placed great importance in Mexico's indigenous population as the foundational basis of a national identity.

125. Eisenstein's difficult and brief stay in the United States while under contract with Paramount Pictures further fueled his desire to work in Mexico, especially after he quickly came to the realization that rabid anticommunist elements in Hollywood would work to ensure that he never would complete a film project. Eisenstein remained bitter about his short time in Hollywood, stating that, although he had been invited to California to produce motion pictures of a "different" sort, he had been denied the "opportunity to take a single foot of film." "Russian Director Quits U.S. Movies, and He Tells Why," *Chicago Daily Tribune*, 20 April 1932, 16. Eisenstein's thorny artistic and business corroboration with the U.S. film industry lasted only a few short months, and soon fears over possible Russian propaganda forced Eisenstein to return to the Soviet Union for a brief stay before he left again to begin his work in Mexico. "Movie Gossip from Hollywood," *Chicago Daily Tribune*, 29 June 1931, 17.

126. Pease further argued that Eisenstein directed a "school of propaganda" in Moscow, which was "uniquely responsible for the avalanche of young people with twisted ideas that are flooding the world, revolutionary graduates of this school, [that are] responsible for the disturbances in China, India, Indochina, and in the end in the rest of the world." Even worse, according to Pease, Eisenstein looked to destroy the world as a "bloody enemy of all guardians of humanity." Letter from Major Frank Pease, president of the Instituto de Directores Técnicos de Hollywood, to the American Citizens of Los Angeles and the Vicinity; Letter from Major Frank Pease and the Instituto de Directores Técnicos de Hollywood to the Jefe de Policía in Mexico City, AGN, DGIPS, caja 273, exp. 6, 26 December 1930.

127. U.S. immigration officials refused to allow Eisenstein to return to the United States for any length of time after his Mexican trip. U.S. officials stopped him at the U.S.-Mexico border in February 1932, and held him there for five weeks before they allowed him to travel to New York on his way back to Moscow. "Eisenstein Is Barred under the Alien Law," *New York Times*, 22 February 1932, 15; "Film Made in Mexico Given Russian Slant," *Chicago Daily Tribune*, 21 May 1933, SA8.

128. "David A. Siqueiros Expulsado del Partido Comunista," *El Machete*, (no day) April 1930, 2, 4.

129. Stein, *Siqueiros*, 66–67.

130. Although Amador originally planned to attend the meetings in Montevideo with her husband, economic difficulties kept her at home. While there, the painter even sent Amador a cryptic wire where he suggested that their days apart had been a "huge error." Although the time passed slowly for Amador, Siqueiros finally sent her a cable with the details of his arrival. While Amador's mother prepared a "sumptuous" meal, she went to the station to meet his train. When he failed to appear, Amador returned to her mother, devastated and fearful that police had arrested her husband. Although he eventually appeared at their house, she soon discovered the truth. Amador, "Gachita Amador, la fiel y la extraña," Parte 2 de 2, 100–102.

131. A strong woman, Amador eventually recovered. Ibid., 103.

132. Amador, "Gachita Amador, la fiel y la extraña," Parte 1 de 2, 84.

133. "David A. Siqueiros Expulsado del Partido Comunista," *El Machete*, (no day) April 1930, 2, 4.

134. Report of the Central Executive Committee, CA, Fond 495, Opis' 108, reel 17, file 130, 9. Report dated 5 January 1930. Caps in original quotation.

135. Ibid., 9–10.

136. Ibid., 10–11.

137. "Declaración del compañero D. A. S. sobre la decisión del C. C. relativa a su caso," CA, Fond 495, Opis' 108, reel 17, file 128, 11–12. Report dated 29 January 1930.

138. "Resolución adoptada por el C. C. del PCM en su sesión de Marzo 27 de 1930, sobre el caso de David Alfaro Siqueiros," CA, Fond 495, Opis' 108, reel 17, file 128, 21. Report dated (no day) March 1930.

139. Ibid.

140. Despite other issues, Siqueiros's relationship with Brum concerned the Central Committee the most, especially after she appeared at the Party's illegal and secret offices. Even though Siqueiros stated that he had "absolute faith" in Brum, Party members remained concerned that police would follow her movements to their offices, and thus her presence would give away their location. Ibid.

141. "ASUNTO: Se informa del resultado de la manifestación que desfilo el día 1 de mayo, para conmemorar los asesinatos de Chicago," AGN, DGIPS, caja 259, exp. 35, 2 May 1930.

142. Ibid.

143. Ibid.

144. "David A. Siqueiros Expulsado del Partido Comunista," *El Machete*, (no day) April 1930, 2, 4.

145. "Boletín de '*El Machete*,'" 2 May 1930, AGN, DGIPS, caja 259, exp. 35.

146. "David A. Siqueiros Expulsado del Partido Comunista," *El Machete*, (no day) April 1930, 2, 4.

147. The Party's Central Committee discussed Siqueiros's arrest and his expulsion from the PCM in a report dated 17 May 1930. AGN, DGIPS, caja 260, exp. 4.

148. While in Taxco, Siqueiros met Eisenstein, and their friendship influenced the muralist's approach to art. Rochfort, *Mexican Muralists*, 145.

149. Folgarait, *So Far from Heaven*, 34.

150. For more on Siquerios's relationship with Brum, see Campos, *Siqueiros y Blanca Luz Brum*.

Chapter Two

1. "Tina Modotti Dies in Taxi," *Excélsior*, 7 January 1942, section 2a, 5.

2. "Olvidada y Envejecida ha Fallecido Tina Modotti M.," *Excélsior*, 7 January 1942, 1. Contreras was an alias for Vittorio Vidali.

3. "Tina Modotti falleció en forma extraña y repentina en un automóvil," *El Universal*, 7 January 1942, Section 1a, 1, 7. Also see "Tina Modotti murió anoche en forma extraña a bordo de un automóvil," *El Universal*, 6 January 1942, Section 1a, 5. Not surprisingly, headlines offered a critical appraisal of the returning Modotti as well, seeming to take delight that a once beautiful Modotti had died "forgotten and aged." "Olvidada y Envejecida ha Fallecido Tina Modotti M.," *Excélsior*, 7 January 1942, 1.

4. Scott argues that the source of unequal gender relationships lies in liberalism. Scott, *Only Paradoxes to Offer*, 63–65.

5. See Smith, *Gender and the Mexican Revolution*, 4.

6. Mraz, *Looking for Mexico*, 77.

7. Of course, Kahlo and her work recently have attracted tremendous interest. For a discussion on the relationships between Frida Kahlo and Diego Rivera, as well as Antonieta Rivas Mercado and José Vasconcelos, see Franco, "Body and Soul." Gerda Taro (born Gerda Pohorylle) is an example of a photographer whose legacy, until recently, was defined by her relationship with Robert Capa, the eminent war photographer. A series of major exhibitions and books have begun to redefine Taro (who died while photographing the Spanish Civil War) as a major artist in her own right. Beyond her art, of course, is the fact that Taro was one of the first women to photograph a war from the front lines, and to die while working.

8. Vaughan, "Introduction: Pancho Villa," 27. Mexican women were excluded from the Mexican muralist movement until 1936, although a few non-Mexican women participated on a limited basis. See Argenteri, *Tina Modotti*, 52.

9. Besides Modotti, other politically radical women also played important roles in creating Mexico's postrevolutionary identity. For instance, Lola Álvarez Bravo, the painters Frida Kahlo, Aurora Reyes, and Nahui Olin (María del Carmen Mondragón Valseca), the writers Anita Brenner and Katherine Anne Porter, the artist and puppeteer Lola Cuento, the muralists Grace and Marion Greenwood, the art patron Antonieta Rivas Mercado, and the founder of *Mexican Folkways*, Frances (Paca) Toor, all either associated directly with the Party as members or else collaborated

with PCM colleagues on artistic projects. While this chapter—and chapter 4—focuses on women associated with the PCM, other women, such as María Izuierdo, avoided interpretations of leftist ideology in their works but still contributed significantly to Mexico's cultural history. As a painter, though, Izuierdo still expressed the difficulties of being a talented woman painter in a male-dominated profession. Del Conde, "A Nostalgic Melancholy," 12.

10. Olcott, "'Take Off That Streetwalker's Dress,'" 37–38.

11. Ibid., 38. Also see Cano, "The Porfiriato and the Mexican Revolution, Constructions of Feminism and Nationalism," 107.

12. Clements, *Bolshevik Women*, 18.

13. Hartmann, "The Unhappy Marriage of Marxism and Feminism," 2.

14. Lenin, "Women in the Struggle for Socialism," 46. Also see Kollontai, *Sexual Relations and the Class Struggle*, 9. First published in 1919 as *The New Morality and the Working Class*.

15. Clements, *Bolshevik Women*, 105–6.

16. According to Olcott, in 1934 Concha Michel left the Party in frustration over the "woman question." Olcott, "'Take Off That Streetwalker's Dress,'" 48.

17. Carr, *Marxism and Communism in Twentieth-Century Mexico*, 36. Also see Hooks, *Tina Modotti*, 81.

18. "Se informa de las actividades comunistas. . . . ," AGN, DGIPS, caja 260, exp. 6, 20 July 1915. Rashkin, *The Stridentist Movement in Mexico*, 68. Jocelyn Olcott points out that Consuelo Uranga was an editor at *El Machete* during the early 1930s. Olcott, "The Center Cannot Hold: Women on Mexico's Popular Front," 237.

19. "Frente único de la mujeres," *El Machete*, 12 October 1935, 3.

20. Tuñón Pablos, *Mujeres que se organizan*, 25; Monsiváis, "When Gender Can't Be Seen amid the Symbols," 14.

21. "A la Mujer Mexicana," *La Mujer*, 12 January 1920, 4. *La Mujer* can be located in the *Centro de Estudios del Movimiento Obrero y Socialista*, caja de mujeres.

22. "EXTRACTO," AGN, DGIPS, caja 260, exp. 6, no date.

23. Anne E. Gorsuch analyzes the construction of gender difference and the "difficulties of restructuring gender relations even in the most conscious of revolutionary environments," in Gorsuch, "'A Woman Is Not a Man,'" 638.

24. *Ley Sobre Relaciones Familiares*; Macías, *Against All Odds*, 76; Morton, *Woman Suffrage in Mexico*, 9.

25. Engel, "New Directions in Russian and Soviet Women's History," 50–51. For an analysis of images of women in Soviet art, see Bonnell, *Iconography of Power*, 65–85.

26. Clements, "Bolshevik Women," 195–99.

27. "Some Important Dates and Events in the Life of Alexandra Kollontai," 214.

28. Hooks, *Tina Modotti*, 133.

29. Beals, *Glass Houses*, 343.

30. Brenner, *Avant-Garde Art and Artists*, vol. 1, 428; Hooks, *Tina Modotti*, 136.

31. Alexandra Kollontai, "Women's Day, February 1913," 64. First published in *Pravda*, no. 40, 17 February 1913.

32. Carleton, "Writing-Reading the Sexual Revolution in the Early Soviet Union," 233.

33. For more on Kollontai's struggles for women's rights, and the Bolsheviks' attitudes toward the issue of women's appropriate roles, see Wood, *The Baba and the Comrade*, 30–39.

34. Carleton, "Writing-Reading the Sexual Revolution in the Early Soviet Union," 235–37.

35. Zetkin, "My Recollections of Lenin (An Interview on the Woman Question)," 103. Also see "Clara Zetkin ha Muerto!," *El Machete*, 13 March 1933, 1, 4. The government closed *El Machete* on 6 June 1929 until 1934, and *El Machete Ilegal* took its place during the interim period. Nonetheless, the name "El Machete" remained on the newspaper's masthead.

36. Dazhina, "An Impassioned Opponent of War and Champion of Peace and Female Emancipation," 13.

37. Kollontai, *Sexual Relations and the Class Struggle*, 1–2.

38. "La Revolución Rusa y las mujeres," *El Machete*, 5 November 1927, Número especial dedicado al 7 de noviembre, 2. Also see "La Mujer en la Unión Soviética," *El Machete*, 30 October and 10 November 1932, 5.

39. "8 de marzo, Día Internacional de la Mujer Trabajadora," *El Machete*, 2a. quincena de febrero de 1931, 4.

40. "Organicemos a la Mujer Trabajadora," *El Machete*, 2a. quincena de abril de 1931, 5.

41. *Gobierno Federal de México, Instituto Nacional de las Mujeres, "Boletín Desarrollo Local,"* http://generodesarrollolocal.inmujeres.gob.mx/node/267.

42. "8 de marzo, Día Internacional de la Mujer Trabajadora," *El Machete*, 2a. quincena de febrero de 1931, 4.

43. Ibid.

44. For example, *El Machete* reported that only fifty women and twenty men attended the 1932 Women's Day events in Mexico City. "¡La Jornada del 8 de Marzo ha Sido Celebrada por las Obreras y Mujeres Revolucionarias del País!," *El Machete*, 30 March 1932, 2.

45. Olcott, *Revolutionary Women in Postrevolutionary Mexico*, 47–51.

46. "¡Alerta, mujeres trabajadoras!," *El Machete*, 20–29 February and 10 March 1932, 2.

47. "Fue Desenmascarado el Congreso de Mujeres que Organizo el P.N.R," *El Machete*, 10 October 1931, 1.

48. Ibid.

49. "El Trabajo del Partido en el Congreso de las Mujeres," *El Machete*, 30 October 1931, 2.

50. Olcott, *Revolutionary Women in Postrevolutionary Mexico*, 51, 111.

51. "Primera Conferencia de Mujeres, Invitación al Congreso Mundial de Mujeres contra la Guerra y el Fachismo," CEMOS, PCM, caja 6, folder 27, November 1934.

52. The earlier meeting, *El Congreso contra el Fachismo y la Guerra Imperialista*, or "The Congress Against Fascism and the Imperialist War," was held in Mexico City in August 1934. "Liga Nacional Contra el Fachismo y la Guerra Imperialista," CEMOS, PCM, caja 6, folder 21, September 1934.

53. "Primera Conferencia de Mujeres, Invitación al Congreso Mundial de Mujeres contra la Guerra y el Fachismo," CEMOS, PCM, caja 6, folder 27, November 1934. The Paris meetings took place 4–7 August 1934.

54. Dimitrov, *Against Fascism and War*, 92–93. Italics in the original.

55. Olcott, *Revolutionary Women in Postrevolutionary Mexico*, 109–10.

56. Carr, *Marxism and Communism in Twentieth-Century Mexico*, 104.

57. Dimitrov, *Against Fascism and War*, 64–65.

58. Ibid., 65.

59. *Tesis sobre el Trabajo Femenil del Partido Comunista*, 14; Tuñón Pablos, *Mujeres que se organizan*, 63, 68–89. For much more on the FUPDM, see Olcott, "The Center Cannot Hold," 223–40.

60. "Frente único de la mujeres," *El Machete*, 12 October 1935, 3.

61. *Tesis sobre el Trabajo Femenil del Partido Comunista*, 14; Olcott, *Revolutionary Women in Postrevolutionary Mexico*, 111–14.

62. Chapa, *El derecho de voto para la mujer*. The pamphlet can be found in CEMOS, caja de mujeres. Also see Olcott, *Revolutionary Women in Postrevolutionary Mexico*, 163–64.

63. Chapa, *El derecho de voto para la mujer*, 10–11.

64. Olcott, "The Center Cannot Hold," 237.

65. "Consuelo Uranga," CEMOS, PCM, caja 10, folder 1, 12 January 1938.

66. Ibid. Caps in the original quotation.

67. Monsiváis, "When Gender Can't Be Seen amid the Symbols," 17. In 1942, the FUPDM became the *Comité Coordinador de Mujeres para la Defensa de la Patria*, or the Coordinating Committee of Women in Defense of the Fatherland.

68. Olcott, *Revolutionary Women in Postrevolutionary Mexico*, 237–38.

69. "Oggetto: Saltarini Modotti," ACS, *Ministero Dell'Interno, Direzione Generale Di Pubblica Sicurezza, Divisione Affari Generali e Riservati*, Busta #4540, 7 August 1929.

70. Wolfe, *Diego Rivera*, 213.

71. Hooks, *Tina Modotti: Photographer and Revolutionary*, 14, 26–31.

72. Letter dated 27 January 1922 from Tina Modotti to Edward Weston. Modotti, *Una mujer sin país*, 99.

73. Unsigned, handwritten letter from Modotti to Edward Weston dated 27 January 1922 (Letter 22.1), "The Letters from Tina Modotti to Edward Weston," *The Archive*, 14–15.

74. Hooks, *Tina Modotti*, 51.

75. Robo died in February 1922. Argenteri, *Tina Modotti*, 55; Hooks, *Tina Modotti*, 53; Albers, *Shadows, Fire, Snow*, 87.

76. Lowe, *Tina Modotti and Edward Weston*, 17–18.

77. Argenteri, *Tina Modotti*, 61–62; Hooks, *Tina Modotti*, 60.

78. Constantine, *Tina Modotti*, 61–62.

79. González Cruz Manjarrez, "Tina Modotti y el muralismo, un lenguaje común," 179–81.

80. Rivera, "Edward Weston and Tina Modotti," 16.

81. Ibid., 17.

82. Weston, *The Daybooks of Edward Weston*, Part I, 202. Weston continued with his Mexico connections after returning to the United States. For example, in 1929 he

received an unsolicited series of photographs from Manuel Álvarez Bravo. Álvarez Bravo was unknown to Weston, and he wrote the Mexican photographer to thank him, but also to let him know how important he considered his photographs to be. "Edward Weston to M Álvarez Bravo," CCP, LAB, box AG154:1, Correspondence: Edward Weston, 30 April 1929 (photocopy).

83. Noble, *Tina Modotti*, xv.

84. Vidali, "A Testimony by Vittorio Vidali," 6.

85. Hooks, *Tina Modotti: Photographer and Revolutionary*, 146.

86. Hatzky, *Julio Antonio Mella*, 181, 189.

87. Ibid., 193.

88. Hatzky discusses the lingering debates surrounding Mella's assassination and puts forward several popular explanations. According to Hatzky, the "official" version argues that Machado's henchmen killed Mella, but other accounts rest on Modotti's supposed "amorous" or "immoral" behavior and contend that jealousy motivated the crime. Although this theory was popular in the Mexico City newspapers at the time, Modotti was cleared of any involvement. Additionally, Hatzky points out that some sectors also consider the possibility of the Mexican government's involvement, while still others question the involvement of the communists in Mella's death. According to the latter theory, members of the Comintern planned the attack and Vittorio Vidali executed it, even though Hatzky also reminds us that Vidali's role in the Comintern continues to remain unclear. Hatzky, *Julio Antonio Mella*, 330–54. Also see Whitney, *State and Revolution in Cuba*, 42; Hooks, *Tina Modotti: Photographer and Revolutionary*, 163.

89. "Crimen que causa sensación," *El Universal*, 11 January 1929, 9.

90. On the establishment of the International Red Aid, see Ryle, "International Red Aid and Comintern," 43.

91. Guanche, *Julio Antonio Mella*, 23.

92. "ASUNTO-Informan sobre la manifestación llevada a cabo por elementos del Partido Comunista de México con motivo del sepelio del cadaver [*sic*] de Julio Antonio Mella," AGN, DGIPS, caja 59, exp. 45, 12 January 1929.

93. "El asesinato de Julio Antonio Mella produjo sensación profunda en la capital de la República el día de ayer," *Excélsior*, 12 January 1929, 1.

94. "Tina Modotti y 'Excélsior,'" Comunicado del Secretariado del Centro Internacional de Mujeres, CEMOS, AMV, PCM3, 17 January 1929.

95. Albers contends that police released José Magriñat only a few days after his arrest, although he later was assassinated in 1933 in Cuba after the overthrow of Machado, possibly for his role as Machado's "henchman." Albers, *Shadows, Fire, Snow*, 201.

96. "Portes Gil Organizó el Asesinato de Mella," *El Machete*, October 1930, 4. In 1930, *El Machete* only printed the month and year on their masthead, without a date.

97. "Informa Nombres y Domicilios de algunos comunistas," AGN, DGIPS, caja 259, exp. 35, 4 June 1930.

98. "Informa Nombres y Domicilios de algunos comunistas," AGN, DGIPS, caja 62, exp. 27, 4 June 1930.

99. Robinson, *A Wall to Paint On*, 86.

100. Ibid., 91–92.

101. "Oggetto: Modotti, Tina," ACS, *Ministero Dell'Interno, Direzione Generale Di Pubblica Sicurezza, Divisione Affari Generali e Riservati*, Busta #4540, num. 441/03488, 27 February 1929.

102. Hooks, *Tina Modotti: Photographer and Revolutionary*, 183. The full name of the newspaper was *Mella: Revista Mensual del Secretariado del Caribe del Socorro Rojo Internacional.*

103. "Embajada de Cuba," AGN, DGIPS, caja 33, exp. 41, 30 April 1929.

104. *Mella: Revista Mensual del Secretariado del Caribe del Socorro Rojo Internacional*, 1 May 1929, 1.

105. "Embajada de Cuba," AGN, DGIPS, caja 33, exp. 41, 30 April 1929.

106. *Cuba Libre! Para los trabajadores*, May 1929, 1.

107. Portes Gil to García Téllez, AGN, EPG, caja 82, exp. 5–302, 9 December 1929.

108. Printed manifesto, AGN, EPG, caja 82, exp. 5–302.

109. See de los Reyes, "Últimas fotografías de Tina Modotti," 137–38.

110. Typed, signed letter from Modotti to Edward Weston dated 25 February 1930 (Letter 30.1), Modotti, "The Letters from Tina Modotti to Edward Weston," *The Archive*, 69; AGN, DGIPS, caja 259, exp. 35, 20 May 1930.

111. "Que se encuentran detenidos el Dr. Wilkings Hans y la Sra. Tina Modotti a disposición de esa Secretaría," AGN, DGIPS, caja 259, exp. 34, 12 February 1930.

112. "Regia Legazione d'Italia Messico," ACS, *Ministero Dell'Interno, Direzione Generale Di Pubblica Sicurezza, Divisione Affari Generali e Riservati*, Busta #4540, num. 509/66, 22 February 1930.

113. Letter from the Socorro Rojo Internacional to Portes Gil, AGN, DGIPS, caja 259, exp. 34, 9 February 1930.

114. Federación Obrera de Tamaulipas to Presidente de la República Mexicana, AGN, DGIPS, caja 259, exp. 34, 10 February 1930; Sindicato de Obreros Panaderos y Similares to Presidente de la República, AGN, DGIPS, caja 259, exp. 34, 11 February 1930.

115. "Se remite con el Agente Fidel Álvarez a los extranjeros Windish Hans, Icek Rosenblum, y Tina Modotti," AGN, DGIPS, caja 259, exp. 34, 18 February 1930.

116. "CUENTA COMPROBADA que rinde el Suscrito al Departamento Confidencial de los gastos erogados en la expulsión de varios extranjeros," AGN, DGIPS, caja 260, exp. 4, 1 March 1930. Caps in original title.

117. Typed, signed letter from Modotti to Weston dated 25 February 1930 (Letter 30.1), Modotti, "The Letters from Tina Modotti to Edward Weston," *The Archive*, 69.

118. Argenteri, *Tina Modotti*, 153.

119. Letter from Frank Pease and the Instituto de Directores Técnicos de Hollywood to the Jefe de Policía in Mexico City, AGN, DGIPS, caja 273, exp. 6, 26 December 1930; "Eisenstein Under New Suspicion: Russian Film Director Again Watched by Police in Mexico as Red Suspect," *Los Angeles Times*, 24 December 1920, 1.

120. Hooks, *Tina Modotti*, pages unnumbered in the foreword, but would be xi.

121. Toor also wrote that Modotti discussed "a new man in her life whom she loves and who loves her." Letter from Frances Toor to Joseph Freeman, HIA, JF, box 38, folder 45, 12 November 1931.

122. Hooks, *Tina Modotti: Photographer and Revolutionary*, 152, 155.

123. Typed, signed letter from Modotti to Weston dated 18 September 1929 (Letter 29.3), Modotti, "The Letters from Tina Modotti to Edward Weston," *The Archive*, 68–69.

124. Modotti, "On Photography," 196–97. The article by Modotti was a reprint of her manifesto for her December 1929 exhibition at the *Universidad Nacional Autónoma de México.*

125. Gallo, *Mexican Modernity*, 43–44.

126. Constantine, *Tina Modotti*, 172–73.

127. Neruda, *Memoirs*, 255; Albers, *Shadows, Fire, Snow*, 261.

128. However, in this same note, Modotti also asked her former lover if he could find a buyer for her camera so that she could obtain another, more appropriate model for working in the Soviet Union. Handwritten, signed letter from Modotti to Weston dated 12 January 1931 (Letter 31.1), Modotti, "The Letters from Tina Modotti to Edward Weston," *The Archive*, 75–76.

129. Hooks, *Tina Modotti: Photographer and Revolutionary*, 220.

130. Typed, signed letter from Modotti to Edward Weston dated 5 April 1929 (Letter 29.1), Modotti, "The Letters from Tina Modotti to Edward Weston," *The Archive*, 65.

131. Typed, unsigned letter from Modotti to Weston dated 4 July 1929 (Letter 29.2), Modotti, "The Letters from Tina Modotti to Edward Weston," *The Archive*, 66–67.

132. Bonnell, "The Peasant Woman in Stalinist Political Art of the 1930s," 58.

133. The decree occurred in April 1932. Bown, *Art under Stalin*, 69.

134. Bonnell, "The Peasant Woman in Stalinist Political Art of the 1930s," 67; Bonnell, *Iconography of Power*, 14.

135. Hooks, *Tina Modotti: Photographer and Revolutionary*, 219–20.

136. Ibid., 221.

137. Modotti, *5,000,000 Widows, 10,000,000 Orphans, Women! Do You Want That Again?*, 19. Pamphlet originally published in 1932.

138. Hooks, *Tina Modotti: Photographer and Revolutionary*, 223–24.

139. Albers, *Shadows, Fire, Snow*, 275, 307–10.

140. For Vidali's immigration forms, see AGN, GSM, Sección Departamento de Migración, Series Italianos, caja 14, exp. 269. For Modotti's immigration forms from an April 1940 trip, see AGN, GSM, Sección Departamento de Migración, Series Italianos, caja 9, exp. 168.

141. "Rinde informe de los datos obtenidos hasta la fecha, acerca de la localización de la Sra. María Cortes (Tina Modotti)," AGN, DGIPS, caja 69, exp. 3.

142. Noble, *Tina Modotti*, xix.

143. 1939 letter from Edward Weston to Miriam Lerner, as cited in Modotti, "The Letters from Tina Modotti to Edward Weston," *The Archive*, 64.

144. Vidali, "A Testimony by Vittorio Vidali," 6.

145. "Rinde informe de los datos obtenidos hasta la fecha, acerca de la localización de la Sra. María Cortes (Tina Modotti)," AGN, DGIPS, caja 69, exp. 3. According to the report, Coronel Adalberto Tejeda also provided references for Modotti. The PCM soon expelled Laborde in 1940 because of his views on the Trotsky situation. Carr, *Marxism and Communism in Twentieth-Century Mexico*, 69–73.

146. On Martínez Cartón, see Hooks, *Tina Modotti: Photographer and Revolutionary*, 241, 254.

147. Letter to Rose Baron, TLRW, CPA, Series I–Letters, box 1, folder 13, 19 January 1942. All money and comments were to be sent to Mexico City in the care of a longtime friend of Modotti's, Adelina Zendejas.

148. Neruda, "Tina Modotti is Dead."

149. Hooks, *Tina Modotti: Photographer and Revolutionary*, 247.

150. Vidali, *Retrato de mujer*, 57.

151. Ibid.

152. "Rinde informe de los datos obtenidos hasta la fecha, acerca de la localización de la Sra. María Cortes (Tina Modotti)," AGN, DGIPS, caja 69, exp. 3.

153. Hooks, *Tina Modotti: Photographer and Revolutionary*, 252–53.

154. As quoted in Hooks, *Tina Modotti: Photographer and Revolutionary*, 224.

155. Carr, *Marxism and Communism in Twentieth-Century Mexico*, 67.

156. This discussion took place soon after Congress finally granted women the right to vote in October 1953. Olcott, *Revolutionary Women in Postrevolutionary Mexico*, 234.

157. "Conferencia Nacional Femenil del PCM," *La Voz de México*, 10 November 1956, 1–2. *La Voz de México*, the official organ of the PCM, proudly reported that the "National Women's Conference of the PCM" took place on November 3rd and 4th, with large groups of working women, campesinas, and others attending the various meetings. In 1962 the PCM and the Central Committee continued with the "self-criticism" of their past errors in regard to women; in response, they produced the pamphlet, *Thesis on Women's Work of the Communist Party*.

Chapter Three

1. "Escándalo en el Teatro de Bellas Artes," *Excélsior*, 30 August 1935, 1, 5; "Gran escándalo en el Palacio de Bellas Artes," *El Universal*, 30 August 1935, 1, 7; "Sensacional encuentro Diego Rivera-Siqueiros," *El Universal Gráfico*, 30 August 1935, 1.

2. Eisenberg, "Battle of the Century," *New Masses*, 10 December 1935, 18. Coffey also discusses the great debate in Coffey, *How a Revolutionary Art Became Official Culture*, 38–42.

3. González Cruz Manjarrez, *La polémica Siqueiros-Rivera*, 25.

4. Eisenberg, "Battle of the Century," 18.

5. Ibid.

6. González Cruz Manjarrez, *La polémica Siqueiros-Rivera*, 27; Eisenberg, "Battle of the Century," 18.

7. Eisenberg, "Battle of the Century," 19.

8. "Alfaro Siqueiros y su polémica con Diego Rivera sobre el arte pictórico," *El Universal Gráfico*, 31 August 1935, 3.

9. Eisenberg, "Battle of the Century," 19.

10. "Diego y Siqueiros no tuvieron local donde proseguir los debates," *Excélsior*, 31 August 1935, 1, 4.

11. According to Raquel Tibol, the talks occurred on 6, 7, and 10 September. Tibol, *Siqueiros: Introductor de realidades*, 69–71; González Cruz Manjarrez, *La polémica Siqueiros-Rivera*, 27–28; Prignitz-Poda, *El Taller de Gráfica Popular en México*, 33.

12. Eisenberg, "Battle of the Century," 19. González Cruz Manjarrez reprints the nine points signed by Siqueiros and Rivera in González Cruz Manjarrez, *La polémica Siqueiros-Rivera*, 161. Also see Prignitz-Poda, *El Taller de Gráfica Popular en México*, 33–34.

13. Prignitz-Poda, *El Taller de Gráfica Popular en México*, 33–34.

14. For Rivera's position see "Raíces políticas y motivos personales de la controversia Siqueiros-Rivera. Stalinismo vs. Bolchevismo Leninista," in Rivera, *Obras. Textos polémicos, 1921–1949*, 87–103. Also see Rivera, "Defensa y ataque con los Stalinistas," in Tibol, ed., *Documentación sobre el arte mexicano*, 65–82.

15. As proof of his position, Rivera cited statistics that revealed that his work accounted for 60 percent of all paintings sold in Mexico, José Clemente Orozco followed with 20 percent, and Siqueiros only 8 percent. In this regard, Rivera further argued that the Stalinists hoped to damage Rivera's reputation, and thus reduce the number of Rivera's overall painting sales, in order to limit the monetary contributions to the opposition movement of the Fourth International. Rivera, "Lo que opina Diego Rivera sobre la pintura revolucionaria," 50–53.

16. Eisenberg, "Battle of the Century," 18.

17. Bertram D. Wolfe contends that the attack on Rivera's art began only after his expulsion from the PCM. Wolfe, *Diego Rivera and His Life and Times*, 259.

18. Carr, *Marxism and Communism in Twentieth-Century Mexico*, 36–37.

19. David Alfaro Siqueiros, "Rivera's Counter-Revolutionary Road," *New Masses*, 29 May 1934, 17; Commentary on Rivera, GRI, DAS, box 1, folder 15.

20. Rivera, *Raíces políticas y motivos personales de la controversia Siqueiros-Rivera*, 4. Taken from the original pamphlet located in GRI, DAS, box 1, folder 37.

21. Rivera, "Raíces políticas y motivos personales de la controversia Siqueiros-Rivera," in Rivera, *Obras. Textos polémicos, 1921–1949*, Tomo II, 95.

22. "ASUNTO: Informa sobre conflicto de la Escuela Normal," AGN, DGIPS, caja 75, exp. 1, 20 October 1937.

23. "El 'Mano a Mano' entre Diego Rivera y su opositor Alfaro Siqueiros, se llevo en calma," *El Universal Gráfico*, 30 August 1935, 2.

24. Siqueiros, *Me llamaban el Coronelazo*, 364–65; "Documents against Rivera," GRI, DAS, box 1, folder 15.

25. Sánchez Salazar, *Murder in Mexico*, xiii.

26. Along with André Breton, Trotsky discussed his views on the subject in "Manifesto for an Independent Revolutionary Art," written 25 July 1938. Diego Rivera signed the statement along with Breton, but in actuality, only Breton and Trotsky, rather than Rivera, worked together as coauthors. Breton and Rivera [Leon Trotsky], "Manifesto for an Independent Revolutionary Art," 472. Also see Gall, *Trotsky en México y la vida política en el periodo de Cárdenas*, 207; Patenaude, *Trotsky*, 167; van Heijenoort, *With Trotsky in Exile*, 128–29.

27. Nothing illustrates this point more clearly than the arrival of Leon Trotsky in Mexico after Rivera pressured President Cárdenas to facilitate Trotsky's asylum in

Mexico. Although Rivera's support of Trotsky as well as debate within the PCM concerning the muralist's acceptance of government funding further alienated Rivera from the PCM, he nonetheless continued to stand by the exiled former leader until the late 1930s.

28. Rivera even claimed to be amused when former comrades first labeled him a Trotskyite. Rivera, *My Art, My Life*, 99; Wolfe, *Diego Rivera and His Life and Times*, 257.

29. Eisenberg, "Battle of the Century," 18; Wolfe, *Diego Rivera and His Life and Times*, 257.

30. Wolfe, *Diego Rivera and His Life and Times*, 257; Rivera, *My Art, My Life*, 141 (originally published by the Citadel Press, New York, in 1960). Of course, as Rivera's autobiography, this source must be utilized as just that: Rivera's memory or interpretation of past events. Also see Patenaude, *Trotsky*, 86.

31. "Documento que elabora Diego Rivera a indicación de la Comisión de Control del Partido Comunista de México en respuesta a las preguntas formuladas por ella," CENIDIAP, FR, DR, caja 17, exp. 16, Trotzkismo; Rivera, "Documento que elabora Diego Rivera a indicación de la comisión de control del Partido Comunista de México en respuesta a las preguntas formuladas por ella," 347.

32. Trotsky to Rivera, CENIDIAP, FR, DR, caja 17, exp. 16, Trotzkismo, 7 June 1933.

33. Richardson, *Mexico Through Russian Eyes*, 198.

34. Juan de Dios Bojórquez's undersecretary, J. Ramírez Villarreal, signed the memo. AGN, LCR, caja 904, exp. 546.6/7.

35. Gall, *Trotsky en México*, 19.

36. Richardson, *Mexico Through Russian Eyes*, 197.

37. Brenner also would become a member of the American Committee for the Defense of Leon Trotsky and part of the Dewey Commission. Glusker, *Anita Brenner*, 161. Rivera received the telegram on 21 November 1936. Richardson, *Mexico Through Russian Eyes*, 197.

38. Rivera, *My Art, My Life*, 141.

39. Ibid.

40. Ibid.

41. Letter from Eduardo Hay, Secretary of Foreign Relations to President Cárdenas, AGN, PLCR, microfilm, roll 19, "Derecho de Asilo, Caso: Trotzky." The date of the document was 30 November 1936.

42. Letter from President Cárdenas to Eduardo Hay, Secretary of Foreign Relations, AGN, PLCR, Roll 19, "Derecho de Asilo, Caso: Trotzky." The date of the document was 4 December 1936.

43. Patenaude, *Trotsky*, 19.

44. Ibid.

45. Letter from Eduardo Hay, Secretary of Foreign Relations to President Cárdenas, AGN, PLCR, microfilm, roll 19.

46. Letter from President Cárdenas to Eduardo Hay, AGN, PLCR, microfilm, roll 19.

47. Still, labor remained divided over the Trotsky situation, and a number of unions supported Trotsky. In the days preceding (and following) the president's official decision, Cárdenas received hundreds of telegrams supporting Trotsky's asylum.

Several of those who sent the messages not only made the case for Trotsky's arrival, but also took the opportunity to criticize the "libelous whim" of the CTM as an "agent of the Russian Government." Telegrama, El Sindicato de Obreros Panaderos Bizcocheros y Reposteros del Distrito Federal, AGN, PLCR, microfilm, roll 19, "Derecho de Asilo, Caso: Trotzky." The date of the quoted telegram was 1 December 1936.

48. Carr, *Marxism and Communism in Twentieth-Century Mexico*, 49, 54–55, 62, 65, 68–69, 104. The PCM's adoption of the 1937 Popular Front program, "Unity at All Costs," also led to disagreements between the PCM and the CTM.

49. Letter from the Partido Comunista de México (Sección de la Internacional Comunista) to President Cárdenas, AGN, PLCR, microfilm, roll 19, "Derecho de Asilo, Caso: Trotzky." The date of the document was 9 December 1936.

50. *Labor Condemns Trotskyism*, 3.

51. Carr, *Marxism and Communism in Twentieth-Century Mexico*, 48–56.

52. *Labor Condemns Trotskyism*, 15–17.

53. Ibid., 21.

54. Tibol, "Cronología de David Alfaro Siqueiros," in Tibol, *Palabras de Siqueiros*, 509–10; Patenaude, *Trotsky*, 247–48. Vidali assumed the alias "Carlos Contreras" while in Spain.

55. Siqueiros, *Me llamaban el Coronelazo*, 364–65.

56. Trotsky and his wife arrived on 9 January 1937. Gall, *Trotsky en México y la vida política en el periodo de Cárdenas*, 20.

57. Trotsky, "Statements in Tampico," 9 January 1937; Trotsky, *Writings of Leon Trotsky (1936–37)*, 103.

58. Immigration document signed by "Leon Sedoff Trotsky," HL, TEP, reel 30, document 15789.

59. In addition to other security measures, Cárdenas also assigned six "detectives" to watch over Trotsky and his wife. "Trotsky, Stalin and Cárdenas," *Time*, 25 January 1937, 16.

60. Kahlo, *Querido Doctorcito*, 160.

61. "Documento que elabora Diego Rivera a indicación de la Comisión de Control del Partido Comunista de México en respuesta a las preguntas formuladas por ella," CENIDIAP, FR, DR, caja 17, exp. 16, Trotzkismo.

62. Serge and Sedova Trotsky, *The Life and Death of Trotsky*, 211.

63. Letter dated 4 March 1937 to "Comrade Rivera" signed by Jean van Heijenoort and Bernard Wolf, HL, TEP, reel 22, document 12264.

64. Patenaude, *Trotsky*, 19.

65. Letter from Leon Trotsky to President Cárdenas, AGN, PLCR, microfilm, roll 19. The date of the document was 18 November 1937.

66. Patenaude, *Trotsky*, 19; van Heijenoort, *With Trotsky in Exile*, 106.

67. "ORDERS FOR SECURITY," HL, TEP, reel 30, document 15762. Caps in original.

68. Serge and Sedova Trotsky, *The Life and Death of Trotsky*, 213.

69. Patenaude, *Trotsky*, 37. Van Heijenoort states that "Shortly after his arrival in Mexico, Trotsky had asked for the formation of an international inquiry commission that would examine the false accusations made against him and his son in the Moscow trials." Van Heijenoort, *With Trotsky in Exile*, 108.

70. Trotsky, *I Stake My Life*, 7. Trotsky was to give his speech via telephone to the American Committee for the Defense of Leon Trotsky crowd waiting in the New York Hippodrome theatre, but at the last minute, the telephone connection failed. In 1934, the GPU was dissolved, and the NKVD took its place. Regardless, Trotsky continued to refer to the Soviet secret police as the GPU.

71. Patenaude, *Trotsky*, 38–39.

72. Dewey, *Truth Is on the March*, 6.

73. Herrera, *Frida*, 207.

74. Van Heijenoort, *With Trotsky in Exile*, 109–10.

75. Serge and Sedova Trotsky, *The Life and Death of Trotsky*, 227. In 1938 all four hundred pages of the report were published by Harper & Brothers as *Not Guilty: Report of the Commission of Inquiry into the Charges Made against Leon Trotsky in the Moscow Trials.*

76. "ASUNTO: Informa sobre conflicto de la Escuela Normal," AGN, DGIPS, caja 75, exp. 1, 20 October 1937.

77. "Documento que elabora Diego Rivera a indicación de la Comisión de Control del Partido Comunista de México en respuesta a las preguntas formuladas por ella," CENIDIAP, FR, DR, caja 17, exp. 16, Trotzkismo.

78. For more on Rivera's political inconsistencies concerning Trotskyism, see Herrera, *Frida*, 247.

79. Trotsky, "Letter to James P. Cannon," 30 October 1938, Trotsky, *Writings of Leon Trotsky (1938–39)*, 345–46.

80. "Documento que elabora Diego Rivera a indicación de la Comisión de Control del Partido Comunista de México en respuesta a las preguntas formuladas por ella," CENIDIAP, FR, DR, caja 17, exp. 16, Trotzkismo.

81. Ibid.

82. Charles Curtiss memo, 12 August 1940, HL, TEP, reel 31, document 15935.

83. Van Heijenoort, *With Trotsky in Exile*, 136–37.

84. Trotsky, "A Necessary Statement," 4 January 1939, Trotsky, *Writings of Leon Trotsky (1938–39)*, 349.

85. Ibid., 354.

86. Serge and Trotsky, *The Life and Death of Trotsky*, 254.

87. Ibid.

88. According to Jean van Heijenoort, Curtiss also served as the representative in Mexico of the Pan-American Bureau of the Fourth International. Van Heijenoort, *With Trotsky in Exile*, 137.

89. Charles Curtiss memo dated 12 August 1940, HL, TEP, reel 31, document 15935.

90. "REPORT OF MEETING WITH RIVERA ON MARCH 11, 1939," HL, TEP, reel 31, document 15934. Caps in original title.

91. This quote is from Charles Curtiss. HL, TEP, reel 31, document 15935.

92. Dugrand, *Trotsky in Mexico*, 141.

93. Trotsky, "The Source of the Problem," 1 January 1939, Trotsky, *Writings of Leon Trotsky (1938–39)*, 355.

94. Trotsky, "Letter to Frida Rivera," 12 January 1939, Trotsky, *Writings of Leon Trotsky (1938–39)*, 359–60.

95. Trotsky, "Letter to Charles Curtiss," 18 January 1939, Trotsky, *Writings of Leon Trotsky (1938–39)*, 362–63.

96. "REPORT OF MEETING WITH RIVERA ON MARCH 11, 1939," HL, TEP, reel 31, document 15934. Caps in original title.

97. "MEMORÁNDUM OF DIEGO RIVERA—CURTISS CONVERSATION of 20 January 1939," HL, TEP, reel 31, document 15933. Caps in original title.

98. Patenaude, *Trotsky*, 171.

99. Van Heijenoort, *With Trotsky in Exile*, 139–41.

100. "Documento que elabora Diego Rivera a indicación de la Comisión de Control del Partido Comunista de México en respuesta a las preguntas formuladas por ella," CENIDIAP, FR, DR, caja 17, exp. 16, Trotzkismo. Rivera did not provide the date of Trotsky's request for the return of his love letters, but in her letter to Carlos Chávez, dated 29 April 1936, Frida Kahlo describes Rivera's eye problems and his doctor's orders to remain in a darkened room. According to Kahlo, Rivera's eye ailments began in March 1936 and clearly continued after Trotsky's arrival in Mexico. Kahlo, *Frida by Frida*, 175–76. Raquel Tibol assets that Kahlo's and Trotsky's affair did not motivate Rivera to ask for a divorce from Kahlo in 1940. Instead, Tibol argues that the "reasons, impossible to document, must be found in the role played by Rivera in the first and second attempts on Trotsky's life, Siqueiro's failure, and Trotsky's execution by Ramón Mercader." Tibol, *Frida Kahlo*, 162.

101. Soon after he broke with Trotsky, Rivera accused his former friend of attacking his position on art in a letter to nonparty individuals, an act that Rivera found particularly distasteful. "REPORT OF MEETING WITH RIVERA ON MARCH 11, 1939," HL, TEP, reel 31, document 15934. Caps in original title.

102. Van Heijenoort, *With Trotsky in Exile*, 127–28.

103. Rivera, *Obras. Textos de Arte*, Tomo I, 186–87.

104. Trotsky insisted on paying rent for the Blue House, or at least until he could rent another home. Although Rivera accepted payment for the first month, he subsequently refused further compensation, stating that the house belonged to Kahlo. Charles Curtiss memo dated 12 August 1940, HL, TEP, reel 31, document 15935.

105. Patenaude, *Trotsky*, 240.

106. "ORDERS FOR SECURITY," HL, TEP, reel 30, document 15762. Caps in original title.

107. "Memorándum, La actividad de la G. P. U. en México," AGN, DGIPS, caja 126, exp. 28. The date of the memo was 28 January 1938. Also see Patenaude, *Trotsky*, 124.

108. "Memorándum, La actividad de la G. P. U. en México," AGN, DGIPS, caja 126, exp. 28. Krivitsky later defected to the United States, where he died on 11 February 1941, under mysterious circumstances—a bullet to the head—in a Washington hotel room. The question remains as to whether the shot was self-inflected. Serge and Sedova Trotsky, *The Life and Death of Trotsky*, 263, n. 15.

109. Patenaude, *Trotsky*, 246–50.

110. Siqueiros, *Me llamaban el Coronelazo*, 360; Patenaude, *Trotsky*, 252.

111. Siqueiros, *Me llamaban el Coronelazo*, 367.

112. Sánchez Salazar, *Murder in Mexico*, 63. According to Sánchez Salazar, Barradas Hernández was married to David Barradas Hernández. The *New York Times* listed

the women's names as "Anita Lopez and Julia Barranda de Serrano" [*sic*]. "21 Held in Mexico for Trotsky Attack," *New York Times*, 19 June 1940, 8.

113. Siqueiros, *Me llamaban el Coronelazo*, 367.

114. Siqueiros contended that thirty-five armed Mexican policemen surrounded the Trotsky compound. He also wrote that he never denied that his participation in the assault on Trotsky's house constituted an offense according to prevailing law, and one that resulted in long periods in prison, three years of exile, and "an offensive derogatory character on an international scale." Ibid., 369.

115. "EL ASALTO DEL 24 DE MAYO, La Noche del Asalto," signed Leon Trotsky, AGN, PLCR, microfilm, roll 19, 8 June 1940. Caps in original title. Also see Trotsky, "Stalin seeks my death," 8 June 1940, Trotsky, *Writings of Leon Trotsky (1939–40)*, 311–14.

116. U.S. Federal Bureau of Investigation. Memo from the FBI on "Communist Activities, Assault on Leon Trotsky," Part 1 of 5, 4 June 1940, http://vault.fbi.gov/leon-trotsky/, 30/247.

117. "MEMORÁNDUM. EL ASALTO A LA CASA DE TROTSKY," AGN, DGIPS, caja 126, exp. 28, 25 May 1940. Caps in original title.

118. "ASUNTO-Vista al Sr. Trotsky," AGN, DGIPS, caja 126, exp. 28, 30 May 1940. This was a report written by two agents from the Dirección General de Investigaciones Políticas y Sociales.

119. "Memo from El Inspector PS-15 to C. Cipriano Arriola, Jefe de la Oficina de Información Política y Social Secretaría de Gobernación," AGN, DGIPS, caja 126, exp. 28, 28 May 1940. It is interesting to note the inspector informed the director of DGIPS about the investigation of the Trotsky assault within the police headquarters. In other words, information passed between the two agencies.

120. "EL ASALTO DEL 24 DE MAYO, La Noche del Asalto," signed Leon Trotsky, AGN, PLCR, microfilm, roll 19, 8 June 1940, 14, 15. Caps in original title.

121. Letter to Sr. Coronel Leandro A. Sánchez Salazar, AGN, DGIPS, caja 126, exp. 28, 31 May 1940.

122. Report to C. Lic. Ignacio García Téllez, Secretario de Gobernación, AGN, DGIPS, caja 115, exp. 2, 7 December 1939.

123. "MANIFESTO," AGN, DGIPS, caja 20, exp. 1, 1 June 1940.

124. And indeed, presenting himself as a keen, balanced observer of Mexican politics, Rivera raised serious concerns with the upcoming 1940 presidential elections between Manuel Ávila Camacho and Juan Andreu Almazán. A supporter of Almazán, who ultimately lost in a landslide, Rivera asked, "Will the national and international powers representing the interests of the Mexican people fight for them before or after July 7?" In a move also intended to inflame the PCM, Rivera contended that the "Stalinists and Nazis" in Mexico backed Camacho, while the "Mexican Government dyed itself with the pinkish-red Communist coloring" for the past thirty years. "Rivera Foresees Strife in Mexico," *New York Times*, 19 May 1940, 30.

125. Rivera, *My Art, My Life*, 139–40.

126. Ibid.

127. "Police Hunt for Rivera," *New York Times*, 30 May 1940, 5.

128. "Se rinde informe previo un incidente de suspensión relativo al Amparo 273/940 promovido por Diego Rivera, contra actos de esta Oficina y otras autoridades," AGN, DGIPS, caja 126, exp. 26, 1 June 1940.

129. U.S. Federal Bureau of Investigation. Memo from the FBI on "Communist Activities, Assault on Leon Trotsky," Part 1 of 5, 4 June 1940, http://vault.fbi.gov/leon-trotsky/, 30/247.

130. Trotsky, "Letter to the Mexican Attorney General," 27 May 1940, Trotsky, *Writings of Leon Trotsky (1939–40)*, 303.

131. "21 Held in Mexico for Trotsky Attack," *New York Times*, 19 June 1940, 8.

132. "Asunto: Trotsky," AGN, DGIPS, caja 126, exp. 28.

133. Patenaude, *Trotsky*, 265.

134. Sánchez Salazar, *Murder in Mexico*, 184–85.

135. "Mexican Police Keep Eye on Russian Vessel at Manzanillo," *New York Times*, 24 July 1940, 5.

136. As cited by Sánchez Salazar, *Murder in Mexico*, 99.

137. On 24 August, just three days after Trotsky's death, President Cárdenas offered Natalia his condolences. In her letter to the president to convey her "profound gratitude" for his visit and words of moral support, Trotsky's widow also thanked him for his "sincere feelings" and "unalterable conviction in the honesty of Leon Trotsky." Clearly revealing her anger at the loss of her husband, she continued, "To date, there has not been a time in history like ours so obscured by lies, slander, crime and inhumanity. The honored fighters fall as victims. Their memory, however, will be eternal." Although Natalia expressed regret that her husband never met the president personally, she still affirmed that their lives were forever linked through the support of the Mexican people at a time when no other country dared to help the exiled couple. Indeed, Mexico's offer of asylum prolonged Trotsky's life by forty-three months, not only for Natalia, but also for "hundreds of thousands of pure fighters, who struggle for the renewal of humanity." Letter from Natalia Sedoff Trotsky to Lázaro Cárdenas, AGN, PLCR, microfilm, roll 19, 12 September 1940.

138. Sánchez Salazar, *Murder in Mexico*, 102.

139. "El Juzgado de Primera instancia de Coyoacán, decretando la libertad por desvanecimiento de datos de la procesada por el delito de homicidio Silvia [*sic*] Ageloff Maslow," AGN, TSJ, caja 3265, exp. 602993, 11 December 1940, 1–2; Patenaude, *Trotsky*, 205–7, 228–29.

140. Patenaude, *Trotsky*, 244–45.

141. Ibid., 266.

142. Ibid., 284–86.

143. Betty Kirk, "The Trotsky Murder: Some International Ramifications," *The Washington Post*, 1 September 1940, B7. The article also argued that Vittorio Vidali, alias Carlos Contreras, represented the most dangerous of all GPU agents operating in Mexico. Vidali, who lived with Tina Modotti during many of her last years, supposedly killed his victims with one clean shot to the back of the head or temple.

144. *La Voz de México*, 23 June 1940; *Excélsior*, 20 September 1953, 2, cited in Stein, *Siqueiros*, 120; White, *Siqueiros*, 224.

145. Caplow, *Leopoldo Méndez*, 155–56.

146. "Que Alfaro Siqueiros fue Capturado en Guadalajara," *El Nacional*, 25 June 1940, 1.

147. According to White, although Siqueiros's "true" motives are unclear, the artist insisted that he never intended to kill Trotsky; instead he only wanted to demonstrate that the Russian was not safe in the country and therefore force the Mexican government to revoke his asylum. White, *Siqueiros*, 225–26.

148. "El Juzgado de Primera instancia de Coyoacán, decretando la libertad por desvanecimiento de datos de la procesada por el delito de homicidio Silvia [*sic*] Ageloff Maslow," AGN, TSJ, caja 3265, exp. 602993, 11 December 1940, 25.

149. Ibid., 75.

150. Ibid., 74.

151. "El Juzgado de Primera instancia de Coyoacán, decretando la libertad por desvanecimiento de datos de la procesada por el delito de homicidio Silvia [*sic*] Ageloff Maslow," AGN, TSJ, caja 3265, exp. 602993, 11 December 1940, 9–12. In 1943, Mercader was given thirty years in prison for three crimes: improper possession of prohibited weapons, dangerous attack and aggravated homicide, and danger to society. "Treinta Anos de Prisión para Mornard, El Asesino de Trotsky," *El Universal*, Segunda Sección, 5 February 1943, 1. In 1960, he finally left prison and traveled to Cuba and eventually to the Soviet Union. Patenaude, *Trotsky*, 295.

152. Sánchez Salazar, *Murder in Mexico*, 107.

153. "No Quiero Volver a Verlo, Dijo la Amante de Frank: Entrevista exclusive de 'Novedades,'" *Novedades*, 31 August 1940, 1.

154. "El Juzgado de Primera instancia de Coyoacán, decretando la libertad por desvanecimiento de datos de la procesada por el delito de homicidio Silvia [*sic*] Ageloff Maslow," AGN, TSJ, caja 3265, exp. 602993, 11 December 1940, 17–18, 21. Because Mercader's true identity was not yet known, the testimonies also referred to him as "Jacques Mornard Vandendresch" or "Franck Jackson." Patenaude writes that it was only in 1950 that his true identity was uncovered, although he never admitted to being a GPU agent. Patenaude, *Trotsky*, 295.

155. "El Juzgado de Primera instancia de Coyoacán, decretando la libertad por desvanecimiento de datos de la procesada por el delito de homicidio Silvia [*sic*] Ageloff Maslow," AGN, TSJ, caja 3265, exp. 602993, 11 December 1940, 35.

156. Ibid., 66.

157. "Mexican Judge Rules Release of Sylvia Ageloff," *Schenectady Gazette*, 20 December 1940, 1.

158. The *New York Times* announced the date of Siqueiros's capture as 5 October 1940. See "TROTSKY SUSPECT CAUGHT," *New York Times*, 6 October 1940, 14. Caps in original title. As a side note, on 23 June 1940, Agent Number 24 from the DGIPS reported that Siqueiros had been discovered in the state of San Luis Potosí on a ranch called Ébano, also known as *El Gringo* ranch. Memo from PS-24 dated 23 June 1940, AGN, DGIPS, caja 126, exp. 28.

159. "JEFATURA DE POLICÍA DEL DISTRITO FEDERAL. SERVICIO SECRETO. Se rinde informe de la comisión confidencial conferida," AGN, DGIPS, caja 126, exp. 27, 8 October 1940; Sánchez Salazar, *Murder in Mexico*, 184–201. Caps in original title.

160. "Mexican Artist Acquitted in Shooting Prior to Assassination," *New York Times*, 18 April 1941, 4.

161. Patenaude, *Trotsky*, 297.

162. "Ayer Abandonó la Penitenciaría el Asaltante de León Trotsky: Bajo Fianza de 4,000 Pesos Salió Siqueiros," *Novedades*, Segunda Sección, 29 March 1941, 1.

163. Patenaude, *Trotsky*, 297.

164. "Declaración de Diego Rivera," CENIDIAP, FR, DR, caja 17, exp. 14, D/19.2; Marnham, *Dreaming with His Eyes Open*, 311.

165. Stein, *Siqueiros*, 173; Tibol, "Cronología de David Alfaro Siqueiros," in Tibol, *Palabras de Siqueiros*, 507–13.

166. Rivera, *My Art, My Life*, 157–61; Tibol, "Datos biográficos," 445–46. The mural remained hidden behind the screen for eight years, although the public could view the work by offering a generous tip to those who worked at the hotel. Toward the end of his life, in 1956, Rivera painted over the quotation. Stein, *Siqueiros*, 177–78.

167. The conference was titled, "The Art of Mexico in the Ranks of the People." For more, see the introduction.

168. Gustavo Castañares, "Alfaro Habló de Arte y del Mural que Pintó Rivera," *Excélsior*, 4 June 1948, 3.

169. "ASUNTO-Informan sobre el 'mitin' auspiciado por el 'Partido Comunista de México,' a favor del pintor David Alfaro Siqueiros," AGN, DGIPS, caja 20, exp. 3, 4 June 1948; "ASUNTO: Informan sobre el 'mitin' auspiciado por el 'Partido Comunista de México,' a favor del pintor David Alfaro Siqueiros," AGN, DGIPS, caja 80, exp. 1, 4 June 1948.

Chapter Four

1. Re: Marín v. Knopf, et al., HIA, BW, box 26, folder 2, no date. Kahlo's biographer, Hayden Herrera, places Kahlo's time in New York City to provide her testimony as around November 1940. Herrera, *Frida*, 299.

2. United States District Court, Southern District of New York, Guadalupe Marín, Plaintiff, against Alfred A. Knopf, Alfred A. Knopf, Inc., and Bertram D. Wolfe, Defendants, HIA, BW, box 26, folder 2, 10 August 1940.

3. Ibid., 2–3. The book referenced during the trial was Wolfe, *Diego Rivera*. Although this passage originally appeared on pages 200–201 in the 1939 edition, the 1943 edition of the book was amended to say only, "Gladly she consented to model for the nude in his mural, and for several of the other symbolical figures appearing in the complex allegory," thus removing the offending words "yielding her body as well as posing." Wolfe, *Diego Rivera*, 200–201. In fact, after the 1942 ruling on the case, Wolfe removed several sentences judged to be libelous.

4. Wolfe, *Diego Rivera*, 197–98 (1939 and 1943 editions).

5. Wolf to Stern, HIA, BW, box 26, folder 2, 22 February 1940, 2. Bertram Wolfe writes that the couple did not carry out a civil wedding, but instead they married in the Church of Saint Michael, and the witnesses were "María Michel and Xavier Guerrero." Wolfe, *Diego Rivera*, 202. The final court decision stated that Rivera and

Marín married in the "Church of San Miguel Arcangel" in Mexico City. United States District Court, Southern District of New York, Guadalupe Marín, Plaintiff, against Alfred A. Knopf, Alfred A. Knopf, Inc., and Bertram D. Wolfe, Defendants, HIA, BW, box 26, folder 2, 19 January 1942, 2. Herrera also notes that Rivera and Marín married in 1922. Herrera, *Frida*, 31.

6. Katherine Bliss examines the politicization of sexual behavior, including the discourses surrounding prostitution in Mexico City from 1910 to 1940, to analyze the issues—for example, the reluctance to regulate masculine sexuality—that blocked women's opportunities for true change during the revolutionary and postrevolutionary era. Despite the various legal reforms directed at women, Bliss notes that the Mexican Revolution "largely consolidated male authority at all social levels." Bliss, *Compromised Positions*, 8.

7. Wolf to Stern, HIA, BW, box 26, folder 2, 22 February 1940, 1.

8. United States District Court, Southern District of New York, Guadalupe Marín, Plaintiff, against Alfred A. Knopf, Alfred A. Knopf, Inc., and Bertram D. Wolfe, Defendants, HIA, BW, 1903–1999, box 26, folder 2, 10 August 1940, 5. Wolfe amended this section for subsequent editions.

9. Ibid., 6; Wolfe, *Diego Rivera*, 277, n. 1 (1939 and 1943 editions). The passage in both editions continued with judgmental disapproval, "the great number of homosexuals among the journalists and poets perhaps helps to explain the catty spitefulness of much of the prose and the preciousness and lack of strength in much of the poetry published there. Lupe, in later years, moved much in these circles."

10. Salvador A. Oropesa points out that the "magic circle" carries two connotations during this era: men who had same-sex relations, and the "group of gay intellectuals protected by Narciso Bassols, the secretary of education, including Salvador Novo, Xavier Villaurrutia, Jaime Torres Bodet, and Jorge Cuesta." Oropesa, *The Contemporáneos Group*, 106. Marín discusses the gay writers, including her ex-husband Cuesta, in her thinly veiled autobiographical novel, *La única*, written in 1938.

11. The couple had a baby, Lucio Antonio, born in 1930.

12. Zavala, "María Izquierdo," 67–69.

13. Irwin, "As Invisible as He Is: The Queer Enigma of Xavier Villaurrutia," 117–18.

14. For example, in his Ministry of Education mural, *El que quiera comer que trabaje* (He who wants to eat ought to work), Rivera theoretically portrayed Novo as an elite, out-of-touch artist, sporting long mule ears, and being kicked to his knees by a soldier. Argenteri, *Tina Modotti*, 51–52; Barrera, *Salvador Novo*, 169–72. Novo also criticized Rivera in his 1926 satirical poem titled *La Diegada*. Oropesa, *The Contemporáneos Group*, 61–62; Barrera, *Salvador Novo*, 172–77. Besides Rivera, however, *La Diegada* critiqued both Marín and Cuesta, especially Marín's "voice of a sergeant." Monsiváis, *Jorge Cuesta*, 12.

15. Zavala, "María Izquierdo," 69. For more on concepts of sexuality in Mexico, see Macías-González and Rubenstein, *Masculinity and Sexuality in Modern Mexico*.

16. Anita Brenner noted in her diary that the Contemporáneos poet, Salvador Novo, was "reforming his preferences and now has more use for females, among them Lupe, beautiful in electric blue with her dark skin and large deep gray eyes and black close-cropped hair." Brenner, *Avant-Garde Art and Artists*, vol. 1, 136, 16 April 1926.

17. Re: Marín v. Knopf, et al., HIA, BW, box 26, folder 2, no date.

18. Kahlo and Rivera's first marriage took place on 21 August 1929. Herrera, *Frida*, 99.

19. Herrera, *Frida*, 272, 302.

20. Ibid., 299–302.

21. Wolf to Stern, HIA, BW, box 26, folder 2, 22 February 1940, 1.

22. Toor to Ella Wolfe, HIA, BW, box 14, folder 62, 28 October 1939. Stories abounded concerning the reasons why Kahlo and Rivera ended their marriage, but the causes were as complex as their marriage.

23. "Kahlo to Emmy Lou Packard," Kahlo, *Frida by Frida*, 239–40, 24 October 1940. After their remarriage, Kahlo and Rivera reached a détente of sorts, with fewer arguments but also "fewer nagging inquiries" from Kahlo concerning Rivera's liaisons with other women. Kahlo, *Querido Doctorcito*, 204, dated 18 July 1941. According to Dr. Leo Eloesser, Rivera and Kahlo's close friend and Kahlo's doctor, Rivera's propensity to "embrace with impartiality" any woman who would allow him caused both Marín and Kahlo great distress. Ibid., 271.

24. The trial was held at the U.S. Courthouse at Foley Square, New York, before Judge Hulbert. Stern & Reubens to Wolfe, HIA, BW, box 26, folder 2, 8 December 1941.

25. United States District Court, Southern District of New York, Guadalupe Marín, Plaintiff, against Alfred A. Knopf, Alfred A. Knopf, Inc., and Bertram D. Wolfe, Defendants, HIA, BW, box 26, folder 2, 19 January 1942.

26. Ironically, Rivera and Marín's daughter, "Lupita" (Guadalupe Rivera Marín), came to live with Kahlo and Rivera as a teenager after Marín "exploded," as Kahlo wrote. According to Kahlo, though, she and her stepdaughter got along well. Kahlo, *The Letters of Frida Kahlo*, 118. Dated 1944.

27. Of course, Mexico was home to many artists and writers besides Kahlo, Toor, Reyes, and Brenner. Of particular interest for future research is Lola Álvarez Bravo. The purpose of this chapter, however, is not to offer an exhaustive examination of each individual artist, but to analyze their relationship to the PCM, the Mexican state, and to each other.

28. Kahlo's painting, "Two Women," appeared in *Mexican Folkways* 5, no. 2 (April–June 1929): 73, and Álvarez Bravo also provided her photograph for *Mexican Folkways* 9, no. 8 (August 1935): 53. As discussed in chapter 2, Tina Modotti's photographs appeared fairly often in *Mexican Folkways*.

29. Because Brenner lived in New York from autumn 1927 to 1930 where she attended Columbia University and earned her PhD in 1930, she and Kahlo became friends after Brenner's return to Mexico City. Glusker, *Anita Brenner*, 58.

30. Out of a total student population of around two thousand, only thirty-five young women attended. Geis, "The Struggles of Modernizing Mexico and the Mural of Aurora Reyes at the Centro Escolar Revolución," 158. Also see Zavala, *Becoming Modern, Becoming Tradition*, 5; and Herrera, *Frida*, 15–22. As a painter and poet, Reyes would remain close to Kahlo throughout her life, often exchanging letters when Kahlo traveled.

31. Not all female artists supported communism, including, for example, María Izquierdo. Even though she rarely spoke out about politics, however, Izquierdo still

recognized the need for the increased opportunities for women within Mexican society. Lozano, "Regarding Modern Mexican Painting," 45–47.

32. According to Brenner's daughter, Brenner sympathized with aspects of revolutionary ideology, especially the Mexican Revolution, and she also expressed an interest in Marxist theory. Glusker, *Anita Brenner*, 154–55.

33. See Olcott's discussion of Concha Michel's confrontation of this issue in Olcott, "'Take Off That Streetwalker's Dress,'" 48.

34. Aurora Reyes, quoted in Patricia Cardona, "Aurora Reyes ingresó a la Academia de San Carlos por una golpiza que dio a una prefecta de la prepa," 2nd part, *Periódico Unomásuno*, 30 December 1985, as cited in Mirkin, "Aurora Reyes's 'Ataque a la Maestra Rural,'" 20.

35. Debroise, "Like Cut Glass," 27. Although Lola Álvarez Bravo was married to the photographer Manuel Álvarez Bravo from 1925 to 1934, she remained artistically and politically active during the years of her marriage. After her divorce, she lived with the artist María Izquierdo for several years and remained friends with many of Mexico's most significant artists and intellectuals for the rest of her life. Wright-Rios, *Searching for Madre Matiana*, 197.

36. For example, Kahlo, Brenner, and Toor lived for extended periods in adopted countries, and Kahlo's father and Brenner's parents also experienced the uncertainties of being an immigrant. Zavala, *Becoming Modern, Becoming Tradition*, 234.

37. Miller and Brenner, "An Interview with Anita Brenner," 114–15.

38. Brenner first attended the University of Texas for two semesters. During 1926 and 1927 Brenner worked as an assistant for the journalist and former *Nation* editor, Ernest Gruening. Armed with a letter of introduction from Gruening, Brenner requested data from the minister of the interior, Adalberto Tejeda, and covered such issues as Mexico's recent religious situation and the number of priests per state. Ernest Gruening letter, AGN, DGG, caja 26, exp. 23, 18 February 1927. In Mexico, Brenner also introduced Gruening to Concha Michel, and in return he gave her opportunities to meet leftists from the United States. Glusker, *Anita Brenner*, 40–41.

39. Glusker, *Anita Brenner*, 16. Brenner's immigration identification cards over the years listed her nationality as "North American." See AGN, GSM, Series Estadounidenses, caja 19, exp. 156.

40. Katherine Elaine Bliss and Ann S. Blum discuss the growth of Mexico City, as well as the gathering of young people in the city's public spaces during this exciting era of change. Bliss and Blum, "Dangerous Driving."

41. For more on Toor and *Mexico Folkways*, see Stern, "Frances Toor and the Mexican Cultural Renaissance," 200–219.

42. Delpar, *The Enormous Vogue of Things Mexican*, 36.

43. Glusker, *Anita Brenner*, 33, 70. López also points out that mystery surrounds Toor's early years and the status of her relationship remains uncertain. López, *Crafting Mexico*, 101. For Toor's account of her early years, see Toor, "Mexican Folkways," 208. The Mexico City newspaper *Excélsior* also wrote that Toor came to Mexico with her husband, "Dr. A. Weinburg." "ELLA GOLDBERG NO ES OTRA QUE LA ESPOSA DE BERTRAM WOLFE, EL COMUNISTA ROJO," *Excélsior*, 29 May 1927, 1, 4. Caps in original title.

44. "Mexico: First Week (1929)," HIA, JF, box 71, folder 12, dated 1935.

45. Glusker, *Anita Brenner*, 58–58, 70–72; López, "Anita Brenner and the Jewish Roots of Mexico's Postrevolutionary National Identity," 124–25.

46. Monsiváis, "Foreword, Anita Brenner and the Mexican Renaissance," xiv.

47. López, "Anita Brenner and the Jewish Roots of Mexico's Postrevolutionary National Identity," 124. Jewish immigration to Mexico from the United States increased throughout the 1920s and the 1930s. For more on Jewish immigration to Mexico during these years, see Gojman de Backal, *Camisas, escudos y desfiles militares*, 101–19; Glusker, *Anita Brenner*, 150–51. Through her examination of Mexico's immigration policies toward Jewish exiles, Daniela Gleizer challenges the vision of Mexico as a country that welcomed all immigrants equally during the 1930s and 1940s, especially when compared to the Spanish Civil War refugees. Gleizer, *Jewish Latin America*, 2014.

48. López, "Anita Brenner and the Jewish Roots of Mexico's Postrevolutionary National Identity," 124–25.

49. Glusker, *Anita Brenner*, 34–35; López, "Anita Brenner and the Jewish Roots of Mexico's Postrevolutionary National Identity," 125. Brenner's 1926 immigration identification card for Mexico listed her religion as "none." Brenner, Anita, Servicio de Migración, AGN, GSM, Series Estadounidenses, caja 19, exp. 156, 6 December 1926. However, her immigration identification card in 1930 listed her religion as Jewish. Ibid., 29 October 1930.

50. As members of Toor's inner circle of friends, many of *Mexican Folkways*'s contributors also shared the editor's creative vision and thus readily worked with her and other staff members to produce the journal. Many of the group claimed Mexico as their birthplace, but others adopted the country as their transplanted home. Originally from Mexico, the painters Dr. Atl, Diego Rivera, José Clemente Orozco, Carlos Mérida; photographer Manuel Álvarez Bravo; musician Concepción (Concha) Michel; anthropologist Manuel Gamio; the printmaker Leopoldo Méndez; and others provided art and articles. Foreign contributors included the art historian Anita Brenner; artists Pablo O'Higgins and Jean Charlot; photographers Edward Weston and Tina Modotti; journalist Carleton Beals; and others. From the beginning, Toor acted as the editor, and for the first four issues, Jean Charlot was art editor. By the fifth issue, Diego Rivera took on the task of art editor, a title he held until the journal's demise. Still, Raquel Tibol notes that Rivera continued as art editor only until October 1927, although his name officially remained until the final issue in 1937. Tibol, *Diego Rivera*, 21.

51. López, *Crafting Mexico*, 142. Alexander Dawson argues that along with the journal *Ethnos* and Diego Rivera's public art, *Mexican Folkways* represented the "popular voice" of *indigenismo*, the Mexican reformist movement that both celebrated indigenous cultures and at other times labeled them as primitive. Dawson, "From Models for the Nation to Model Citizens," 279–81.

52. Volume 7 was published in 1932, volume 8 in 1933, and volume 9 in 1937. Additionally, in November 1934, Toor produced a special issue dedicated to children's drawing and painting in the primary schools. This special issue was bound in volume 8. Volume 9 also contained two special issues. During its first two years, Toor

issued the journal in a fairly small format, although she increased the size beginning in 1927 with volume 3.

53. For a discussion of Modotti at *Mexican Folkways*, see Hooks, *Tina Modotti*, 132.

54. Anita Brenner as cited in Glusker, *Anita Brenner*, 70.

55. Although this chapter focuses on the visual artists, other contributors to *Mexican Folkways*, including the singer Concha Michel, were members of the PCM. Issue number 4, in 1929, reproduced nine of Rivera's more radical murals from the *Secretaría de Educación Pública* building, and it also printed a ballad, "Thus Will Be Proletarian Revolution," to accompany the paintings. See *Mexican Folkways* 5, no. 4 (October–December, 1929): 164–72.

56. In 1927 Modotti provided one of the more powerful examples of an image with ideological connotations when *Mexican Folkways* included her photograph of a hammer and sickle still life. Composed of a bandolier crossed with an ear of corn and sickle, the stark composition paired the revolutionary action of the bullets with the symbols of Mexico's traditional peasant worker. *Mexican Folkways* 3, no. 4 (August–September, 1927): 189.

57. Hooks, *Tina Modotti*, 238.

58. "ELLA GOLDBERG NO ES OTRA QUE LA ESPOSA DE BERTRAM WOLFE, EL COMUNISTA ROJO," *Excélsior*, 29 May 1927, 1, 4. Caps in original title. After arriving in Mexico in 1923, Bertram Wolfe, Ella's husband, was detained in Mexico during 1925 for his activities related to the Communist Party and left the country upon his release. Ella also left Mexico soon afterward. Hooks, *Tina Modotti: Photographer and Revolutionary*, 111.

59. As quoted in Glusker, *Avant-Garde Art and Artists*, vol. 1, 424. Diary entry dated Sunday, 29 May 1927.

60. Delpar, *The Enormous Vogue of Things Mexican*, 50–51.

61. "Se informa de las gestiones empleadas para saber que persona es el arrendataria del Apartado Postal Núm 1994 en esta ciudad," AGN, DGIPS, caja 254, exp. 12, 22 October 1925.

62. Hooks, *Tina Modotti: Photographer and Revolutionary*, 131. According to Hooks, Modotti moved to the building in late 1926.

63. For accounts of the group's get-togethers, see Anita Brenner's diaries in Glusker, *Avant-Garde Art and Artists*.

64. Glusker, *Avant-Garde Art and Artists*, vol. 1, 334. Diary entry dated Wednesday, 16 March 1927. Although Brenner attended parties and worked with Toor, she still professed that the writer "irritate[d] her often." Glusker, *Avant-Garde Art and Artists*, vol. 1, 129. Diary entry dated Friday, 9 April 1926.

65. Modotti to Freeman, HIA, JF, box 30, folder 36, 4 November 1929.

66. Robinson, *A Wall to Paint On*, 84–85; "Mexico: First Week (1929)," HIA, JF, box 71, folder 12, dated 1935.

67. Mirkin, "Aurora Reyes's 'Ataque a la Maestra Rural,' "19.

68. Herrera, *Frida*, 94.

69. Ibid., 80.

70. Ibid.

71. Modotti to Kahlo, ©Archivo Diego Rivera y Frida Kahlo, Banco de México, Fiduciario en el Fideicomiso relativo a los Museos Diego Rivera y Frida Kahlo,

ADRFK, Sección 1: Frida Kahlo, Serie 3: Correspondencia, Subserie 1: Amigos, Expediente 76, Modotti, Tina, Imagen 436. 7 June, no year.

72. Herrera, *Frida*, 94–95.

73. Siqueiros also stands to the far left of the panel, as does Vittorio Vidali in the far right.

74. Both Kahlo and Rivera would apply for readmittance to the Party in 1946. In 1948, the PCM approved Kahlo's application, but it would take until 1954 before the PCM once again accepted Rivera. Herrera, *Frida*, 341–42, 395–96.

75. Ibid., 101.

76. *Mexican Folkways* 5, no. 1 (January–March, 1929): 78.

77. Ibid., 66. Caps in original quotation.

78. See de los Reyes, "Últimas fotografías de Tina Modotti," 137–38.

79. Toor to Freeman, HIA, JF, box 38, folder 45, 29 November 1929.

80. Toor to Freeman, HIA, JF, box 38, folder 45, 7 June 1930.

81. Ibid.

82. Hooks, *Tina Modotti*, 213.

83. Ibid., 121–24.

84. Glusker, *Anita Brenner*, 98, 112. Brenner's continued research from 1934 to 1943 resulted in the publication of her book, *The Wind That Swept Mexico*, in 1943 by Harper's.

85. Glusker, *Anita Brenner*, 138, 150, 204. Brenner also made trips to Spain in 1933 and 1936 to cover the Spanish Civil War. Glusker, *Anita Brenner*, 10, 175.

86. Herrera, *Frida*, 116, 126–28, 131.

87. Kahlo to Eloesser, *Querido Doctorcito*, 98, dated 26 November 1931.

88. "Letters to Clifford and Jean Wight," Frida Kahlo, *Frida by Frida*, 128–29.

89. Toor to Kahlo, HIA, BW, box 114, folder 8, 16 December 1930. Just as Toor voiced her frustration with Rivera's seeming possessiveness concerning Kahlo, she often declared her irritation with Rivera and his procrastination in delivering promised work for *Mexican Folkways*. Western Union telegram from Frances Toor to Diego Rivera, HIA, BW, box 115, folder 3, 22 November 1930.

90. Volume 7 included a healthy four numbers that spanned the complete year. For the editions, Toor called upon the work of her longtime colleagues, including Concha Michel, Carleton Beals, Robert Redfield, Manuel Álvarez Bravo, Rufino Tamayo, Leopoldo Méndez, and others. Although lacking Rivera's articles, Number 1 still included several photographs and close-up details of his murals in the National Palace. Additional pieces also covered the typical topics, including studies of rural toys and games, plays and music, the lotería, archeological discoveries, and rituals, but also analyses of the art of Rivera, Tamayo, María Izquierdo, and Carlos Mérida.

91. Toor also wrote to Rivera during the previous March that she also had experienced two attacks of "colecistitis," or inflammation of the gallbladder. Toor to Rivera, HIA, BW, box 115, folder 1, 21 March 1931.

92. Toor to Freeman, HIA, JF, box 38, folder 45, 4 December 1931.

93. Toor to Freeman, HIA, JF, box 38, folder 45, 9 March 1933.

94. Stein, *Siqueiros*, 71.

95. Toor to Kahlo, ADRFK, Sección 1: Frida Kahlo, Serie 3: Correspondencia, Subserie 1: Amigos, exp. 112 Toor, Frances (Paca), imagen 157–58, 26 January 1932. To provide them with a chance to evaluate the show and "laugh at their enemies," the very next day Toor sent Rivera and Kahlo a catalog of Siqueiros's art show. Ibid., imagen 159, 27 January 1932.

96. For example, Toor supported Rivera, Orozco had Alma Reed, and Brenner followed Siqueiros. Ibid., imagen 159, 27 January 1932.

97. Anita Brenner, "Siqueiros Is the Aesthetic Revelation of the Greatest Importance in the Artistic Movement of Mexico," GRI, DAS, box 3, folder 17, 15 February 1932.

98. Glusker, *Anita Brenner*, 154–55, 161–62.

99. Ibid., 52–53.

100. Hooks, *Tina Modotti*, 238; Glusker, *Anita Brenner*, 161.

101. Hooks, *Tina Modotti*, 238.

102. Glusker, *Anita Brenner*, 205–6.

103. "ASUNTO: Informa arribo a esta Capital de la señorita A. Bremenn" [*sic*], AGN, DGIPS, caja 78, exp. 9, 1 July 1938.

104. Although the undercover agents' accounts of Brenner's activities attempted to undermine her credibility, they proved to be even harsher when discussing the other woman known as "Güera." Writing that Güera came from Mexico, Clavé noted that she used her "personal attractiveness" to "conquer" a few of the presidential aides and to seduce other high-level officials. During Cárdenas's stay in San Luis, she even appeared on the scene, flirting with the presidential aides until her suspected activities forced the president, officials, and their close friends to move from their hotel. "José Clavé: Su expediente como Inspector de esta Oficina," AGN, DGIPS, caja 81, exp. 3, 1 July 1938.

105. Letter to Carlos Chávez, AGN, CC, Sección Correspondencia, vol. 5, caja 2, exp. 82, 28 September 1941.

106. Miller and Brenner, "An Interview with Anita Brenner," 115, 117.

107. Mirkin, "Aurora Reyes's 'Ataque a la Maestra Rural,'" 19.

108. López Moreno and Ocharán, *Aurora Reyes*, 64.

109. Marrufo Huchim, "El arquetipo de la Gran Madre en *Espiral en retorno* de Aurora Reyes," 13.

110. Geis, "The Struggles of Modernizing Mexico and the Mural of Aurora Reyes at the Centro Escolar Revolución," 159.

111. Marion and Grace Greenwood also painted murals before Reyes, but they came from the United States. Oles, "Painting in the Shadow of the Big Three," 79–89.

112. Mirkin, "Aurora Reyes's 'Ataque a la Maestra Rural,'" 19. For more on Reyes's life as a young woman, see "Aurora Reyes, feminista y pionera del PCM, pasó su infancia entre tarántulas y animales del desierto," *unomásuno*, 1st part, 29 December 1985, 20.

113. Mirkin, "Aurora Reyes's 'Ataque a la Maestra Rural,'" 20.

114. López Moreno and Ocharán, *Aurora Reyes*, 63, 76–77.

115. Mirkin, "Aurora Reyes's 'Ataque a la Maestra Rural,'" 22.

116. López Moreno and Ocharán, *Aurora Reyes*, 63.

117. Ibid., 77.

118. Mirkin, "Aurora Reyes's 'Ataque a la Maestra Rural,'" 20.

119. The endorsement took place during the Seventh Congress. Dimitrov, *Against Fascism and War*, 92–93.

120. Olcott, *Revolutionary Women in Postrevolutionary Mexico*, 109–10.

121. See chapter 2 for more information. *Tesis sobre el Trabajo Femenil del Partido Comunista*, 14; Olcott, "The Center Cannot Hold," 223–40.

122. Chapa, *El derecho de voto para la mujer*, 28 June 1938. No publisher listed. Pamphlet located in CEMOS, Caja de mujeres. Olcott, *Revolutionary Women in Postrevolutionary Mexico*, 163–64.

123. Tuñón Pablos, *Mujeres que se organizan*, 118.

124. "Consuelo Uranga: Instructivo para el trabajo femenil que servirá de orientación a los organizadores del Partido que salgan a los estados, México," CEMOS, PCM, caja 10, folder 1, La comisión dictaminadora, 12 January 1938.

125. Ibid. For more, see chapter 2.

126. The conference was held from 16 February to 18 February.

127. Olcott, *Revolutionary Women in Postrevolutionary Mexico*, 180–83.

128. "Rinden informe acerca de la Conferencia Especial de Mujeres, verificada en el Teatro Hidalgo y temas que se trataron durante este acto," AGN, DGIPS, caja 30, exp. 29, 17 February 1938.

129. Ibid.

130. Michel ultimately left the Party in 1934. Olcott, "'Take Off That Streetwalker's Dress,'" 48.

131. "Rinden informe acerca de la Conferencia Especial de Mujeres, verificada en el Teatro Hidalgo y temas que se trataron durante este acto," AGN, DGIPS, caja 30, exp. 29, 17 February 1938.

132. "Relación de mujeres delegadas asistentes al VII Congreso del Partido Comunista de México celebrado en la segunda quincena del mes de enero de 1930," AGN, DGIPS caja 20, exp. 1.

133. VII Congreso Nacional del Partido Comunista, México, 1939, HIA, CNPC, 1 vol. Talk dated 31 January 1939. During the Congress, comrades elected twenty-four members, plus the secretary general and two other secretaries, to the Central Committee; Consuelo Uranga, appeared among this group. "Lista de miembros del Comité Central del Partido Comunista de México elegidos en el VII Congreso de enero de 1939," AGN, DGIPS caja 20, exp. 1.

134. Dra. Esther Chapa, "LA MUJER MEXICANA EN LA DEFENSA DE LA PATRIA," *La Voz de México*, 15 September 1942, 8. Caps in original title.

135. Adelina Zendejas Gómez, "La mujer y la Revolución," *La Voz de México*, 22 November 1942, 11.

136. The name change occurred in late 1945. Miller, *Latin American Women and the Search for Social Justice*, 117. In 1942, the FUPDM became the *Comité Coordinador de Mujeres para la Defensa de la Patria*, or the Coordinating Committee of Women in Defense of the Fatherland.

137. Almaguer, *Por un Partido de 50,000 Miembros*, 16–17. Located in HIA, REM, box 17, folder 10.

138. "El Bloque Nacional de Mujeres Revolucionarias de México," Circular in *El Popular*, 7 March 1949. Located in AGN, DGIPS, caja 21, exp. 1.

139. Almaguer, *Por un Partido de 50,000 Miembros*, 16–17.

140. Encina, *Unidad Democrática Antiimperialista por la soberanía de México*, 60. Located in HIA, REM, box 17, folder 10.

141. "HAGAMOS UN PARTIDO DE MASA: Reclutemos más mujeres," *Mujeres: Boletín Quincenal de la Comisión Femenil del C. del D. F. del P.C.M.*, 15 January 1949, 1–2. Located in AGN, DGIPS, caja 21, exp. 1. Caps in original title. And even though the Party often found itself at odds with government officials, the PCM also reminded its members that it complied precisely with the Ley Federal del Trabajo, or the federal labor law, with its codes directed at women. Regulations covered hygienic conditions in workplaces where women labored, social security, factory dining rooms, children centers, and other areas. Ibid., 3.

142. "Expulsados del Partido Comunista de México," *La Voz de México*, 1 June 1940, page unknown. Located in AGN, DGIPS, caja 20, exp. 1.

143. Olcott, " 'Take Off That Streetwalker's Dress,' " 48.

144. Tuñón Pablos, *Mujeres que se organizan*, 118–19.

145. Reyes to Kahlo, ©Archivo Diego Rivera y Frida Kahlo, Banco de México, Fiduciario en el Fideicomiso relativo a los Museos Diego Rivera y Frida Kahlo, ADRFK, Sección 1: Frida Kahlo, Serie 3: Correspondencia, Subserie 1: Amigos, Expediente 96, Reyes, Aurora, Imagen 26793, 24 December 1946. Reyes even painted a painting of her friend titled, "Retrato de Frida Frente al Espejo," which portrayed a thin Kahlo, without clothing from the front, boldly confronting her naked image in a mirror. For an image of the painting, see López Moreno and Ocharán, *Aurora Reyes*, 108. Reyes painted her Kahlo image in oil in 1953.

146. Mirkin, "Aurora Reyes's 'Ataque a la Maestra Rural,' " 23.

147. A catalog, including Breton's preface, of Kahlo's show at the Julien Levy Gallery can be found in the PCBK, AD, Section Réserve, box-RLPF 8880. The gallery exhibited twenty-five of her paintings, and, according to Kahlo, she sold twelve. "Kahlo to Chávez," Kahlo, *The Letters of Frida Kahlo*, 105. Dated 1939.

148. Herrera, *Frida*, 241–42.

149. "Kahlo to Nickolas Muray," Kahlo, *Frida by Frida*, 197–201, 16 February 1939 and 27 February 1939.

150. Ibid., 198, 16 February 1939.

151. The exhibition catalog, titled *Mexique: Exposition organisée par André Breton*, is located in the PCBK, AD, Frida Kahlo Dossier, Section-Réserve, box-AP KAHL. Once again Breton wrote the descriptions of the art for the catalog.

152. Ibid. "Kahlo to Nickolas Muray," Kahlo, *Frida by Frida*, 198, 16 February 1939.

153. "Invitation from Frida Kahlo to her Individual Exhibition in the Galería de Arte Contemporáneo on April 13, 1953," Kahlo, *Frida by Frida*, 378–79.

154. Herrera, *Frida*, 341–42, 395–96.

155. From Kahlo's conversation with Rosa Castro, as cited in Herrera, *Frida*, 396.

156. Carrasco (Secretario de Organización) to Kahlo, ©Archivo Diego Rivera y Frida Kahlo, Banco de México, Fiduciario en el Fideicomiso relativo a los Museos Diego

Rivera y Frida Kahlo, ADRFK, Sección 1: Frida Kahlo, Serie 3: Correspondencia, Subserie 7: Instituciones, Expediente 10, Partido Comunista de México, Imagen 4625, no date.

157. Recibo, ADRFK, Sección 1: Frida Kahlo, Serie 3: Correspondencia, Subserie 7: Instituciones, Expediente 10, Partido Comunista de México, Imagen 4627, 15 June 1950.

158. Herrera, *Frida*, 342.

159. Ibid., 396.

160. "Kahlo to Bertram and Ella Wolfe," Kahlo, *The Letters of Frida Kahlo*, 117–18. Dated 1944.

161. "Kahlo to Boytlers," Tibol, *Frida Kahlo*, 78.

162. Encina to Kahlo, ©Archivo Diego Rivera y Frida Kahlo, Banco de México, Fiduciario en el Fideicomiso relativo a los Museos Diego Rivera y Frida Kahlo, ADRFK, Sección 1: Frida Kahlo, Serie 3: Correspondencia, Subserie 7: Instituciones, Expediente 10, Partido Comunista de México, Imagen 4632, 7 July 1954.

163. Herrera states the student was Arturo García Bustos. Herrera, *Frida*, 435.

164. "Ha muerto Frida. Ha muerto Frida Kahlo," HIA, BW, box 117, folder 27, 27 July 1954.

165. Herrera, *Frida*, 435–36.

166. Ibid., 436–37.

167. Typed talk by Iduarte, HIA, BW, box 117, folder 27, 14 July 1954.

168. Herrera, *Frida*, 436–37.

169. *Excélsior* editorial cited in "Rites for Rivera's Wife Cost Art Head His Job," *New York Times*, 17 July 1954, 3.

170. Statement by Professor Andrés Iduarte about the burial of Frida Kahlo de Rivera, HIA, BW, box 117, folder 27, 27 July 1954.

171. Ibid.

172. In addition to *Mexican Folkways*, her publications included *Frances Toor's Guide to Mexico* (1934), *Mexican Popular Arts* (1939), *Frances Toor's New Guide to Mexico* (1944), *A Treasury of Mexican Folkways* (1947), *Three Worlds of Peru* (1949), *Festivals and Folkways of Italy* (1953), *The Golden Carnation, and Other Stories Told in Italy* (1960), among other works.

173. "Mexico Honors Miss Toor," *Los Angeles Times*, 13 June 1948, C6. Brenner was also awarded the same honor, although she refused to accept it on the grounds that she was not a foreigner. Glusker, *Anita Brenner*, 17.

174. Highlighting her work throughout Mexico, and her incessant desire to learn more about the art of Mexico's indigenous groups, the *New York Times*'s obituary categorized Toor as "a leading ambassador to the rest of the world for Mexican crafts, arts and culture." "Frances Toor, 66, 'Wrote on Mexico,'" *New York Times*, 18 June 1956, 25. The *Los Angeles Times* also emphasized Toor's key role in promoting Mexico's artists and offering them their first publication opportunity in *Mexican Folkways*. According to the obituary in the *Los Angeles Times*, Toor even sold Rufino Tamayo's and Siqueiros's first paintings, and promoted Rivera in the United States. "Frances Toor's Funeral Rites Will Be Today," *Los Angeles Times*, 5 August 1956, B26.

175. Diego Rivera, "(Paquita Torre) nuestra amiga yankee, como Thoreau," in *Textos de Arte*, Tomo 1, 421–22; first published as Diego Rivera, "Francis Toor," México en la cultura: Suplemento cultural de *Novedades*, 22 July 1956, 1.

176. The strict regulations required Brenner to register within thirty days of entering the country and to devote her work to journalism and writing her popular history of Mexico. Tarjeta Forma 5, No. 159565 a favor de la Sra. Anita Brenner Glusker, de nacionalidad Norteamericana, AGN, GSM, Series Estadounidenses, caja 19, exp. 156, 16 May 1944.

177. Ibid., 19 September 1945; 12 April 1946; 8 July 1947.

178. "Anita Brenner, Wrote on Mexico," *New York Times*, 3 December 1974, 44.

179. Miller and Brenner, "An Interview with Anita Brenner," 117.

180. Ibid., 117–18. Also see Glusker, *Anita Brenner*, 217–23.

181. "Anita Brenner, Wrote on Mexico," *New York Times*, 3 December 1974, 44.

Chapter Five

1. Azuela, "*El Machete* and *Frente a Frente*," 87.

2. TGP artists also came together in a roundtable organized by the art historian, Raquel Tibol, to celebrate the twenty years of their existence. Throughout their talks, the artists discussed their early involvement in LEAR, followed by their 1937 transition into the TGP. "Twenty Years of the Taller de Gráfica Popular." Round Table Organized by Raquel Tibol, *artes de méxico*, 5–6. The TGP also commemorated twenty years of artistic production through workshops and exhibitions, including one organized by the *Instituto Nacional de Bellas Artes* (National Institute of Fine Arts), which opened on 19 November. "Letter to Sr. Carlos Rojas Juanco," TGP, reel 13, box 3, folder 14, 9 November 1957.

3. "TRASCENDENCIA HISTÓRICA DEL TALLER DE GRÁFICA POPULAR," TGP, reel 13, box 3, folder 9, 1957. Caps in original title.

4. "RECORDACIÓN EN HOMENAJE AL T. D. G. P. [*sic*] DE MÉXICO," ibid., 27 July 1957. Caps in original title.

5. Letter from the Graphic Art Group of the Union of Chinese Artists, Peking, China, ibid., no date.

6. Letter addressed to Sr. Leopoldo Méndez, ibid., 2 November 1957.

7. The later group highlighted the TGP's use of realistic art to express "the ideas of humanism." Letter to the Taller de Gráfica Popular, Mexico, 12 September 1957; "A los artistas del Taller de Grafica [*sic*] Popular," ibid., 1957.

8. Visiting artists paid a ten-peso fee each year they remained in the TGP, and in return, they received technical help, could participate in TGP group exhibitions, and could sell their work through the TGP. "ESTATUTOS DEL TALLER DE GRÁFICA POPULAR," TGP, reel 12, box 3, folder 1, January 1956. Caps in original title.

9. Craven, *Art and Revolution in Latin America*, 71.

10. Azuela, "*El Machete* and *Frente a Frente*," 85; Caplow, *Leopoldo Méndez*, 93. Azuela argues that LEAR formed in early 1934, while Caplow places the date in 1933. Moreover, April 1934 is the date given in the *Declaración de Principios y Estatutos de la Liga de Escritores y Artistas Revoluciomarios* [*sic*], *LEAR*, 3. The pamphlet, dated 20

June 1936, can be found in CEMOS, caja Liga de Escritores y Artistas Revolucionarios, 1936–1937, folder 8.

11. Azuela, "*El Machete* and *Frente a Frente*," 87; Caplow, *Leopoldo Méndez*, 93.

12. Caplow, "Leopoldo Méndez, A Revolutionary Spirit in Art," 30; Vogel, *Becoming Pablo O'Higgins*, 109; Rankin, *¡Mexico, la patria!*, 23–24.

13. Reyes Palma, "La LEAR y su revista de frente cultural," 5.

14. Reyes Palma, *Leopoldo Méndez: El oficio de grabar*, 15; Caplow, *Leopoldo Méndez*, 70–73. Méndez remained in the Party until 1946. Caplow, *Leopoldo Méndez*, 156.

15. Vogel, *Becoming Pablo O'Higgins*, 64, 69.

16. Ibid., 133–34; Stein, *Siqueiros*, 106, 121; Patenaude, *Trotsky*, 259–60. Siqueiros was married to Angélica Arenal, who also was a PCM member.

17. Reyes Palma, "La LEAR y su revista de frente cultural," 5. Many of LEAR's original members belonged to the much earlier Union of Technical Workers, Painters, and Sculptors, or SOTPE. Caplow, *Leopoldo Méndez*, 95.

18. "Principios Declarativos de la Lucha Intelectual Proletaria (LIP)," *Llamada, periódico de pared* (Mexico City), October 1931. Found online at the Documents of 20th-century Latin American and Latino Art: A Digital Archive and Publications Project at the Museum of Fine Arts, Houston, Registration ICAA: 822380, accessed 26 January 2015.

19. Reyes Palma, "La LEAR y su revista de frente cultural," 5.

20. *Declaración de Principios y Estatutos de la Liga de Escritores y Artistas Revoluciomarios* [*sic*], *LEAR*, 3–5.

21. As an essential requirement for being an active LEAR member, the principles also obliged all participants to recognize and promote the class struggle through a vigorous and broad intellectual campaign dedicated to workers and campesinos. "Síntesis De Los Principios Declarativos De La LEAR," *Frente a Frente*, November 1934, no. 1, 3. Edición facsimilar.

22. *Declaración de Principios y Estatutos de la Liga de Escritores y Artistas Revoluciomarios* [*sic*], *LEAR*, 7.

23. Ibid., 7–11.

24. Reyes Palma, *Leopoldo Méndez*, 15. The PCM continued to publish sporadic editions of *El Machete Ilegal* with difficulty.

25. Report on the LEAR Congress, HIA, JF, box 174, folder 2, read before the American Artists Congress, 22 March 1937.

26. Beloff, *Memorias*, 86–87; Caplow, *Leopoldo Méndez*, 93–94.

27. Reyes Palma, "La LEAR y su revista de frente cultural," 5–6.

28. "Comité Ejecutivo de la Liga de Escritores y Artistas Revolucionarios (LEAR) to Joseph Freeman, National Secretary of the John Reed Club (JRC)," 22 January 1935. Found online at the Documents of 20th-century Latin American and Latino Art: A Digital Archive and Publications Project at the Museum of Fine Arts, Houston, Registration ICAA: 800989, accessed 1 February 2015.

29. Caplow, *Leopoldo Méndez*, 121.

30. List is dated from 11 February 1937. Other visual artists, photographers, architects, and sculptors listed in the LEAR roster were José Chávez Morado, Olga Costa, Raúl Anguiano, Julio Castellanos, Isabel Villaseñor, Frances Zalce, Kilagawa (listed

as a single name), Feliciano Peña, Jorge Enciso, Manuel Echauri, Francisco Gutiérrez, Roberto Reyes Pérez, Federico Cantú, Celia Calderón, Santos Balmori, Rosendo Soto, Jesús Guerrero Galván, Jaime Colson, Carlos Orozco Romero, Jesús Bracho, Abelardo Ávila, Roberto Guardia Berdecio, Enrique Godiener, Armando García Franqui [*sic*], Manuel Piña, Franco (indio Soma), Pedro Rendón, Francisco Dosamantes, Ernesto Cortés Juárez, Jesús Escobedo, Ramón Alva de la Canal, Gabriel Fernández Ledesma, Francisco Díaz de León, Isidoro Ocampo, Gonzalo de la Paz Pérez, Julio Prieto, Everardo Ramírez, Ramón Arroyo, Enrique Gutmann, Gabriel Figueroa, Emilio Amero, Agustín Lazo, Raúl Cacho, Carlos Leduc, Germán Cueto, Esperanza Hoffman, Dolores Cueto, Luis Ortiz Monasterio, Federico Canesi, Juan Olaguíbel, Tomás Chávez Morado, and Oliverio Martínez. "Nomina de los integrantes de la Liga de Escritores y Artitas [*sic*] Revolucionarios (LEAR), durante su mayor apogeo: 1937," CEMOS, Caja Liga de Escritores y Artistas Revolucionarios, 1936–1937, folder 8. Also see Cortés Zavala, "La Liga de Escritores y Artistas Revolucionarios durante Cardenismo," 118–20. Cortés Zavala also mentions the artists Jorge Overa, Roberto Lago, Mariano Paredes, Elena Huerta, Francisco Mora Francis, Ramón Sosa Montes, Martín Fulier, Adolfo Mexiac, Valderrama, Carlos Leduc, and Enrique Goodman.

31. Ibid.

32. "Comité Ejecutivo de la Liga de Escritores y Artistas Revolucionarios (LEAR) to Joseph Freeman, National Secretary of the John Reed Club (JRC)," 22 January 1935. Found online at the Documents of 20th-century Latin American and Latino Art: A Digital Archive and Publications Project at the Museum of Fine Arts, Houston, Registration ICAA: 800989, accessed 1 February 2015.

33. Ibid.

34. "Secretario del Comité Ejecutivo de la Liga de Escritores y Artistas Revolucionarios (LEAR) to New Masses Magazine, México D.F.," 6 June 1935. Found online at the Documents of 20th-century Latin American and Latino Art: A Digital Archive and Publications Project at the Museum of Fine Arts, Houston, Registration ICAA: 801041, accessed 1 February 2015.

35. Azuela, "*El Machete* and *Frente a Frente*," 86.

36. "Editorial," *Frente a Frente*, November 1934, no. 1, 5. Edición facsimilar.

37. Reyes Palma, "La LEAR y su revista de frente cultural," *Frente a Frente*, 5–6.

38. Caplow, *Leopoldo Méndez*, 263, n. 3; Pereira, *Diccionario de literatura mexicana: Siglo XX*, 194–95.

39. The second phase began with the March 1934 issue. Reyes Palma, "La LEAR y su revista de frente cultural," *Frente a Frente*, 5–6, 10; Caplow, *Leopoldo Méndez*, 102.

40. Javier Durán discusses three major themes throughout *Frente a Frente*'s existence: (1) to promote international socialism and in this respect to criticize Trotsky's arrival in Mexico; (2) to provide educational information to the working classes; (3) and beginning in March 1936, to promote antifascism. Durán, "México, la Guerra Civil española y el cardenismo," 108–10.

41. Although Trotsky moved to Mexico City in January 1937, the criticism directed at the Russian within the pages of *Frente a Frente* began much earlier.

42. David Alfaro Siqueiros, "Diego Rivera, pintor de cámara del gobierno de México," *Frente a Frente*, May 1935, no. 3, 8. Edición facsimilar.

43. Eisenberg, "Battle of the Century," 18.

44. Azuela, "*El Machete* and *Frente a Frente*," 85–86. Mexico would not reestablish relations with the Soviet Union until the mid-1940s. Carr, *Marxism and Communism in Twentieth-Century Mexico*, 45.

45. Caplow, *Leopoldo Méndez*, 94; Azuela, "*El Machete* and *Frente a Frente*," 86.

46. As quoted in Caplow, *Leopoldo Méndez*, 102; Durán, "México, la Guerra Civil española y el cardenismo," 110.

47. Letter from the Sindicato Revolucionario de Obreros y Obreras de la Fábrica de Jauja, AGN, LCR, caja 1289, exp. 704/15, 8 March 1935.

48. "A TODAS LAS ORGANIZACIONES . . . ," CA, Fond 495, Opis' 108, reel 24, file 182, 22 February 1935. Caps in original title.

49. Carr, *Marxism and Communism*, 46–47.

50. Letter signed "M S/." to Al Ciudadano, Presidente de la República, AGN, LCR, caja 1289, exp. 704/15, 1 April 1935.

51. Letter with several signatures to Precidente [*sic*] de la República, ibid., dated 25 March 1935.

52. Letter from Socorro Rojo Internasional [*sic*] to S. Gral. Lazaro [*sic*] Cardenas [*sic*], ibid., dated 18 March 1935; Letter from Felipe Percasteguí to Presidente de la República, ibid., 14 March 1935. The last letter originated from San Juan Tepa, Hidalgo.

53. Letter from *El Machete* to C. Presidente de la Republica [*sic*], ibid., 10 March 1935.

54. McClean, "Committed to Print," 28.

55. Charmion von Wiegand, "Building the Popular Front in Mexico," HIA, JF, box 174, folder 2, 9 April 1937.

56. The following November, sixteen members again set out for Guadalajara, where they held meetings, gave lectures, and presented a variety of arts. Report on the LEAR Congress, HIA, JF, box 174, folder 2, read before the American Artists Congress, 22 March 1937.

57. "Exposiciones de la LEAR Llamamiento a los Pintores, Dibujantes, Grabadores y Escultores," *Frente a Frente*, November 1934, no. 1, 7. Edición facsimilar.

58. "Editorial," *Frente a Frente*, November 1934, no. 1, 5. Edición facsimilar.

59. Reyes Palma, "La LEAR y su revista de frente cultural," *Frente a Frente*, 14. Reyes Palma provides an excellent discussion of the complex issues surrounding LEAR's first art show. Ibid., 12–14. Also see "Arte y revolución: Una polémica en la LEAR," *Memoria: Revista del Centro de Estudios del Movimiento de Obreros Socialistas* (CEMOS, Mexico City), no. 38 (January 1992): 40. Found online at the Documents of 20th-century Latin American and Latino Art: A Digital Archive and Publications Project at the Museum of Fine Arts, Houston, Registration ICAA: 779783, accessed 21 February 2015.

60. Chano Urueta, "La trascendental exposición de la LEAR," *Todo: Semanario enciclopédico* 3, no. 142 (May 1936), n.p. Found online at the Documents of 20th-century Latin American and Latino Art: A Digital Archive and Publications Project at the Museum of Fine Arts, Houston, Registration ICAA: 770220, accessed 1 February 2015.

61. Even more damning, Cardoza y Aragón wrote that LEAR often had been considered "as the only organization created in Mexico against Art." Luis Cardoza y

Aragón, "Exposición de pintura organizada por la LEAR: Divagaciones y pretextos," *El Machete*, 23 May 1936, 3–4. Found online at the Documents of 20th-century Latin American and Latino Art: A Digital Archive and Publications Project at the Museum of Fine Arts, Houston, Registration ICAA: 779286, accessed 7 February 2015.

62. Juan de la Cabada, "Las sugestiones de Cardoza," *El Machete*, 30 May 1936, 3–4. Found online at the Documents of 20th-century Latin American and Latino Art: A Digital Archive and Publications Project at the Museum of Fine Arts, Houston, Registration ICAA: 779292, accessed 7 February 2015.

63. "Exposiciones," *Frente a Frente*, January 1937, no. 7, 7. Edición facsimilar.

64. Urueta, "La trascendental exposición de la LEAR," Registration ICAA: 770220, accessed 1 February 2015.

65. "La exposición de artes plásticas de la LEAR," *Frente a Frente*, July 1936, no. 4, 21. The LEAR exhibit ran from 24 July to 7 August 1936.

66. Julio de la Fuente, "Insistimos en nuestro programa de reivindicaciones en el arte," *Frente a Frente*, August 1936, no. 5, 18–19. Edición facsimilar.

67. Caplow, *Leopoldo Méndez*, 104, 110, 116–17.

68. Dimitrov, *Against Fascism and War*, 92–93; Olcott, *Revolutionary Women in Post-revolutionary Mexico*, 109–10.

69. "CIRCULAR G. NO. 82," 6 September 1935, CA, Fond 495, Opis' 108, reel 24, file 182.

70. See *Frente a Frente*, May 1936, no. 3.

71. Esther Merrill, "Las Tres K: Kínder, los niños; kirche, la iglesia; kiiche [*sic*]; la cocina. La situación de la mujer en la alemania de hoy," *Frente a Frente*, May 1936, no. 3, 10.

72. Caplow, *Leopoldo Méndez*, 120. The American Artists' Congress was founded in 1936.

73. Charmion von Wiegand, "Building the Popular Front in Mexico," HIA, JF, box 174, folder 2, 9 April 1937.

74. "RESUMEN del CONGRESO," *Frente a Frente*, March 1937, no. 8, 22. Edición facsimilar.

75. Charmion von Wiegand, "Building the Popular Front in Mexico," HIA, JF, box 174, folder 2, 9 April 1937.

76. Letter to Sr. Gral. Lázaro Cárdenas, AGN, LCR, caja 456, exp. 433/145, dated 2 January 1937.

77. Charmion von Wiegand, "Building the Popular Front in Mexico," HIA, JF, box 174, folder 2, 9 April 1937.

78. Ibid.

79. Report on the LEAR Congress, HIA, JF, box 174, folder 2, read before the American Artists' Congress, 22 March 1937.

80. "RESUMEN del CONGRESO," *Frente a Frente*, March 1937, no. 8, 24. Edición facsimilar. Besides these five points, the artists also recommended that they request state funding for a number of projects, including the painting of murals in the country's capitals; the creation of a permanent and conveniently located gallery; the creation of a large-scale popular edition of monographs covering painting, drawing, printmaking, and photography, all with a clear message for the country's working

people; a fine arts workshop that would promote the development of Mexico's youth; and other suggestions.

81. "Address by Joe Jones to the Mexican Artists' and Writers' Congress, Opening Session, Mexico City, D.F. January 17th, 1937," HIA, JF, box 174, folder 2.

82. Ibid.

83. Charmion von Wiegand, "Building the Popular Front in Mexico," HIA, JF, box 174, folder 2, 9 April 1937.

84. Caplow, *Leopoldo Méndez*, 121.

85. Prignitz-Poda, *El Taller de Gráfica Popular en México*, 46.

86. Reyes Palma, "La LEAR y su revista de frente cultural," *Frente a Frente*, 14.

87. Correograma to C. Secretario de Educación Pública, AGN, LCR, caja 356, exp. 415.13/18, 7 July 1937.

88. "Informe de algunas cuestiones de Mejico [*sic*] tomadas del Nacional de los días 18 al 21 de julio." CA, Fond 495, Opis' 108, reel 24, file 192. In October 1937, José Pomar, acting as a representative of LEAR, traveled to the National Palace to request both "economic and moral support." Specifically, with the use of government funds, Pomar hoped to initiate a series of four concerts, including two orchestrated symphonies written by Mexican composers, created to "stimulate the working class in its daily struggles against all of its internal and external enemies." LEAR members planned to hold the musical activities in workplaces, unions, peasant organizations, nursing homes, and other gathering places. Although LEAR hoped to receive permission from the institutions' directors to charge a small price for the events, all profits would serve as seed money for future performances. Letter from the Palacio Nacional to C. Secretario de Educación Pública, AGN, LCR, caja 1065, exp. 568.3/47, 19 October 1937.

89. Azuela, "*El Machete* and *Frente a Frente*," 87. Azuela states that the members resigned from LEAR in 1938. Also see Caplow, *Leopoldo Méndez*, 121.

90. "Twenty Years of the Taller de Gráfica Popular," *artes de méxico*, 5–6.

91. Ibid., 6.

92. Poniatowska, "Los 60 años de Leopoldo Méndez," 11.

93. Caplow, *Leopoldo Méndez*, 123.

94. Meyer, "The Workshop for Popular Graphic Art in Mexico," vii. O'Higgins and Arenal had been members of LEAR's Plastic Arts Section, and Méndez was the section's director. Caplow, "El Libro Negro del Terror Nazi en Europa," 19.

95. "Twenty Years of the Taller de Gráfica Popular," *artes de méxico*, 6. Additionally, the "SÍNTESIS HISTÓRICA DEL TALLER DE GRÁFICA POPULAR" states, "Some have said that David Alfaro Siqueiros had some involvement but [this] has been denied by the founders." TGP, reel 12, box 3, folder 9, June 1957, 2. Caps in original title. According to the "SÍNTESIS HISTÓRICA DEL TALLER DE GRÁFICA POPULAR," the initial group consisted of: Leopoldo Méndez, Luis Arenal, Pablo O'Higgins, Alfredo Zalce, Ángel Bracho, Ignacio Aguirre, Raúl Anguiano, Gonzalo de la Paz Pérez, Everardo Ramírez, and Antonio Pujol. Ibid.

96. Caplow, *Leopoldo Méndez*, 123. Also see "Twenty Years of the Taller de Gráfica Popular," *artes de méxico*, 15. According to Méndez, Zalce, Chávez Morado, Castro Pacheco, among others, officially left the TGP but continued to work with the

printmaking workshop. "Twenty Years of the Taller de Gráfica Popular," *artes de méxico*, 6.

97. Craven, *Art and Revolution in Latin America*, 64.

98. "SÍNTESIS HISTÓRICA DEL TALLER DE GRÁFICA POPULAR," TGP, reel 12, box 3, folder 9, June 1957; "Twenty Years of the Taller de Gráfica Popular," *artes de méxico*, 4. Caps in original title. Only Mariana Yampolsky, Celia Calderón, Andrea Gómez, Sarah Jiménez, María Luisa Martín, and Fanny Rabel participated in the roundtable discussion organized by Raquel Tibol and reproduced in the *artes de méxico*.

99. Richards, "Imaging the Political," 213–14.

100. Caplow, "Mariana Yampolsky and the Taller de Gráfica Popular," 50.

101. Oles, *South of the Border*, 201; Herzog, *Elizabeth Catlett*, 56, 112–13.

102. For example, along with more recent arrivals, in 1957, many of the original male members remained, including Leopoldo Méndez, Pablo O'Higgins, Luis Arenal, Raúl Anguiano, Jesús Álvarez Amaya, Alberto Beltrán, Guillermo Bonilla, Ángel Bracho, Oscar Frías, Arturo García Bustos, Cutberto Galván, Lorenzo Guerrero, Javier Iñiguez, Marcelino Lorenzo Jiménez, Carlos Jurado, Francisco Luna, Adolfo Mexiac, Francisco Mora, Adolfo Quinteros, Amado Salazar, and Ramón Sosamontes. "SÍNTESIS HISTÓRICA DEL TALLER DE GRÁFICA POPULAR," TGP, reel 12, box 3, folder 9, June 1957. Caps in original title. From 1937 to the 1960s, more than three hundred artists worked with the TGP, although Craven notes that the TGP generally enjoyed about fifteen active members. Craven, *Art and Revolution in Latin America*, 64.

103. Of the men, only Alfredo Zalce never joined the PCM, and in fact he opposed any form of official alliance between the PCM and the TGP. Prignitz-Poda, *El Taller de Gráfica Popular en México*, 77; Caplow, *Leopoldo Méndez*, 145; Craven, *Art and Revolution in Latin America*, 68.

104. Caplow, *Leopoldo Méndez*, 125.

105. Tensions increased after the PCM expelled Méndez in 1946 during a purge of supposedly disloyal members. Caplow, *Leopoldo Méndez*, 156, 211–12.

106. The art collector Michael T. Ricker argues that "many of these [TGP] artists were artists first and Communists second." But he also continues that the "workshop's overriding interest was in the well-being of the Mexican people, and Communism was, in their eyes, the clearest path to their goal." Ricker, "A Collector's Notes on the Taller de Gráfica Popular," 9–10.

107. "Declaration of Principles of the People's Graphics Workshop (T.G.P.)," in Ades, *Art in Latin America*, 326.

108. Byant Foundation Brochure, CENIDIAP, FR, LM, caja 29, exp. 1852, Sección Taller de Gráfica Popular, Subsección Publicaciones, 1, dated 2 December 1947.

109. "Twenty Years of the Taller de Gráfica Popular," *artes de méxico*, 6.

110. Vogel, *Becoming Pablo O'Higgins*, 121.

111. Prignitz-Poda, *El Taller de Gráfica Popular en México*, 56.

112. "Twenty Years of the Taller de Gráfica Popular," *artes de méxico*, 6.

113. Meyer, "The Workshop for Popular Graphic Art in Mexico," in *TGP Mexico*, vii.

114. "Twenty Years of the Taller de Gráfica Popular," *artes de méxico*, 6.

115. Ibid.

116. Prignitz-Poda, *El Taller de Gráfica Popular en México*, 56; "Twenty Years of the Taller de Gráfica Popular," *artes de méxico*, 7.

117. "Twenty Years of the Taller de Gráfica Popular," *artes de méxico*, 9.

118. Richards, "Imaging the Political," 43–44.

119. "Twenty Years of the Taller de Gráfica Popular," *artes de méxico*, 9.

120. Additionally, many key members of the TGP, including Méndez, credited José Guadalupe Posada for providing their foundational inspiration on both an artistic and political front. For one, Posada firmly grounded his images in a Mexican tradition; he focused on Mexico's politics and culture, and his work reflected Mexico's history rather than a European past. Second, as the "best example of contemporary Mexican engraving," the TGP printmakers drew upon Posada's imaginings of the country and the human condition as motivation for their own work. And third, Posada's highly critical approach to the country's political problems offered a powerful model for the TGP to follow. Here, the TGP and Posada followed similar goals in that both sought out the popular masses as their audience rather than elite art collectors or the exhibition galleries. "Twenty Years of the Taller de Gráfica Popular," *artes de méxico*, 8.

121. "Twenty Years of the Taller de Gráfica Popular," *artes de méxico*, 11.

122. Ibid., 10.

123. Traditionally the Communist Party promoted similar techniques of self-criticism to promote reflection and fix errors. As members of the PCM, and utilizing similar methods as those found in the Party, TGP engravers would have been familiar with the group criticism process. "Twenty Years of the Taller de Gráfica Popular," *artes de méxico*, 9–10.

124. Byant Foundation Brochure, CENIDIAP, FR, LM, caja 29, exp. 1852, Sección Taller de Gráfica Popular, Subsección Publicaciones, 1, dated 2 December 1947; Caplow, *Leopoldo Méndez*, 127–29.

125. Byant Foundation Brochure, CENIDIAP, FR, LM, caja 29, exp. 1852, Sección Taller de Gráfica Popular, Subsección Publicaciones, 1, dated 2 December 1947.

126. The exhibition was titled "Twenty Centuries of Mexican Art." Richards, "Imaging the Political," 56.

127. "Estatutos del Taller de Gráfica Popular," CENIDIAP, FR, LM, caja 25, exp. 1462, Sección Taller de Gráfica Popular, Subsección Estatutos.

128. Ibid.

129. Ibid.

130. The other artists were Raúl Anguiano, Francisco Dosamantes, Isidoro Ocampo, Antonio Pujol, Alfredo Zalce, and Ignacio Aguirre.

131. Printed exhibition invitation, CENIDIAP, FR, LM, caja 28, exp. 1804, Sección Taller de Gráfica Popular, Subsección Exposiciones, 1–4; Prignitz-Poda, *El Taller de Gráfica Popular en México*, 67.

132. García Bustos, "El Taller de Gráfica Popular: A Personal History," 12–13.

133. Prignitz-Poda, *El Taller de Gráfica Popular en México*, 69–70.

134. Caplow, *Leopoldo Méndez*, 157, 211–12; Prignitz-Poda, *El Taller de Gráfica Popular en México*, 92.

135. Prignitz-Poda, *El Taller de Gráfica Popular en México*, 95–96.

136. Caplow, "El Libro Negro del Terror Nazi en Europa," 19. Beth Merfish notes that in 1939 there were approximately seven thousand German citizens in Mexico. Merfish, "Stars in Complex Constellations," 66.

137. Merfish, "Stars in Complex Constellations," 65–66.

138. "Comentarios sobre LAS INVESTIGACIONES DE LA POLICÍA DEL DISTRITO FEDERAL, EN RELACIÓN CON ACTIVIDADES NAZIS," AGN, IPS, caja 83, exp. 7, 4 November 1940. Caps in original title.

139. Even worse, the DGIPS agents complained that the Mexico City police failed to adequately carry out their jobs. Agent Number 10 criticized just this point when he argued that the "[Mexico City police] reports often repeat data that are of public knowledge, they investigate details that this Office knows very well, and follow inconsequential leads without the slightest idea of the organization and the Nazi people." Although he continued that his office had better knowledge and valuable links to the German community in Mexico, his department lacked the necessary staff to investigate the Nazi threat within the country. The agent ended his report with a plea for either a greater number of agents for his department, or a top commander responsible for anti-Nazi activities of the police, but "under no circumstance should the two parallel services continue." "Comentarios sobre LAS INVESTIGACIONES DE LA POLICÍA DEL DISTRITO FEDERAL, EN RELACIÓN CON ACTIVIDADES NAZIS," AGN, IPS, caja 83, exp. 7, 4 November 1940. Caps in original title.

140. Prignitz-Poda, *El Taller de Gráfica Popular en México*, 74–78; Richards, "Imaging the Political," 60–61.

141. Richards, "Imaging the Political," 74–75; Prignitz-Poda, *El Taller de Gráfica Popular en México*, 83.

142. "Twenty Years of the Taller de Gráfica Popular," *artes de méxico*, 6; Caplow, *Leopoldo Méndez*, 159.

143. Merfish, "Stars in Complex Constellations," 119–20.

144. Traditionally, individual artists donated to the preservation of the collective group by dedicating one-third of the profits from the sale of their personal work, by donating 20 percent of the earnings derived from any contract between the TGP and other organizations, and even through their personal gifts. Byant Foundation Brochure, CENIDIAP, FR, LM, caja 29, exp. 1852, Sección Taller de Gráfica Popular, Subsección Publicaciones, 3, dated 2 December 1947; "Twenty Years of the Taller de Gráfica Popular," *artes de méxico*, 6.

145. "Twenty Years of the Taller de Gráfica Popular," *artes de méxico*, 6.

146. Prignitz-Poda, *El Taller de Gráfica Popular en México*, 84–85.

147. Ibid., 86–87; Caplow, *Leopoldo Méndez*, 177.

148. *El libro negro del terror nazi en Europa*, title page; Caplow, "El Libro Negro del Terror Nazi en Europa," 21. Caplow explains that the number of illustrations increases to ninety-five with the inclusion of the smaller images. As Merfish notes in her dissertation, these smaller illustrations originated from previously published sources. Merfish, "Stars in Complex Constellations," 166.

149. Caplow, "El Libro Negro del Terror Nazi en Europa," 21; Richards, "Imaging the Political," 74–75; Prignitz-Poda, *El Taller de Gráfica Popular en México*, 83.

150. Caplow, "El Libro Negro del Terror Nazi en Europa," 19.

151. *El libro negro del terror nazi en Europa*, inside pages; Pérez Montfort, "Apuntes sobre el exilio alemán en México," 53.

152. The TGP joined the Bonestell Gallery in 1940. Richards, "Imaging the Political," 102.

153. Letter to "Ignacio" of the TGP from Edwin L Mayer, TGP, reel 1, box 1, folder 17, 14 November 1943.

154. Prignitz-Poda, *El Taller de Gráfica Popular en México*, 103.

155. Theresa Avila argues in her dissertation that the TGP remained independent from their patrons who held ideologically contradictory positions, even while accepting their funding. Avila, "Chronicles of Revolution and Nation," 35. Susan Richards points out in her dissertation that the TGP "actively curried favored with the two conservative presidents of the decade, Manuel Ávila Camacho and Miguel Alemán." Richards, "Imaging the Political," 2.

156. Of special relevance was point two, which now stressed, "The Taller de Gráfica Popular makes a constant effort so that its production benefits the progressive and democratic interests of the Mexican people, mainly in their struggle against the fascist reaction." "DECLARACIONES DE PRINCIPIOS DEL TALLER DE GRÁFICA POPULAR," CENIDIAP, FR, LM, caja 25, exp. 1464, Sección Taller de Gráfica Popular, Subsección Estatutos, dated March 1945. Caps in original title. The other points included the following: "The Taller de Gráfica Popular is a collective work center for the functional production and study of the different branches of engraving and painting. . . . Whereas the social purpose of an artwork is inseparable from its good artistic quality, the Taller de Gráfica Popular strives to develop the technical capabilities of its individual members. The Taller de Gráfica Popular will lend its professional cooperation to other workshops or cultural institutions, to the workers' organizations and all progressive movements and institutions in general. The Taller de Gráfica Popular will defend the professional interests of the artists."

157. "MEXICAN PRESIDENT THWARTS ASSASSIN," *New York Times*, 11 April 1944, 1. Caps in original.

158. Prignitz-Poda, *El Taller de Gráfica Popular en México*, 88–89.

159. Letter from Dionicio Encina to Manuel Ávila Camacho, AGN, MAC, caja 425, exp. 433/111, 27 March 1944.

160. Ibid.

161. Memo to Palacio Nacional, AGN, MAC, caja 425, exp. 433/111, 4 April 1944.

162. Prignitz-Poda, *El Taller de Gráfica Popular en México*, 104.

163. Caplow notes that the exact circumstances of Méndez's expulsion remain murky. Caplow, *Leopoldo Méndez*, 211–12; Vogel, *Becoming Pablo O'Higgins*, 69.

164. Caplow, *Leopoldo Méndez*, 212.

165. Carr, *Marxism and Communism in Twentieth-Century Mexico*, 148, 159.

166. Prignitz-Poda, *El Taller de Gráfica Popular en México*, 123.

167. "Acuerdos," TGP, reel 7, box 2, folder 1, 20 February 1948; Richards, "Imaging the Political," 177.

168. Some government backing was in exchange for their work in support of President Miguel Alemán's (1946–1952) election campaign. Avila, "Chronicles of Revolution and Nation," 35.

169. "Letter of Sr. Lic. Miguel Alemán Valdés, Presidente Constitucional de los Estados Unidos Mexicanos," TGP, reel 13, box 3, folder 14, no date.

170. Craven, *Art and Revolution in Latin America*, 68.

171. "Letter of Sr. Lic. Miguel Alemán Valdés, Presidente Constitucional de los Estados Unidos Mexicanos," TGP, reel 13, box 3, folder 14, no date.

172. Carr, *Marxism and Communism in Twentieth-Century Mexico*, 181–83.

173. Caplow, *Leopoldo Méndez*, 221.

174. Moreover, Siqueiros, at this point a longtime critic of the TGP, continued his reproach of the *Taller* and specifically of Méndez as an overly controlling leader who spurned more modern printmaking techniques. Ibid., 221–21.

175. For example, in 1950 TGP and PCM members Arturo García Bustos and Oscar S. Frías, writing as representatives of the Party's Silvestre Revueltas cell, sent a letter to the TGP executive committee in protest of *Taller*'s accusations against García Bustos. García Bustos and Frías concluded that the charges' true intent was to portray the PCM as a "band of political degenerates." "A LA REUNIÓN ORDINARIA DEL TALLER DE GRÁFICA POPULAR," CENIDIAP, FR, LM, caja 25, exp. 1471-D3066/13.2, Sección Taller de Gráfica Popular, Subsección Acuerdos y sesiones, 1–3, dated 21 April 1950. Caps in original title. This letter was headed with: "PCM, Célula Silvestre Revueltas," or the Silvestre Revueltas cell of the Mexican Communist Party. Caplow notes that "Newer members of the Taller, young artists who belonged to the Silvestre Revueltas cell of the Communist Party, began to agitate for a greater role for the party in internal TGP affairs and to challenge Méndez's role in the group." Caplow, *Leopoldo Méndez*, 221.

176. Vogel, 214; *Becoming Pablo O'Higgins*; Avila, "Chronicles of Revolution and Nation," 30.

177. "Twenty Years of the Taller de Gráfica Popular," *artes de méxico*, 7, 13.

178. "RESPUESTA DE LOS ARTISTAS AL LLAMAMIENTO DEL PARTIDO COMUNISTA MEXICANO," CENIDIAP, FR, LM, caja 38, exp. 2496, Sección Actividades políticas, Subsección Escritos y notas, June 1950. Caps in original title.

179. Typewritten note signed by Rivera, Siqueiros, and Méndez, CENIDIAP, FR, LM, caja 36, exp. E2460, Sección Congreso Mundial por la Paz, Subsección Escritos, notas y conferencias, 3 April 1955.

Epilogue

1. "C. LAMBERTO ORTEGA PEREGRINA," AGN, DGIPS, caja 20, exp. 3, 6 June 1948. Caps in original title.

2. "DIEGO RIVERA Solicita su reingreso al Partido Comunista," CEMOS, PCM, caja 24, folder 5, Diego Rivera, 16 November 1952. Caps in original title; Rivera, "Solicitud de reingreso al Partido Comunista," 339–43.

3. Apel, "Diego Rivera and the Left," 70.

4. "DIEGO RIVERA Solicita su reingreso al Partido Comunista," CEMOS, PCM, caja 24, folder 5, Diego Rivera, 16 November 1952. Caps in original title.

5. Ibid.

6. In this respect, Rivera argued, "This example should be useful for all producers of art, as a demonstration of the absolute necessity of the artist and generally any

intellectual worker to remain in a human, clear and correct progressive political line, that in our time cannot be otherwise than the Marxist-Leninist-Stalinist line." Ibid.

7. Ibid.

8. "Partido Comunista Mexicano. Comité Central," ADRFK, Sección 2: Diego Rivera, Serie 5: Correspondencia, Subserie 16: Partidos Políticos, exp. 1, Partido Comunista Mexicano, Legajo 1, Imagen: 14952, 11 March 1954.

9. "Documento que elabora Diego Rivera a indicación de la Comisión de Control del Partido Comunista de México en respuesta a las preguntas formuladas por ella," ©Archivo Diego Rivera y Frida Kahlo, Banco de México, Fiduciario en el Fideicomiso relativo a los Museos Diego Rivera y Frida Kahlo, ADRFK, Sección 2: Diego Rivera, Serie 5: Correspondencia, Subserie 16: Partidos Políticos, exp. 1: Partido Comunista Mexicano, Legajo 1, Imagen: 14954, no date. Also see Rivera, "Documento que elabora Diego Rivera a indicación de la comisión de control del Partido Comunista de México en respuesta a las preguntas formuladas por ella," 347–55. This document is dated 17 May 1954.

10. Ibid., 351–52.

11. Tibol, "Datos biográficos," 452–55; Marnham, *Dreaming with His Eyes Open*, 311.

12. Marnham states that this was Rivera's fifth application. *Dreaming with His Eyes Open*, 311. However, the PCM document states that Rivera had applied only twice before his successful attempt.

13. Tibol, "Datos biográficos," 453–55.

14. Marnham, *Dreaming with His Eyes Open*, 311.

15. In 1952, Rivera was diagnosed with penis cancer and in 1957 he lost of the use of his right arm as a result of a stroke. Ibid., 312.

16. "RESPUESTA DE LOS ARTISTAS AL LLAMAMIENTO DEL PARTIDO COMUNISTA MEXICANO," CENIDIAP, FR, LM, caja 38, exp. 2496, Sección Actividades políticas, Subsección Escritos y notas, June 1950. Caps in original title.

17. Manuel Terrazas (director of *La Voz de México*) also remained as a member of the Excutive Committee, and Dionicio Encinas was reelected. Memo, AGN, IPS, caja 21, exp. 2, 29 November 1950.

18. "ASUNTO: COMUNISMO," AGN, DGIPS, caja 21, exp. 2, 22 November 1950. Caps in original title.

19. "MEMORÁNDUM CONFIDENCIAL," AGN, DGIPS, caja 21, exp. 2, 22 November 1950. Caps in original title.

20. "ACONTECIMIENTOS DEL PRIMERO DE MAYO, 1952," AGN, DGIPS, caja 23, exp. 24, 2 May 1952. Caps in original title. Just a few days later, Mexico City newspapers reported that Rivera, Siqueiros, and other "prominent leaders of the communist movement in Mexico" were identified as directly responsible for the "bloody rumpus" that occurred on 1 May. "Acusan a Diego Rivera, Siqueiros y Otros Cabecillas Comunistas, por el Zafarrancho," *El Novedades*, 6 May 1952, 1, 7.

21. White, *Siqueiros*, 329.

22. Marnham, *Dreaming with His Eyes Open*, 311–12; White, *Siqueiros*, 326.

23. Letter signed by TGP members, TGP, reel 13, box 3, folder 9, 25 November 1957.

24. Folgarait, *So Far from Heaven*, 38, 40.

25. Ibid., 41–42, 44.

26. "Siqueiros, Muralist and Exponent of New World Proletarian Art, Dies at 77," *New York Times*, 7 January 1974, 27.

27. Ibid.

28. Ibid.

29. Ibid.

30. Folgarait, *So Far from Heaven*, 53–54. Stein argues that at the time of Siqueiros's death, the PCM was "attempting to have Siqueiros posthumously expelled from his Party." Stein, *Siqueiros*, 354. In this respect White writes, "Even in death, however, his differences with his Party continued to haunt him. Some members wanted him expelled posthumously because of his support of Echeverría." White, *Siqueiros*, 453.

31. Arenal, *Paginas Sueltas con Siqueiros*, 270; White, *Siqueiros*, 453.

32. Clearly Rivera experienced difficulties in juggling both his art and PCM duties, even as he argued that his murals influenced more people than his labor within the Party. "Diego Rivera to the National Executive Committee of the Communist Party of Mexico," HIA, JF, box 180, folder 3, 26 April 1925.

33. Folgarait, *So Far from Heaven*, 54.

Bibliography

Archival Sources

Amsterdam

Internationaal Instituut voor Sociale Geschiedenis
Partido Comunista Mexicano Archives

Mexico City

Archivo Diego Rivera y Frida Kahlo, Museo Frida Kahlo
Archivo General de la Nación
Archivo Particular de Lázaro Cárdenas del Río
Archivos Presidenciales, Manuel Ávila Camacho
Archivos Presidenciales, Lázaro Cárdenas del Río
Archivos Presidenciales, Emilio Portes Gil
Dirección Federal de Seguridad
Dirección General de Investigaciones Políticas y Sociales
Fondo Carlos Chávez
Fondo Dirección General de Gobierno
Fondo Gobernación Siglo XX, Departamento de Migración
Fondo Tribunal Superior de Justicia del D.F.
Archivo Histórico de la Secretaría de Educación Pública
Biblioteca Miguel Lerdo de Tejada
Archivos Económicos
Centro de Documentación, Información e Investigación Arkheia, Museo Universitario Arte Contemporáneo de la Universidad Nacional Autónoma de México
Fondo Olivier Debroise
Centro de Estudios del Movimiento Obrero y Socialista
Fondo Arnoldo Martínez Verdugo
Fondo Partido Comunista Mexicano
Centro Nacional de Investigación, Documentación e Información de Artes Plásticas
Fondo Reservado
Archivo Diego Rivera
Fondo Documental Leopoldo Méndez
Hemeroteca Nacional de México
Instituto del Derecho de Asilo-Museo Casa de León Trotsky, Biblioteca Rafael Galván
Sala de Arte Público Siqueiros, Acervo Documental

Paris

Pompidou Center, Bibliothèque Kandinsky
Archives et dossiers

Rome

Archivio Centrale dello Stato

United States

Center of Creative Photography, University of Arizona
Lola Álvarez Bravo Archive
The Comintern Archives: Files of the Communist Party of Mexico, 1919–1940 (Microfilm)
The Getty Research Institute, Special Collections
David Alfaro Siqueiros Papers, 1920–1991
The Hoover Institution Library and Archives, Stanford University
Alexander H. Buchman Papers, 1920–2003
Congreso Nacional del Partido Comunista, 1939
Charles Curtiss Papers, 1938–1987
Rodolfo Echeverría Martínez Collection, 1911–1986
Leo Eloesser Papers, 1861–1994
Joseph Freeman Papers, 1904–1966
Mexican Subject Collection, 1918–1998
Leon Trotsky Collection, 1917–1995
Bertram D. Wolfe Papers, 1903–2000
The Houghton Library, Harvard University
Leon Trotsky Exile Papers
Sterling Memorial Library at Yale University
Taller de Gráfica Popular Records, Mexico City, 1937–1960 (Microfilm)
Tamiment Library and Robert F. Wagner Labor Archives
Communist Party of America Records

Journals, Newspapers, and Bulletins

Mexico City

artes de méxico
Cuba Libre! Para los trabajadores
Excélsior
Frente a Frente
El Machete
El Machete Ilegal
Mella: Revista Mensual del Secretariado del Caribe del Socorro Rojo Internacional
Mexican Folkways

El Nacional
Novedades
Periódico Unomásuno
El Popular
La Prensa
El Universal
El Universal Gráfico
La Voz de México

United States

Chicago Daily Tribune
Los Angeles Times
The Nation
The New Masses
The New York Times
Schenectady Gazette
The Washington Post

Primary Material

Almaguer, Prisciliano. *Por un Partido de 50,000 Miembros* (Tercer punto de la Orden del Día), Informe al X Congreso del Partido Comunista Mexicano. México, DF: Fondo de Cultura Popular, 1947.

Amador, Graciela. "Gachita Amador, la fiel y la extraña." Parte 1 de 2. *CURARE: Espacio Crítico para las Artes*. Compiled by Miguel Ángel Echegaray. No. 20 (July–December 2002): 82–110.

———. "Gachita Amador, la fiel y la extraña." Parte 2 de 2. *CURARE: Espacio Crítico para las Artes*. Compiled by Miguel Ángel Echegaray. No. 21 (January–June 2003): 90–107.

Arenal, Angélica. *Paginas Sueltas con Siqueiros*. México, DF: Editorial Grijalbo, 1980.

Beals, Carleton. *Glass Houses: Ten Years of Free-Lancing*. Philadelphia, PA: J. B. Lippincott, 1938.

Beloff, Angelina. *Memorias*. México: Coordinación de Difusión Cultural Dirección de Literatura/UNAM/SEP, 1986.

Brenner, Anita. *Avant-Garde Art and Artists: Anita Brenner's Journals of the Roaring Twenties*. Edited by Susannah Joel Glusker. 2 Vols. Austin: University of Texas Press, 2010.

Breton, André, and Diego Rivera [and Leon Trotsky]. "Manifesto for an Independent Revolutionary Art." In *Manifesto! A Century of Isms*, edited by Mary Ann Caws, 472–77. Lincoln: University of Nebraska Press, 2001.

Brum, Blanca Luz. *Amor, me hiciste amarga: Poemas, cartas y memorias de México*. México, DF: Consejo Nacional para la Cultura y las Artes (CONACULTA) Breve Fondo Editorial 2002.

Campa, Valentín S. *Mi testimonio: Memorias de un comunista mexicana*. México, DF: Ediciones de Cultura Popular, 1978.
Chapa, Esther. *El derecho de voto para la mujer*. México: No publisher listed, 1938.
La C. T. M. y Trotsky (Resolución adoptada en el 1er. Congreso General Ordinario de la C.T.M., Febrero de 1938). México, DF: Editorial Popular, 1938.
Declaración de Principios y Estatutos de la Liga de Escritores y Artistas Revolucioмarios [sic], LEAR. México, DF, 1936.
Dewey, John. *Truth Is on the March: Report and Remarks on the Trotsky Hearings in Mexico*. New York: American Committee for the Defense of Leon Trotsky, 1937.
Encina, Dionisio. *Unidad Democrática Antiimperialista por la soberanía de México* (Primer punto de la Orden del Día), Informe al X Congreso del Partido Comunista Mexicano. México, DF: Fondo de Cultura Popular, 1947.
Freeman, Joseph. *An American Testament: A Narrative of Rebels and Romantics*. London: Victor Gollancz, 1938.
Gobierno Federal de México, Instituto Nacional de las Mujeres. "Boletín Desarrollo Local." http://generodesarrollolocal.inmujeres.gob.mx/node/267. July 8, 2011.
Kahlo, Frida. *The Diary of Frida Kahlo: An Intimate Self-Portrait*. New York: Abrams, in association with México: La Vaca Independiente, 2005.
———. *Escrituras*. Selección, proemio y notas de Raquel Tibol. México: Plaza y Janés, 2004.
———. *Frida by Frida*. Selection of Letters and Texts, Foreword and Notes by Raquel Tibol. Translated by Gregory Dechant. México: Editorial RM, 2006.
———. *The Letters of Frida Kahlo: Cartas Apasionadas*. Compiled by Martha Zamora. San Francisco: Chronicle Books, 1995.
———. *Querida Doctorcita: Frida Kahlo–Leo Eloesser, correspondencia*. México, DF: DGE Ediciones: Consejo Nacional para la Cultura y las Artes, 2007.
Kollontai, Alexandra. *Sexual Relations and the Class Struggle*. Edited and translated by Alix Holt. Montpelier, Bristol: The Falling Wall Press, 1972.
———. "Women's Day, February 1913." In *Alexandra Kollontai: Selected Articles and Speeches*, edited by I. M. Dazhina, M. M. Mukhamedzhanov, and R. Y. Tsivlina, 62–65. New York: International, 1984.
Labor Condemns Trotskyism: Resolution Unanimously Adopted by First National Congress of the Mexican Confederation of Labor. New York: International, 1938.
Lenin, V. I. "On Proletarian Culture." In *The Lenin Anthology*, edited by Robert C. Tucker, 675–76. New York: W. W. Norton, 1975.
———. "Women in the Struggle for Socialism." In *Women and Communism: Selections from the Writings of Marx, Engels, Lenin and Stalin*, edited by Harry Pollitt and Clara Zetkin, 42–47. Westport, CT: Greenwood Press, 1975.
Ley Sobre Relaciones Familiares, Expedida por el Primer Jefe del Ejército Constitucionalista, Encargado del Poder Ejecutivo de la Nación, el 9 de abril de 1917. México: Editorial Andrade, 1964.
El libro negro del terror nazi en Europa: Testimonios de escritores y artistas de 16 naciones. México: Editorial "El Libro Libre," 1943.
El Machete Ilegal: 1929–1934. Edición Facsimilar. Puebla, México: Instituto de Ciencias Universidad Autónoma de Puebla, 1975.

Mexique: Exposition organisée par André Breton. Paris: Renou & Colle, 1939.
Meyer, Hannes. "The Workshop for Popular Graphic Art in Mexico." In *T.G.P México: El Taller de Gráfica Popular, doce años de obra artística colectiva/The Workshop for Popular Graphic Art, a Record of Twelve Years of Collective Work*. México: La Estampa Mexicana, 1949.
Modotti, Tina. *5,000,000 Widows, 10,000,000 Orphans, Women! Do You Want That Again?* San Diego, Vancouver: Parentheses Writing Series, 1996.
———. "The Letters from Tina Modotti to Edward Weston." Edited by Amy Stark. In *Archive*, No. 22. University of Arizona: Center for Creative Photography, January 1986.
———. "On Photography." *Mexican Folkways* 5, no. 4 (1929): 196–97.
Modotti, Tina, Edward Weston, Antonio Saborit. *Una mujer sin país: Las cartas a Edward Weston y otros papeles personales*. Translation, notes, introduction by Antonio Saborit. México: Cal y arena, 2001.
Neruda, Pablo. *Memoirs*. Translated by Hardie St. Martin. New York: Farrar, Straus and Giroux, 1977.
Partido Comunista de México, Sección de la Internacional Comunista, *III Congreso Celebrado en la Ciudad de México del 7 al 12 de abril de 1925*. México, DF: Talleres Gráficos "Soria," 1925.
Rivera, Diego. "Defensa y ataque con los Stalinistas." In *Documentación sobre el arte mexicano*, edited by Raquel Tibol, 65–82. México, DF: Fondo de Cultura Económica, 1974.
———. "Documento que elabora Diego Rivera a indicación de la comisión de control del Partido Comunista de México en respuesta a las preguntas formuladas por ella." In *Arte y política, Diego Rivera: Selección, prólogo, notas y datos biográficos por Raquel Tibol*, 347–55. México, DF: Editorial Grijalbo, 1979.
———. "Edward Weston and Tina Modotti." *Mexican Folkways* 2, no. 6 (April–May, 1926): 16–17.
———. "Lo que opina Diego Rivera sobre la pintura revolucionaria." *Octubre: La Revista del Marxismo Revolucionario*, no. 1 (October 1935): 50–53.
———. *My Art, My Life: An Autobiography*. With Gladys March. New York: Dover, 1991.
———. *Obras. Correspondencia*. Tomo III. Edited by Esther Acevedo, Leticia Torres Carmona, and Alicia Sánchez Mejorada. México: El Colegio Nacional, 1999.
———.*Obras. Textos de arte*. Tomo I. Edited by Xavier Moyssén. México: El Colegio Nacional, 1996.
———. *Obras. Textos polémicos, 1921–1949*. Tomo II. Edited by Esther Acevedo, Leticia Torres Carmona, and Alicia Sánchez Mejorada. México: El Colegio Nacional, 1999.
———. "(Paquita Torre) nuestra amiga yankee, como Thoreau." In *Textos de Arte*, edited by Xavier Moyssén, 421–22. México: Universidad Nacional Autónoma de México, 1986.
———. *Raíces políticas y motivos personales de la controversia Siqueiros-Rivera: Stalinismo vs. Bolshevismo Leninista*. México: Imprenta Mundial, 1935.

———. "Solicitud de reingreso al Partido Comunista." In *Arte y política, Diego Rivera: Selección, prólogo, notas y datos biográficos por Raquel Tibol*, 339–43. México, DF: Editorial Grijalbo, 1979.

Robinson, Ione. *A Wall to Paint On*. New York: E. P. Dutton, 1946.

Siqueiros, David Alfaro. *Art and Revolution*. Translated by Sylvia Calles. London: Lawrence and Wishart, 1975.

———. *Me llamaban el Coronelazo*. México, DF: Editorial Grijalbo, 1977.

———. *No hay mas ruta que la nuestra*. México: SEP, 1945.

———. *Raíces políticas y motivos personales de la controversia Siqueiros-Rivera: Stalinismo vs. Bolshevismo Leninista*. México: Imprenta Mundial, 1935.

———. "Tres llamamientos de orientación actual a los pintores y escultores de la nueva generación americana." *Vida-Americana: Revista Norte Centro y Sud-Americana de Vanguardia*, no. 1 (May 1921): 2–3.

Strategy of the Communist: A Letter from the Communist International to the Mexican Communist Party. Chicago: Workers Party of America, 1923.

Taller de Gráfica Popular. *Estampas de la revolución mexicana*. México, DF: Taller de Gráfica Popular, 1947.

Toor, Francis. "Mexican Folkways." *Mexican Folkways* 7, no. 4 (October–December, 1932): 205–11.

Trotsky, Leon. *Art and Revolution: Writings on Literature, Politics, and Culture*. New York: Pathfinder, 1970.

———. *I Stake My Life*. New York: Labor Publications, 1977.

———. *My Life: An Attempt at an Autobiography*. Mineola, NY: Dover, 2007.

———. *Writings of Leon Trotsky (1936–37)*. New York: Pathfinder, 2010.

———. *Writings of Leon Trotsky (1938–39)*. New York: Pathfinder, 2010.

———. *Writings of Leon Trotsky (1939–40)*. New York: Pathfinder, 2011.

"Twenty Years of the Taller de Gráfica Popular," Round Table Organized by Raquel Tibol. *artes de méxico* 3, no. 18 (July and August 1957).

U.S. Federal Bureau of Investigation. *History of the Special Intelligence Service Division (of the FBI)*, Vol. 3. Washington, DC: United States Department of Justice, 1947. http://vault.fbi.gov/special-intelligence-service/special-intelligence-service-history-3/view. October 20, 2013.

———. "Memo from the FBI on "Communist Activities, Assault on Leo Trotsky." Leon Trotsky. Part 1 of 5. http://vault.fbi.gov/leon-trotsky/. November 24, 2012.

———. "Special Intelligence Service History." Part 4 of 8. https://vault.fbi.gov/special-intelligence-service/SIS%20History%20Part%2004%20of%2008/view. October 21, 2016.

van Heijenoort, Jean. *With Trotsky in Exile: From Prinkipo to Coyoacán*. Cambridge, MA: Harvard University Press, 1978.

Vidali, Vittorio. *Comandante Carlos*. Roma: Editori Riuniti, 1983.

Weston, Edward. *The Daybooks of Edward Weston*. Part I: *Mexico*. Edited by Nancy Newhall. New York: An Aperture Book, 1973.

Zetkin, Clara. "My Recollections of Lenin (An Interview on the Woman Question)." In *The Emancipation of Women from the Writings of V. I. Lenin*, 97–123. New York: International Publishers, 1995.

Secondary Material

Adès, Dawn. *Art in Latin America: The Modern Era, 1820–1980*. New Haven, CT: Yale University Press, 1989.

———. "The Many Revolutions of Rivera." Review of *Dreaming with His Eyes Open*, by Patrick Marnham. *Times Literary Supplement* (TLS), no. 4988 (6 November 1998): 17.

Aguayo Quezada, Sergio. *La charola: Una historia de los servicios de inteligencia en México*. México, DF: Grijalbo, 2001.

———. "Intelligence Services and the Transition to Democracy in Mexico." In *Strategy and Security in U.S.-Mexican Relations beyond the Cold War*, edited by John Bailey and Sergio Aguayo, 139–55. San Diego: Center for U.S.-Mexican Studies, University of California, San Diego, 1996.

———. *1968: Los Archivos de la Violencia*. México, DF: Editorial Grijalbo, 1998.

Albers, Patricia. *Shadows, Fire, Snow: The Life of Tina Modotti*. New York: Clarkson Potter, 1999.

Alcántara, Isabel, and Sandra Egnoff. *Frida Kahlo and Diego Rivera*. Munich: Prestel Verlag, 2008.

A.M.E., "A New Folklore Journal." *Hispania* 8, no. 4 (October 1925): 282.

Anhalt, Diana. *A Gathering of Fugitives: American Political Expatriates in Mexico, 1948–1965*. Santa Maria, CA: Archer Books, 2001.

Anreus Alejandro. "Los Tres Grandes: Ideologies and Styles." In *Mexican Muralism: A Critical History*, edited by Alejandro Anreus, Robin Adèle Greeley, and Leonard Folgarait, 37–55. Berkeley: University of California Press, 2012.

Apel, Dora. "Diego Rivera and the Left: The Destruction and Recreation of the Rockefeller Center Mural." *Left History: An Interdisciplinary Journal of Historical Inquiry and Debate* 6, no. 1 (1999): 57–75.

Argenteri, Letizia. *Tina Modotti: Between Art and Revolution*. New Haven, CT: Yale University Press, 2003.

"Aurora Reyes: 1908–1985, Mexico." In *Women Artists of Modern Mexico: Frida's Contemporaries*, edited by Dolores Mercado, 150–54. Chicago: National Museum of Mexican Art, 2008.

Avila, Theresa. "Chronicles of Revolution and Nation: El Taller de Gráfica Popular's *Estampas de la Revolución Mexicana* (1947)." PhD diss., University of New Mexico, May 2013.

Azuela, Alicia. "Graphics of the Mexican Left, 1924–1938." In *Art and Journals on the Political Front, 1910–1940*, edited by Virginia Hagelstein Marquardt, 247–68. Gainesville: University of Florida Press, 1997.

———. "*El Machete* and *Frente a Frente*: Art Committed to Social Justice in Mexico," *Art Journal* 52, no. 1 (Spring 1993): 82–87.

———. "Public Art, Meyer Schapiro and Mexican Muralism." *Oxford Art Journal* 17, no. 1 (1994): 55–59.

———. "Rivera and the Concept of Proletarian Art." In *Diego Rivera: A Retrospective*, 125–29. New York: Founders Society, Detroit Institute of Arts, in association with W. W. Norton, 1986.

Baki, Peter, Jean-François Chévrier, and Estrella de Diego, eds. *Kati Horna.* México, DF: RM/Museo Amparo/Jeu de Paume, 2014.
Barbosa Heldt, Antonio. *La mujer en las luchas por México.* México: Editora y Distribuidora, 1972.
Barrera, Reyna. *Salvador Novo: Navaja de la inteligencia.* México, DF: Plaza y Valdés, 1999.
Bartelik, Marek. "Concerning Socialist Realism: Recent Publications on Russian Art." *Art Journal* 58, no. 4 (Winter 1999): 90–95.
Battat, Erin Royston. *Ain't Got No Home: America's Great Migrations and the Making of an Interracial Left.* Chapel Hill: University of North Carolina Press, 2014.
Beloff, Angelina. *Angelina Beloff: Trazos de una vida.* Edited by María Monserrat Sánchez Soler. México: Instituto Nacional de Bellas Artes, 2012.
Bergan, Ronald. *Eisenstein: A Life in Conflict.* Woodstock, NY: Overlook Press, 1999.
Bliss, Katherine Elaine. *Compromised Positions: Prostitution, Public Health, and Gender Politics in Revolutionary Mexico.* University Park: Pennsylvania State University Press, 2001.
Bliss, Katherine Elaine, and Ann S. Blum. "Dangerous Driving: Adolescence, Sex, and the Gendered Experience of Public Space in Early-Twentieth-Century Mexico City." In *Gender, Sexuality, and Power in Latin America Since Independence,* edited by William E. French and Katherine Elaine Bliss, 163–86. Lanham, MD: Rowman & Littlefield, 2007.
Bonnell, Victoria E. *Iconography of Power: Soviet Political Posters under Lenin and Stalin.* Berkeley: University of California Press, 1997.
———. "The Peasant Woman in Stalinist Political Art of the 1930s." *American Historical Review* 98, no. 1 (February 1993): 55–82.
Bown, Matthew Cullerne. *Art under Stalin.* New York: Holmes & Meyer, 1991.
———. *Socialist Realist Painting.* New Haven, CT: Yale University Press, 1998.
Bruce-Novoa, Juan. "Offshoring the American Dream." *New Centennial Review* 3, no. 1 (Spring 2003): 109–45.
Caballero, Manuel. *Latin America and the Comintern, 1919–1943.* Cambridge, UK: Cambridge University Press, 1986.
Cacucci, Pino. *Tina Modotti: A Life.* Translated by Patricia J. Duncan. New York: St. Martin's Press, 1999.
Campos, Esteban. *Siqueiros y Blanca Luz Brum: Una pasión tormentosa.* México: L.D. Books, 2010.
Cano, Gabriela. "Las mujeres en el México del siglo xx: Una cronología mínima." In *Miradas feministas sobre las mexicanas del siglo XX,* edited by Marta Lamas, 21–75. México, DF: Fondo de Cultura Económica, 2007.
———. "The Porfiriato and the Mexican Revolution: Constructions of Feminism and Nationalism." In *Nation, Empire, Colony: Historicizing Gender and Race,* edited by Ruth Roach Pierson and Nupur Chaudhuri, 106–20. Bloomington: Indiana University Press, 1998.

Caplow, Deborah. "Leopoldo Méndez, A Revolutionary Spirit in Art." In *El Taller de Gráfica Popular: Vida y Arte*, exhibition catalogue, 27–39. Athens: Georgia Museum of Art at University of Georgia, 2015.

———. *Leopoldo Méndez: Revolutionary Art and the Mexican Print*. Austin: University of Texas Press, 2007.

———. "El Libro Negro del Terror Nazi en Europa." In *El Taller de Gráfica Popular: Vida y Arte*, exhibition catalogue, 18–26. Athens: Georgia Museum of Art at University of Georgia, 2015.

———. "Mariana Yampolsky and the Taller de Gráfica Popular." In *El Taller de Gráfica Popular: Vida y Arte*, exhibition catalogue, 50–53. Athens: Georgia Museum of Art at University of Georgia, 2015.

Carleton, Greg. "Writing-Reading the Sexual Revolution in the Early Soviet Union." *Journal of the History of Sexuality* 8, no. 2 (October 1997): 229–55.

Caronia, María, and Vittorio Vidali. *Tina Modotti Photographs*. Translated by C. H. Evans. New York: Idea Editions & Belmark, 1981.

Carr, Barry. "The Fate of the Vanguard under a Revolutionary State: Marxism's Contribution to the Construction of the Great Arch." In *Everyday Forms of State Formation: Revolution and the Negotiation of Rule in Modern Mexico,* edited by Gilbert M. Joseph and Daniel Nugent, 326–52. Durham, NC: Duke University Press, 1994.

———. "Hacia una historia de los comunismos mexicanos: Desafíos y sugerencias." In *El comunismo: Otras miradas desde América Latina*, edited by Elvira Concheiro Bórquez, Massimo Modonesi, and Horacio Crespo, 521–26. México, DF: Centro de Investigaciones Interdisciplinarias en Ciencias y Humanidades, 2007.

———. *Marxism and Communism in Twentieth-Century Mexico*. Lincoln: University of Nebraska Press, 1992.

Clements, Barbara Evans. *Bolshevik Women*. Cambridge, UK: Cambridge University Press, 1997.

———. "Bolshevik Women." In *The Russian Revolution: The Essential Readings*, edited by Martin A. Miller, 182–205. Malden, MA: Blackwell, 2001.

———. "New Directions in Russian and Soviet Women's History." In *Making Women's Histories: Beyond National Perspectives*, 38–50. New York: New York University Press, 2013.

Coffey, Mary K. *How a Revolutionary Art Became Official Culture: Murals, Museums, and the Mexican State*. Durham, NC: Duke University Press, 2012.

Condés Lara, Enrique. *Los últimos años del Partido Comunista Mexicano (1969–1981)*. Puebla: Universidad Autónoma de Puebla, 2000.

Constantine, Mildred. *Tina Modotti: A Fragile Life*. New York: Rizzoli International, 1983.

Corrigan, Philip, and Derek Sayer. *The Great Arch: English State Formation as Cultural Revolution*. Oxford: Basil Blackwell, 1985.

Cortés Zavala, María Teresa. "La Liga de Escritores y Artistas Revolucionarios durante el Cardenismo." *Tzintzun. Revista de Estudios Históricos*, no. 13 (January–June, 1991): 115–30.

Craven, David. *Art and Revolution in Latin America, 1910–1990*. New Haven, CT: Yale University Press, 2002.
Dawson, Alexander S. "From Models for the Nation to Model Citizens: Indigenismo and the 'Revindication' of the Mexican Indian, 1920–40." *Journal of Latin American Studies* 30, no. 2 (May 1998): 279–308.
———. *Indian and Nation in Revolutionary Mexico*. Tucson: University of Arizona Press, 2004.
Dazhina, I. M. "An Impassioned Opponent of War and Champion of Peace and Female Emancipation." In *Alexandra Kollontai: Selected Articles and Speeches*, edited by I. M. Dazhina, M. M. Mukhamedzhanov, and R. Y. Tsivlina, 5–15. New York: International, 1984.
Debroise, Olivier. "Action Art: David Alfaro Siqueiros and the Artistic and Ideological Strategies of the 1930s." In *Portrait of a Decade: David Alfaro Siqueiros, 1930–1940*, exhibition catalog. Mexico City: Museo Nacional de Arte, Instituto Nacional de Bellas Artes, 1997.
———. "Like Cut Glass: Approach to the Photography of Lola Álvarez Bravo." In *Lola Álvarez Bravo: In Her Own Light*, 11–33. English Version by James Oles. Tucson: University of Arizona, Center for Creative Photography, 1994.
———. *Mexican Suite: A History of Photography in Mexico*. Austin: University of Texas Press, 2001.
de Lara Rangel, María Eugenia. *Dolores Olmedo Patiño (1908–2002)*. México: Museo Dolores Olmedo Patiño, 2003.
del Conde, Teresa. "A Nostalgic Melancholy." In *María Izquierdo, 1902–1955*, exhibition catalog. Chicago: Mexican Fine Arts Center Museum, 1996.
de los Reyes, Aurelio. "Últimas fotografías de Tina Modotti." *Archivo General de la Nación* 6, no. 9 (2005): 136–44.
Delpar, Helen. *The Enormous Vogue of Things Mexican: Cultural Relations between the United States and Mexico, 1920–1935*. Tuscaloosa: University of Alabama Press, 1992.
de Neymet, Marcela. *Cronología del Partido Comunista Mexicano: Primera parte, 1919–1939*. México, DF: Ediciones de Cultura Popular, 1981.
Dickerman, Leah, and Anna Indych-López. *Diego Rivera: Murals for the Museum of Modern Art*, exhibition catalog. New York: Museum of Modern Art, 2011.
Dimitrov, George. *Against Fascism and War*. New York: International, 1986.
Dugrand, Alain. *Trotsky in Mexico, 1937–1940*. Great Britain: Carcanet Press, 1992.
Durán, Javier. "México, la Guerra Civil española y el cardenismo: La revista *Frente a frente*." *La Palabra y el Hombre, Revista de la Universidad Veracruzana*, no. 109 (January–March, 1999): 107–18.
Eisenberg, Emanuel. "Battle of the Century." *New Masses* 10 (December 1935): 18–20.
Engel, Barbara Alpern. "New Directions in Russian and Soviet Women's History." In *Making Women's Histories: Beyond National Perspectives*, edited by Pamela S. Nadell and Kate Haulman, 38–60. New York: New York University Press, 2013.
Fattal, Laura Felleman, and Carol Salus, eds. *Out of Context: American Artists Abroad*. Westport, CT: Praeger, 2004.

Ferrer, Elizabeth. *Lola Álvarez Bravo*. México: Fondo de Cultura Económica, 2006.
Folgarait, Leonard. *Mural Painting and Social Revolution in Mexico, 1920–1940s: Art of the New Order*. New York: Cambridge University Press, 1998.
———. *Seeing Mexico Photographed: The Work of Horne, Casasola, Modotti, and Álvarez Bravo*. New Haven, CT: Yale University Press, 2008.
———. *So Far from Heaven: David Alfaro Siqueiros'* The March of Humanity *and Mexican Revolutionary Politics*. Cambridge, UK: Cambridge University Press, 1987.
Fort, Ilene Susan, and Tere Arcq, eds. *In Wonderland: The Surrealist Adventures of Women Artists in Mexico and the United States*. With Terri Geis. New York: Prestel, 2012.
Foster, William Z. *History of the Communist Party of the United States*. New York: International, 1952.
Franco, Jean. "Body and Soul: Women and Postrevolutionary Messianism." In *Plotting Women: Gender and Representation in Mexico*, 102–28. New York: Columbia University Press, 1989.
Gall, Olivia. *Trotsky en México y la vida política en el periodo de Cárdenas, 1937–1940*. México, DF: Ediciones Era, 1991.
Gallo, Rubén. *Mexican Modernity: The Avant-Garde and the Technological Revolution*. Cambridge, MA: MIT Press, 2010.
García Bustos, Arturo. "El Taller de Gráfica Popular: A Personal History." In *El Taller de Gráfica Popular: Vida y Arte*, exhibition catalogue, 14–15. Athens: Georgia Museum of Art at University of Georgia, 2015.
García Canclini, Néstor. *Anthropology for a Society without a Story Line*. Translated by David Frye. Durham, NC: Duke University Press, 2014.
Garrido, Luis Javier. *El partido de la revolución institucionalizada: La formación del nuevo estado (1928–1945)*. México, DF: Siglo Veintiuno Editores, 1984.
Geis, Terri. "The Struggles of Modernizing Mexico and the Mural of Aurora Reyes at the Centro Escolar Revolución." In *Women's Contributions to Visual Culture, 1918–1939*, edited by Karen E. Brown, 157–72. Aldershot, England: Ashgate, 2008.
Gleizer, Daniela. *Jewish Latin America: Unwelcome Exiles. Mexico and the Jewish Refugees from Nazism, 1933–1945*. Translated by Susan Thomae. Leiden, Germany: Brill, 2014.
Glusker, Susannah Joel. *Anita Brenner: A Mind of Her Own*. Austin: University of Texas Press, 1998.
Gojman de Backal, Alicia. *Camisas, escudos y desfiles militares: Los Dorados y el antisemitismo en México (1934–1940)*. México, DF: Fondo de Cultura Económica, 2000.
Gómez, Nadia Ugalde, and Juan Rafael Coronel Rivera. *Frida Kahlo: The Metamorphosis of the Image*. México: Editorial RM, 2006.
González Cruz Manjarrez, Maricela. *La polémica Siqueiros-Rivera: Planteamientos estético políticos, 1934–1935*. México, DF: Museo Dolores Olmedo Patiño, 1996.
———. "Tina Modotti y el muralismo, un lenguaje común." *Anales del Instituto de Investigaciones Estéticas* 23, no. 78 (Spring 2001): 175–88.
Gorsuch, Anne E. "'A Woman Is Not a Man': The Culture of Gender and Generation in Soviet Russia, 1921–1928." *Slavic Review* 55, no. 3 (Autumn 1996): 636–60.

Grimberg, Salomon. *I Will Never Forget You: Frida Kahlo and Nickolas Muray*. San Francisco: Chronicle Books, 2006.
Guanche, Julio César. *Julio Antonio Mella: Líder comunista cubano y latinoamericano; un imprenta traspasa fronteras para convertirse en icono de las revoluciones del continente*. México: Ocean Press y Ocean Sur, 2009.
Hartmann, Heidi. "The Unhappy Marriage of Marxism and Feminism: Towards a More Progressive Union." In *Women and Revolution: A Discussion of the Unhappy Marriage of Marxism and Feminism*, edited by Lydia Sargent, 1–42. Cambridge, MA: South End Press, 1981.
Hatzky, Christine. *Julio Antonio Mella (1903–1929): Una biografía*. Santiago de Cuba: Editorial Oriente, 2008.
Heale, M. J. *American Anti-Communism: Combating the Enemy Within, 1830–1970*. Baltimore, MD: The Johns Hopkins University Press, 2009.
Hemingway, Andrew. *Artists on the Left; American Artists and the Communist Movement, 1926–1956*. New Haven, CT: Yale University Press, 2002.
———. "Introduction." In *Marxism and the History of Art: From William Morris to the New Left*, edited by Andrew Hemingway, 1–8. London: Pluto Press, 2006.
Herman, Donald L. *The Comintern in Mexico*. Washington, DC: Public Affairs Press, 1974.
Herrera, Hayden. *Frida: A Biography of Frida Kahlo*. New York: Harper Perennial, 1984.
Herzog, Melanie Anne. *Elizabeth Catlett: An American Artist in Mexico*. Seattle: University of Washington Press, 2000.
Hooks, Margaret. *Frida Kahlo: Portraits of an Icon*. New York: Throckmorton Fine Art, 2002.
———. *Tina Modotti*. New York: Phaidon, 2002.
———. *Tina Modotti: Photographer and Revolutionary*. London: Pandora, 1993.
Indych-López, Anna. *Muralism without Walls: Rivera, Orozco, and Siqueiros in the United States, 1927–1940*. Pittsburgh, PA: University of Pittsburgh Press, 2009.
Irwin, Robert McKee. "As Invisible as He Is: The Queer Enigma of Xavier Villaurrutia." In *Reading and Writing the Ambiente: Queer Sexualities in Latino, Latin American, and Spanish Culture*, edited by Susana Chávez-Silverman and Librada Hernández, 114–46. Madison, WI: University of Wisconsin Press, 2000.
Joseph, Gilbert M., and Daniel Nugent. "Popular Culture and State Formation in Revolutionary Mexico." In *Everyday Forms of State Formation: Revolution and the Negotiation of Rule in Modern Mexico*, edited by Gilbert M. Joseph and Daniel Nugent, 3–21. Durham, NC: Duke University Press, 1994.
Kaltmeier, Olaf. "Mexican *Indigenismo* in a Hemispheric Context—Elements for a Historiography of Inter-American Entanglements in the First Half of the Twentieth Century." In *Mobile and Entangled America(s)*, edited by Maryemma Graham and Wilfried Raussert, 283–300. London: Routledge, 2016.
Karttunen, Frances. *Between Worlds: Interpreters, Guides, and Survivors*. New Brunswick, NJ: Rutgers University Press, 1994.
Kettenmann, Andrea. *Frida Kahlo: Pain and Passion, 1907–1954*. Los Angeles: Taschen, 2008.

Knight, Alan. "Weapons and Arches in the Mexican Revolutionary Landscape." In *Everyday Forms of State Formation, Revolution and the Negotiation of Rule in Modern Mexico*, edited by Gilbert M. Joseph and Daniel Nugent, 24–66. Durham, NC: Duke University Press, 1994.

Lear, John. *Picturing the Proletariat: Artists and Labor in Revolutionary Mexico, 1908–1940*. Austin: University of Texas Press, 2017.

———. "Representing Workers, the Workers Represented: Artists, Unions and Print Production in the Mexican Revolution." *Third Text* 28, no. 3 (2014): 235–55.

———. "La revolución en blanco, negro y rojo: Arte, política, y obreros en los inicios del periódico *El Machete*." *Signos Históricos*, no. 15 (January–June, 2006): 108–47.

Liga de Escritores y Artistas Revolucionarios. *Homenaje a Rubén Romero*. México: Imprenta Mundial, 1937.

Lindauer, Margaret A. *Devouring Frida: The Art History and Popular Celebrity of Frida Kahlo*. Middletown, CT: Wesleyan University Press, 1999.

Lola Álvarez Bravo and the Photography of an Era, edited by James Oles. México: Editorial RM, 2012.

Lola Álvarez Bravo: Recuento fotográfico. México: Editorial Penélope, 1982.

López, Rick A. "Anita Brenner and the Jewish Roots of Mexico's Postrevolutionary National Identity." In *Open Borders to a Revolution: Culture, Politics, and Migration*, edited by Jaime Marroquín Arredondo, Adela Pineda Franco, and Magdalena Mieri, 123–30. Washington, DC: Smithsonian Institution Scholarly Press, 2013.

———. *Crafting Mexico: Intellectuals, Artisans, and the State after the Revolution*. Durham, NC: Duke University Press, 2010.

———. "The Noche Mexicana and the Exhibition of Popular Arts: Two Ways of Exalting Indianness." In *The Eagle and the Virgin: Nation and Cultural Revolution in Mexico, 1920–1940*, edited by Mary Kay Vaughan and Stephen E. Lewis, 23–42. Durham, NC: Duke University Press, 2006.

López Guzmán, Rafael, Gloria Espinosa Spínola, and Teresa Suárez Molina. "La oposición artística desde México al régimen franquista." In *Dos décadas de cultura artística en el franquismo (1936–1956): Actas del congreso*, 623–39. Vol. 1. Granada, Spain: Universidad de Granada, 2001.

López Moreno, Roberto, and Leticia Ocharán. *Aurora Reyes: La sangre dividida*. Chihuahua, México: Gobierno del Estado Chihuahua, Consejo Nacional para la Cultura y las Artes, 1990.

Lowe, Sarah M. *Tina Modotti and Edward Weston: The Mexico Years*. London: Merrell, 2004.

Lozano, Luis-Martín. "Regarding Modern Mexican Painting: María Izquierdo." In *María Izquierdo: 1902–1955*, exhibition catalog, 20–50. Chicago: Mexican Fine Arts Center Museum, 1996.

Macías, Anna. *Against All Odds: The Feminist Movement in Mexico to 1940*. Westport, CT: Greenwood Press, 1982

Macías-González, Víctor M., and Anne Rubenstein, eds. *Masculinity and Sexuality in Modern Mexico*. Albuquerque: University of New Mexico Press, 2012.

Mahoney, Harry Thayer, and Marjorie Locke Mahoney. *Espionage in Mexico: The 20th Century*. San Francisco: Austin & Winfield, 1997.

Marín, Lupe. *La Única: Novela*. México: Editorial Jalisco, 1938.
Marnham, Patrick. *Dreaming with His Eyes Open: A Life of Diego Rivera*. Berkeley: University of California Press, 1998.
Marrufo Huchim, Karla Lili. "El arquetipo de la Gran Madre en *Espiral en retorno* de Aurora Reyes." Thesis, Universidad Veracruzana, 2011.
Martínez Verdugo, Arnoldo, ed. *Historia del Comunismo en México*. México, DF: Editorial Grijalbo, 1985.
Masacchio, Humberto. *Taller de Gráfica Popular*. México: Fondo de Cultura Económica, 2007.
McClean, Alison. "Committed to Print: Printmaking and Politics in Mexico and Beyond, 1934–1960." In Dawn Adès and Alison McClean, *Revolution on Paper: Mexican Prints 1910–1960*, edited by Mark McDonald, 27–42. Austin: University of Texas Press, 2009.
McLemee, Scott. "The Re-Assassination of Leon Trotsky." *Inside Higher Ed* (8 July 2011). http://www.insidehigher.com. 28 November 2015.
Meijer, Jan M. ed. *The Trotsky Papers*. 2 Vols. London: Mouton, 1964.
Mercado, Dolores, ed. *Women Artists of Modern Mexico: Frida's Contemporaries*. Chicago: National Museum of Mexican Art, 2008.
Merfish, Beth. "Stars in Complex Constellations: Mexico City's Taller de Gráfica Popular through Inside and Outside Histories." PhD diss., New York University, May 2013.
Miles, Jonathan. *The Dangerous Otto Katz: The Many Lives of a Soviet Spy*. New York: Bloomsbury, 2010.
Miller, Beth, and Anita Brenner. "An Interview with Anita Brenner." *Bilingual Review/La Revista Bilingüe* 4, no. 1/2 (January–August 1977): 113–18.
Miller, Francesca. *Latin American Women and the Search for Social Justice*. Hanover, NH: University Press of New England, 1991.
Mirkin, Dina Comisarenco. "Aurora Reyes's 'Ataque a la Maestra Rural': The First Mural Created by a Mexican Female Artist." *Women's Art Journal* 26, no. 2 (Autumn 2005–Winter 2006): 19–25.
Monsiváis, Carlos. "Foreword, Anita Brenner and the Mexican Renaissance." In Susannah Joel Glusker, *Anita Brenner: A Mind of Her Own*, ix–xvi. Austin: University of Texas Press, 1998.
———. *Jorge Cuesta (Grandes Maestros Mexicanos)*. México, DF: Editorial Terra Nova, 1985.
———. "When Gender Can't Be Seen amid the Symbols: Women and the Mexican Revolution." In *Sex in Revolution: Gender, Politics, and Power in Modern Mexico*, edited by Jocelyn Olcott, Mary Kay Vaughan, and Gabriela Cano, 1–20. Durham, NC: Duke University Press, 2006.
Morton, Ward M. *Woman Suffrage in Mexico*. Gainesville: University of Florida Press, 1962.
Mraz, John. *Looking for Mexico: Modern Visual Culture and National Identity*. Durham, NC: Duke University Press, 2009.
———. *Photographing the Mexican Revolution: Commitments, Testimonies, Icons*. Austin: University of Texas Press, 2012.

Musacchio, Humberto. *El Taller de Gráfica Popular*. México: Fondo de Cultura Económica, 2007.
Navarro, Aaron W. *Political Intelligence and the Creation of Modern Mexico, 1938–1954*. University Park: Pennsylvania State University Press, 2010.
Neruda, Pablo. "Tina Modotti is Dead." In *Frida Kahlo and Tina Modotti*, exhibition catalog, 34. London: Whitechapel Art Gallery, 1982.
Noble, Andrea. *Tina Modotti: Image, Texture, Photography*. Albuquerque: University of New Mexico Press, 2000.
Nonaka, Masayo. *Remedio Varo: The Mexican Years*. México: Editorial RM, 2014.
Olcott, Jocelyn. "The Center Cannot Hold: Women on Mexico's Popular Front." In *Sex in Revolution: Gender, Politics, and Power in Modern Mexico,* edited by Jocelyn Olcott, Mary Kay Vaughan, and Gabriela Cano, 223–40. Durham, NC: Duke University Press, 2006.
———. *Revolutionary Women in Postrevolutionary Mexico*. Durham, NC: Duke University Press, 2005.
———. "'Take Off That Streetwalker's Dress': Concha Michel and the Cultural Politics in Postrevolutionary Mexico." *Journal of Women's History* 21, no. 3 (2000): 36–59.
Oles, James. "The Mexican Murals of Marion and Grace Greenwood." In *Out of Context: American Artists Abroad*, edited by Laura Felleman Fattal and Carol Salus, 113–34. Westport, CT: Praeger, 2004.
———. "Painting in the Shadow of the Big Three: The Mexican Experience of Marion and Grace Greenwood." In *The Eagle and the Virgin: Nation and Cultural Revolution in Mexico, 1920–1940*, edited by Mary Kay Vaughan and Stephen E. Lewis, 79–94. Durham, NC: Duke University Press, 2006.
———. *South of the Border: Mexico in the American Imagination, 1914–1947*. Washington, DC: Smithsonian Institution Press, 1993.
O'Mahony, Mike. *Sergei Eisenstein*. London: Reaktion Books, 2008.
Oropesa, Salvador A. *The Contemporáneos Group: Rewriting Mexico in the Thirties and Forties*. Austin: University of Texas Press, 2003.
Padilla, Tanalís, and Louise E. Walker. "In the Archives: History and Politics." *Journal of Iberian and Latin American Research* 19, no. 1 (2013): 1–10.
Patenaude, Bertrand M. "Trotsky: A Biography. In Defense of Leon Trotsky." *American Historical Review* 116, no. 3 (June 2011): 900–902.
———. *Trotsky: Downfall of a Revolutionary*. New York: HarperCollins, 2009.
Peláez, Gerardo. *Partido Comunista Mexicano: 60 años de historia*. 2 Vols. Sinaloa, México: Universidad Autónoma de Sinaloa, 1980.
Pendleton, David. "Eisenstein, Sergei: Filmmaker." In *Routledge International Encyclopedia of Queer Culture*, edited by David A. Gerstner, 201–2. London: Routledge, 2006.
Pereira, Armando, ed. *Diccionario de literatura mexicana: Siglo XX*. México: Universidad Nacional Autónoma de México, 2004.
Pérez Montfort, Ricardo. "Apuntes sobre el exilio alemán en México." In *Mexico, país refugio: La experiencia de los exilios en el sigo XX*, edited by Pablo Yankelevich, 49–54. México, DF: Instituto Nacional de Antropología e Historia, 2002.

Poniatowska, Elena. "Los 60 años de Leopoldo Méndez." *Artes de México*, no. 45 (July 1963): 3–20.
———. *Tinísima*. Translated by Katherine Silver. Albuquerque: University of New Mexico Press, 1992.
Prignitz-Poda, Helga. *El Taller de Gráfica Popular en México, 1937–1977*. Translated by Elizabeth Siefer. México: Instituto Nacional de Bellas Artes-Centro Nacional de Investigación, Documentación, 1992.
Rankin, Monica A. *¡Mexico, la patria! Propaganda and Production during World War II*. Lincoln: University of Nebraska Press, 2009.
Rashkin, Elissa J. *The Stridentist Movement in Mexico: The Avant-Garde and Cultural Change in the 1920s*. Lanham, MD: Lexington Books, 2009.
Reyes Palma, Francisco. "La LEAR y su revista de frente cultural." In *Frente a Frente, 1934–1938*, Edición facsimilar, 5–16. México City: Centro de Estudios del Movimiento Obrero y Socialista, 1994.
———. *Leopoldo Méndez: El oficio de grabar*. México, DF: Consejo Nacional para la Cultura y las Artes, Dirección General de Publicaciones, 1994.
Richards, Susan Valerie. "Imaging the Political: El Taller de Gráfica Popular in Mexico, 1937–1949. PhD diss., University of New Mexico, July 2001.
Richardson, William Harrison. "The Dilemmas of a Communist Artist: Diego Rivera in Moscow, 1927–1928." *Mexican Studies/Estudios Mexicanos* 3, no. 1 (Winter 1987): 49–69.
———. *Mexico Through Russian Eyes, 1806–1940*. Pittsburgh, PA: University of Pittsburgh Press, 1988.
Ricker, Michael T. "A Collector's Notes on the Taller de Gráfica Popular." In *El Taller de Gráfica Popular: Vida y Arte*, exhibition catalogue, 8–11. Athens: Georgia Museum of Art at University of Georgia, 2015.
Rochfort, Desmond. *Mexican Muralists: Orozco, Rivera, Siqueiros*. San Francisco: Chronicle Books, 1993.
———. "The Sickle, the Serpent, and the Soil: History, Revolution, Nationhood, and Modernity in the Murals of Diego Rivera, José Clemente Orozo, and David Alfaro Siqueiros." In *The Eagle and the Virgin: Nation and Cultural Revolution in Mexico, 1920–1940*, edited by Mary Kay Vaughan and Stephen E. Lewis, 43–57. Durham, NC: Duke University Press, 2006.
Rouverol, Jean. *Refugees from Hollywood: A Journal of the Blacklist Years*. Albuquerque: University of New Mexico Press, 2000.
Rupprecht, Tobias. *Soviet Internationalism after Stalin: Interaction and Exchange between the USSR and Latin America during the Cold War*. Cambridge, UK: Cambridge University Press, 2015.
Ryle, J. Martin. "International Red Aid and Comintern." *International Review of Social History* 15, no. 1 (1970): 43–66.
Salazkina, Masha. *In Excess: Sergei Eisenstein's Mexico*. Chicago: University of Chicago Press, 2009.
Sánchez Salazar, Leandro A. *Murder in Mexico: The Assassination of Leon Trotsky*. Westport, CT: Hyperion Press, 1950.

Sanders, Nicole. *Gender and Welfare in Mexico: The Consolidation of a Postrevolutionary State*. University Park: Pennsylvania State University Press, 2011.
Schaefer, Claudia. *Frida Kahlo: A Biography*. Westport, CT: Greenwood Press, 2009.
Schmitt, Karl M. *Communism in Mexico: A Study in Political Frustration*. Austin: University of Texas Press, 1965.
Schreiber, Rebecca M. *Cold War Exiles in Mexico: U.S. Dissidents and the Culture of Critical Resistance*. Minneapolis: University of Minnesota Press, 2008.
Scott, Joan. *Only Paradoxes to Offer: French Feminists and the Rights of Man*. Cambridge, MA: Harvard University Press, 1996.
Serge, Victor, and Natalia Sedova Trotsky. *The Life and Death of Trotsky*. Translated by Arnold J. Pomerans. New York: Basic Books, 1975.
60 años TGP: Taller de Gráfica Popular. México: Instituto Nacional de Bellas Artes, 1997.
Sluis, Ageeth. *Deco Body, Deco Body: Female Spectacle and Modernity in Mexico City, 1990–1939*. Lincoln: University of Nebraska Press, 2016.
Smith, Bernard. *Modernism's History: A Study in Twentieth-Century Art and Ideas*. New Haven, CT: Yale University Press, 1998.
Smith, Stephanie J. *Gender and the Mexican Revolution: Yucatán Women and the Realities of Patriarchy*. Chapel Hill: University of North Carolina Press, 2009.
"Some Important Dates and Events in the Life of Alexandra Kollontai." In *Alexandra Kollontai: Selected Articles and Speeches*, edited by I. M. Dazhina, M. M. Mukhamedzhanov, and R. Y. Tsivlina, 200–215. New York: International, 1984.
Spenser, Daniela. *The Impossible Triangle: Mexico, Soviet Russia, and the United States in the 1920s*. Durham, NC: Duke University Press, 1999.
———. *Stumbling Its Way through Mexico: The Early Years of the Communist International*. Translated by Peter Gellert. Tuscaloosa: University of Alabama Press, 2011.
Starn, Randolph. "Seeing Culture in a Room for a Renaissance Prince." In *The New Cultural History*, edited by Lynn Hunt, 205–32. Berkeley: University of California Press, 1989.
Stein, Philip. *Siqueiros: His Life and Works*. New York: International Publishers, 1994.
Stephan, Alexander. *"Communazis": FBI Surveillance of German Emigré Writers*. Translated by Jan van Heurck. New Haven, CT: Yale University Press, 2000.
Stern, Peter A. "Frances Toor and the Mexican Cultural Renaissance." In *Documenting Movements, Identity, and Popular Culture in Latin America: Papers of the Forty-Fourth Annual Meeting of the Seminar on the Acquisition of Latin American Library Materials, Nashville, Tennessee, May 30–June 3, 1999*, edited by Richard F. Phillips, 200–219. Austin, TX: Seminar on the Acquisition of Latin American Library Materials, 2000. http://works.bepress.com/peter_stern/6.
Taibo II, Paco Ignacio. *Los Bolshevikis: Historia narrativa de los orígenes del comunismo en México (1919–1925)*. México, DF: Editorial Joaquín Mortiz, 1986.
Tesis sobre el Trabajo Femenil del Partido Comunista. México, DF: Fondo de Cultura Popular, 1962.
Tibol, Raquel. "Datos biográficos." In *Arte y política, Diego Rivera: Selección, prólogo, notas y datos biográficos por Raquel Tibol*, 423–60. México, DF: Editorial Grijalbo, 1979.

———. *Diego Rivera: Great Illustrator*. México: Editorial RM, Museo Nacional de Arte, 2008.
———. *Documentación sobre el arte mexicano*. México, DF: Fondo de Cultura Económica, 1974.
———. *Frida Kahlo: An Open Life*. Translated by Elinor Randall. Albuquerque: University of New Mexico Press, 1993.
———. *Palabras de Siqueiros*, Selección, prólogo y notas de Raquel Tibol. México, DF: Fondo de Cultura Económica, 1996.
———. *Siqueiros: Introductor de realidades*. México, DF: UNAM, 1961.
———. *Textos de Siqueiros*. México, DF: Fondo de Cultura Económica, 1974.
Togliatti, Palmiro. *Lectures on Fascism*. New York: International, 1976.
Toor, Frances. "Editor's Foreword." *Mexican Folkways* 1, no. 1 (June–July 1925): 3–4.
Tuer, Dot, and Elliott King, eds. *Frida and Diego: Passion, Politics and Painting*. Art Gallery of Ontario/High Museum of Art Atlanta, 2012. Exhibition catalog.
Tuñón Pablos, Esperanza. *Mujeres que se organizan: El Frente Único Pro Derechos de la Mujer, 1935–1938*. México, DF: Universidad Nacional Autónoma de México, 1992.
Vaughan, Mary Kay. *Cultural Politics in Revolution: Teachers, Peasants, and Schools in Mexico, 1930–1940*. Tucson: University of Arizona Press, 1997.
———. "Introduction: Pancho Villa, the Daughters of Mary, and the Modern Woman: Gender in the Long Mexican Revolution." In *Sex in Revolution: Gender, Politics, and Power in Modern Mexico,* edited by Jocelyn Olcott, Mary Kay Vaughan, and Gabriela Cano, 21–32. Durham, NC: Duke University Press, 2006.
Vaughan, Mary Kay, and Stephen E. Lewis. "Introduction." In *The Eagle and the Virgin: Nation and Cultural Revolution in Mexico, 1920–1940*, edited by Mary Kay Vaughan and Stephen E. Lewis, 1–20. Durham, NC: Duke University Press, 2006.
Vázquez Ramírez, Esther Martina. *Organización y resistencia popular en la ciudad de México durante la crisis de 1929–1932*. México, DF: Instituto Nacional de Estudios Históricos de la Revolución Mexicana, 1998.
Vidali, Vittorio. *Retrato de mujer: Una vida con Tina Modotti*. México: Universidad Autónoma de Puebla, 1993.
———. "A Testimony by Vittorio Vidali." In *Tina Modotti Photographs*. Translated by C. H. Evans, 6–7. New York: Idea Editions and Belmark, 1981.
Vogel, Susan. *Becoming Pablo O'Higgins: How an Anglo-American Artist from Utah Became a Mexican Muralist*. San Francisco: Pince-Nez Press, 2010.
White, D. Anthony. *Siqueiros: Biography of a Revolutionary Artist*. Charleston, SC: BookSurge, 2009.
Whitney, Robert. *State and Revolution in Cuba: Mass Mobilization and Political Change, 1920–1940*. Chapel Hill: University of North Carolina Press, 2001.
Williams, Daryle. *Culture Wars in Brazil: The First Vargas Regime, 1930–1945*. Durham, NC: Duke University Press, 2001.
Wolfe, Bertram D. *Diego Rivera: His Life and Times*. New York: Alfred A. Knopf, 1943.
———. *The Fabulous Life of Diego Rivera*. New York: Stein and Day, 1963.
Wood, Elizabeth A. *The Baba and the Comrade: Gender and Politics in Revolutionary Russia*. Bloomington: Indiana University Press, 1997.

Wright-Rios, Edward. *Searching for Madre Matiana: Prophecy and Popular Culture in Modern Mexico*. Albuquerque: University of New Mexico Press, 2014.
Yankelevich, Pablo, ed. *México, país refugio: La experiencia de los exilios en el siglo XX*. México, DF: Instituto Nacional de Antropología e Historia, 2002.
Zamora, Martha. *Frida Kahlo: The Brush of Anguish*. San Francisco: Chronicle Books, 1990.
Zavala, Adriana. *Becoming Modern, Becoming Tradition: Women, Gender, and Representation in Mexican Art*. University Park: Pennsylvania State University Press, 2010.
———. "María Izquierdo." In *The Eagle and the Virgin: Nation and Cultural Revolution in Mexico, 1920–1940*, edited by Mary Kay Vaughan and Stephen E. Lewis, 67–79. Durham, NC: Duke University Press, 2006.

Index

Note: Illustrations are indicated by page numbers in *italics*.

www.ingramcontent.com/pod-product-compliance
Ingram Content Group UK Ltd.
Pitfield, Milton Keynes, MK11 3LW, UK
UKHW011043190826
474455UK00004B/264

9 781469 635682